Dilemmas of China's Growth in the Twenty-First Century

Dilemmas of China's Growth in the Twenty-First Century

Ligang Song (ed.)

Australian
National
University

E PRESS

ANU E PRESS

Published by ANU E Press
The Australian National University
Canberra ACT 0200, Australia
Email: anuepress@anu.edu.au
This title is also available online at http://epress.anu.edu.au

National Library of Australia Cataloguing-in-Publication entry

Title: Dilemmas of China's growth in the twenty-first century /
            Ligang Song (ed.).

ISBN: 9781922144584 (pbk.) 9781922144591 (ebook)

Notes: Includes bibliographical references and index.

Subjects: World Trade Organization.
            China--Economic conditions--2000-
            China--Foreign economic relations.

Other Authors/Contributors:
            Song, Ligang.

Dewey Number: 330.951

First published by Asia Pacific Press, 2002
This edition © 2012 ANU E Press

Contents

Illustrations

Tables

Figures

Boxes

Symbols used in Tables

..	not available
n.a.	not applicable
-	zero
.	insignificant

Abbreviations

ABC	The Agricultural Bank of China
ACMs	asset management companies
AEZ	agro-ecological zones
AIC	Asian Info-communications Council
ANOVA	analysis of variance
APCs	Asia Pacific countries
ATM	automatic teller machine
BOC	The Bank of China
BOF	basic oxygen furnace
CAB	current account balance
CADB	The China Agricultural Development Bank
CBC	The Construction Bank of China
CCP	Chinese Communist Party
CDR	crude death rate
CDU	Clean Development Scheme
CEIB	The China Export-Import Bank
CES	crop-mix index
CETA	Carbon Emissions Trajectory Assessment
COP	conference of parties
CPI	CP Industries
ECL	Energy Conservation Law
EDU	employment educational attainment
EEFSU	Eastern Europe and the Former Soviet Union
EU	European Union
FAO	Food and Agriculture Organization
FDI	foreign direct investment
FIEs	foreign-invested enterprises
GAMS	grants application management system
GDP	gross domestic product
GHG	Greenhouse Gas
GNP	gross national product
GOV	gross output value
HFDI	high foreign direct investment
HOV	Heckscher-Ohlim-Vanek Theorem
HRS	household responsibility system
HSBC	The Hongkong and Shanghai Banking Corporation
ICBC	The Industry and Commerce Bank
ICEA	industrial classification of economic activity

IFPRI	International Food Policy Research Institute
IMF	International Monetary Fund
IPB	Intellectual Property Bulletin
IT	information technology
JI	joint implementation
LDCs	less-developed countries
LFDI	low foreign direct investment
LTS	least-trimmed square
LUC	land-use change
MFDI	medium foreign direct investment
MFN	most-favoured nation
MMT	million metric tonnes
MPCs	marginal propensity to consume
NAPF	Neoclassical Aggregate Production Function
NDB	National Development Bank
NICs	newly industrialised countries
NLS	non-linear squares
NOV	net output value
NPLs	non-performing loans
NTBs	non-tariff barriers
OECD	Organization for Economic Co-operation and Development
OHF	open hearth furnace
OTP	overseas training program
PBC	People's Bank of China
PIH	permanent income hypothesis
PPP	purchasing power parity
RCA	revealed comparative advantage
RCC	rural credit cooperatives
RCRE	Research Centre for Rural Economy
ROW	rest of world
SBCs	soft budgetary constraints
SECIC	State Energy Conservation Investment Corporation
SITC	standard international trade classification
SLA	State Land Administration
SOEs	state-owned enterprises
SSIC	Social Survey Institute of China
TVEs	township-village enterprises
UCC	urban credit cooperatives
UNESCO	United Nations Educational Scientific and Cultural Organization
UNFCCC	United Nations Fieldwork Convention on Climate Change
VA	value added
WTO	World Trade Organization

Contributors

Peter Albersen is a research analyst at The Centre for World Food Studies, Free University (SWO-VU), Amsterdam.

John P. Bonin is at the Department of Economics, Wesleyan University, Middletown, CT. Research Fellow, William Davidson Institute, University of Michigan, School of Business, Ann Arbor, MI.

Deborah Cass is at the London School of Economics, Law Department. L.LB (Melbourne) LL.M (Harvard). Chief Investigator, China and the WTO Project, Law Faculty, The Australian National University.

Yu Chen is at the Centre for Studies and Research on International Development in France.

Günther Fischer is a research analyst at the International Institute for Applied Systems Analysis (IIASA) in Austria.

Fan Gang is at the National Economic Research Institute, China Reform Foundation.

Wen Hai is at The China for Economic Research (CCER) and Peking University, Beijing, China.

Yiping Huang works with Asia Pacific Economic and Market Analysis, Citibank, Hong Kong.

Tingsong Jiang is with The Economics Division, at the Research School of Pacific and Asian Studies and the Asia Pacific School of Economics and Management, The Australian National University, Canberra.

Ding Jianping is at The Shanghai University of Finance and Economics, Shanghai, People's Republic of China.

Michiel A. Keyzer is Professor of Mathematical Economics and Director of the Centre for World Food Studies, Free University (SOW-VU), Amsterdam.

Hyunok Lee is at the Department of Agricultural and Resource Economics, The University of California, Davis.

Jordan Shan is at The Victoria University of Technology, Melbourne and The Guanghua School of Management, Peking University.

Ligang Song is at the Asia Pacific School of Economics and Management at The Australian National University.

Daniel A. Sumner works in The Department of Agricultural and Resource Economics, The University of California, Davis.

Laixiang Sun is a senior researcher, mathematician and economist, at the International Institute for Applied Systems Analysis (IIASA), Austria and project director at The United Nations University, WIDER, in Helsinki, Finland.

Guanghua Wan is with The Department of Agricultural Economics, The University of Sydney, NSW, Australia.

Brett Williams LL.B, BEc, PhD (law) (Adelaide) is a Lecturer in the Faculty of Law at the University of Sydney.

Wing Thye Woo is at The Economics Department, The University of California, Davis.

Yanrui Wu is at The Department of Economics, The University of Western Australia, Nedlands, WA.

Qing Zhang is at The School of Economics, The University of Tasmania.

Zhang Yue Zhou is with the Asian Agribusiness Research Centre, The University of Sydney, Orange.

1

Conditions and prospects for sustaining China's economic growth

Dilemmas of economic growth

Ligang Song

Sustaining economic growth has been of paramount importance for securing social stability in China while the economic system has been undergoing fundamental transformation. Growth not only creates more employment opportunities, but relatively high growth rate for a sustained period of time during the transition, largely through raising the standard of living, has demonstrated convincingly that the gradualist approach to reform adopted in China since the late 1970s has worked.[1] This success provides confidence and assurance for the government in silencing resistance to reform and overcoming difficulties in the reform process.

Yet, various dilemmas of economic growth exist in the context of reform and transformation. Some are more transitory and likely to be resolved with deepening reform and ongoing structural change, such as the dilemma of decontrolling prices while preventing inflation from rising as in the early period of reform.[2] Similarly reforms such as the liberalisation of interest rates and the capital account, which is yet to be materialised, falls into this category of dilemmas. Some dilemmas are more deep-seated and likely to have some long-term implications in that they are unlikely to be resolved easily with the progression of the reform and in some cases may become major obstacles to reform if not be dealt with well. Thus, failure to resolve these dilemmas may pose serious threats to the reform process itself and the long-term growth prospects of the Chinese economy. Some stem from the dynamic change in the reform process, shifting institutional settings, and changing macroeconomic environment.[3]

Dilemma 1: to balance the goal of efficiency with that of equity to maintain a sustainable growth in the process of reform.

- Can economic growth with per capita income growing over time be sustainable from the standpoint of social stability with increasing and widening regional and income disparities?
- What does the government need to do to strike a balance between efficiency and equity in the context of reform?
- Do measures such as high income taxes, increased government expenditure on social welfare and transfer payments across provinces to reduce regional and income disparities at this stage of development affect incentives and therefore undermine the current growth momentum?

Dilemma 2: to ease unemployment pressures while deepening the reform programs especially with regard to the restructuring of SOE, opening up more domestic industrial sectors to foreign competition, and in the likelihood of slowing down of rural industries:

- To what extent does rising urban unemployment hold back the pace and depth of SOE reform?
- In what ways can productivity growth resulting from reform and industrial restructuring lead to job creation?
- Will increased foreign competition adversely affect domestic employment?
- What are the long-term solutions to the problem of a large rural surplus labour force, and what are the major constraints?
- What are conditions for maintaining stability while deepening the structural reform?

Dilemma 3: to achieve the goal of quality growth while pursuing growth targets amid growing structural problems in the economy.

- How to achieve the goal of quality growth against the background of an oversupply of manufactured goods on a large scale?
- How to deal with the situation in which demand becomes satiated with a relatively low per capita income?
- Is the government's investment-driven growth strategy against domestic deflation sustainable on efficiency and fiscal terms in a long run?
- What conditions are needed to revive non-government investment?
- What needs to be done in order to realise an optimal economic (industrial) structure by which quality of growth can be achieved?

Dilemma 4: to transform the widespread informal business practice into more rules-based business behaviour and operation without negatively affecting business transactions in the transition.

- Will the shift to formality required by conforming to WTO rules affect business transactions, and negatively affect growth?
- What are the compromises needed in society where doing business through informal means, through connections, is the norm?

- Can traditional networks and social relations be transformed and institutionalised in new forms needed for a market economy?

Dilemma 5: to overcome the existing ideological and institutional barriers to allow the dynamic private sector to play a more important and wider role in reforming SOEs and SOBs and sustaining growth.

- Is more dramatic reform of ownership required for deepening the structural changes for the next crucial stage of reform?
- What institutional reforms are needed to accommodate the rise of the private economy?
- What conditions are needed for the private sector to become the new source for growth?
- What are the consequences of delaying reform measures aimed at dismantling the existing institutional barriers for private sector development?

Dilemma 6: to build market compatible institutions against the remaining legacy of the former planning system, which still affects the behaviour of government and the way in which it functions at different levels.

- What are the discrepancies between the substantial and procedural rules required by the WTO and current institutional settings in China?
- In what way does China's extant legal and regulatory system and associated political and institutional restrictions constrain the development of open market competition?
- What are the most effective and practical ways of reducing the discrepancies and dealing with consequent adjustment costs?
- What are the political and economic implications of building market-compatible institutions for sustaining China's long-term growth?

These dilemmas result from a gradualist and complex process of reform. At the heart of the economic transformation is structural change and the best way to deal with the structural problems in the economy is to reform the entire economic system. But there are the impracticalities in carrying out all reform programs at the same time. When pushing for a reform in one area, the gradualist approach tends to leave other parts of the economic system unattended thereby producing various kinds of discords and conflicts during the process. Frictions caused by such an approach usually lead to the identified dilemmas, exacerbated by other factors such as institutional incompatibility, demographic structure, macroeconomic instability, and social, custom and culture influences.

Dealing with these dilemmas requires skilful management of the reform process in terms of the sequencing and depths of the reform program. Adjustment costs have to be minimised in order to keep reform on track against the backdrop of the resistance to reform. It is evident that incremental changes resulting from the implementation of such an approach can gradually pave the way for further reform in the system. This is the key consideration in implementing the gradualist reform approach. In so doing, various kinds of compromises and adjustments have to be made, affecting ongoing structural changes and incentives, and consequently the efficiency and growth potential of the Chinese economy.

Structural change is required in order to create those conditions in which incentives can be raised and macro and microeconomic efficiency can be improved. Dealing with structural change, especially its side effects such as rising unemployment, is an important component of the reform strategy. China has managed to make the necessary compromises and adjustments to overcome different kinds of impediments to reform and in doing so to maintain the growth momentum in the past. However, the economic imperatives at the turn of the century, such as the binding commitments and the changes required by China's accession to the WTO, have made it more difficult for the government to manoeuvre in dealing with some of the key dilemmas facing the economy. It is also anticipated that China's accession to the WTO will produce some significantly positive impacts on the structural adjustment and reform (Drysdale and Song 2000).

In the past, the government could simply delay the reform program in certain areas when tensions resulting from the reform became so great that they had the potential to derail the reform process. But, the reality now is that the government has less degree of freedom because of binding constraints imposed by its accession to the WTO. Apart from the commitments China has made for its accession, requiring a comprehensive reform of the economic system in a timely manner, there are also areas of domestic reform where more radical reform programs need to be carried out to enable the government to overcome bottlenecks to further reform.

The remaining reform agenda involves those parts of the economic system which have been most difficult to tackle. For example, much-needed reform of banking sector has been tied up with the progress in reforming state-owned enterprises (SOEs), which in turn has been subject to unemployment pressures, the development of a social security system as well as some political constraints on ownership reform. Government attempts to slash state-owned banks' (SOBs) bad loans by converting a large amount of bad assets into equity have lessened the problem of bad debts for major SOBs, but not resolved it in a fundamental way.

There has also been macroeconomic shift from China being 'a seller's market to a buyer's market' taking place during the reform period of the 1990s. The resulting over-supply of manufactured goods has made the task of structural change even more difficult. The situation has worsened because of stagnant domestic demand and weak external markets, which have plunged the economy into a persistent period of deflation from the last quarter of the 1990s and into the new century.

The reform programs implemented in the earlier period of reform especially in the 1980s tended to be more inflationary such as freeing up the price control

4

and decentralisation. In contrast, reform programs put into practice since the mid 1990s have had a propensity to be more deflationary including increased taxation, strengthened financial regulation and supervision, rising unemployment from SOE reform, and housing and pension system reform. These reforms and associated uncertainties, coupled with the slow growth of rural incomes in recent years are the main causes for China's persistent deflation.

Under these circumstances, the government has no other choice but to rely primarily on fiscal means to boost domestic demand and to offset external shocks in order to reach growth targets. Such requirement is particularly pronounced when China faces weak external markets for its exports as it experienced in the aftermath of the Asian crisis in the late 1990s and the recent slowdown of the global economy. However, it is doubted that whether this kind of debt-driven growth strategy is sustainable given the fiscal capacity it has and possible distortion it might create. It is generally accepted that the real hope lies at the revival of non-governmental investment especially from the private sector, but again this requires further changes in policies and institutions.

> The emergence and development of the private economy is the most significant outcome of reform in that the sector has been most responsive to changes in market prices and market-oriented institutions with respect to incentives and efficiency. Despite constraints, the private sector has become the most dynamic sector in the economy, and has, since the early 1990s, made important contributions to growth and reform. It increases employment, creates competition, nurtures entrepreneurship and instigates innovation. It helps channel an increasing proportion of investment into more efficient uses and hence increases the overall efficiency of the economy. It helps derive the regulatory and institutional framework into becoming more compatible with a market system. It also accelerates growth with less risk to macroeconomic stability than would expansion of SOEs since private enterprises are subject to budget constraints (Garnaut *et al.* 2001).

However, there still exist some institutional barriers, which prevent the government taking full advantage of the developing private economy. It is evident that the emerging sector has had the greatest impact on the process of marketisation and played an increasingly important role in reforming SOEs and SOBs through purchasing and holding the share of state assets and increased competition. Nevertheless, there is still not an unreserved endorsement of the role of the private sector in restructuring the economy. Many issues of reform with respect to the development of the private economy remain. Some are structural in nature. For example, the formally registered private enterprises receive only less than one per cent of the total state bank lending while having produced more than one-third of industrial outputs by the end of the 1990s (Song 2002).[4]

The private sector genuinely needs a level-playing field, which put enterprises on an equal footing in competing with other firms, including foreign firms. In this sense, the building of market-compatible institutions is the most important factor for the continued development of the private sector. Right institutions reduce the transaction costs for business activities by reducing frictions and uncertainties. Specifically, ownership and property rights need to be formalised and made more secure. Regulatory policies that affect, among other things, entry, exit, markets (especially financial markets) and government functions need to be enhanced. Reform in these areas will help overcome the remaining constraints on the development of the private sector, leading it to make an even greater contribution to the reform and growth of the Chinese economy (Song 2002:101).

The commitments on accession to the WTO are presenting the new challenges for China. In particular, WTO entry requires transparent and formal procedures in the conduct of business and trade, property rights to enhance incentives and facilitate business transactions, level-playing fields to fulfil the obligation for 'national treatment' and ensure fair competition, and rule of law to provide a legal environment in which businesses can operate. Informalities widely practised in China are therefore in principle inconsistent with the WTO requirements. The challenges thus stress the role of institutions and formalities in determining economic outcomes, through among other ways, their effect on transactions costs, and the societal benefits that flow from the use of property rights in a competitive marketplace.

Hence, it is safe to say that the biggest challenge facing China's entry to the WTO is not its sectoral impact, but its impact on the institutions of government itself. The task is to build a modern, open and transparent, and efficient system of government management in line with the requirements of the WTO and the broader objectives of the economic transformation. Failing to accomplish this objective will not only impede the reform process in China, but will also undermine the functioning of the WTO itself given the size and increasing influence of the Chinese economy.

This book describes some of the main features of China's economic growth in the context of reform at the turn of the new century. The main message is that the prospects for China's economic growth will, to a great extent, depend on how the authorities can successfully handle the key dilemmas it faces given the constraints that both internal and external environments have imposed. The first 5–10 years of the twenty-first century will be crucial for testing whether China's growth and reform strategies will work well through this difficult and complex period of transition. A key criterion is whether these strategies are capable of producing sustained growth.

Conditions to be met

None of the dilemmas mentioned in the previous section are likely to trigger an immediate crisis, nor is the failure to resolve them in the short term likely to put the reform on hold indefinitely. However, because of their potential long-term consequences, these dilemmas do require solutions by which conditions for a sustainable growth and development can be met. In particular, solutions to some of the key dilemmas do demand the political commitments and determination as well as skilful management in guiding the economy going through the uncertain path of the ongoing reform and economic transformation. Chapters in this book discuss some of these conditions from different angles.

Chapter 2 focuses on China's legitimate worries about its WTO membership by discussing its implications for continued high growth and for internal security. Based on the 'convergence school' of thought,[5] Woo argues that WTO-induced acceleration in the convergence of Chinese economic institutions to those in rich market economies will sustain China's economic growth in the twenty-first century, as long as severe political instability does not occur. But the view is premised on the maintenance of domestic stability dependent on whether the increase in China's exports and the increase in foreign direct investment into China can offset enough of the temporary negative unemployment created by import liberalisation. Woo concludes that this occurrence will improve the tradeoff in the state enterprise sector between restructuring and job losses.

Chapter 3 provides an analysis of the dynamics of incremental reform with special respect to the relationship between the growth of the non-state sector, the change of the ownership structure of the economy as a whole and the reform process of the state sector. In particular, Fan discusses the issue of sustainable growth in the context of gradualist reform by asking whether the problems of the SOEs have dragged the whole economy down and to what extent the development of the non-state sector lessens the burden of SOEs. His model suggests that as long as the non-state sector keeps growing, the conditions for reforming the state sector will improve and the institutional transition will be achieved in the long run. The major risk is however that the state sector may use its state power to control income redistribution and the allocation of resources and consequently slow down the structural change in ownership. Viewed from this angle, he points out that the worsening financial situation is actually the ultimate driving force for the reform program.

Chapter 4 looks at China's WTO issues in the context of domestic reform particularly with respect to the reform of the SOEs and private sector development. Apart from the gains from trade, China's WTO membership may help the government to break through political, economic and ideological deadlocks and set up the ultimate goal and road map for economic transition. In particular, pressures from internal and external economies may push China to complete the last and most difficult stage of reform—ownership reform.

Chapter 5 discusses the impact of foreign entry in Chinese banking based on the experience of the Central European transition economies and taking account of the current situation in China and the prospects for reform. The key message is that competitive pressure from foreign entry evolves only gradually and depends on foreign banks' share of credit markets becoming significantly large. This suggests that domestic banks in China do have a window of opportunity to adjust to competition. They point out that the more quickly the government removes restrictions from the credit and deposit markets, the more likely it is that domestic banks will learn how to price risk appropriately, leading to a significant improvement in the quality of their assets.

Chapter 6 discusses the legal implications for regulation of trade in service sectors. Under the General Agreement on Trade in Services (GATS), any treatment afforded to foreign service suppliers by China under any bilateral arrangement will have to be offered on the same terms to service suppliers from any WTO member. However, whether the theoretical opportunities to compete using a joint venture by foreign suppliers actually result in competitive markets will depend to some extent upon the way that the government sets and administers domestic regulations. Williams and Cass pointed out, that depending on the extent to which the GATS commitments actually achieve increases in competition, it is possible that the rent accruing to the existing producers in the more restricted markets will increase. There is the possibility that in some areas the commitments may not result in a significantly more competitive environment.

Chapter 7 deals with income distribution issues using a macroeconomic approach to examine the causal linkage between macro factors and income disparity in China in a dynamic context. The estimation results show that unemployment/population growth and the dispersion of fiscal spending across different provinces played a prominent role in widening income inequality in China while monetary factors had a less significant role. Interestingly, the findings do not support the view that income disparity will prevent further economic growth. A policy implication of the results is that a sound macroeconomic environment is crucial to reducing income inequality in China.

With an impressive record in raising its agricultural production, it is not entirely clear to what extent China can, or should, maintain food self-sufficiency, and whether eventual imports should consist of meat or feed grains. Chapter 8 tries to lay the ground work for dealing with these issues by adopting a Land Use Change (LUC) approach that seeks to identify alternative options for agricultural policy through a spatially explicit intertemporal model. Their findings show that the marginal value of labour is high in the Northern regions and low in densely populated areas of the Central and Southern regions where marginal returns to land are relatively high for both irrigated and rain-fed land. It also appears that the marginal productivity of agricultural labour is usually higher in the neighbourhood of large urban areas.

Gain storage is an integral component of the food system. The area of household grain stocks is particular pronounced in China since it is estimated that some 60–70 per cent of China's annual output of grains are held as household stocks in rural China having profound implications for the design and implementation of domestic policies. And yet, the area has received little attention.

Chapter 9 tries to fill in this gap by analysing the determinants of household grain stocks in China based on household survey data. Wan's main finding is that price does matter, suggesting that rural farmers in China do engage in speculative activities by storing grains.

The labour force that is in excess of farming requirements in China is estimated in the order of over 200 million. To sustain China's economic development, this labour force needs to be absorbed into non-farming activities. Chapter 10 deals with this issue by discussing part-time farming trends and their policy implications. Zhou, Summer and Lee point out that there are two major paths through which labour can be shifted out of farming activities: leaving the farm completely and moving to other industries; or remaining farm-based and where possible engaging in non-farming activities, which is referred to as part-time farming. Since any large-scale relocation of farm labour is not likely to happen in the near future, encouraging more farmers to engage in part-time farming may be a solution to lessen the employment pressure in rural areas.

Chapter 11 attempts an interesting question about whether China is abundant in unskilled labour. Ding's findings show that China is neither rich in all of its low-educated, unskilled labour, nor poor in its entire high-educated profession due to many constraints. The most abundant factor in China is manufacturing manual workers not the large number of agricultural workers. A trade-off is that low income in agriculture impedes the application of advanced technology to agricultural sectors because more labour needs to be employed instead of machinery. Another trade-off is that the rapid growth of the manufacturing industry leaves less room for development of agriculture because both sectors demand land and capital. For China, the real bottlenecks are highly skilled workers such as technicians and managerial personnel and physical capital.

Chapter 12 examines the role of foreign direct investment (FDI), exports and spillover effects in regional development in China. The study found that while FDI and exports have in general a positive and significant impact on economic growth in China, the role of export expansion varies across different regions. Export growth significantly contributed to economic growth on the most developed coastal region, while its impact was insignificant in the less developed Central region and negative or marginally significant in the poorest West. The results indicate that the role of exports in economic growth depends largely on the individual situation of each region such as the level of development, industrial structure, policy orientation and degree of openness.

Decentralisation can positively affect economic growth through its impact on the mobility and allocation of resources and the provision of local public goods. However, as Chapter 13 shows, fiscal decentralisation in China during the period 1979–93 had a positive impact on the provision of local public goods, but a negative impact on provincial economic growth. As Chen points out, the negative impact of decentralisation on provincial economic growth may be due

9

to the inappropriate degree or the badly adapted form of the decentralisation. However, in terms of the government-enterprise relationship, decentralisation may not have gone far enough for enterprises to have true autonomy or hard budget constraints.

In finding out the determinants of regional economic growth, Chapter 14 provides some empirical evidence from a panel data of Chinese provinces. Wu found that the growth of physical capital, infrastructure, labour productivity, human capital and foreign investment is positively related to China's economic growth in the 1980s and 1990s. The study also confirms that China's economic reform and openness have made positive contributions to economic growth.

Chapter 15 discusses China's role in international action on climate change by analysing the bargaining power and set, and comparing emission tax and permit trading schemes. A key question to be addressed is whether a decentralised and differentiated emission tax scheme improves global welfare. Jiang's theoretical and numerical models show that the emission tax and tradable permit policies are different for a tradable permit policy allows cross-border income transfers while a tax does not. To achieve the Pareto optima, an emission tax policy should be accompanied by a net transfer of income from rich to poor countries, while a tradable emission permit policy requires that rich countries are allowed a negative number of permits. The second-best outcome lies at a differentiated tax system which can be justified by the fact that China and the rest of the world have different preferences about the environment and consumption, and different production technologies.

Notes

1 China experienced an average of 9 per cent annual growth rate in the twenty years of economic reform (1978–98) and only in recent years since the end of 1990s the average annual growth rate has been lowered to around 7 per cent.

2 Resolving this dilemma involved a series of government retrenchment programs leading to a stop-go cycle of the economic growth in the early period of reform. With the deepening of the reform programs, the 'dual price system', which was essentially a compromise in freeing up prices, has been gradually replaced by the unified market prices. Consequently, the cycle of macroeconomic movement has become less volatile over time.

3 The list does not mean to be complete. Major issues such as growth with environment degradation are not included.

4 See the share of the total non-state sector in the total bank credits over the 1997–98 period in Table 3.1.

5 See Sachs and Woo (1994), Sachs and Woo (2000) and Woo (2001) for a more detailed background of the debate between the 'experimentalist school' and the 'convergence school' about the different interpretations of the way in which institutional change has affected China's economic success.

2

What are the legitimate worries about China's WTO membership?

Wing Thye Woo

There can be no dispute that China's admission into the World Trade Organization (WTO) will result in an important improvement in its external economic security. Trade and foreign investment have constituted an important engine of growth since 1978. The annual review made by the US Congress concerning China's normal trading relationship with the United States has made China's economic growth vulnerable to the vagaries of American domestic politics. Now with WTO membership, the United States will not be able to shut off this engine of growth unilaterally without the action being a major violation of international law.

While the case for external security is clear, WTO membership does raise serious questions about its implications for continued high growth and for internal security. The possibility that WTO membership could be detrimental to China's long-term growth flows directly from the conclusion of some China watchers that the source of China's high growth in the last two decades was a policy of experimentation that had induced unique institutional innovations that were optimal for China's economic circumstances.[1] From this experimentalist interpretation of China's growth, it is troubling that WTO not only specifies, but also enforces, a common norm on the economic institutions of its members. The logical possibility from the experimentalist perspective is that WTO's emphasis on institutional harmonisation could lower future growth in China.

The possibility that WTO membership could also be detrimental to China's internal security flows from the comprehensive trade deregulation that China has agreed to undertake. The average industrial tariff will fall from 24.6 per cent to 9.4 per cent in 2005, the average agricultural tariff will fall from 31.5 per cent to 14.5 per cent in 2004, and foreign participation in many service sectors, including telecommunications and banking, will be given national treatment—put on the same legal status as local firms—within five years. Since over a third of all state-owned enterprises (SOEs) have been operating with zero or negative profits in the past eight years, and since China with its high man-land ratio is naturally a food importer, the large-scale import liberalisation could result in very high temporary unemployment. This will be politically explosive if not handled correctly.

This chapter seeks to analyse the validity of these worries about China's WTO membership. Our first conclusion is that WTO membership will increase rather than decrease the probability of continued high growth in China. Our second conclusion is that the maintenance of domestic stability is crucially dependent on whether the increase in China's exports and the increase in foreign direct investment into China, can offset enough of the temporary negative unemployment created by import liberalisation.

What is the view from the ivory tower?

Broadly speaking, there are two schools of thought about the wellsprings of China's growth; the experimentalist school (E-school) and the convergence school (C-school).[2] The debate between the two schools started off with different explanations as to why the introduction of market-oriented reforms generated large output collapse in Eastern Europe and the Former Soviet Union (EEFSU) but sustained growth in China. The E-school has ventured the hypothesis that the rapidity and broadness of EEFSU reforms constituted a big negative shock to their economic systems. This hypothesis has fallen out of favour in recent years because the speed and scope of reforms actually varied widely within EEFSU, and there was no relationship between speed-and-scope and degree of output collapse. Furthermore, no such relationship was observed in the communist regimes within Asia. The big-bang style reforms in Laos and Vietnam in 1989 produced higher growth rates instantly and in a sustained manner, while super-gradualist North Korea has veered from one economic disaster to another.

The E-school has recently emphasised that the output collapse in EEFSU was the result of uncritical adoption of western economic institutions that turned out to be inappropriate for the economic circumstances of EEFSU. China, on the other hand, according to the E-school, boldly experimented with different economic institutions and relied on the process of induced innovation to generate new economic institutions that were optimal for its specific economic conditions. Three of the new non-capitalist institutions that are alleged to have produced capitalist-style efficiency without introducing private ownership are

- the introduction of 15-year leases of farmland to households has caused significant productivity increases, thus suggesting that privatisation of farm land is unnecessary
- the introduction of dual-track pricing (sales of above-quota production at market-determined prices) and the devolution of operational

autonomy to the SOEs have improved SOEs' efficiency, suggesting that China has found the right form of enterprise contract that would make market socialism work

- the emergence of rural enterprises that are collectively owned by the local communities and supervised by the local authorities (commonly known as township-village enterprises, TVEs) has produced dynamic growth, suggesting that localised socialism not centralised socialism is the true viable alternative to capitalism.

The convergence school (C-school), on the other hand, sees China's high growth in the 1978–2000 period to be the product of its economic institution being allowed to converge to those of the capitalist market economy. Hence, the C-school cautions that unless the convergence process is continued, China's growth will slow down in the near future. According to the C-school, China did not adopt standard capitalist market institutions, like in EEFSU, primarily because of ideological and political considerations, and only secondarily because of the desire to discover new economic institutions through experimentation.[3]

In short, the C-school views the so-called new economic institutions identified by the E-school to be political adaptations of the standard institutions in the rich market economies. New growth-generating institutions based on fundamentally different economic principles may appear in China in the future, especially after its full transformation to a market-based economy where all ownership forms are voluntarily embraced. Contrary to the E-school's assertions they claim that no such institutions have been evident in the 1978–2000 period. The C-school points out that

- productivity in the grain sector has slowed down drastically since 1984. The government has responded by lengthening the duration of the land lease from 15 years to 30 years; an action that is consistent with the convergence prediction
- the reform of the SOE sector has failed.[4] Economic efficiency has not improved, and there is rampant stripping of enterprise assets by managers and workers. As a result the Chinese government is now in the process of privatising all but the largest SOEs; a development that is in line with the convergence hypothesis
- the dynamism of the collectively-owned rural enterprises has flagged considerably since 1991. Most of the collectively-owned enterprises have been corporatised and their shares distributed to the original workers or the original residents. This move toward insider privatisation supports the convergence interpretation.

Possibly because of post 1992 developments in China, some members (and sympathisers) of the E-school have appeared to change their positions, or at least their emphasis, on Chinese economic conditions being the primary reason for the unusual nature of these new institutions. These (former) members of the E-school now recognise the imperfect nature of these hybrid institutions, and acknowledge that ideological constraints could have been important factors in determining the non-capitalist characteristics of these hybrid institutions. Despite these changes, the debate between the two schools is still far from over.

To be consistent with the fundamental axiom that it was the newly-discovered economic mechanisms (like localised socialism) that generated the post 1978 growth, the remaining members of the E-school should regard China's joining the WTO, an international organisation that ensures institutional harmonisation, to be a mistake. The logical deduction from the E-school's fundamental axiom is that WTO membership could cause a decline in the future dynamism of the Chinese economy.

To members of the C-school, however, the WTO-induced acceleration in the convergence of Chinese economic institutions to those in rich market economies will sustain China's economic growth in the twenty-first century as long as severe political instability does not occur. The C-school believes that China's deep integration into the international economy will make it politically easier within China to borrow and adapt foreign institutions for its own use. They also believe it will give China the right to help shape the infrastructural institutions that regulate international markets to accommodate its own interests better. The C-school predicts that as a globalised China begins to join the rank of other global economic leaders, the rest of the international community may then re-import from China its adaptations and improved versions of its economic institutions. As the developed China of the future is still likely to account for a quarter of the world's population, and hence its brain power, China will certainly become a significant source of institutional innovations in the world.

The Chinese government's verdict on the debate

WTO membership marks a watershed in the Chinese government's public recognition of the primary source of its impressive growth in the last two decades. China's willingness to join such an institution reflects its realisation that the active ingredient in Deng Xiaoping's recipe for growth was the convergence of China's economic institutions with the economic institutions of modern capitalist economies, in particular East Asian capitalist economies. At the early stages of China's reform, when most of the intelligentsia did not know the full extent of the economic achievements of their capitalist neighbours, and when most of the top leaders were ideologically committed to Stalinist-style communism, it was important for the survival of the reformist faction of that time that changes to China's economic institutions were comfortingly gradual, conveniently located in areas far from Beijing, and cloaked in the chauvinistic rhetoric, 'experimentation to discover new institutional forms that are optimal for China's socialist system and particular economic circumstances'.

After 20 years of evolution in economic institutions, rotation in political leadership, and tectonic change in the political fortune of the communist parties in Eastern Europe and the former Soviet Union, the only organised opposition today to the continued convergence of China's economic institutions to international forms comes from a few sentimental Stalinists.[5] The social and political landscape in China has changed so much that the political leadership now incurs only minimal ideological liability when they introduce more capitalist incentives (such as differentiated pay, leveraged buy-outs, and stock options for managers) and capitalist tools (such as joint-stock companies, bankruptcy laws and unemployment insurance). The leadership is confident that its explicit embrace of capitalist institutions under the auspices of the WTO will be seen by the general Chinese public (and the Chinese élite) as a step forward in the reform process, rather than as the surrender of China's sovereignty in economic experimentation. China's intelligentsia has now gone well beyond the ideologically insecure stage of questioning whether the surname and ancestry of any proposed economic mechanism is socialist or capitalist. They are now at the intellectually confident stage of assessing whether the proposed economic mechanism will increase the productive capacity and resilience of the economy.

The integration of China into the world economy has enabled its exports to industrialise the Chinese countryside, and pay for the import of new technology. The large inflow of foreign direct investments (FDI) has increased the export capacity of the country and enhanced its technological base. Many rigorous studies have confirmed that international integration has been an important reason for the acceleration of growth in China.[6] Since partial integration has been so favourable for China, total integration will only increase the benefits.

The luck of an initially favourable economic structure

Luckily for China, economic restructuring was not required in order for growth to occur in the early years of the reform. This is because unlike the urbanised Central European and Russian economies in 1989, which had an overabundance of heavy industries, in 1978 China was still an undeveloped economy dominated by self-subsistence peasant agriculture. This meant that the introduction of market forces caused economic development in China, but caused economic restructuring in Poland and Russia, which translated, respectively, into output growth and output decline.[7]

The movement of Chinese labour from low-productivity agriculture to higher-productivity industry, and from the poor inland provinces to the richer coastal provinces, produced an average annual growth rate of 10 per cent between 1978 and 1995. The Chinese state sector certainly did not wither away in this period. It employed 18.6 per cent of the workforce in 1978 and 18.0 per cent in 1995, and there were 38 million more state workers in 1995 than in 1978.[8] There was a reallocation of labour from agriculture to industry, but reallocation of labour from state to non-state enterprises. China in 1978 was very different from Russia in 1991: while extensive growth was still possible in China, it had run its course in Russia.[9]

Since China was in the fortunate situation of being able to postpone most of the pain of restructuring, it was understandable that it did so. The result is that after two decades of 'reform and opening,' the job of economic restructuring is far from done. These are some of the many daunting problems that remain

- a government sector that is still too large (despite recent reductions in the central bureaucracy), too intrusive, and susceptible to corruption
- a state-owned enterprise system that has proved itself resistant to numerous efforts to increase its efficiency and profitability
- a state-dominated financial system in which the banks lack the ability to assess the economic merits of proposed projects, and, worse, have shied away from lending to non-state enterprises, the most dynamic component of the economy
- a lack of established institutional infrastructure that allows the smooth running of a market economy—for example, an efficient commercial court system, speedy bankruptcy procedures, independent mechanisms to mediate labour conflict, uniform accounting standards, and social safety nets.

Facing inevitable restructuring

The trade-off between stability and restructuring so starkly brought to the forefront by China's admission into the WTO is not a new tradeoff. China's WTO membership has accentuated an existing dilemma rather than introduced a new one. The government has always realised that the soft budget constraint of the inefficient state-owned enterprise sector is a constant threat to price stability, and the diversion of resources to keep this sector afloat is a drag on economic growth. But serious restructuring of SOEs means much more than facing higher urban unemployment. It also means confronting the politically powerful industrial-military complex and the industrial-bureaucratic complex. Economic rents now pose a bigger obstacle to restructuring than ideological sentimentality, and the rents, unlike the ideology, will not lose their power with the mere passing of time.

The appropriate analogy of China prior to its accession to the WTO, is that of a goat standing at the edge of a chasm. The goat sees that the grass on the other side appears not only greener, but also seems to extend infinitely toward the horizon. The goat also sees a wooden bridge spanning the chasm. The goat faces at least two questions: is the bridge strong enough to carry its weight?; and would it be able to walk steadily enough on the bridge so it does not fall off?

The analogy is obvious. The goat is China, the grass on its side is the half-reformed centrally planned Chinese economy, the grass on the other side of the chasm is the dynamic capitalist market economy, and the bridge is the WTO. When China signed the trade accord with the United States in November 1999, it has in effect agreed to walk across the bridge to the other side.

Is the WTO bridge strong enough to hold China's weight?

Entry into the WTO has set in motion two events that could break the beams that are holding the bridge. The first event is the lowering of tariffs. This will increase imports, which could cause the yuan to devalue and raise unemployment in the politically sensitive urban areas. For example, China has over 30 car-making firms—a large number compared to the five in Japan, the most efficient car manufacturer in the world. China is clearly not exploiting the economies of scales in its automobile industry. China's excess capacity exists because the tariff rate on cars, which used to be 200 per cent, is still 100 per cent. But the tariff on cars is scheduled to be drastically lowered in the next five years.

Thus, one of the first consequences of WTO membership could be a flood of imports into China, turning the current account negative, and possibly rendering the present value of the yuan unsustainable. Would a yuan devaluation spark off another Asian currency crisis?

There is, however, another side to this scenario. China's entry into the WTO will not only permit the entry of more imports into China, it will also allow several big Chinese exports greater access to markets in the United States and Western Europe—for example, the multi-fibre agreement is ended. Instead of China losing its shirt because of its entry into the WTO, the Chinese textile industry would expand. Labour-intensive exports will expand more generally to offset some of the increase in imports.

In the event that the current account does turn negative, it still need not be a source of serious concern. After the November 1999 signing of the Sino-United States trade accord, there has been a sharp rise in the contracted FDI into China. The capital account is expected to show a much larger surplus than before, and this is likely to keep the overall balance of payments in surplus, allowing the yuan peg to be sustainable.

What if the preceding prediction is wrong and China's balance of payments does turn negative? At that point, it would not be a bad thing for the yuan to be devalued, for all of China's biggest competitors have experienced devaluation from 1997–2000. China did not have an excuse to devalue during the 1997–2000 period because its trade account and capital account were positive. Had China devalued the yuan to take into account what had happened in Southeast Asia, the

United States Treasury and the IMF, among others, would have accused it of exchange rate manipulation. In the unlikely event of a devaluation of the yuan in the aftermath of tariff cuts, it is unlikely to cause competitive devaluations across Asia, because the market will take into account that the tariff cuts would also open China's markets to the Southeast Asian economies, resulting in no major loss of competitiveness for these economies.

Another important issue arising from tariff reductions is the loss of jobs, which could translate into political instability. The net loss of jobs depends on two factors: how large the rise in exports will be in the face of better market access to the foreign markets; and, how large the job creation will be from the increase of FDI into China? As long as these two factors are substantial, the loss of jobs will not be as disastrous as some commentators have suggested. Since 1994, China has been laying off workers in the small to medium SOEs on a large scale. Most of the industrial northeastern provinces have had relatively high rates of unemployment for the last five years, and yet social stability has been maintained. From this post 1994 experience, the government appears confident that it is sufficiently capable of containing the domestic disturbances from higher unemployment.

Besides tariff reduction, another post WTO event that could knock off one of the bridge's beams, is the entry of foreign-owned banks into China. One of the aspects of the trade agreement that has always been commented upon with some surprise, is how much the Chinese appear to have conceded in the financial sector. The question is whether the WTO will finally bring about the meltdown of the state-banking system as the newsletters of some Hong Kong based investment banks have been predicting since 1997. The bank meltdown scenario is based on the fact that all the state banks are effectively insolvent (Lardy 1998). Hence, there is the danger that depositors, realising the insolvency of the banks, would start a run for the deposits and precipitate a credit crisis that would reduce production and create a recession. This is the oft-predicted gloom-and-doom scenario that has not happened. Now, with WTO membership, will competition from foreign-owned banks make the insolvency of the state-banks so obvious to the general public, that the long-expected bank run will at last occur?

It is far from Panglossian to state that even if the profits of the state banks are further decreased, thereby worsening their insolvency, this situation is well within the technical capacity of the Chinese government to handle. A run on the Chinese banking system is a run from M2 to M0 (M2 is cash plus banking deposits and M0 is cash). This transformation from M2 to M0 need not cause the banks to fail, as it could easily be accommodated by the central bank acting as the lender of last resort to the banks. The banking crisis takes a more serious turn only if the increase in M0 is switched into foreign currencies, because then the exchange rate would plummet. But, given the existing capital controls in China, the switch from M0 into foreign currencies cannot take place, and the exchange rate will not collapse.

What are the legitimate worries about China's WTO membership?

Because M0 cannot run into foreign currencies, it could run into goods. The frightful scenario is that this would spark off an inflation that would decrease the willingness of the Chinese government to accommodate the bank run. However, given that China is still in a deflationary situation and is expected to remain so in 2001, inflation would not take off even it there were a run from M0 to goods. In a weak domestic economy, it is a good thing if people run from M0 to goods because this will boost aggregate demand.

The last technical detail is that since M0 cannot run into the US dollar, and if M0 does not run into goods, it will then have to run under the pillows. Money under the pillows is good news because it means that the crisis will soon blow over, provided that the central bank has prevented any bank from failing during the bank run and, hence, has avoided undermining public confidence in the government's commitment to ensuring the safety of bank deposits. Just leave the M0 alone under the pillows, and it will, like Little Bo-Peep's sheep, return to the banks with their tails behind them.

Can China walk steadily on the WTO bridge?

The basis for this question is that the Chinese economy has recently been proceeding unsteadily on two fronts. China has been wobbling on the macroeconomic front because it has found it exceedingly hard to utilise the traditional instruments of macroeconomic stabilisation. China has also been wobbling on the political front because of the difficulties of reforming the state enterprise sector.

China's wobbly gait on the macroeconomic front is caused by two Keynesian maladies; the liquidity trap and the paradox of thrift. The liquidity trap refers to the phenomenon of the last few years where monetary policy does not seem to work. China has tried to boost the domestic economy with successive cuts in interest rates, but the rise in credit creation has been disappointing. Credit growth has been much lower than expected, except for brief intervals when the central bank leaned heavily upon the banks.

The paradox of thrift refers to the steady decline in private aggregate demand because the private saving rate has been increasing. The Chinese government has concluded that, because private aggregate demand is falling and monetary policy seems incapable of stimulating it, the key to maintaining macroeconomic stability is government spending.

However, fiscal stimulus may not be the most efficient way to deal with the current problem of weak domestic demand. The solution lies in eliminating the liquidity trap and ending the paradox of thrift. I argue that both of these phenomen spring from the same cause, which is the absence of adequate financial intermediation in China.

Why is China suffering from the liquidity trap? State bank managers have been told that if the ratio of non-performing loans were to go up in two consecutive years, they will lose their jobs. The traditional client-base of the state banks is state enterprises, of which, half to two-thirds, are reporting zero or negative profits. By extending more loans to state enterprises, the non-performing loan ratio will inevitably rise.

At the same time, and for very good reasons, state banks are also unwilling to lend to non-state enterprise. First, the accounting practices of the non-state enterprises are neither uniform nor transparent. Second, it is politically more risky to do so. A loan to a state-owned enterprise may be a bad economic decision, but a loan to non-state enterprise that goes bad could also be a potentially bad political decision. A bank manager could be accused of consorting with the private sector to embezzle the state.

The Chinese government has sought to increase bank lending to private individuals by encouraging banks to establish mortgage loans, which are perceived as less risky because of their seemingly fully collateralised nature. Mortgage lending, however, is a totally new product to be provided to a totally new set of customers, and so the state banks have, understandably, been slow in setting up this market.

The liquidity trap arises because the banks are not willing to lend money to either SOEs or the private enterprises. The only activity that the banks are happy to use their funds for is buying the state bonds to finance the government's deficit spending. The fundamental step to eliminating the liquidity trap is to end the bias against lending to the private sector.

In the paradox of thrift, some observers have interpreted the rise in the saving rate to be a sign of general pessimism by the Chinese public. These observers claim that urban workers are afraid of losing their jobs as a result of the forthcoming state enterprise reform. With the forthcoming cancellation of free housing, free medical care and subsidised education, workers are now saving more for the future. There is something wrong with this reasoning—there has also been a rise in the rural saving rate, which should not be the case if this line of reasoning were correct. This is because rural residents have little to fear about the loss of jobs in the state-enterprise sector as none of them are employed there. They do not have to fear losing free housing because they have never had free housing. They do not have to fear losing their pension and other subsidies because they have never had it.

The reason why the rural sector has increased its savings rate is quite straightforward. The most dynamic industrial expansion in China since 1984 has occurred in the rural areas. Since non-state firms in the rural areas cannot borrow from the bank, the only way they could establish themselves was through self-financing, which required the would-be entrepreneurs to save first. In the initial phase of rural industrialisation, the amount of capital that was needed to start a factory workshop was very low. After 16 years of rapid industrial growth, the Chinese countryside is saturated with labour-intensive enterprises. Competition is fierce. It now makes no sense to invest and open the same type of factory workshop, and rural enterprises have to move up to the next stage of value added production. This new generation of rural enterprises will be much more capital-intensive, thus requiring a much larger amount of startup investment.

Rural residents have responded to the higher capital requirements by increasing their saving rates. The rising rural saving rate reflects optimism about the future. This phenomenon of investment-induced savings is not new,[10] it has happened earlier in Taiwan. Up until the mid 1980s, all Taiwanese banks were state-owned. Every Taiwanese loan officer was personally responsible for any loan that went bad, and so every loan officer minimised lending to small and medium sized enterprises, and only lent readily to big business groups. Between 1960 and 1985, there was a steady rise in the saving rate in Taiwan.

Total fixed investment was 30 per cent of GDP in 1987, and 33 per cent of GDP in 1997. It rose 3 percentage points in 10 years. Fixed investment in the rural sector was 9 per cent of GDP in 1987 but was only 8 per cent in 1997. The investment–GDP ratio went up at the national trend, but went down in the rural sector, the most dynamic part of the Chinese economy. The investment ratio in the rural sector has gone down because it makes no sense to establish another labour-intensive factory, and rural entrepreneurs cannot borrow the money to undertake the more capital-intensive investments required for the next generation of rural enterprises. The investment–GDP ratio went up at the national level because FDI went up while state investments (through either the budget or state enterprises) utilised the domestic savings fully.

The solution to insufficient domestic demand in the Chinese economy is not for the government to use up the private savings in public investments, but to set up mechanisms to channel private savings into private investments. This is where the entry of foreign banks will be exceedingly important. Foreign banks will be concentrating their activities in the large coastal cities, where the state-owned banks now make the bulk of their profits. This increased competition will force the state-owned banks to focus on areas of banking where they have a comparative advantage over the foreign banks; in the inner provinces and the rural areas where they have extensive existing branch systems. The state banks have traditionally neglected the inland provinces and the rural areas. The most dynamic part of the Chinese economy is located in the rural areas, and yet formal financial intermediation has decreased there—the number of rural banks has actually decreased in the 1985–95 period. This trend is directly against the sustenance of growth, and has occured because the regulated interest rate for loans in China made it unprofitable to extend small loans. Large and small loans require the same amount of paperwork and time to process. It is only natural that rural banks should charge a higher interest rate since the cost of monitoring and processing the loan is higher. But since rural branches have to charge the same lending rates on small loans as urban branches on large loans, banks have retreated from lending in the rural areas. The liberalisation of interest rates combined with increased competition in the coastal urban markets will motivate the state banks to expand their activities in the long-neglected inland provinces and rural areas.

What has happened in the face of strong rural industrial growth is that a lot of informal rural financial institutions have sprouted up to meet the financing needs of the rural industries. Given the illegal nature of these rural financial institutions, they live under constant threat of closure, and so tend to focus only on the short run and take more risks. It is not surprising that these risky rural financial institutions often fail. Whenever they fail, the government has to bail them out in order to maintain political stability. Subsequently, the government has been clamping down even harder on these illegal financial intermediaries, as it does not want to choose between the risk of bailing them out or the risk of social instability. The government's increasingly strict enforcement of the ban on private financial intermediation is exactly the opposite to what ought to be done. The efficient solution is to allow private financial intermediaries in the rural area, and bring them under proper prudential supervision.

The general principle, and a trend that the Chinese government will find increasingly costly to prevent, is to reduce interest rate controls and allow private banks to come into existence. The improvement in financial intermediation will eliminate the liquidity trap and reduce the paradox of thrift. The entry of foreign banks will also improve financial intermediation by enabling the transfer of modern banking technology through a seldom-mentioned channel. In the future, when a successful Chinese enterprise group establishes a bank, it will do so by hiring the local managers employed by the foreign owned banks. This has been the Southeast Asian experience, where the top managers of all the biggest domestic banks were all ex-employees of foreign banks. This is perhaps what the Chinese leadership sees and why it is willing to allow the entry of foreign banks, giving them national treatment within five years of WTO membership. The Chinese leadership is betting that in the short run, there could be significant displacement of Chinese state banks by foreign banks, but in the long run, Chinese banks (most likely private ones) will increase in importance. Twenty years from now, the international financial world will have more to fear from Chinese banks than vice-versa.

China's walk across the bridge is also wobbly because of the uncertainty as to how the privatisation process should continue. The state enterprise sector is simply too large, and, like its cousins the world over, is losing money on a large scale. Most state enterprises are already economically dead. Obviously, the Chinese leadership agrees with this description, because it has been expanding SOE privatisation. But the Eastern European experience warns that mass privatisation is an exceedingly dangerous business politically no matter how it is done, be it outsider privatisation through vouchers as in the Czech Republic or insider privatisation through shares for loans as in Russia.

Corruption leading to political demise appears to be an inevitable by-product of mass privatisation, for example Vaclav Klaus in the Czech Republic and Anatoli Chubais in Russia. China has so far avoided widespread organised public dissatisfaction with its partial privatisation of the small and medium state enterprises. The central government has given itself an indirect role in the privatisation process in order to avoid bearing the brunt of any negative fallout. It works through passing to local governments the financial responsibility for most of the state enterprises located in their areas. In the case of loss-making enterprises, the local government is forced to either come up with a subsidy or to privatise them. The second option is the common choice. The party secretary who gets rid of the loss-makers without arousing local resentment is promoted. If there is substantial public resentment over the privatisation, then the party secretary is reprimanded or replaced for inept implementation of state policy.

The question is whether this strategy can continue to shelter the central government from the public backlash over inept privatisation, especially when the large state enterprises are privatised? Given the fact that every manager, after the implosion of the Soviet Union in 1991, knows that privatisation is inevitable, he recognises that this is the last chance for him to steal. This end game consideration may be responsible for the recent escalation of corruption across China, creating a situation that Party Secretary, Jiang Zemin, has called the biggest threat to the continued rule of the Communist Party. In short, the ongoing acceleration of the privatisation process (both formal and informal) could create a political storm over corruption that would make it difficult for China to walk steadily across the bridge to the greener grass of a private market economy.

Conclusion

It is important to be reminded that the apparent trade-off faced by China between stability and restructuring is not caused by its accession to WTO membership but by the need to move from a planned economy to a market economy. Joining the WTO now is really not bringing forward the date of confronting this trade-off. Most SOEs have been economically dead for almost a decade, and the fiscal burden and the corruption problem of the state enterprise sector have become too heavy to bear.[11] The two key WTO-induced developments that are crucial to the successful crossing of the WTO bridge are the rise in Chinese exports and the rise in FDI. Their occurrence will improve the tradeoff in the state enterprise sector between restructuring and job losses.

While keeping balance on the macroeconomic and political fronts would enable China to walk steadily across the bridge, we must point out that the absence of a strong wind is also crucial for making it over to the other side. There are three types of typhoon that would make the crossing more difficult for China.

- Substantial slowdown in the US economy: the US economy has been the engine of growth for the world economy. Recent data suggest that continued fast expansion of the United States economy is unlikely. Japan seems likely to plunge back into recession. Western Europe shows no signs of dynamic growth that would rival that of the United States. So, a significant slowdown of the US economy means that there would be a fall in Chinese exports and a drop of FDI into China, both of which are important for keeping the bridge strong enough for the goat to walk on. More importantly, the slowdown in the United States economy could give impetus to protectionism within the United States, and this would make the WTO adjustment process in China much more painful.

- Political conflicts in the Pacific Rim: three such conflicts come readily to mind: the Chinese occupation of islands in the South China Sea; mainland-Taiwan tensions over political union; and the resolution of the Korean question, if the North Korean regime were to collapse from a worsening of its already disastrous economic situation. In the case of an acrimonious political conflict, trade sanctions by the United States and other Western European countries will hamper Chinese economic performance.

- Drop in FDI: FDI in China may not grow as rapidly as expected. This scenario depends on changes in the attractiveness of places like India. India has been unusually hostile to FDI—for example, foreigners cannot hold more than 51 per cent of equity in a firm. If this were to change, a significant diversion of FDI into India, a country with an English-speaking labour force, could happen.

Acknowledgments

I am grateful Ligang Song and Wei Men of The Australian National University, and Geng Xiao of the University of Hong Kong for very helpful conversations on the Chinese economy, the reform of state-owned enterprises, and the impact of WTO.

Notes

1 Prominent examples of this experimentalist line of thought are Naughton (1994) and Rawski (1995).
2 Sachs and Woo (2000) surveys this debate in detail.
3 Chang and Wang (1994) is an early recognition of this point.
4 Chen (1998) provides an excellent picture of the difficulties in reforming SOEs in her case study on Chongqing. One of her most interesting findings is that new managers bring improvements in the first two years but then they begin to focus on asset-stripping.

5   For recent warnings from this faction against what is perceived as suicide by the Communist Party, see 'Elder warns on economic change', *South China Morning Post*, 13 January 2000, and 'Leftists make late bid to slow reforms', *South China Morning Post*, 10 February 2000.

6   For a recent study on the large impact of FDI on China's growth, see Demurger (2000).

7   This argument is developed in Sachs and Woo (1994).

8   The 18.0 per cent for 1995 is calculated from the *China Statistical Yearbook 1996* because the total workforce data from 1990 onward was revised upward in the *China Statistical Yearbook* of the succeeding years by increasing the size of the rural workforce. The revised data are inconsistent across time. The growth in labour force between 1989 and 1990 is now 15.5 per cent (!), while the old data show an increase of 2.5 per cent. Using the revised data, the SOEs employed 17 per cent of the total labour force.

9   Easterley and Fischer (1994) shows that extensive growth came to a quicker end in Russia than would have occurred in capitalist market economies because the elasticity of substitution between capital and labour in Russia was much lower. Woo (1998) suggests that the intersectoral reallocation of labour contributed 1.3 percentage points to the annual GDP growth rate in the 1985–93 period.

10 See Liu and Woo (1994) for theoretical discussion and empirical verification of investment-induced saving.

11 The combination of mounting losses in the state enteprises, the inability of the government to raise revenue significantly, and the need to increase state spending to maintain aggregate demand is creating a fiscally alarming situation. See Gamble (2000) on the difficulties of tax collection in China.

3

The dynamics of transition in ownership structure

Fan Gang

Much research has shown how and why the non-state sector has been growing in China and the contribution it has made to the overall growth and development of the market system. Other research focuses on the problems of state-owned enterprises (SOEs) and how they should be further reformed.

However, one aspect of the reform process seems to have not yet been fully explored in discussions about the economic transition in China: how the growth of the non-state sector has changed the conditions for the reform of SOEs in particular, and the state sector in general, and why it is necessary to reform SOEs if we want continued growth in the non-state sectors and the economy as a whole. These questions are crucial to an understanding of the current situation in China and the future of China's economic transition and development.

This chapter provides an analysis of the dynamics of incremental reform with special respect to the relationship between the growth of the non-state sector, the change of the ownership structure of the economy as a whole and the reform process of the state sector.[1]

Ownership structure and institutional transition

The key characteristic of the gradual approach to transition is not the slowness of transition, but that it starts with the development of elements of the new system, such as private sector and market pricing, while keeping the old system, such as SOEs and state banks, unchanged. In comparison, radical reform (as in Russia) started with the reform of the old system, where the new elements started to grow on the ruins of the old structures. Comparisons do not include any value judgments.

One way or another, both approaches to transition require a change of economic structure. The fundamental structure of the economy is the ownership structure. Institutional transition from a planned economy to a market economy requires structural changes from the domination of the state-owned sector to that of private (non-state) ownership.

The most important issue for transition: developing the non-state sector

We define the following ratio as the ownership structure (J) of an economy in transition

$$J_0 = \frac{S_0}{N_0}$$

where S stands for the state sector, N the non-state sector, subscript indicates the time and 0 here refers to the initial state.

The institutional transformation can be defined by the change of J from somewhere close to one to somewhere close to zero. This process can be done by the privatisation of S into N, but can also be done by simply developing N without changing S in the long run.

Let g^s and g^n be the growth rates of state sector and non-state sector respectively. By assuming that the new system, the non-state sector, is more efficient than the old state sector, we have $g^s < g^n$. We may call this inequality the fundamental presumption of reform, because otherwise the reform is not economically rational. Under such a presumption, if the period of time is long enough, that is, $t \rightarrow \infty$ we have

$$J_t = \frac{S_0(1+g^s)^t}{N_0(1+g^n)^t} = J_0 \frac{(1+g^s)^t}{(1+g^n)^t} \xrightarrow[t \rightarrow \infty]{} 0 \tag{3.1}$$

This means that no matter how big the state sector was at the beginning of the transition, or is at any point of time, as long as the non-state sector can grow, the transition will succeed in the long run, simply by the assumption that $g^s < g^n$.

Here we can see that first and foremost the whole process of transition is to allow growth to begin in the non-state sector. Everything starts from there, no matter which reform approach is taken. Mass privatisation may be the way to start growth in the private sector.

The possibility of transition without SOE reform

We can also see that transition, indicated by the diminishing J, may take place without any reform of the state sector. This is justified by the feasibility of the gradual approach, which starts the transition with an initially unreformed state sector. Theoretically, as long as the non-state sector is growing, the position of the state sector will, in the long run, shrink to zero. In a more real sense, for a period of one generation it is feasible that SOEs may operate as before and the state employees may be paid just as before, until they all retire. In the period of one generation, the state sector may disappear and the transition may be completed.

This seems to be the least painful process and an ideal program.

Of course, such a picture looks unrealistic. But it does reveal the key elements of the economic transition: developing the private sector and limiting the expansion of the state sector. No matter how big the state sector is and how big its problems at the moment or at any time in its history, it will be unimportant as long as the private sector is able to grow. The focus of attention should always be on the growth of new institutions. As long as the structure of the economy continues to change, problems can eventually be solved in a comparatively painless fashion.

In China transition started with the growth of the non-state sector that made the J value change from more than 9 in 1979, to 0.3 in 1998 in terms of the value-added industrial output (Figure 3.1). The most important achievement of China's economic transition in the past 20 years is the development of the non-state sector. Meanwhile, reform of the state sector has only begun recently. During the 20-year course of transition, the state sector also grew in absolute terms. At the same time, its problems became more severe, including lower profitability, more loss-making enterprises and huge non-performing loans owed to the state banks. All the difficulties of the economy are related to the problems of the state sector. But the reason that the economy continues to grow and the overall situation of financial and social stability is still manageable is simply because the importance of the state sector is diminishing, as it only contributes about 30 per cent of national income.

In a more extreme example of the no-reform transition, in some coastal regions where the non-state sector already accounts for over 90 per cent of economic activities, people do not even bother to reform the SOEs. They simply leave SOEs alone and continue to pay them subsidies. We call this the simple transition or no-reform approach to transition.

In general, this may not actually be possible because the state sector does not give up. Interest groups in the state sector do their best to protect themselves and use their political monopoly to get more resources in order to expand and resist shrinkage. They will try all available means to stop the growth of the private sector. Thus, while the no-reform approach is theoretically feasible, it is impossible from the point of view of real-life political economy.

Development of the non-state sector

Changes of conditions for SOE reform

A more realistic possibility in the practice of reform, is that the conditions for the reform of SOEs will be improved because of growth in the non-state sector for following reasons.

- Growing competition by the non-state sectors breaks down the

Figure 3.1 **Political economy dynamics of China's transition**

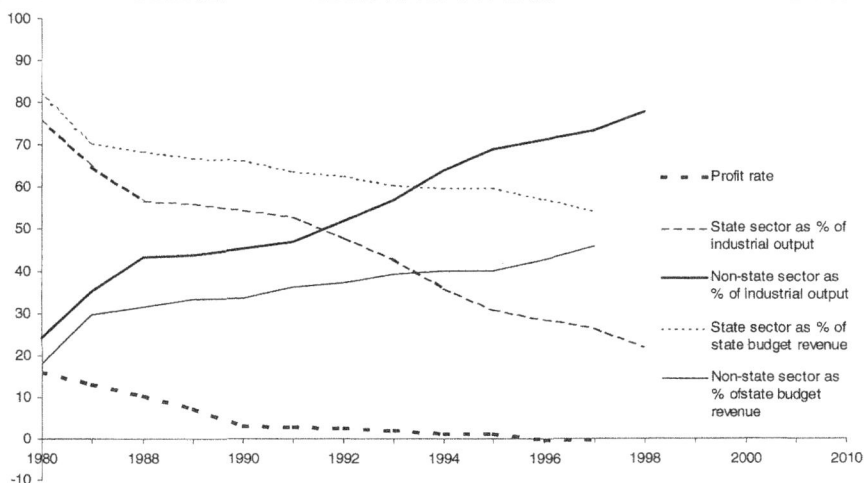

monopoly position of SOEs and pulls down their monopolistic profits. The worsening financial situation is actually the ultimate driving force for the reform program. In real life, reform only takes place when there is no other alternative for survival.

• The development of the non-state sector supports the growth of the economy as a whole and, therefore, provides more job opportunities to absorb laid-off state employees, and/or it makes it possible for the government to mobilise resources to subsidise unemployment compensation for laid-off workers. The higher the share of the non-state sector, the more lay-offs can take place in accordance with regional experiences.

• Growing private financial assets make the capital restructuring and privatisation of SOEs through market mechanism possible.

• The growing entrepreneurial capability of the private sector makes it possible for the remaining assets of SOEs to be taken over for more productive and efficient uses, rather than simply being wrecked in non-productive hands.

For these reasons, small-sized SOEs are the first to have been reformed. While non-state business is still mostly small, they increase competition mainly against the small SOEs, while they are only at the stage of being able to take over SOEs that are not too big or too complicated in terms of both capital and management. Some preliminary data from the provinces shows that in some regions over 70 per cent of small, local SOEs have already been privatised or reformed in one way or another.

According to the same logic of dynamism, the conditions for reforming the bigger SOEs should be ready, sooner or later, along with further growth of the non-state sectors. This is the basis of the so-called step-by-step of the incremental transition, and is different from the step-by-step in the theory of sequencing. As long as the development of the non-state sector continues, large SOEs will be reformed, even though doubts exist among those who hold a static vision.

It would be an ideally smooth transition if things progressed this way. In drawing an analogy, it seems a 'West Germany' has been growing and taking over 'Eastern Germany' in China. Such an analogy is drawn because the German transition can be seen as the smoothest among the Eastern European economies, even though the Germans still think their course has been very costly.

The political economy of the government's reform policy

In many cases, the way of reform depends very much on the political willingness of the government. But it is arguable that such a political willingness is in reality, determined by the economic conditions.

Figure 3.1 also shows that all the major break-through(s) in the policies of SOE reform were only adopted after turning points changed the structure of the economy, that is, the J_t, or the performance of the different sectors relating to the J_t. For example, the Central Committee of the Chinese Communist Party (CCP) wrote into its Reform Decisions, the restructuring of property rights for the first time in 1993. It happened in that year as the J_t reached one for the first time, meaning that the non-state sector surpassed the state sector in terms of the proportion of the industrial value-added output. Another example occurred between 1996–97. The SOEs as a whole registered a net loss in the first half of 1996 and 1997. The CCP then adopted a new reform decision at its Fifteenth Party Congress, announcing that the non-state sector should have equal legal status with the SOEs and that small SOEs should be fully subject to market competition, even if this meant their privatisation. In many coastal regions, the government reform policy changed sharply when the private sector surpassed the state sector as the main source of local fiscal revenue. Nothing was accidental about this process.

Theoretically, government policy depends on how much it stands to gain from reform and how much it stands to lose if it reforms. The most important thing here is that all of the factors relating to policymaking are the variables of the J_t, and therefore, that the policy itself is a dependent variable of the J_t. Such a correlation may be summarised in the following simplified model.

Suppose a local government can make its own reform policies on its own economic calculation. Its basic behavioural model can be written as

$z^n (J_t) \geq z^s (J_t)$

where $z^s (J_t)$ = that which the government receives if not reforming SOEs

all kinds of Government revenues provided by the SOEs concerned (profits,

taxes , plus any 'off-budget revenues')
+ wage income generated by the SOEs for the employees (J_t)
- fiscal subsidies to SOEs (J_t)
- non-performing loans owed by SOEs to the state banks (J_t)
- all the troubles of dealing with SOEs' debts and unemployment and daily
 operations (J_t)

And $z^n(J_t)=$ if the government goes with reforms
all kinds of government revenues from the non-state companies concerned (J_t)
+ proceeds from privatisation (J_t)
+ wage income provided by the non-state undertakings (J_t)
- expenditures for clearing up the debts of SOEs (J_t)
- expenditures on unemployment compensation due to the lay-off of state
 employees (J_t)
- premium of the political risks that reform may be faced with (J_t).

Theoretically, the government will choose to 'reform' when the inequality holds and choose to stay with 'no change' if it does not.

It can be demonstrated in detail that the components of both sides of the inequality are somehow variables of J_t and so, the inequality changes with changes to the J_t. This explains the evolution of the government policy—from a planning economy dominated by state ownership, to the recent market economy with diversified investors and mixed ownership.

Some may argue for the reversed causality. That is, it seems that it was the (previous) government policies that led to the change of economic structure, rather than vice versa. In some sense, causality may not be important as long as the correlation is clear. But the time lag between the development of reality and the progress of policies does hint at the causal relationship. Since the early 1990, China's reforms, particularly SOE reforms, have featured the bottom-up and crisis push processes, and most reforms were actually initiated by local people and local enterprises. In most cases and at all levels, the government has failed to take the lead but instead has been waiting until the conditions (determined by J_t) change making the situation clearer and more favorable.

The dynamics of the political economy of 'lay-off'

More than 100 million state employees used to enjoy life-time employment and the many privileges offered by the government. Although the SOEs were 20–30 per cent over-staffed, even according to the government's official estimation, the lay-off (particularly the mass lay-off of millions of people per year) was unthinkable even five years ago. But since 1995, over 15 million state employees have been laid off at an accelerated rate. It has become so common that almost every SOE has laid off employees.

The question is, why have state employees, who are perhaps the most powerful interest group in China and who refused to be laid-off for such a long time, now accepted the reform packages? It has, of course, been dependent on the development of, and reforms to, the social security system and increased government expenditures on unemployment insurance. But it also depends on the development of the non-state sectors and the J_t, because that determines the opportunity costs of accepting the lay-off. The behavioural model of a state employee is written as following

$w^n(J_t) \geq w^s(J_t)$

$w^n(J_t)=$ (if being laid off from the SOEs and going to the private sector)

money and non-money wage income from private undertakings (J_t)

+ social security income

- suffering from higher working efforts

- suffering from discrimination against the private sectors (J_t)

- risk premium of job uncertainty in private sectors

+ what a state employee can keep from the SOEs (housing, pension program and so on)

- losses in period of unemployment (J_t)

+ unemployment compensations from the government.

$w^s(J_t)=$ (if staying with SOEs)

money and non-money wage income from SOEs (J_t)

+ income in forms of free housing, pension, medical care and so on

- losses because of the delay of wage payment or any payment from the financially troubled SOEs (J_t)

+ the pleasure of less working efforts

+ satisfaction from the social status of being a state employee (J_t).

Some of the factors of inequality are hard to measure quantitatively and make any monetary equivalent (such as suffering, pleasure or satisfaction), but they still play a role in the decision-making process. The various possible directions of correlation between the independent variables of the inequality and the J_t should also be noted. For example, the higher the J_t, the less possible it is for an SOE to delay its payment to its workers because SOEs may still be in a monopolistic position. But for some regions that have lagged behind, the higher the J_t, the more probable the delay might be because in such a region more SOEs may suffer from financial difficulties. The issue is worth a great deal of further study, both theoretically and empirically.

The possibility of a reversed course or crisis

So far we have presented a relatively rosy picture of economic transition. As long as the non-state sectors grow, the conditions for reforming the state sector will improve and the institutional transition will be achieved in the long run, no matter how big the state sector or how long the transition process takes.

But where is the problem? In reality, reforms are faced with tremendous difficulties and people always worry about the possibility that the reforms may stop and the transition process may be reversed and then, as the result, economic growth may stop too. So where are the risks?

The key problem which has not been captured in the above model is the fact that the state sector may use its state power to control income redistribution and the allocation of resources, and consequently, slow down the change of J_t.

Subsidies to SOEs

What is missing in the simplified model above is income redistribution. The state sector may have a lower growth rate, but it may still be able to rely on government power to control the distribution and resource allocation in order to subsidise SOEs. In China, the government not only has taxation power but has also kept the monopoly of state banks and state financial institutions in the financial sectors. Therefore, redistribution and subsidies take place in various forms such as

- fiscal subsidies—this kind of subsidy has been minor since the mid 1980s when the government shifted most of its fiscal responsibilities (equity

---

Box 3.1	Gradual reform since 1978

Date	Reform
1978–79	Planned economy using the law of market exchange value
1979–10.84	Planned economy supplemented with some market elements
10.1984–10.87	The planned commodity economy
10.1987–06.89	State regulating the market and market regulating enterprises
06.1989–91	Organic integration of planned economy and market regulations
1992	Shareholding system and security market (started) can be used by socialism
10.1992	Socialist market economy
1994	Corporatisation of SOEs and reform of property rights
1997	Developing the state sector together with all other kinds of ownership. Improving large SOEs while letting small ones go to the market
1998	Constituional Amendment. Private ownership should be equally promoted and protected
10.1999	SOEs withdrawing from competitive industries. Diversification of ownership of corporate and mixed ownership. Executive stock options for SOEs

Source: Central Committee of CCP, 1985. 'Ten policies of the CCP Central Committee and the State Council for the further invigoration of the rural economy', in *The Agricultural Yearbook of China*, China Statistical Publishing House, Beijing:1–3.

---

investment and subsidies) to the state banks. But recently this kind of subsidy has risen as the government has started to use a debt-equity swap program to reduce the non-performing loan burdens on SOEs

- non-performing loans between the SOEs and the state banks—this may also be called quasi-government debt
- non-performing foreign debts owed by the SOEs directly, or by the state financial institutions or by some government agencies that borrow in international market for the state sector.
- part of the funds raised from the security market for SOEs—it was officially claimed that one of the main roles of the current stock markets is to raise funds for SOEs that continue to be controlled by the government, as it holds unchangeable majority shares. The fact that most state-controlled companies listed on the stock market have since turned out to be loss-making indicates that a great deal of funds raised from the market are a form of public subsidy for the SOEs.

Non-state sector as the source of subsidy to the state sector

If the subsidy is not only the nominal one (taken back by inflation, for instance), it must come from somewhere in the economy. In a two-sector model, the subsidy to the state sector must come from the non-state sector. In this model the government is in the state sector. Even if we take the government as a third party, it still only channels the transfer between the two sectors.

To understand this, it is important to keep in mind the equality issue. If the non-state sector could get bank loans or foreign loans equally and could have an equally high non-performing loan ratio, or, if the non-state sector could go to the stock market to raise funds proportional to its contribution to GDP with equality, then there would be no real subsidy. It would be only equivalent to certain level of inflation in such a model. But, at least in China, equality is not the case. The most serious distortion of resource allocation is that the non-state sector, which contributes more than 70 per cent of output, uses less than 30 per cent of bank credits (Table 3.1). The most serious policy mistake in the past 20 years of reform has been the lack of development of the non-state financial institutions which would more adequately have served the growth of the non-state sector.

It is such subsidies that create the risk that the transition (indicated by a decreasing J_t) may be stopped or reversed. This can be seen when we bring such a redistribution factor into the model.

Let D stand for a form of taxation on the non-state sector which includes formal taxes and various levies, such as fees and contributions, bank deposits which would become non-performing loans, and public investment in the state controlled companies listed in the stock market. ΣD_I then stands for the comprehensive taxation on non-state sectors and d for the comprehensive tax rate on non-state sector. We then have

$$d = \frac{\sum D_i}{N}$$

The d actually indicates the total transfer from the non-state sector to the state sector, or the total subsidies that the SOEs receive. Therefore, we can call it the subsidy-transfer rate between the two sectors.

We then have Equation (3.2)

$$J_t = \frac{S_0(1+g^s)^t}{N_0(1+g^n-d)^t} \tag{3.2}$$

Equation (3.2) is actually no longer an output function of J but is a resource allocation function of J, which describes the economic structure in terms of income redistribution and resource allocation between the two sectors. The existence of d makes it possible that $(1+g^s) > (1+g^n - d)$, if $d > 0$ and $d > g^n - g^s$.

Without doubt, the growth rates will be affected by the resource allocation. That is

$$g_t^n(d) = f(d_t, d_{t-1}, d_{t-2} \ldots \ldots)$$

As long as $d > 0$, the growth rate of the non-state sector will slow down to a certain extent. If the d is big enough, we may have $g^n(d) < g^s$, although we always have $g^s < g^n$ as the fundamental presumption of reform. We then have

$$J_t = J_0 \frac{(1+g^s)^t}{[1+g^n(d)]^t} \xrightarrow[t \to \infty]{} \infty \tag{3.3}$$

That is, the J_t will be reversed, if not exploded. We call the situation described by (3.3) the possibility of reversal of the transition.

Table 3.1   Economic structure of China, 1997–98 (per cent of total)

	State sector	Non-state sector
GDP	37.8	62.2
Industrial value-added	26.47	73.53
Investment	54.1	45.9
Bank credit	68.2	31.8
Export	52.7	47.3
Total increase in employment	-101.52	201.52

Note: Some figures are data of 1997.
Source: State Statistical Bureau of China (SSB), 1999. *China Statistical Yearbook*, China Statistical Publishing House, Beijing (in Chinese).

Controlling *d*: the real reason for SOE reform

We have discussed the possibility of not reforming SOEs under the fundamental presumption of reform, that is $g^s < g^n$. Having introduced *d*, that is, the taxation on the non-state sector and subsidies to the state sector, we see why we have to reform the state sector. It is necessary in order to prevent *d* from becoming big in the real life of political economy. If the old sector could pass away naturally due to less efficiency, transition would be much less painful because it is possible to simply wait without reforming. But those people with a vested interest in the old system may use their political influence to resist the process of passing away, by taking subsidies from other sectors and stopping or even reversing the process of transition. People will have to reform the old sector with additional costs of reform, simply because others have exerted their efforts to survive.

The crucial point here is the size of *d*. The non-state sector may stop growing totally if *d* gets too big, that is, if the economic surplus for growth of the non-state sector is taxed away. In any circumstances, the size of *d* actually captures all possible factors that may cause the crisis and reversal of the transition. Therefore, the issue as to whether or not transition can continue and economic growth be sustained from the point of view of institutional change, boils down to the question of whether *d* can be controlled without an explosion.

There are many reform policies that suggest ways to prevent *d* from getting too big, so we shall avoid discussing them again here.

A comparison of different approaches to transition

The size of *d* may be determined by the following factors
- the size of the state sector in the relation to the non-state sector at the initial stage and any particular time afterward: the bigger the state sector, the bigger the *d* may be
- the financial situation of the state sector—the less efficient and less profitable (the two are not the same) the state sector as a whole, the bigger the *d* may be. Historical experience justified by theoretical logic, shows that the longer the state economy exists, the worse its financial situation and the lower its profitability.

We can now compare the approaches to transition in different countries. In Russia, for instance, the almost entire domination of the state sector and a 70-year history of a planned economy left it with no choice but mass privatisation at the very beginning of transition. Otherwise the private sector would not grow because any economic surplus they received might immediately be taxed away (by inflation at least). In China, the relatively small size of the state industries (in terms of employment) at the initial stage of transition has made it possible to postpone the

Table 3.2   **Comprehensive public-sector liability as a measure of overall financial risk in the Chinese economy**

	1997	1998	1998*
Total NPL (% of GDP)	25.05	27.19	..
Government domestic debt (% of GDP)	7.32	8.78	..
Total foreign debt (% of GDP)	14.70	14.57	..
Comprehensive government liability ratio (%)	47.07	50.53	37.45
Inflation RPI (%)	0.8	-2.6	..
Total short-term foreign debt / GDP	1.53	1.5	..

Notes: 1988 includes short-term foreign debt only; NPL is non-performing loans.
Source: State Statistical Bureau of China (SSB), 1999. *China Statistical Yearbook*, China Statistical Publishing House, Beijing (in Chinese).

reform of SOEs for quite a long time. The relatively better financial situation of the SOEs (due to a shorter history) have made the d relatively small, and have even enabled the government to give non-state companies some tax reductions in their early stages of growth. A similar argument may also be applicable to some Eastern European economies.

Measuring overall financial risks and preventing a crisis

The Chinese government has kept tax revenue below 15 per cent as a proportion of GDP in most years since the late 1980s. Therefore, subsidy transfer mainly takes the form of various kinds of public or quasi-public debts, including government debt, non-performing bank loans and foreign debt borrowed by government or SOEs. All of these debts are transferred from the private sector or the general public (as individuals) to loss-making SOEs (as long as they are still operating).

Therefore, the approximate measurement of the ΣD_i and d is the sum of the three kinds of debts: government debt, non-performing loans and the foreign debts, and the ratio of this sum over GDP.

$$CLP = \frac{NPL + government\ domestic\ debt + total\ foreign\ debt}{GDP}$$

We take a rough, but popular, estimation of the non-performing loans as 25 per cent of total bank credits at the end of 1998. It was equivalent to about 27 per cent of GDP. At the same time, the government debt over GDP ratio was about nine per cent and the foreign debt over GDP ratio was about 14 per cent. Adding these up, the comprehensive public-sector liability (CPL), as it may be termed, is about 50 per cent over GDP (Table 3.2).

Compared to similar indicators of other economies (Table 3.3), China's overall

Table 3.3   International comparison of comprehensive public-sector liability, 1997

	Japan	Thailand	Indonesia	Korea
(1) Total foreign debt (Balance, billions) WB &ADB data base	..	91.8	136.2	155.4
(2) Total foreign debt (Balance, billions of local currency, based on annual average exchange rate)	..	3151.0	412760.0	140170.0
(3) Government domestic debt, balance (in billions of local currency, balance at year end)	508354.3	69.3	6278.5	28543.0
(4) NPL/total banks' loans (%) (JPM 1998:2 estimate)	12.3	26.6	32.5	25.2
(5) Total bank loans (billions of local currency, Merryl-Lynch 1998:4)	624864.0	7723.6	361736.9	558481.0
(6) Total NPL (billions of local currency, (6)+(5)×(4))	76858.3	2054.5	117564.5	140737.2
(7) GDP (billion of local currency, IMF1998 annual report)	511864.0	4827.0	578779.0	410647.9
(8) Comprehensive Public-sector Liability Ratio (CPL) (NCL=((2)+(3)+(6))/(7))×100)	114.3	109.3	92.7	75.4
(9) Inflation (RPI, %, GDP deflator)	1.7	5.6	11.1	4.5
* Exchange rate ($1=X local currency) (annual average)	119.4	34.3	3035.0	902.0

Sources: (1)http://www.boj.or.jp/en/link/link_f.htm
(2)http://www.bi.go.id/
(3)http://www.worldbank.org/html/extdr/data.htm
(4)http://www.bot.or.th/research/public/DataBank/databank.htm
(5)http://bok.or.kr/kobank/owa/stats3_ei_top=stats&i_subject

Figure 3.2   **Percentage change of non-state sector's contribution to the industrial output**

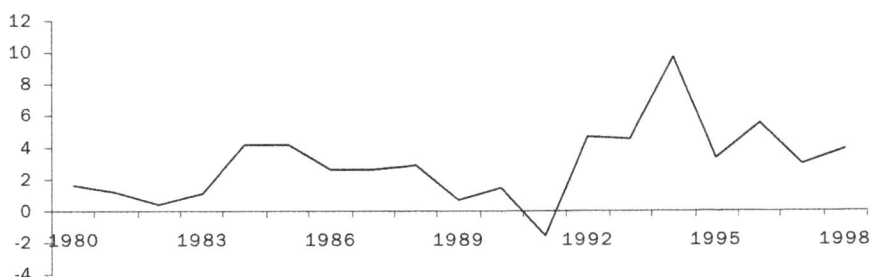

financial situation measured by CPL seems to be not as bad as the non-performing loans indicate, and it can be said that China is still not in danger of financial crisis within the foreseeable future.

In addition, looking at recent trends in economic structure, the J is still steadily decreasing while the non-state sector keeps growing as the major contributor to output at a rate of one to two percentage points annually (Figure 3.2). This indicates the continuation of the process of transformation continues rather than its reversal.

Concluding remarks

This chapter tries to identify the causes of institutional transition and the factors that may lead to a crisis, stop, or even reversal at the transition process. It demonstrates that transition may gain its own momentum once it has started (fundamental assumption of the transition), but that there are possibilities that the process may not proceed successfully due to dislocation (subsidy-transfer).

While the theoretical analysis proves the possibility of reversal, the statistical evidence shows that economic transformation in China has been steadily going forward, as measured by the change of the ownership structure (J). These statistics also show that transition will continue without the threat of crises or collapse in the foreseeable future. The future of China's institutional transition depends on the progress made preventing crises in the next stage of transition.

Note

1   By the state sector we mean the combination of the SOEs, state-banking system and the government.

4

China's WTO membership

Implications for the domestic economy

Wen Hai

After more than 20 years of reform and 13 years of negotiation, China finally signed the agreement on World Trade Organization (WTO) accession with the United States on 15 November 1999, and with the European Union (EU) on 19 May 2000 and has now joined the WTO.

Needless to say, China's accession to the WTO will have a significant impact on both China and the world economy. There are at least three important reasons for economists, as well as policymakers, to study and understand the significance and implications of its WTO accession. First, China is a big economy, any changes will most likely affect the equilibrium of the world market, even the world economic system. It is obvious that WTO membership will bring big changes to China's economic performance and structure. In turn, these changes will effect world economic performance and business structures. This is one of the reasons why the WTO negotiations with the United States and the EU took so long. Second, China is a developing country. China's decisions and actions regarding the WTO will affect the decisions and actions of other developing countries. If China opens its markets more than most developing countries, it will bring pressure on them to do likewise. On the other hand, if China maintains protection for its domestic markets, it may increase the bargaining power of developing countries in the world trading system. Third, China is a transitional economy. How the WTO access effects China's economy will provide lessons for other transitional economies.

As the seventh largest economy[1] and an economy in the process of industrialisation and transition, WTO membership will impact significantly on China's economic development and reforms, as well as on other world economies. What will be the impact of China's WTO accession on international trade? How will it affect the scope and pace of China's economic reform and development? What are the implications of China's membership? Although there are many other issues that need to be addressed, this chapter focuses on the possible impact on China's economy.

China's WTO membership will affect its economic reform and development in at least three respects. First, it will increase China's foreign trade. In particular, imports from industrialised countries will increase rapidly. Second, it will significantly change its economic structure. As a result of freer trade, production in highly protected sectors will decrease. On the other hand, opening to foreign direct investment (FDI) will stimulate the development of a modern service sector, the information and technology (IT) industry, and even automobile manufacture. Third, it will accelerate the reform of state-owned enterprises and help develop private enterprises in the Chinese economy. China may be able to complete its economic transition from a planned economy to a market economy through its WTO accession.

Stimulating freer trade

The first and most direct impact of China's WTO membership will be the stimulation of world trade volume. Economists from the World Bank, China and other countries have estimated the possible quantitative impacts of China's WTO accession—all of the studies show that China's accession will make world trade bigger and freer.

The reasons why people believe that China's accession to the WTO will stimulate world trade are simple and clear. Because China is already the seventh largest economy and the ninth largest trading country, further trade liberalisation in China will certainly make a significant contribution to the world trade volume. Being a member of the WTO, China will not only open up more of its markets to foreign goods, but will also be able to export more through an improvement in the external business environment and the development of its economic and export capacity.

Reducing trade protection and increasing imports

Like most of the newly industrialised economies in Asia, China's economic development began with the expansion of its exports. Although China's imports have been growing at a fast rate, they have been restricted by the state. Therefore, while exports are being liberalised and encouraged, imports are still limited and controlled. Table 4.1 shows China's total trade in the last ten years. It is not surprising that it has experienced a trade surplus for all but one year. According to the General Administration of Customs of China, the accumulated trade surplus from these ten years was as high as US$156.4 billion. As trade protection is reduced, China will increase imports significantly.

Tariff reduction. Currently, China's average tariff rate is about 16.4 per cent.

Table 4.1   **China's trade with the world,** 1990–99 (US$ billion)

	1990	1991	1992	1993	1994
Exports	62.1	71.9	84.9	91.7	121.0
Imports	53.3	63.8	80.6	104.0	115.6
Balance	8.8	8.1	4.3	-12.3	5.4
Total	115.4	135.7	165.5	195.7	236.6

	1995	1996	1997	1998	1999	Accumulated
Exports	148.8	151.1	182.7	183.8	194.9	1292.9
Imports	132.1	138.8	142.4	140.2	165.7	1136.5
Balance	16.7	12.3	40.3	43.6	29.2	156.4
Total	280.9	289.9	325.1	324.0	360.6	2429.4

Source: PRC General Administration of Customs, 2000. *China's Customs Statistics*, Beijing, July.

This rate has reduced significantly from more than 40 per cent in the early 1990s, but it is still relatively high compared to the average 6 per cent tariff rate of WTO members and the average rate of 14 per cent for developing countries. To be a member of the WTO, China agreed to make a substantial reduction in tariffs. The average tariff rate will be decreased to about 15 per cent on accession to the WTO and will be further reduced to about 10 per cent by 2005. Table 4.2 shows the projected tariff reductions in major sectors and for selected industrial products. The average tariff rate of industrial products will be reduced more than 60 per cent in 5 years from the current level of 24.6 per cent to 9.4 per cent. The tariff on IT products will be completely eliminated, and the agriculture tariff will be cut more than half from 31.5 per cent to 14.5 per cent by 2004.

Table 4.2 illustrates the significance of these tariff reductions on trade in China and in the world. The fifth column of the table indicates the selected products imported in China as the percentage of China's total imports. The sixth column shows the relative importance of these products in total exports from the United States. The last column calculated the products imported by China as the percentage of the total world export of these products. Partly due to high levels of protection, most of these items accounted for only a small percentage of both China's imports and the total world exports of these products. On the other hand, many of them are major exports from industrialised countries, such as the United States.

Taking the Chinese auto market as an example with an 80–100 per cent tariff rate, the import of automobiles is highly restricted. In 1997, China's total auto imports accounted for less than 1 per cent of world trade in auto products that year. This is small for the world's ninth largest trading country. Imports of cosmetics, furniture, pharmaceuticals, agricultural and medical equipment are also very low as a share of total world trade. The limited imports are mainly due to trade restrictions. Once China enters the WTO and reduces such protection, imports of these products is expected to increase rapidly.

In the China–EU negotiations, China offered an additional reduction of 40 per cent on 150 specific EU products, varying from gin to building materials. Tariffs on 13 leather products, which account for 60 per cent of total EU exports in this sector, will be reduced from 20–25 per cent to 10 per cent. Tariffs on 5 specific footwear products that account for more than 70 per cent of EU footwear exports will be reduced from 25 per cent to 10 per cent. On 52 specific products in the important machinery and appliances sector, which accounts for 26 per cent of total EU exports, tariffs will be cut to 5–10 per cent from the current level of 35 per cent. The rapid tariff reduction on these specific EU products indicates that China's European imports will also increase.

Removal of non-tariff barriers. Besides the reduction of tariffs, China will also remove significant non-tariff barriers (NTBs). Table 4.3 summarises the main changes in non-tariff barriers. Again, we can see in selected industry sectors what type of NTBs will be eliminated—these NTBs include quotas, tendering requirements, trading rights, local content, technology transfer requirements, government procurement, and so on.

All quotas on civil aircraft, medical equipment, and IT products will be eliminated. Quotas on auto packages will grow by 15 per cent annually until completely eliminated. Removal of these quotas and other NTBs will certainly make importing much easier. Sometimes, removal of NTBs has more significant effects on trade than removing tariffs since NTBs are a direct trade restriction while tariffs restrict imports indirectly.

Improving business environment and expanding exports

Although China is already one of the largest exporting countries, WTO membership will help it expand its exports. First of all, through the improvement of export conditions, China may expand its traditional exports such as textiles, toys, footwear, machinery and electronic products. As a member of the WTO, China will face a non-discriminatory and stable environment in the world trade system through its permanent most favoured nation status and participation in a multilateral framework for dispute settlement. Second, China's economic structure will be changed through freer trade and foreign investment. As resources move to those sectors in which China has comparative advantages, exports from those sectors will increase.

Without WTO membership, China did not automatically have MFN status with other trading partners. It must negotiate trade agreements with each individual country. Although China has signed bilateral MFN agreements with most countries, some of these agreements are unstable. Since 1989, the

Table 4.2   Tariff reductions after China's accession to the WTO

Selected items	Current level (%)	Tariff level after WTO accession (%)	Rate of reduction (%)	Share of China's total imports (%)	Share of US exports in US total exports (%)	Share of China's imports in world exports (%)
Industrial tariff	24.6	9.4 (2005)	61.8	..	..	..
IT product tariff	13.3	0.0 (2005)	100.0	..	..	..
Agriculture tariff	31.5	14.5 (2004)	54.0	..	..	..
Agriculture equipment	11.54	5.7 (1.1.2002)	50.6	0.06	0.42	0.98
Auto package	80.0–100.0	25.0 (7.1.2006)	72.2	1.57	8.10	0.63
Construction equipment	13.6	6.4 (2004)	52.9	..	..	..
Civil aircraft	14.7	8.0 (1.1.2002)	45.6	2.03	5.93	4.05
Cosmetics	45.0	10.0–15.0 (2004–05)	72.2	0.06	0.39	0.52
Furniture	22.0	0.0 (1.1.2005)	100.0	0.11	0.69	0.38
Medical equipment	9.9	4.7 (1.1.2003)	52.5	0.24	1.18	1.59
Paper	14.2	5.5 (1.1.2005)	61.3	2.20	1.55	4.30
Pharmaceuticals	9.6	4.2 (1.1.2003)	56.3	0.55	1.20	1.21
Scientific equipment	12.3	6.5 (1.1.2003)	47.2	..	..	..
Steel	10.3	6.1 (1.1.2003)	40.8	1.15	0.58	3.68
Textiles and apparel	25.4	11.7 (1.1.2005)	53.9	11.51	2.59	5.97

Note: For the last two columns, Agriculture equipment includes SITC 721; Auto package includes SITC 781–84; Civil aircraft includes SITC 792; Cosmetic includes SITC 553; Furniture includes SITC 821; Medical equipment includes SITC 872; Paper includes SITC64; Pharmaceuticals includes SITC 541; Steel includes SITC 673, 674, 678 and 679; and textiles and apparel includes SITC 65 and 84.
Source: MOFTEC, The White House, and Statistics Canada.

annual review and debate of China's MFN status in the United States always brought uncertainty to Sino–US business and economic relationships. The establishment of permanent normal trading status brings more certainty and stability in business relations between China and other countries, including the United States.

With WTO membership, an effective multilateral dispute settlement framework will be used to increase business security, fairness and confidence.

Increases in trade with industrialised countries

China's trade with industrialised countries will grow even more rapidly than the average growth rate in China's foreign trade.

If we look at the trade development of the past 20 years (Table 4.4), it is clear that the share of China's imports from most industrialised countries (except Japan) has not changed much in spite of dramatic increases in China's foreign trade. Imports from the United States, Western European countries, Canada, Australia and New Zealand have remained a small percentage of the total exports from these countries. Meanwhile, China's total imports as a percentage of the world total has increased from 0.88 to 3.32 per cent in the same period. Furthermore, the share of imports from these industrialised countries as a percentage of China's total imports has not increased either. From 1980–1996, China's import share of North America exports changed from 19.4 per cent to 20.9 per cent, Western Europe dropped from 24.4 per cent to 14.4 per cent, and Australia changed from 2.0 per cent to 1.1 per cent.[2] Overall, the growth of China's imports from industrialised countries was below the average rate, and trade between China and industrialised countries was restricted.

Part of the reason China did not import much from industrialised countries was due to trade protection, as most of the goods being protected were more efficiently produced in industrialised countries. The expansion of exports to industrialised markets will be one of the important results of China's WTO membership.

Changes in economic structure

If a country is engaged in international trade and foreign investment, it is also engaged in the international division of labour and, therefore, integrates its economy into the world. This results in a series of adjustments to its economy. Driving forces for economic restructuring come from both freer trade and FDI. Freer trade will reduce the production of goods for which a country does not have comparative advantages, and will increase the production of goods that exploit a country's comparative advantages. The impact of FDI on the structure of the country's economy depends on the types of technologies associated with

Table 4.3   Removal of non-tariff barriers

Industry

Agriculture equipment	Tendering requirements for non-government purchases will be eliminated within 4 years of accession. Trading rights and distribution will be changed over 3 years.
Auto package	Quotas will grow 15 % annually until eliminated. Trading rights and distribution will be changed over 3 years. Non-bank financial institutions will be permitted to provide auto financing. Safeguard 12 years after accession. Local content eliminated immediately. No condition on import or investment of technology.
Construction equipment	Tendering requirements will be eliminated within 2 years of accession. Trading rights and distribution will be changed over 3 years. Export performance will not apply after accession. Local content will not apply after accession.
Civil aircraft	Quotas will be eliminated upon accession. Trading rights and distribution will be changed over 3 years. The US could use its unfair trade laws with subsidies.
Cosmetics and Furniture	Trading rights and distribution will be changed over 3 years. Export performance will not apply after accession. Local content will not apply after accession.
Medical equipment	Quotas will be eliminated upon accession. Tendering requirements for non-government purchases will be eliminated within 4 years of accession. Trading rights and distribution will be changed over 3 years. Export performance will not apply after accession. Local content will not apply after accession.
Paper	Trading rights and distribution will be changed over 3 years.
Pharmaceuticals	Trading rights and distribution will be changed over 3 years. Intellectual property rights will be implemented under the Trade-Related Intellectual Property Agreement of the Uruguay Round upon accession.
Scientific equipment	Tendering requirements for non-government purchases will be eliminated within 4 years of accession. Trading rights and distribution will be changed over 3 years. Export performance will not apply after accession. Local content will not apply after accession. Intellectual property rights will be implemented under the Trade-Related Intellectual Property Agreement of the Uruguay Round upon accession.
Steel	Trading rights and distribution will be changed over 3 years. Export performance will not apply after accession. Local content will not apply after accession.
Textiles and apparel	Trading rights and distribution will be changed over 3 years.
Toys	Trading rights and distribution will be changed over 3 years.
IT products	Quotas will be eliminated upon accession. Trading rights and distribution will be changed over 3 years. Export performance will not apply after accession. Local content will not apply after accession.

Source: MOFTEC, The White House.

the investment and the types of industries in which foreign capital is invested. Most of the FDI now comes from multinationals and is associated with particular products and certain types of technology. Technology or product-specific FDI is not just a transfer of resources, but may affect either export or import-competing sectors and change the economic structure of the receiving country.

Although China has been opening up its markets since the beginning of economic reform in late 1970, accession to the WTO is still a big move and further adjustments to its economic structure will be inevitable.

China's comparative advantages

To comprehend the possible impact of China's WTO accession on the structure of the Chinese economy, we must first understand what types of products benefit from China's comparative advantages. The revealed comparative advantage (RCA) index, developed by Balassa (1965) is often used to make international comparisons. To study the comparative advantage in China relative to other countries or regions, we constructed and calculated a series of regional (or bilateral) revealed comparative advantage indices.

The regional revealed comparative advantage index of product 'i' of country 'j' in region 'R' is calculated as follows

$$RRCA_{ij} = (X_{ij}/X_{tj}) / (X_{iR}/X_{TR})$$

where X_{ij} and X_{tj} are the value of product i and the value of total products exported from country j, respectively. X_{iR} and X_{TR} are the value of product i and the value of total products exported from the region, respectively. If $RRCA_{ij} > 1$, it indicates that country j has a comparative advantage of producing good i in the region. The higher the value of RRCA, the greater the comparative advantage. On the other hand, if $RRCA_{ij} < 1$, it means that the country does not have a comparative advantage (or, that it has a disadvantage) in this product.

To calculate the RRCA for China, we used trade data compiled by the Standard Industrial Trade Classification (SITC) in 1997. Table 4.5 shows the values of China's regional revealed comparative advantage index in each sector. Compared with all the industrialised countries in Table 4.5 (including Japan, the United States and Western Europe), China has explicit comparative advantages in SITC 8 and disadvantage in SITC 1, 5 and 7. Compared with the United States and Western Europe, China does not have comparative advantage in SITC 0, 3 or 4.

The goods in SITC 8 include travel goods, clothing, footwear, instruments, watches, clocks, sound recorders and so on. These products are mainly labour-intensive. The products that China does not have comparative advantages are either resource-intensive products (SITC 0, 1, 3 and 4) or are capital/technology-intensive (SITC 5 and 7).

Table 4.4 **Share of China's imports in other economies' total exports** (per cent)

	1980	1983	1987	1990	1993	1997
Hong Kong	5.93	10.71	25.20	26.44	38.33	36.76
Taiwan	0.00	0.00	0.00	4.56	14.29	17.36
South Korea	0.00	0.00	0.00	0.91	7.91	14.02
Japan	4.04	4.19	6.50	2.95	9.11	7.45
Australia	4.06	2.18	4.47	2.98	4.33	4.91
Singapore	1.29	0.74	2.29	1.67	3.18	3.91
Southeast Asian 4	1.01	0.82	3.13	2.11	2.65	3.16
New Zealand	3.12	2.19	2.87	1.15	2.44	2.79
United States	1.64	0.87	1.10	1.17	1.58	1.57
West Europe	0.31	0.41	0.70	0.54	1.08	0.95
Canada	1.31	2.18	1.37	1.20	0.97	0.85
Total market	0.88	0.95	1.69	1.64	3.28	3.32

Note: Southeast Asian 4 includes Malaysia, Indonesia, Thailand and the Philippines.
Source: Statistic Canada (1999).

Production adjustment and resource reallocation

As China enters the WTO, both tariff and non-tariff barriers in resource-intensive products (agriculture, wood, paper and so on) and capital/technology-intensive products (chemicals, automobiles and IT products) will be reduced. Imports of these products from industrialised countries are expected to increase. Consequently, domestic production in these sectors has to be adjusted. Resources will be reallocated to those sectors where China has comparative advantages, or potential comparative advantages, and the newly developed service sectors.

However, the automobile industry may face a different situation. Although currently China does not have comparative advantage in the auto sector, the industry may still not shrink even after protectionist measures are removed. The import of luxury cars or those that are not produced in China will increase, but most economy cars will still be produced in China.

Currently, the major auto companies in China have set up joint ventures with American, European and Japanese automobile producers. The dominating models are manufactured by these joint ventures. On the other hand, there are also more than 100 companies in China producing autos on a very small scale which are protected by high trade barriers. Once the protection is removed, these small-scale companies will disappear, but production of joint venture autos will expand. In other words, auto producers in industrialised countries prefer to produce economy cars in China rather than produce them in their home countries and export them to China. Because of the growing market for small and medium size economy cars, China is attracting FDI from the world's major auto producers. A freer trade will reduce or shut down the small automobile companies' production while a freer FDI will expand the production of Chinese-made foreign cars.

Opening up the service sectors to foreign companies

Less-restricted FDI will also affect China's economy. China has successfully attracted much foreign investment in the past decade, but this has mainly been from Hong Kong, Taiwan and other Asian countries. Most FDI is in labour-intensive manufacturing sectors and has helped China produce and export more labour-intensive products. Little FDI has been in the service sector because it is highly restricted.

One of the major agreements in both Sino–US and Sino–EU, WTO membership negotiations was to open up the service sector in China. Table 4.6 summarises the main points in both agreements. All service sectors, including telecommunications, banking, insurance, retail, transportation and professional services, will be opened up to foreign investment and participation. Through foreign investment and competition, the service sector in China will rapidly develop.

Overall changes in economic structure

Freer trade and market access will change China's economic structure in next 5–10 years. The adjustment of economic structures and the reallocation of resources will follow the principles of comparative advantage and economic dynamics.

In general, the production of goods that use China's scarce resources intensively will decrease, and production of goods that use China's abundant resources intensively will increase. In particular, China will import more land-intensive agricultural products such as grain and will shift production towards more labour-intensive goods. Domestic production of resource-intensive

Table 4.5	Regional revealed comparative advantage between China and selected economies, 1997								
SITC	0	1	2	3	4	5	6	7	8
Tiger 3	3.90	1.60	2.83	2.25	1.69	0.91	1.85	0.45	1.28
Southeast Asian 4	1.22	5.59	0.59	0.55	0.13	2.98	2.25	0.69	0.56
Japan	9.62	0.98	3.93	7.04	3.31	0.62	1.33	0.27	3.17
United States	0.30	0.05	0.24	0.77	0.08	0.34	1.23	0.51	3.78
West Europe	0.49	0.14	1.35	0.36	0.26	0.64	0.92	0.67	2.95

Notes: Tiger 3 includes Korea, Singapore and Taiwan. Southeast Asian 4 includes Malaysia, Indonesia, Thailand and the Philippines.
SITC: 0–food and live animals; 1–beverage and tobacco; 2–crude malts excluding fuels; 3–mineral fuels and so on; 4–animal fat, vegetable oil; 5–chemicals; 6–basic manufactures; 7–machines, transport equipment; 8–miscellaneous manufactured goods.
Source: Statistics Canada 1999.

products (wood, paper) will also decrease.

Production in some highly protected sectors (for example, chemicals, cosmetics and pharmaceuticals) will decrease as imports go up. But some other highly protected sectors (auto, service industries and IT) may develop rapidly as China opens up for FDI. Although at its present development stage China does not have comparative advantage in these sectors, it may have a potential comparative advantage in the near future.

Deepening market-oriented economic reforms

It is obvious that China's WTO membership will bring more business to China as well as to other countries. However, the most significant impact of China's WTO accession is to deepen its economic reform.

Unlike reforms in Russia and other Eastern European countries where the ultimate goal is to create a private market economy, there is no clear and consistent road map for China. Basically, the reform strategy is, as Deng Xiaoping said, a process of 'crossing the river by touching the stones'. China's economic reform is under the leadership of the Chinese Communist Party (CCP). The initial objective of the reform is to improve the efficiency of state-owned enterprises without changing the basic economic system. Chinese leaders have announced that the goal of reforms is to establish a socialist market economy with Chinese characteristics. However, this goal is still not well defined. Each political and economic group can interpret it in a different way depending on their own interests.

Vague reform goals were not a big problem in the early stages because the initial reforms were simple and mainly a Pareto improvement process. In this situation no one is worse off and most people are better off during the reforms. The reforms started in agriculture by reinstating the family farming system. It was relatively easy to implement because family farming had been practised in China for thousands of years. Collective farming in China had a less than 25-year history and was easily reversed. Although land is still collectively owned, farmers are now able to rent land for a long period (30 years). Thus, the initial reforms in the agricultural sector were very successful.

Urban or industrial reforms started in 1984 and are still far from completion. There is no commonly accepted theory to guide the reform process since the ultimate goal of reform is unclear. On the one hand, China wants to establish an efficient modern economic system. On the other hand, political leaders want to maintain public or state ownership of enterprises. China has been moving towards a market economy, but political leaders still reject Western economics. A strongly influential group of people, including economists, hope to develop a non-planning and non-capitalist economic system, but most businesspeople and reformists want to complete the transition and establish a private ownership-based market economy. Since the goals and road map are not clearly stated, many interest groups are also using political force to protect their narrow economic interest. A vague goal now becomes an obstacle to further economic reforms in China.

By joining the WTO, China is able to put all the differences among politicians, interest groups and economists aside, set up a clear goal for further reform and establish a road map to reach that goal. WTO membership forces China to deepen reforms based on the WTO's rules. It enables Chinese leaders to turn a controversial domestic issue into an international commitment. People do not have to spend endless time debating what system China should adopt and what sectors it should protect. The most urgent issue is how to adjust the current system to be consistent with the WTO and determine how to reform Chinese enterprises in order to be ready for international competition.

Development of private enterprises

Private enterprises have experienced remarkable development in China over the past two decades. However, private ownership is still being discriminated

Table 4.6   China's commitment to market access

Sector	Sub-sector	China's Commitment
Telecommunications	Basic services	49% foreign ownership (first year of accession) to 50% (in the second year)
	Mobile/cellular phones	25% foreign ownership on accession, 35% after 1 year, 49% after 3 years
	Leasing markets	Open up in 3 years
	Wireless services	6 years
Finance	Insurance	Eliminate geographic limitation in 3 years; open 85% of the service in 3 years; 50% ownership for life insurance, 51% for non-life (100% in 2 years)
	Banking	Local currency business in 2 years; full market access in 5 years
	Non-banking	Auto financing upon accession
Commerce	Trading and distribution rights	Phased in over 3 years; lift restrictions on joint ventures and size limit for foreign-owned stores
Others	Professional service	Legal: open to foreign law firms; Accountancy: open to foreign accountants
	Travel and tourism	100% foreign ownership in 3 years

Source: MOFTEC and White House.

Table 4.7   Composition of China's exports by enterprise ownership
                 (January–July 2000)

	Total	SOE	FIE	COE	Other
Total exports (US$ billion)	135.95	65.73	63.31	5.63	1.29
Share (%)		48.35	46.57	4.14	0.95
Ordinary trade (US$ billion)	58.20	43.33	10.16	3.77	0.94
Share (%)		74.45	17.46	6.48	1.62

Notes: FIE is foreign-invested enterprises or enterprises with foreign investment (including foreign firms, joint ventures and foreign cooperation); COE is collectively-owned enterprises.
Source: China Monthly Exports and Imports, July 2000.

against in many aspects. In many important sectors, including financial, distribution, international trade, power supply and transportation, private ownership is still prohibited. Under the title of a socialist system, interest groups in these sectors are able to use political, ideological, even legal power to maintain state monopolies. It is very difficult for private enterprises to enter these sectors without domestic political support.

China's WTO accession provides opportunities for private enterprises to enter previously prohibited sectors. In the process of preparing to join the WTO, the government was asked to first open up the financial, telecommunications and other important sectors to Chinese private enterprises. Since China will allow foreign investment in these sectors and all foreign investors are private, it is natural that China should allow domestic private enterprises to invest or operate in the same sectors. Once the government lifts all bans on private ownership, private enterprises will develop even more rapidly.

Ownership reforms in SOEs

China's WTO membership will also bring a serious challenge to the state ownership of the production of tradable goods. One of the major principles of the WTO is to protect fairness in trade and international competition. Any non-market activities like subsidies or state trading are considered as unfair trade and subject to retaliation. As a transitional economy, SOEs in China are still playing an important role in many sectors. Recent data (Table 4.7) shows that almost 50 per cent of exports still come from SOEs. The SOEs share is even higher (almost two-thirds) of exports. China would still be treated as a non-market economy even though it is a WTO member country. Some retaliation measures against Chinese SOEs could be used for another 15 years, or until China becomes a market economy.

China's WTO membership

Membership of the WTO will bring greater pressure for ownership reform in SOEs. In addition to the need to improve efficiency, Chinese SOEs now have more incentives to reform ownership to avoid unfair treatment of the non-market economy and painful default dumping charges. Globalisation and international competition require common rules of the game. As long as a firm wants to participate in the game (international competition), it must follow the same rules. WTO membership will bring a convergence of enterprise ownership in different countries. Unless China is able to change the rules of the game (by entering the WTO, China has already committed to follow its existing rules), ownership reform in SOEs is inevitable.

Conclusion

Many studies of the impact or implications of China's WTO membership have been conducted, clearly indicating the importance of the issue.

As most of the studies point out, trade liberalisation in China will increase both its imports and exports. The sectors being liberalised are those in which industrialised countries have a comparative advantage, and therefore imports from industrialised countries will grow most rapidly. China's WTO membership will increase trade between China and industrialised countries.

In return, the expansion of trade and FDI from industrialised countries will change the industrial structure of the Chinese economy. Resources will move away from land-intensive agriculture, resource-intensive manufacturing, and some capital/technological industries to labour-intensive products or the sectors that have potential comparative advantage and market sizes.

China's WTO membership may help the government to break through political, economic and ideological deadlocks and set up the ultimate goal and road map for economic transition. Pressures from internal and external economies may push China to complete the last and most difficult stage of reform: ownership reform. Through adjustment and reforms, the Chinese economic system may well converge with the system that all WTO members have adopted.

China's WTO membership implies that China is not only integrating with the world market but also converting to the world economic system. China is entering a new stage of reform and development. Like the agricultural reform in 1978, accession to the WTO marks another milestone in China's modern history. China has successfully achieved high growth under a more open environment. Reforms under the WTO framework will take China to another higher level of economic performance.

Notes

1 According to the World Bank (The World Development Indicator Database, World Bank 2000), China's GDP in 1999 was US$991 billion, ranking seventh in the world. China's population is about 1.3 billion. It is the world's most populated country.

2 See Table 2.1 China's geographic trade structure, 1970–96, in Drysdale, P., 2000. 'Open Regionalism, APEC and China's International Trade Strategies', P. Drysdale, Y. Zhang and and L. Song (eds), *APEC and Liberalisation of the Chinese Economy*, Asia Pacific Press, Canberra.

5

China's opening up of the banking system

Implications for domestic banks

John P. Bonin and Yiping Huang

As several of the Asian economies have recovered from the East Asian financial crisis, several lessons have become clear. First, the proximate cause of the financial problems in many countries was a futile attempt to defend an overvalued currency. A second more fundamental cause was allowing a weak banking system to become overexposed to foreign exchange risk. However, the recovery of some but not all economies points to a deeper concern. The countries that had stronger financial institutions and undertook more rapid restructuring of their banking systems coped more successfully with the financial crisis. The clear lesson for China is the importance of strong financial institutions when opening up capital markets.

With the accession of China to the WTO, the main question is whether this event can be the impetus to institution building in the banking sector. Currently China is one of the most monetised economies in the world. At the end of 1999, the loan to GDP ratio was 114 per cent. However, four large state-owned banks that have combined market shares in loans and deposits of over 70 per cent dominate the banking sector. Furthermore, interest rates are set centrally by the government and banks have little leeway in pricing risk. Although a program is in place to remove the stock of old bad debt from these four banks' balance sheets by transferring it to asset management companies, the likelihood of the state retaining ownership of these banks for the foreseeable future is high.

The medium-term solution requires China to develop strong financial institutions that will not be unduly hurt by foreign competition and to develop an interbank market to facilitate the liberalisation of interest rates. The requirements for WTO entry are that foreign banks be allowed to conduct all types of foreign exchange transactions with foreign clients immediately on entry and with Chinese clients within one year of entry in designated cities. The Chinese government has promised to add four cities to the list each year after accession. Foreign banks must be allowed to make corporate loans in local currency within two years of entry and deal with individual Chinese customers five years after entry. Furthermore, foreign banks are allowed to engage in joint ventures and full foreign ownership will be permitted within five years of entry. How to navigate in these potentially turbulent waters is the crucial concern for Chinese policymakers today. The natural tendency is to fear cream-skimming by stronger, more financially savvy foreign banks, leaving weak domestic banks still weaker. In this chapter, we consider the impact of foreign entry in Chinese banking based on the experiences of the Central European fast-track transition economies and taking account of the current situation in China and the prospects for reform. We conclude by taking a tentative glimpse into the future that should allay the worst fears of the Chinese authorities.

Literature and experiences from Central Europe

The literature on foreign bank entry in developing countries indicates that it may be a two-edged sword.[1] Although foreign penetration should enhance the efficiency of the domestic banking sector and hence be welfare-improving, it also puts competitive pressure on weak domestic banks. Early literature concludes that foreign banks have traditionally followed abroad their customers who have already established a position in the host country through FDI. However, more recent literature indicates that foreign banks are being more aggressive and entering domestic markets to acquire business and take market share from domestic banks (Seth *et al.* 1998).

The effects of foreign bank entry in eighty countries, both industrialised and developing, over the period 1988–95 are studied by Claessens *et al.* (1998). These authors find that, while domestic banks do lose market share and become less profitable due to competition, the overall welfare effect on the domestic economy is positive. Goldberg *et al.* (1999) find evidence in Argentina and Mexico that foreign entry increased the stability of the domestic banking sectors as loan growth increased, while the volatility of this growth decreased. Regarding the transition economies, Buch (1997) argues that allowing foreign bank entry improves the production of financial services, promotes competition, facilitates bank privatisation, and transfers know-how and technology to the host countries. Her only caveat is that the domestic banks be fully recapitalised for truly inherited bad loans prior to opening up the banking sector to foreign competition. Since conditions in the banking sectors of the transition economies resemble the situation in China today, we take a more detailed look at foreign entry in the Central European fast-track countries.

The experiences of these countries indicate that foreign banks find it much easier to acquire market share in credit markets than in deposit markets. By mid 1999 in Poland, foreign banks accounted for 10 per cent of all banking offices, 22 per cent of the deposit market, 33 per cent of all net loans and 35 per cent of the banking capital. Included in these aggregates are several Polish banks that were privatised to strategic foreign investors in addition to the greenfield operations of foreign entrants. At the end of 1998 in the Czech Republic, foreign banks accounted for 22 per cent of total credits and 15 per cent of total deposits. Two of the five largest banks in the Czech Republic had been privatised to strategic foreign investors at this time. At the end of 1998 in Hungary, foreign banks held 63 per cent of all banking assets, 67 per cent of registered capital, 76 per cent of total corporate credits but only 36 per cent of household deposits (Buch 2000). Foreign banks' market shares in Hungary are a result both of the privatisation of all major commercial banks to strategic foreign owners and of the early entry of greenfield foreign branches. The only major bank in Hungary that is owned domestically is the former state savings bank OTP, the shares of which are widely held by domestic and foreign portfolio investors. OTP currently holds 40 per cent of all retail deposits. The bank with the second largest market share in retail deposits, Postabank, is currently in state receivership.

The largest foreign bank, ABN-Amro, was created when a large domestic commercial bank, Magyar Hitel Bank, was privatised in a sale to the Dutch bank that subsequently merged the purchase with its own greenfield operation. ABN-Amro, with more than 104 branches, has recently claimed that it holds 10–15 per cent of the retail deposit market (BCE 2000:34). Another Dutch bank, ING, recently sold its unprofitable twelve-branch retail banking operation to Citibank although it had only moved into retail banking in 1997 (BCE 2000:34). Clearly, even in a small country like Hungary, success in retail banking depends on an extensive branch system. Estimates for Central Europe place the cost of building a new branch at US$400,000 (BCE 2000:36). Clearly, domestic banks have a comparative advantage in the old bricks and mortar branch system that collects household deposits. This legacy explains the relatively strong market position maintained by domestic banks in retail banking.

Data on interest spreads indicate that the achievement of a threshold level of foreign ownership of banking assets may be necessary before competitive pricing pressure is felt by domestic banks. Interest rate spreads in Poland and the Czech Republic have been relatively constant from 1995 to 1999 whereas, in Hungary the spread has declined by almost 50 per cent since 1997 (Buch 2000: graph 2). By the end of 1997, the major commercial banks in Hungary had been privatised to strategic foreign investors and foreign banks' share of the corporate credit market exceeded 70 per cent. In Poland and the Czech Republic, this same share was under 20 per cent at the end of 1997. This evidence is consistent with the hypothesis that foreign banks create a more competitive market environment but only when their aggregate market share reaches a critical threshold.

Interestingly, data on classified credits indicate that the mere presence of active foreign banks may have a positive influence on combating soft lending. In Poland and Hungary, the share of classified credits decreased from a peak of around 30 per cent in 1993 to below 10 per cent in 1998 (Buch 2000: graph 1). In the Czech Republic, the share of classified credits has remained high at around 30 per cent reflecting to some extent the restrictive entry practices regarding greenfield foreign operations. However, the passive attitude toward commercial banking taken by the foreign owner of the largest privatised bank, IPB, also contributed to a soft lending environment. IPB bank was taken over by the Czech National Bank after a scandal regarding the tunneling of assets from the bank's investment funds by the foreign owner, the Japanese investment bank, Nomura. This evidence is consistent with the hypothesis that a credible threat of competition from foreign banks disciplines domestic banks and leads to an improvement in the quality of their portfolios so long as the soft lending environment is not tacitly approved.

What are the lessons for China from the experiences of Central European countries regarding foreign entry in the banking sector? Overall, foreign banks' market shares were not large in these countries until these banks became significantly involved in the privatisation of domestic banks. This point is seen from a comparison of Hungary with the other two countries at the end of 1998. Recently, foreign ownership of Polish banks has increased dramatically through privatisation and the large Czech banks are in the process of being privatised by strategic foreign owners. For countries with small, open economies that are aspiring to join the European Union, such an outcome is expected.

However, even when strategic foreign investors acquire existing banks in Central Europe, foreign banks' market shares in the deposit markets are significantly smaller than in the credit markets. Hence, there is room for domestic banks that have a comparative advantage in retail activity in these countries. Most importantly, the experiences of the Central European countries demonstrate that competitive pressure from foreign entry evolves only gradually and depends on the foreign banks' share of credit markets becoming significantly large. Therefore, domestic banks have a window of opportunity to adjust to competition. In a large, relatively closed economy such as China, the adjustment period is likely to be even longer as the competitive pressure will evolve even more gradually and be managed by the authorities. Furthermore, the eventual outcome need not involve market dominance of the banking sector by foreign banks as the situation in many large countries with open capital markets demonstrates.

Foreign bank penetration in China: the current situation

There are already a large number of foreign financial institutions present in China, although the extent and breadth of their business are still relatively restricted. Under the current regulatory framework, the Commercial Bank Law is also applicable to foreign banks in China. However, the establishment and operation of foreign financial institutions are set out mainly in the Regulations of the People's Republic of China on Foreign Financial Institutions. According to this Regulation, a foreign commercial bank may engage in some of the foreign exchange businesses, including deposit-taking, lending, brokerage and settlement, but mainly for foreign-funded enterprises.[2]

In December 1996, the PBC promulgated the Provisional Regulations on the Experimental Renminbi Business by Foreign Financial Institutions in Pudong. Qualified foreign banks in the Pudong District of Shanghai started to conduct local currency business on a trial basis. Currently, foreign financial institutions are allowed to receive RMB deposits from foreign-funded enterprises, foreigners who have lived in China for at least one year, or re-deposits of their RMB loans to non-foreign-funded enterprises only. At the same time, they are allowed to extend RMB loans and provide guarantee services to foreign-funded enterprises or non-foreign-funded enterprises that have received their foreign currency loans or guarantees only. The experiment was later extended to include Shenzhen.

At the end of 1999, thirteen foreign banks had been set up wholly owned (six) or joint venture operations (seven) in China (for a complete list of foreign banks in China at the end of 1998, see Appendix 5.1).[3] In addition, foreign banks were operating 157 branches in the country. The minimum requirement for a foreign bank to set up a wholly owned or joint venture bank was total assets of US$10 billion. The same requirement for opening a branch was assets of US$20 billion. The total assets of foreign banks in China amounted to 262.9 billion RMB (US$31.8 billion) or about 2 per cent of the total bank assets in 1999. Loans by foreign banks were 180.5 billion RMB (US$21.8 billion) and deposits were 43 billion RMB (US$5.2 billion). Regarding local currency affairs, the foreign banks made loans of 6.7 billion RMB or about 3.7 per cent of their total, and held deposits equal to 5.44 biilion RMB or about 12.7 per cent of their total assets.

The data indicate that penetration of Chinese banking by foreign banks to the beginning of the twentieth century had been insubstantial. Loans to total assets was about 69 per cent while the ratio of local currency loans to assets was a mere 0.25 per cent. Deposits to total assets were only 16.4 per cent while the ratio of local currency deposits to assets less than 0.25 per cent. Clearly, foreign banks restricted their activity in China mostly to servicing their own clients and almost exclusively to dealing in foreign currency. The Chinese authorities restricted the ability of foreign banks to engage in local currency business.

The major restriction on foreign banking activities was a locational one. Wholly owned and joint venture banks in addition to foreign branch banks were permitted to set up operations only in cities designated by China's State Council. Foreign financial institutions located only in Shanghai or Shenzhen were allowed to apply for the right to conduct business in the local currency. Thirty-two foreign banks— of which twenty-four were in Shanghai and eight in Shenzhen—were engaged in renminbi affairs. In 1999, about one half of total foreign banking assets, loans and deposits were held by banks in Shanghai. In March 2000, the central bank announced that foreign banks with two or more branches in the country must designate one branch as its main reporting entity to strengthen the PBC's control over foreign banks. Many large banks, for instance Citibank and HSBC, designated their Shanghai branch as the main branch. These policies seem designed to promote Shanghai as an important financial centre in Asia.

A commentary in the April 2000 edition of *Shanghai Jinrong* (available online at <URL:http://ChinaOnline.com> on 9 May 2000) recommended that China adopt a gradual approach to foreign banking to allow the domestic banking sector sufficient time to improve its efficiency and to prevent it from being further weakened by foreign competition. In the first stage, protection, foreign banks are allowed to follow their clients into the country and promote FDI. Significant restrictions on location and the scope of business are imposed during this period. According to the article, China is moving from this stage to the transition period or second stage. In this phase, restrictions are eased and foreign exchange business is completely open. Furthermore some banks are allowed to conduct local currency business and foreign banks are allowed to operate in a larger number of coastal and inland cities. During this stage it is imperative that domestic banks restructure and become more competitive in anticipation of moving to the final stage: maturity. According to the article, foreign banks must be 'managed' during this period to prevent them from bringing overseas financial risks to China and to guide them to support Chinese policies and development strategies.

In June 2000, the president of the China Construction Bank, Wang Xuebing, warned that China must adopt a law that regulated competition between foreign and domestic banks. Mr Wang warned of a worst-case scenario in which domestic banks keep only the unprofitable banking business and foreign banks skim the cream of the profitable business. How far and how quickly the Chinese authorities are prepared to move in the transition period is unclear. To what extent the management of foreign banks referred to above involves the maintenance of restrictions rather than arm's-length supervision will be a crucial determinant of the depth of foreign bank penetration in China. Hence the benefits of foreign entry will depend on the regulatory policies pursued by the Chinese authorities.

In April of the same year, the president of the Bank of China, Liu Mingkang, supported the use of the capital market to reform banks in three stages (see <URL:http://ChinaOnline.com> on 19 April 2000). In the short term, China will focus on developing the interbank capital market and the government bond market. In the medium term, interest rates are to be liberalised. Mr Liu recommended relaxing the upper limit on commercial bank lending first to avoid malignant competition between banks through the efforts of banking associations. Once reform has proceeded, the government can relax the minimum loan interest rates. In the longer term, banks will look to the capital market for funds by issuing shares and mergers between state-owned banks while large international banks can be arranged by stock swaps. Interestingly, this plan does not envision a role for a strategic foreign investor in privatising the four large state-owned banks but rather imagines the outcome to be a merger of equals. For this vision to be realised, Chinese banks must be strengthened institutionally.

The introduction of a market-based interest rate is also on the agenda. Earlier, the PBC liberalised the interbank market interest rate. The next step is to liberalise the lending rate, although commercial banks are already allowed to adjust the lending rate by plus or minus 10 per cent, and plus 30 per cent for loans to small enterprises. The deposit rate, however, is likely to remain highly regulated for an extended period.

On 10 May 2000, the Chinese Association of Banks (CAB) was formed in Beijing as a non-profit self-regulating organisation with a mission of formulating professional conventions and self-regulating standards (see <URL:http:// ChinaOnline.com> on 12 May 2000). Jiang Jianqing, the current president of the Industrial and Commercial Bank of China, was appointed as the head of the CAB. Hence, the institution is already in place to manage the competition on interest rates referred to by Mr Liu. Allowing banks to charge higher rates to commercial clients will permit them to better price the risk of loans but it is likely that the cartel nature of CAB will blunt competition and promote cooperation. This may be a useful in constraining interest rates and may actually encourage the sharing of financial information on clients that is necessary for banks to price risk appropriately. However, when the limit is removed from deposit rates, the CAB is likely to discourage significant competitive reductions in interest rates. Without competition on deposit rates, the banks will retain the benefits of liberalisation through their rent monopoly, rather than sharing them with households as they would if deposit rates were determined competitively.

What is at stake?

Approximately half of China's population of 1.2 billion have bank accounts. The loan to GDP ratio at the end of last year was 114 per cent, one of the highest in the world. The big four domestic banks have a combined market share of about 70 per cent (Table 5.1).

Together, these four major banks have extensive branch networks across the country, with nearly 125,000 branches and 1.6 million employees. However, their financial performance is unsatisfactory. The profitability of these banks has fallen

Table 5.1   China's financial system, end of 1997 (RMB billion)

Financial institutions	Number of branches	Number of employees	Total deposits	Household deposits	Total assets	Total loans
PBC	2,416	188,000	..	..	..	..
NDB	-	1,000	..	..	..	24.00
CADB	2,000	110,000	..	..	66.46	62.50
CEIB	-	500	..	..	1.85	1.42
ICBC	31,400	520,000	179.75	113.13	..	163.30
ABC	55,640	490,000	89.50	61.70	..	77.13
BOC	1,795	195,754	48.64	31.07	..	47.50
CBC	35,895	356,864	103.00	50.90	..	74.57
12 other banks	700	45,211	49.77	6.61	..	33.66
RCCs	50,219	563,000	87.90	..	..	63.64
UCCs	4,243	90,980	29.70	..	..	19.52
TICs	244	32,400	61.82	..	27.34	32.23
FCs	67	..	13.22	..	8.18	6.35
SEC	94	..	..	..	15.90	..

Notes: The three policy banks are the National Development Bank (NDB), the China Agricultural Development Bank (CADB) and the China Export-Import Bank (CEIB). The four major banks include the Industry and Commerce Bank (ICBC), the Agricultural Bank of China (ABC), the Bank of China (BOC) and the Construction Bank of China (CBC). RCCs and UCCs refer to rural and urban credit cooperatives, respectively (UCCs have been transformed into urban commercial banks in some cities). TICs are trust and investment corporations, FCs are finance companies and SEC are stock exchange centres. The 12 other banks referred to are shareholding commercial banks such as CITIC Industry Bank, China Everbright Bank and Minsheng Bank.
Source: People's Bank of China.

consistently since the beginning of the 1990s. Most would have made losses in the mid 1990s if uncollected interest payments had been excluded from the revenues on their income statements (Bonin and Huang 2000). Of the total profits generated by these major banks in recent years, about 95 per cent came from almost half a dozen coastal cities, such as Shenzhen, Guangzhou, Xiamen, Shanghai, Beijing and Tianjin (Yi 2000). Unfortunately, these cities will become the centre of the battlefield when foreign banks compete aggressively for domestic clients. If Chinese banks lose significant market share in these cities, the more dire forecasts of the harmful effects of foreign entry will be realised.

Retail banking is a growth industry in China. Housing loans account for less than 1.5 per cent of all loans made (see <URL:http://ChinaOnline.com> on 28 March 2000). In a survey of 3,900 people from Beijing, Tianjin, Shanghai, Guangzhou, Wuhan and Harbin, conducted by the Social Survey Institute of China (SSIC), 71 per cent ranked buying a house as a top goal (see <URL:http://ChinaOnline.com> on 4 April 2000). An average house costs at least eight times a family's annual income and a downpayment of RMB 100,000 to qualify for a loan. Taken together, this information indicates the significant growth potential of the housing loan market and provides a major reason for the high saving rate in

China. Whether or not significant competition from foreign banks should be expected in this market is unclear. On the one hand, housing loans transactions tend to be concentrated in banks with local knowledge and household clients so that domestic banks have a comparative advantage in this area. On the other hand, collateral on housing loans may be more transparent and secure than collateral on small business loans so that foreign banks in some Central European countries have taken an interest in this market.

Xiong Anping, president of Visa (China), claims that credit card usage is still in its infancy in China and that foreign banks will focus on these rather than the existing debit cards issued by Chinese banks (see <URL:http://ChinaOnline.com> on 26 July 2000). In a survey of 1,678 people from Beijing, Shanghai, Nanjing, Guangzhou, Wuhan and Changsha, conducted by the SSIC, more than 40 per cent have at least one plastic bank card but many didn't bother to use them because of the difficulty in doing so (see <URL:http://ChinaOnline.com> on 2 June 2000). Although major Chinese banks have issued plastic cards, they are not interchangeable and thus not widely accepted because merchants find it impossible to have separate machines for each card. Furthermore these are mostly debit cards. ICBC issues the Peony Card that has a thirty-day overdraft facility but is essentially a debit card. Foreign banks could overcome the interchangeability problem by issuing the Visa cards.

The Bank of China has issued about 200 million debit cards on which the annual transaction volume is RMB 2.42 trillion. Bankcards are beginning to be used as a secondary medium of exchange in China. In Hungary, a country in which the ratio of banking assets to GDP is only 70 per cent, 3 million people or about 35 per cent of the population have credit or debit cards and use them about once a month on average (BCE 2000:36). As with much of Central Europe, China is likely to skip the stage of instituting checks and move directly to plastic money as a co-medium of exchange with cash. Consequently, bankcards and ATMs are likely to be important vehicles for acquiring market share in retail banking in China. In Hungary, the domestic bank OTP is the market leader in ATMs because of its branch network and competes aggressively in the bankcard market. With their extensive branch networks, Chinese domestic banks are well positioned to capture a reasonable share of this new retail business.

According to Zhu Min, the general manager of the BOC's Institute of International Finance, online banking is the direction in which the Chinese banking sector should be expanding (see <URL:http://ChinaDaily.com> on 30 July 2000). Internet use has grown by an average of 80 per cent over the last five years in China, compared with 50 per cent in the rest of Asia. China's commercial banks have launched several online products and the demand has created some technical problems. Octasoft Co. Ltd has offered its business-to-business e-financial solutions—which have been successful in other Asian banks—to Chinese financial institutions to assist in their online banking endeavours. According to Mr Zhu, Chinese banks risk losing out to non-banking institutions in providing certain banking services due to the rapid penetration of the Internet. Given the high cost of building new branches, several foreign-owned banks in Poland are developing e-banking operations. However, there are only 20,000 customers online in Poland (BCE 2000:36). Nonetheless, foreign banks are likely to become an important source of competition in e-banking for China's large banks.

China's response

In order for the domestic financial sector to survive the international competition brought about by WTO membership, the Chinese authorities must step up their efforts to strengthen the domestic banks. In the wake of the East Asian financial crisis, China introduced a number of reform measures to improve the health of the banking sector, mainly through the introduction of better banking practices and a program to deal with the stock of bad loans in the four large banks. In 1998, the Ministry of Finance issued RMB 270 billion of special treasury bonds for the recapitalisation of the four major banks, raising their average capital-adequacy ratio from 4.4 per cent to the 8 per cent required by the Commercial Bank Law.

Another important policy measure was the creation of asset management companies (AMCs) to deal with the bad loans (Bonin and Huang 2000). About RMB 1,300 billion of non-performing loans (NPLs), which is about 19 per cent of the total outstanding loans, are scheduled to be transferred from the banks to the AMCs. By the end of 1999, a total of RMB 350 billion had been transferred, including those resulting in debt-equity swaps. The AMCs are charged with working out the bad loans and using capital markets for asset sales. Since capital markets are still primitive in China and the direction of ownership reform for the large state-owned enterprises is still not clear, the sale of these debts will be a difficult undertaking. Recovery rates on problem assets have not been high in Central Europe. In a Polish program, the recovery rate for a limited number of small loans was less than 25 per cent of face value. In May 2000, the Chinese government made a policy decision to allow AMCs to sell non-performing assets and shares taken in debt-equity swaps to foreign companies. Although this is an important policy change, substantial transactions have not been taken place so far.

While both recapitalisation of the banks and the creation of AMCs for the resolution of bad loans are important steps in improving the health of the domestic banking sector, a more important issue is to stop the creation of new NPLs that lead to a continued deterioration of asset quality. In August 2000, only one and a half years after the first round of recapitalisation to achieve regulatory standards, the central bank called on the four major banks to boost their average capital-adequacy ratio from 6 per cent to above 8 per cent (*Asian Wall Street Journal*, 4

August 2000). This suggests that the quality of the banks' financial assets continued to deteriorate after 1998. In this environment, it is difficult for the authorities to make a credible commitment to a once-off transfer of NPLs to the AMCs.

Loss-making SOEs continue to exist. For example, in the first half of 2001, total losses made by SOEs were RMB 46 billion, which is more than one-half of total SOE profit. Moreover, the state continues to intervene in lending decisions. From 1998–99, the Ministry of Finance spent RMB 200 billion on infrastructure projects in order to achieve the government's growth target. Commercial banks were called on to provide RMB 400 billion in policy loans for companion projects. To prepare the domestic banks for international competition requires a significant improvement in the behaviour of bank lending. SOE reform is a necessary first step. Bank managers' incentives were improved gradually as they were given more responsibility in exchange for more accountability. In mid 2000, the central bank stressed its earlier instruction to the banks to stop lending to loss-making SOEs. Hence, the completion of reforms of both the state sector and the state budget is an important precondition for successful bank restructuring.

Financial supervision of the banks has also gradually strengthened. At the end of 1998, the government introduced international accounting standards to banks, although the nationwide application of this system is still incomplete. On 21 March 2000, the State Council published a new set of regulations for the supervision of state-owned financial institutions (see <URL:http:// ChinaOnline.com> on 23 March 2000). The document states that supervision committees will be sent to state-owned banks to oversee their financial and accounting activities. Included among the mandates of the supervision committees is the evaluation of the chief executives and the responsibility to submit proposals for rewards and punishments including appointments and removals. These committees will inspect the procedures for capital management and oversee the financial affairs of the banks. This document indicates that the State Council through these supervision committees is taking an active role in monitoring and regulating state-owned banks.

The Bank of China (BOC) signed an agreement on 6 June 2000 with Reuters to use the Kondor+ Risk Management System for its financial operations (see <URL:http:// ChinaOnline.com> on 9 June 2000). The system will be customised for the BOC in China and was initially installed in the Beijing and Hong Kong offices. This is the first time that a large Chinese bank has used a third-party vendor to solve IT problems rather than depend on in-house development. Kondor+ is an applications system for risk management that is designed to handle e-commerce, credit and risk management.

The Industrial and Commercial Bank of China (ICBC), the largest of the four state-owned banks, has introduced a centralised system of credit management to monitor and supervise its 400,000 clients (see <URL:http:// ChinaDaily.com>

on 30 July 2000). This system replaces the situation in which local branches were responsible for all loans. As part of this restructuring, ICBC introduced procedural management techniques into its credit department. This reorganisation is designed to solve the problem of soft lending by local branches. During the first six months of 2001, ICBC's lending activity increased by RMB 165.6 billion, which was RMB 71.4 billion more than in the same period in 2000. This increase in activity was coupled with an improvement in the quality of new loans as only 0.66 per cent of these were non-performing, which, according to its president Jiang Jianqing, is the lowest amount in ICBC's history. Consumer loans constituted 21.8 per cent of all new loans, an increase of 6 percentage points from the same period in 2000, indicating that ICBC is becoming more aggressive in retail banking.

Taken together, these observations indicate a willingness on the part of both the regulatory authorities and the major domestic banks to change banking practice in China prior to any serious market penetration through the entry of foreign banks. In a related area, China is also accelerating reforms of the stockmarkets. The China Securities Regulatory Commission (CSRC) is contemplating a number of proposals, including

- opening up the A-share market to foreign companies (or their joint ventures) and, most probably, creating a Taiwan-style QFII system while the capital account is still closed
- merging the Shanghai and Shenzhen stockmarkets (to Shanghai) and setting up a secondary board for growth enterprises (likely to be in Shenzhen)
- and combining A and B shares, and possibly even including H shares.

A key issue left largely untouched to date is the ownership of the large domestic banks. Will it be necessary to privatise these four state-owned banks in some way to improve the efficiency and competitiveness of the banking sector? At the moment, the government appears to favour industry consolidation and internal restructuring rather than seeking strategic foreign investors. However, the smaller state-owned banks are being listed on the stockmarket gradually and sequentially.[4] As the stockmarket deepens and broadens, the possibility of selling small packages of shares in the four major banks arises. Following a policy similar to the one undertaken by the Hungarian government in privatising OTP, the Chinese authorities could gradually privatise these large banks over a reasonable period of time to domestic and foreign portfolio investors. Under this scenario, the four large state-owned banks could be privatised yet remain domestic Chinese banks.

A glimpse into the future

On which edge of the sword is China likely to find itself over the next decade because of its entry into the WTO? Will foreign bank penetration be deep enough to enhance the efficiency of Chinese banking and the welfare of China's economy? Will China's big four state-owned domestic banks lose significant market share under this competitive pressure and become vulnerable to foreign takeover? These are important issues for policymakers in China to address during the five-year transition period afforded by the phase-in provision of removing restrictions in the WTO agreement. By combining our analysis of the experiences of the Central European transition economies with foreign bank entry and our consideration of the current situation in Chinese banking, we conclude with some conjectures on these issues.

Will foreign banks be a stimulus to institution building in China's financial sector? Our answer is yes. Competition will obviously spur domestic banks to develop products and services in order to retain good clients. Less obvious perhaps is the role that foreign banks are likely to play in stimulating the development of the interbank market. The four large state-owned banks in combination with the network of rural and urban cooperative banks are sure to collect more than 95 per cent of all household deposits. From experiences in other countries, foreign banks are not likely to be interested in building bricks and mortar branch networks to collect household deposits in the traditional way. Currently, the foreign banks operating in China make loans in excess of 400 per cent of the deposits that they collect in the country. Clearly, they are using external sources of financing. However, as their business in China grows, foreign banks will look increasingly to domestic sources of funds. Hence, foreign banks will have an incentive to push for the development of an interbank market of which they will be a significant part of the demand side. Under the supervision of China's central bank, the interbank market can be an important ingredient in the liberalisation of interest rates, the pricing of risk and the development of monetary policy.

Will foreign banks be a stabilising factor in the financial sector by facilitating capital outflows and setting up conditions in China for an East Asian-type financial crisis? Interestingly enough, our answer is no. Although an open capital account can lead to ebbs and flows of speculative short-term capital, foreign banks are likely to be a buffer. Because foreign banks actually have a stake in the financial stability of the host country and because they are subject to domestic banking supervision, they are more likely to be a stabilising influence. The traditional concern that foreign banks would respond to economic conditions in their home country and thus be a conduit of financial problems seems to be overshadowed now by concerns about transmission mechanisms in international capital markets. Foreign direct investment in the banking sector is no different from FDI in other sectors in that it constitutes a long-term commitment to the host country. Foreign banks should not be feared as a destabilising factor. On the contrary, they are likely to have a stabilising influence on short-term speculative capital movements.

Are foreign banks likely to compete with domestic banks for profitable corporate clients and wealthy retail clients? Based on experiences in other countries and the likely development of Chinese banking, the answer must surely be yes. Is this cream-skimming avoidable? At least in the longer term it is probably unavoidable. High-profile profitable business clients will have alternatives to the domestic banking sector for raising funds. As the financial sector liberalises, these companies will be able to access domestic and international capital markets for both equity and debt. Once the capital account is open, wealthy retail clients will also have full access to international investment opportunities. The question becomes one of whether it is better to lose this business and these clients to foreign banks operating within a domestic regulatory system or to international capital markets.

Recent government policies and the practices of foreign banks indicate that Shanghai is the financial capital of China and could become an important financial hub in Asia. That Shanghai is one of six coastal cities that provide the vast majority of profitable business for China's major banks, makes the competitiveness of the big four domestic banks in this hub and the other cities crucial. To facilitate the maintenance and development of business in these profitable areas, the government must allow the domestic banks to reallocate resources from non-profitable activities. To the extent that the big four banks are beholden to local governments in their branch network, they can not allocate their resources properly and will be at a competitive disadvantage with respect to foreign banks. To the extent that the big four banks are persuaded by the federal government to support designated projects that are complementary to the government's economic policy, domestic banks will have a competitive disadvantage with respect to foreign banks. Hence, independent bank governance is a necessary condition for the big four banks to compete effectively with foreign entrants. Therefore, a credible commitment to only arm's-length regulation by the government and a gradual divestiture of the state's ownership shares to domestic and foreign portfolio investors should have high priority on the policy agenda in China.

Since retail banking is a growth industry in China, the battle for retail clients will be fierce. Domestic banks have the inside track on housing mortgages due to their established client relationships. However, this informational advantage can be squandered if these banks are not allowed to compete aggressively on pricing and the terms of the contract with foreign banks. Because housing loans afford transparent and relatively secure collateral, foreign banks are attracted to this business. Hence, domestic banks must be allowed to offer mortgages on competitive terms.

Plastic money will be an area of intense competition between foreign and domestic banks. Although the big four have begun to issue debit cards, the infrastructure for easy use is not in place. Because foreign banks issue bankcards that are accepted worldwide, they have a comparative advantage in developing cards that would be accepted universally in China. However, the big four banks have the branch networks in place to provide a complementary product, such as cash machines. By offering a bankcard that can be used both as a debit card and at ATMs, the big four banks can take advantage of their branches by providing clients with both means of exchange. The pre-requisite for domestic banks to compete effectively is the development of information technology (IT) systems to handle such transactions.

The immediate development of IT capabilities is crucial if the big four hope to compete in the nascent, small, but developing area of internet banking. Foreign banks will find e-banking particularly attractive as an alternative to building brick-and-mortar branches to attract retail clients. Even though e-banking is only currently available to a very small number of people in China, it is an area in which foreign banks could engage in significant cream-skimming. Furthermore, as China's capital market develops, the ability to cross-sell investment products to wealthy retail clients has significant profit potential. The big four domestic banks need to develop an integrated IT strategy that takes account of their comparative advantage in branch banking but does not disregard the future evolution of internet banking.

Is the sword of foreign entry likely to pierce the heart of the big four banks in China? The answer depends on how the government and the banks use the window of opportunity provided by the phase-in period. The more quickly the government removes restrictions from the credit and deposit markets, the more likely it is that domestic banks will learn how to price risk appropriately, leading to a significant improvement in the quality of their assets. The more the banks become independent from direct government control, from their inherited portfolios of policy loans and from their implicit obligations to weak clients, the more likely it is that they will be strong enough to compete with foreign banks. The more quickly the government allows capital markets to develop, the more options become available to facilitate the independent governance of the big four domestic banks. Hence, supported by appropriate policy reforms, the big four Chinese banks are capable of taking a firm stand on the battleground created by China's accession to the WTO.

Appendix 5.1

Foreign financial institutions in China (as of 31 December 1998)
1   Wholly-owned foreign banks (6)
    Concord Bank (Ningbo)
    Xiamen Commercial Bank (Xiamen)
    Ningbo International Bank (Ningbo)
    TM International Bank (Shanghai)
    Nantong Bank Ltd (Zhuhai)
    Rabobank China Ltd (Shanghai)

2 Sino–foreign joint venture banks (7)
   First Sino Bank (Shanghai)
   The International Bank of Paris & Shanghai (Shanghai)
   Chinese Mercantile Bank (Shenzhen)
   Zhejiang Commercial Bank (Ningbo)
   Xiamen International Bank (Xiamen)
   Qingdao International Bank (Qingdao)
   Fujian Asia Bank Ltd (Fuzhou)
3 Foreign bank branches (69 banks with 153 branches from 16 countries)
   Australia (1 bank with 2 branches)
       ANZ Banking Group Ltd (Shanghai, Beijing)
   Belgium (2 banks with 3 branches)
       Credit Bank NV (Shanghai)
       Generale Bank (Guangzhou)
   Britain (1 bank with 8 branches)
       Standard Chartered Bank PLC (Shanghai, Shenzhen, Xiamen, Tianjin,
       Zhuhai, Haikou, Nanjing)
   Canada (3 banks with 5 branches)
       Royal Bank of Canada (Shanghai)
       Bank of Nova Scotia (Guangzhou, Chongqing)
       Bank of Montreal (Guangzhou, Beijing)
   France (6 banks with 17 branches)
       Societe Generale (Shanghai, Shenzhen, Guangzhou, Tianjin, Wuhan)
       Credit Lyonnais (Shanghai, Xiamen, Tianjin)
       Credit Agricole Indosuez (Shanghai, Guangzhou, Shenzhen)
       Banque Nationale de Paris (Shenzhen, Tianjin, Guangzhou, Beijing)
       Banque de Paris et des Pays-Bas (Shanghai)
   Germany (5 banks with 8 branches)
       Dresdner Bank AG (Shanghai, Shenzhen, Beijing)
       Commerzbank AG (Shanghai)
       Deutsche Bank AG (Guangzhou)
       Westdeutsche Landesbank (Shanghai)
       Bayerische Landesbank (Shanghai)
   Hong Kong (13 banks with 34 branches)
       The Bank of East Asia Ltd (Shanghai, Shenzhen, Xiamen, Guangzhou,
       Dalian, Zhuhai)
       Nanyang Commercial Bank Ltd (Shenzhen, Guangzhou, Dalian, Haikou,
       Shekou, Beijing)
       Hongkong and Shanghai Banking Corporation Ltd (Shanghai, Shenzhen,
       Xiamen, Tianjin, Qingdao, Beijing, Dalian, Wuhan)
       Po Sang Bank Ltd (Shanghai, Shenzhen, Qingdao)

China's opening up of the banking system

Dao Heng Bank Limited (Shenzhen)
Chiyu Banking Corporation Ltd (Xiamen, Fuzhou)
Wing Hang Bank Ltd (Shenzhen)
Hua Chiao Commercial Bank Ltd (Shantou)
Liu Chong Hing Bank Ltd (Shantou)
Heng Sheng Bank Ltd (Guangzhou, Shanghai)
Asia Commercial Bank Ltd (Shenzhen)
Xin Hua Bank Ltd (Shenzhen)
Kuangtung Provincial Bank (Shenzhen)
Italy (2 banks with 2 branches)
Banca Commerciale Italiana (Shanghai)
Banco di Roma SPA (Shanghai)
Japan (12 banks with 30 branches)
Bank of Tokyo-Mitsubishi Ltd (Shanghai, Shenzhen, Dalian, Beijing)
Sanwa Bank Ltd (Shanghai, Beijing, Shenzhen, Dalian)
Sumitomo Bank Ltd (Shanghai, Guangzhou, Yangpu, Shuzhou)
Sakura Bank Ltd (Shanghai, Guangzhou, Tianjin)
Industrial Bank of Japan Ltd (Shanghai, Dalian, Beijing)
Fuji Bank Ltd (Shenzhen, Dalian, Shanghai)
Dai-ichi Kangyo Bank Ltd (Shanghai, Dalian)
Yamaguchi Bank Ltd (Qingdao, Dalian)
Tokai Bank Ltd (Tianjin, Shanghai)
Daiwa Bank Ltd (Shanghai)
Asahi Bank Ltd (Shanghai)
Long-Term Credit Bank of Japan Ltd (Shanghai)
Korea (7 banks with 9 branches)
Korea Exchange Bank (Tianjin, Dalian, Beijing)
Hanil Bank (Shanghai)
Shinhan Bank (Tianjin)
Korea Development Bank (Shanghai)
Commercial Bank of Korea (Shanghai)
Industrial Bank of Korea (Tianjin)
Cho Hung Bank (Tianjin)
Netherlands (2 banks with 6 branches)
ING Bank NV (Shanghai, Shenzhen, Xiamen)
ABN-Amro Bank (Shanghai, Shenzhen)
Portugal (1 bank with 1 branch)
Banco Nacional Ultramarino SA (Zhuhai)
Singapore (4 banks with 9 branches)
Overseas Chinese Banking Corporation (Shanghai, Xiamen, Tianjin, Chengdu)

United Overseas Bank Ltd (Xiamen, Guangzhou)
Overseas Union Bank Ltd (Shenzhen)
Development Bank of Singapore (Shanghai, Beijing)
Switzerland (1 bank with 1 branch)
Credit Suisse (Shanghai)
Thailand (3 banks with 5 branches)
Bangkok Bank Ltd (Shanghai, Shantou, Xiamen)
Krung Thai Bank Ltd (Kunming)
Thai Farmers Bank Public Company Ltd (Shenzhen)
USA (5 banks with 11 branches)
Bank of America (Shanghai, Guangzhou, Beijing)
Citibank, NA (Shanghai, Shenzhen, Beijing, Guangzhou)
Bank of The Orient (Xiamen)
First National Bank of Chicago (Beijing)
Chase Manhattan Bank, NA (Tianjin, Shanghai)

Notes

1 This section relies heavily on Buch (2000).
2 The 13 areas specified by the Regulation that foreign banks may engage in include: foreign currency deposit-taking, foreign currency lending, foreign currency bill-discounting, approved foreign exchange investments, foreign exchange remittance, foreign exchange guarantee, import and export settlement, foreign currency dealing and brokerage, exchanging of foreign currencies and foreign exchange bills as an agent, foreign currency credit card payment, custodial service, credit verification and consulting, local currency businesses and other foreign exchange businesses approved by the PBC.
3 Information in this section is taken from articles on the internet. See <URL:http://ChinaOnline.com> for 3 March 2000, 6 March 2000, 9 May 2000 and 16 May 2000.
4 Pudong Development Bank and Shenzhen Development Bank are already listed on the domestic stockmarket, while the Bank of Communication and Minsheng Bank are finalising the procedures for listing.

6

Legal implications for regulation of trade in services of China's accession to the WTO

Brett Williams and Deborah Cass

During the Uruguay Round, the creation of a treaty relating to services trade found its way onto the agenda. A number of parties to the General Agreement on Tariffs and Trade (GATT) had observed that the services sector was becoming increasingly important within their economies and that services exports were becoming a larger part of their total exports. Consequently, they argued that further exchanges of market access for goods would not necessarily result in significant gains in trade for them and that in order to achieve a mutually advantageous and reciprocal distribution of benefits from further multilateral liberalisation, it would be necessary to extend the rules to cover services as well as goods. As a result, when the Uruguay Round concluded with the creation of the World Trade Organization (WTO), one of the key elements of the new rules was a new treaty on trade in services. The General Agreement on Trade in Services (GATS) became binding on every Member of the WTO. In all subsequent WTO accession negotiations, the negotiation of access for trade in services has been an essential element of the overall accession negotiation; as important as the negotiation of access for trade in goods.

In the recently completed negotiation for the accession of China to the WTO, the negotiation of access for service provision in China was a major focus. The Chinese economy includes many underdeveloped service industries that represent an enormous opportunity for Chinese and foreign service providers. To foreign service providers, China is one of the last great greenfields of unharvested profits—1.25 billion consumers who until now have not been provided with services that they might purchase if they had the opportunity to do so.[1]

All countries—including China—have laws restricting the way foreigners can provide services (or at least some services) and the way they can conduct the business of providing those services. China's restrictions have been particularly stringent. Though the Chinese government has been liberalising China's foreign trade and investment since 1978, removal of restrictions on foreign trade in services has lagged behind reform of trade in goods. In most cases, the government has restricted the number of foreign entrants. In many cases, it has restricted foreigners to operating through joint venture arrangements with a Chinese partner. It has imposed limits on the geographical area within which the foreign entity or Sino–foreign entity can operate. All such restrictions have been discussed in the accession negotiation.

This chapter provides an overview of the GATS obligations that will apply to China and explain their application in the context of existing Chinese legal regulation.

Foreign participation in services trade in China

Traditionally, the Chinese government has taken a restrictive approach to the supply of services by foreigners in China. The reasons for this restrictive approach arise in part from factors that are common to many countries and in part from factors unique to China.

Common to many countries is a perception that domestic control over certain service industries is integral to national security and sovereignty. This justification for national protection is particularly strong in relation to banking, insurance, telecommunications, transportation and media. In the case of China, there seems to be considerable support for the view that 'foreign control over these industries might pose a threat to China's sovereignty and security' (Wang 1995:519). In many countries also, there is a perception that particular sectors of the economy ought to generate certain proportions of production; that is, the services, agricultural, manufacturing and mining sectors should each generate a target percentage of total GDP. Although completely at odds with the theory of comparative advantage (which suggests that there is no such thing as a wealth maximising formula for sectoral structure) the idea continues to command respect in many countries. It seems that the idea has some influence among policymakers in China, as the Chinese government appears to be trying to increase the role of the services sector in the economy. In addition, the Chinese government seems to be adopting a simple infant industry argument in relation to some services industries, taking the view that protection from

Legal implications for regulation of trade in services

foreign service providers is necessary in order to promote the development of the domestic services sector. Although these justifications for restricting opportunities for foreign service providers have been influential, they are not a complete explanation. Historical factors also play a part in the exclusion of foreigners from the domestic domain.

The restrictive approach to foreign service providers also arises from the economic development model which dominated or substantially influenced Chinese economic policy for many years. The model emphasised the promotion of manufacturing industries, even at the cost of slower development of other sectors, including services. This approach left China with an underdeveloped services sector, and with difficulty in competing with foreign service suppliers.

Clearly, these factors have had an impact on the Chinese government's approach to liberalisation of the economy since 1978 (Wang 1995:518). Even as there has been a progressive liberalisation of imports of goods and of some foreign investment, the government has maintained a restrictive approach to foreigners engaging in service provision in China. Any liberalisation that has been introduced has been carefully controlled.

This more cautious approach to liberalisation of trade in services than to liberalisation of trade in goods is reflected in the provisions of the 1994 *Chinese Foreign Trade Law*.[2] Chapter III of the *Foreign Trade Law*, dealing with import and export of goods, begins with Article 15 that provides, 'the State shall allow free import and export of goods and technologies, however, except as otherwise provided for in laws or administrative rules and regulations'.

In contrast, Chapter IV, dealing with International Service Trade, begins with Article 22 which provides that 'the State shall promote the progressive development of international service trade'.

Article 23 also provides that

> The People's Republic of China shall, in international service trade, grant other signatories and acceding parties market access and national treatment according to the commitments made in the international treaties or agreement it has signed or acceded to.

Thus, in respect of trade in goods, Chinese government policy has shifted its underlying position from one of a prohibition on foreign trade subject to specific exceptions, to a position under which trade should be permitted unless specific restrictions provide otherwise. In contrast, in relation to services trade, the basic position remains that foreign trade in services is prohibited except to the extent that the state specifically allows it.

Despite this generally restrictive approach, the Chinese government has introduced a steady flow of initiatives for liberalising services trade, although this process has occurred in a measured way. Some examples of initiatives taken before the WTO came into existence at the end of 1994 are[3]

- in the financial services sector, the licensing of 100 foreign banks to conduct business in foreign currency, in one or more of 13 Chinese cities
- in the shipping sector, the Chinese Ministry of Communications permitted foreign shipping companies to set up wholly foreign-owned or Sino–foreign joint ventures to ship export and import goods
- in the airport sector, foreign firms had been permitted to invest in airport facilities
- in the legal services sector, foreign law firms were able to set up offices in five coastal cities.

In the succeeding years, China has continued to gradually open its services sector to foreigners but with continuing limits on the participation of foreign service providers in various ways. These have included limiting their number, requiring them to operate in joint ventures with Chinese partners, limiting the share of equity foreigners may hold in joint ventures and imposing limits on the type of businesses foreigners may operate and on the geographic areas of operation of their businesses.

In sum, foreign participation in services trade in China is a product of both Chinese history and traditional Chinese economic thinking and of protectionism like that in any other country. As a result, services have not been liberalised at the same rate or to the same extent as trade in goods.

The requirements of GATS

This section sets out the principal rules of the GATS which are now binding upon China.

Non-discrimination among WTO Members—the MFN rule

One of the central rules of the GATS is the most favoured nation (MFN) rule (GATS, Article II). Under the MFN rule, China will be obliged to treat services and service providers from any other WTO Member no less favourably than it treats like services and service providers from any other country. However the MFN obligation is subject to an exception for preferential measures as long as they are included in a Members' List of Annex II Exemptions. China has listed possible future arrangements in the field of international maritime transport of freight and passengers. For so long as this listing remains, China will be able to afford preferential treatment to providers of international sea transport from particular countries without having to extend that treatment to providers of international sea transport services from all WTO Members. In all other service sectors, any treatment afforded to foreign service suppliers by China under any bilateral arrangement will have to be offered on not less favourable terms to service suppliers from any WTO Member.

The MFN rule will also protect China from discrimination from its trading partners. Other WTO Members will have to treat services and service providers from China no less favourably than they treat services and services from any other country, except in circumstances covered by their Annex II Exemptions.

Specific commitments on market access

In addition to the MFN rule, the GATS contains a framework for reducing barriers to foreign service providers. The GATS provides a mechanism by which each WTO Member can make specific commitments relating to the way that foreigners can supply particular services to the Member's domestic market. These specific commitments arise from negotiations between Member states and are placed in a Schedule of Specific Commitments by each Member thus forming part of that Member's GATS obligations.

Sectors and sub-sectors. The Uruguay Round participants divided their negotiation on services into 12 services sectors

- business (including professional and computer) services
- communication services
- constructions and related engineering services
- distribution services
- educational services
- environmental services
- financial (insurance and banking) services
- health-related and social services
- tourism and travel-related services
- recreational, cultural and sporting services
- transport services
- other services not included elsewhere.

Each of the 12 sectors are divided into sub-sectors making a total of 160 sub-sectors.[4]

Horizontal and vertical commitments. Specific commitments that relate to a particular service sector or sub-sector are commonly called vertical commitments. In addition to sector-specific vertical commitments, Members can make commitments that apply across all sectors. These are commonly called horizontal commitments. Typically, horizontal commitments relate to the movement of capital and people. Sub-sectors which are the subject of commitments are commonly described as being bound or having bindings using the same language as is applied to tariff bindings under the GATT. Correspondingly, sub-sectors that are not subject to any commitment are commonly described as unbound.

In practice, the horizontal commitments section of the GATS Schedule tends to be filled not with commitments but with limitations on commitments given under the vertical commitments part of the Schedule, and contains access limitations and national treatment derogations which apply across all of the specific sectoral commitments made in the vertical commitments section of the schedule.

Modes of service. Members can subdivide services and service provision into four modes of service (GATS, Article I:1). Explained in relation to China, the four modes of service are

- Mode 1—Cross-border provision of services. This relates to the situation in which the foreign service suppliers remaining in their foreign territory provide services to customers located in China.
- Mode 2—Consumption abroad. This relates to the situation in which foreign service suppliers provide services in their own territory to Chinese nationals who have travelled to that territory.
- Mode 3—Provision of service through commercial presence. This relates to the situation in which foreign service providers supply services through establishing a commercial presence in China. This includes the establishment of branches, Chinese subsidiaries, minority shareholdings in Chinese companies, and unincorporated partnerships and joint ventures.
- Mode 4—Provision of service through the presence of natural persons. This relates to the situation in which foreign service providers supply services through the temporary presence of natural persons in China.

In general, Members' Schedules deal separately with each of the four modes of service. A Member's Schedule may contain a commitment in respect of a service sub-sector that relates only to one mode of service and not others. In those cases, the modes of service upon which no commitment is included are usually described as unbound.

In negotiating commitments under the various modes of service, the Chinese government displayed caution—evidence of an awareness of the way that the commitments could affect the government's control over China. Commitments for provision of services through the first mode (cross-border provision) affect China's capacity to regulate Chinese people receiving services from outside the country. Commitments under the third mode (commercial presence) affect China's capacity to restrict foreign ownership.[5] Commitments under the fourth mode (presence of natural persons) affect China's ability to restrict the entry of people into China.

Renegotiation of specific commitments. Once a specific commitment has been in force for three years, a Member may renegotiate it. The Member may negotiate the withdrawal or modification of the commitment by offering one or more alternative commitments to liberalise services in its place. These alternative liberalisation commitments brought into effect to compensate for the withdrawal of the original commitment are called 'compensatory adjustments' to the Member's Schedule, or simply 'compensation'. If agreement cannot be reached on the compensatory adjustments, then they may be determined through an arbitration of what adjustments would be necessary to maintain a general level of mutually advantageous commitments not less favourable to trade than those originally in the Schedule. If a Member proceeds to modify a Schedule without agreement and without implementing compensatory adjustments as determined through arbitration, then affected Members who actually participated in the arbitration may exclude the modifying Member from the benefits of some of their own specific commitments (GATS, Article XXI).

The GATS rules on market access

There are three broad GATS rules on market access. The operation of each rule in relation to China is determined by the exact content of China's scheduled commitments.

- Rule 1—Treatment no less favourable than scheduled: Article XVI:1. China is required to accord services and service suppliers from any other WTO Member treatment no less favourable than the treatment specified in its Schedule (GATS, Article XVI:1).
- Rule 2—Qualified prohibition of quantitative restrictions and some other restrictions: Article XVI:2. China must not apply any of the six types of restrictions that are listed in Article XVI:2 to any service sectors in respect of which China has made a market access commitment, unless the otherwise proscribed restrictions are specified in China's Schedule.[6]

The six prohibited types of restrictions are

a limits on the number of service suppliers

b limits on the total value of service transactions or assets

c limits on the total quantity of service output

d limits on the number of persons that can be employed in a sector or by a particular service provider

e restrictions on the type of legal entity or joint venture through which a service supplier may supply a service

f limitations on the participation of foreign capital in terms of maximum percentage or maximum value of individual or aggregate foreign investment.

The first four paragraphs of this second rule constitute a prohibition on quantitative restrictions in sectors in which market access commitments are made but the prohibition is subject to an exception for scheduled restrictions (effectively permanently grandfathering the scheduled quantitative restrictions). Paragraph (e) constrains the use of legal restrictions on the vehicle that can be used to carry on a business of providing services. The approach taken by paragraph (e) of Article XVI(2) is to prohibit any such restrictions subject to an exception for scheduled restrictions. Paragraph (f) relates to the foreign ownership of businesses providing services.

The application of these six rules to China and the content of China's obligations under this rule depends on the content of China's Schedule but two comments can be made. First, these rules do not apply to a sector at all if China's Schedule does not contain any specific commitments with respect to that sector. Where China's Schedule contains specific commitments for some but not all sub-sectors within a sector, these rules apply with respect to the sub-sectors in which a specific commitment has been made and do not apply with respect to the other sub-sectors.[7] Second, even for the subsectors in which China has made specific commitments and, consequently, to which these rules do apply, the rules do not proscribe such restrictions as China's specifies in its Schedule.

- Rule 3—Qualified national treatment. In sectors which China has listed in its Schedule, it is required to apply all measures affecting the supply of services no less favourably to services and service suppliers of any other Member than such measures are applied to Chinese services and service suppliers, except for such instances of less favourable treatment as are listed in China's Schedule (GATS, Article XVII:1).

However, as for Rule 2, both the application of this national treatment rule to China and the content of China's obligations under it depend upon the content of China's Schedule. First, as for Rule 2, the national treatment rule does not apply to a sector if China has not made a specific commitment with respect to the sector. Nor does it apply to any sub-sector if China has not made a specific commitment with respect to that sub-sector (even if China has made specific commitments in relation to other sub-sectors within the sector). Second, even for the subsectors in which China has made specific commitments and, consequently, to which the national treatment rule does apply, the rule does not proscribe such derogations from national treatment as China has listed in its Schedule.

Negotiability of scheduled commitments. Thus the dependence of the above obligations upon the content of a Member's Schedule means that the GATS allows considerable room for Member states to negotiate the level of liberalisation that they are obliged to provide. The framework for making commitments allows China, like other countries, considerable flexibility to control the pace and extent of the process of liberalising services trade.

Additional GATS rules. In addition to the above commitments there are some other rules which apply once a sector has been scheduled. These latter obligations cannot be qualified by anything in the Schedule of Commitments.[8]

- Members must deal with applications for authorisation to provide a service, upon which a specific commitment has been made, within a reasonable time, must inform the applicant of the decision and must maintain tribunals or procedures to provide for prompt, objective and impartial review of the decision (GATS, Article VI(2), (3)).
- Members must not restrict international payments for current transactions relating to specific commitments, nor (with some exceptions) for capital transactions inconsistently with their specific commitments regarding such transactions (GATS, Article XI).
- Members cannot grant monopoly rights in relation to supply of a service covered by a specific commitment without having to negotiate compensatory adjustments in accordance with the usual procedures for withdrawing or modifying a specific commitment (GATS, Article VIII:4).
- Members must permit foreign suppliers of services subject to specific commitments to have access to public telecommunications networks for the purposes of supply of those services (GATS, Annex on Telecommunications, Article 5).

Violation of GATS obligations

In the event that China violates an obligation under the GATS, other Members will be able to resort to the provisions of the WTO dispute settlement system (see GATS, Article XXII and the *Understanding on Dispute Settlement* (DSU)). In the event that the WTO Dispute Settlement Body (DSB) adopts a decision that China is in violation of a GATS obligation, then it will request China to comply with the relevant obligation (DSU, Article 19). If China fails to conform with the obligation, and fails to reach agreement with the affected Members on compensatory liberalisations, then the DSB will be able to authorise the Member having invoked the dispute settlement procedure to suspend the application to China of an equivalent level of obligations (DSU, Article 22(2), (4)).

The evolution of China's proposed GATS schedule and post Uruguay round services negotiations

A brief chronology: raising the bar for China and services

China's Schedule of Commitments under the GATS evolved against a background of rapid change. This process has two aspects: Chinese liberalisation and alteration of Member states' expectations. Within China, the process of economic liberalisation led by the government enabled it to gradually improve the scope and depth of market access included in the succeeding drafts of the proposed Schedule of Commitments. At the same time, China had to react to the demands of WTO Members. These demands from other WTO Members were shaped by the growing economic importance of service exporters and their consequent increased influence over governments. The demands of other WTO Members were also shaped by the further liberalisations of trade in services by WTO Members that occurred through the post Uruguay Round program for further GATS negotiations.

During the Uruguay Round, China submitted a schedule of GATS commitments as part of its attempt to complete its accession process in time to become one of the founding Members of the WTO. This schedule ('China's 1994 Draft GATS Schedule') is reproduced as part of the Final Act of the Uruguay Round of 15 April 1994, even though China was not accepted as a Member.[9]

China's 1994 offer did not include any commitments relating to a number of sectors. To a limited extent, these omissions corresponded to similar omissions in the schedules of other countries. Like all Uruguay Round participants, China had not offered any commitments at all on basic (real time voice transmission)[10] telecommunications services and its offer on financial services was extremely limited. Like a number of other countries, China had scheduled a MFN derogation for maritime services. In these respects China's offer of commitments was no weaker than the commitments made in 1995 by all WTO Members. In the Uruguay Round these parts of the services negotiation had simply been too difficult and part of the final agreement had been that these matters would be the subject of further negotiations. As a result no commitments were made by any Member state in the field of basic telecommunications (as distinct from value-added communications) and it was agreed that negotiations in this field would continue. Nor did many of the original WTO Members make comprehensive commitments in relation to financial services and it was similarly agreed that negotiations in this field would continue. Similarly, all Members agreed that the MFN rules would not apply to maritime services and that negotiations on this issue should also continue. China's position on these critical service sectors was equivalent to the position of all WTO Members at that time.

However, since the Uruguay Round, Member states have negotiated additional service commitments. As each negotiation has been completed and existing WTO Members have made more commitments, there has been a corresponding increase in the scope and level of commitments that other WTO Members have requested of applicants for accession, like China. Therefore, the price of accession has gone up since 1 January 1995 as each round of additional

Legal implications for regulation of trade in services

GATS negotiations has been completed.

Despite the equivalence in 1994 between China's offer and other Member states in relation to basic telecommunications, maritime and financial services, there were some other serious omissions from China's 1994 offer. In particular, China made no offer at all in the areas of retail and wholesale distribution, and given the existence of many restrictive distribution arrangements, that omission impacted on the value of their offer of tariff concessions on goods.

Following the establishment of the WTO on 1 January 1995 and a WTO Working Party on the Accession of China, China continued negotiating with WTO Members on its accession. At the same time the WTO Members, amongst themselves, commenced four tracks of negotiations for further liberalisation in trade in services: financial services, basic telecommunications services, movement of natural persons, and maritime services. By July 1995, some further limited liberalisations had been achieved. The negotiation on financial services produced an interim result which was brought into effect under the Second Protocol to the GATS,[11] with improvements in the schedules of 29 Members in relation to financial services and in some cases removal or reduction of the scope of the MFN exemption for financial services.[12] Also in July 1995, WTO Members completed negotiations on the movement of natural persons and these commitments were brought into effect under a Third Protocol under the GATS.[13] These achieved additional commitments from only six Members on the temporary entry of personnel for the purpose of providing a service (Ruggiero 1995:5–17).

In December 1996, China circulated to WTO Members a revised version of its proposed GATS schedule dated 21 November 1996 which was made public (China's 1996 Draft GATS Schedule).[14] Like most Members' GATS schedules at that time, China's 1996 Draft GATS Schedule contained no commitments on basic telecommunications. In addition, China's commitments on value-added telecommunications were extremely limited. They did not contain any commitment relating to provision of valued-added telecommunications services through commercial presence and cross-border telecommunications services could only be provided through the Ministry of Posts and Telecommunications. Soon after, in February 1997, 72 of the existing WTO Members completed their negotiations on basic telecommunications services signing the Fourth GATS Protocol, also known as the Basic Telecoms Agreement.[15] Under this Fourth Protocol, the MFN rule came into force in the sector, and commitments in each of local, domestic, long distance and international voice services were made by more that 50 Members, with 61 Members agreeing to permit at least two suppliers of basic telecommunications services and 57 parties agreeing to abide by rules on interconnection.[16] Clearly, the signature of the Fourth Protocol increased the pressure on China to enhance its offer on services to include commitments on basic telecommunications.

China circulated a revised services offer to Members of the Working Party on 20 November 1997.[17] Neither the Chinese government nor the WTO released the document to the public at the time. The substance of the 1997 offer was still regarded as inadequate by the other WTO Members. In particular it was criticised because it still did not contain any commitments with respect to basic telecommunications and made extremely limited advances on the proposed commitments on financial services.[18]

On 12 December 1997, less than a month after China had distributed its 1997 services offer, the second series of WTO negotiations on financial services came to a conclusion.[19] Seventy WTO Members agreed on new commitments in the financial services sector.[20] Fifty-two of these Members brought those commitments into force under the Fifth Protocol to the GATS on 1 March 1999. [21] At the conclusion of the financial services negotiations, the other WTO Members had again raised their expectations with respect to the liberalisations that China would have to make before they would agree to China's accession.[22]

No doubt, as China continued bilateral negotiations with a number of countries during 1998 and 1999, it must have considered adding further liberalisations to its proposed services schedule. In particular, it is clear that at the April 1999 meeting in Washington between President Clinton and Premier Zhu Rongji, possible revisions to the services offer must have been under consideration by China and the United States. No new draft Schedule was made public. However, the US Trade Representative made a press release giving some details about the services commitments that China purportedly had offered.[23] In particular, it set out allegedly agreed liberalisations that made significant advances on previous positions in relation to the sensitive sectors of financial services and telecommunications. The Chinese disassociated themselves from the press releases saying that the concessions described in them had not been agreed.[24] However, it seems that the Chinese did not backtrack very much (if at all) on their April 1999 offer, for within the next few months Japan and Australia made separate announcements that they were satisfied with China's services offer, though despite a few fragments in press releases no new version of the draft GATS schedule was made public.[25] The United States and China finally reached a bilateral agreement on market access on 15 November 2000.[26] An agreement with the Canadians followed in that same month.[27] However, once again no revised draft services schedule was released. It was not until March 2000 after the Sino–US bilateral agreement had been tabled in US legislative processes that a revised draft Services Schedule became public.[28] Two months later in May 2000, the European Union and China announced that they had reached a bilateral agreement on market access which included some improvements on some parts of the offer on services but they did not release a new version of the proposed Schedule.[29]

Over the next year, the US and the EU continued to press for some clarifications and extensions, particularly in the insurance sector and the retail distribution sector. In relation to the insurance sector, there was a controversy over whether the commitments that China had offered to the EU were consistent with the commitments that China had offered the USA and also some deliberation over the insertion of a definition of the term 'large scale commercial risk'. In relation to retailing, where China's offer to permit wholly foreign owned stores excluded chain stores, clarification was sought over the meaning of 'chain stores. China and the USA reached agreement on these matters together with various other matters affecting the Chinese accession during talks in Shanghai between 4 and 8 June 2001.[30] The completion of the accession process in the WTO Working Party continued for a few months with the remaining outstanding matters being agreed in September 2001. The decision to admit China was finally made at the Doha Ministerial meeting in November. On 10 November 2001, China signed the Protocol of Accession [31] to which was annexed the Schedule of Specific Commitments under the GATS. [32] The Protocol came into force on 10 December 2001.

Limitations in China's offer

This chronology may give the impression that the evolution of the Chinese draft services schedule involved little more than the addition of more sectors to the offer as time passed. However, the evolution of the offer was significantly more complex. At various stages of the negotiation, the Chinese offer was criticised because of a variety of limitations in the offer. These limitations included

- quantitative limitations on the number of licences that could be issued to foreigners
- conditions for eligibility for licences including conditions related to registered capital, annual trade volume or the prior existence of a representative office
- limitations on conducting business in particular economic zones or in particular cities
- limitation of participation through commercial presence to minority shareholdings in joint ventures with Chinese entities.[33]

These aspects of China's offer of liberalisation of foreign service providers also evolved as the accession negotiation has progressed. Some of these characteristics of the Chinese offer bear similarities to restrictions in many other countries but some of these restrictions are reflections of the particular process of transition from planned to market economy that China has been undergoing since 1978. In order to understand the limitations in China's offer, it is necessary to consider how the transition to market economy has involved the gradual development of a legal framework for business.

The transition in Chinese regulation of business

While some restrictions set out in China's services offer—particularly the earlier versions—may seem strange by Western standards, they are predictable manifestations of a society in which in the past, everything was planned and controlled by the state. According to the socialist philosophy, the corollary of control was responsibility. Therefore, although vested interests no doubt influenced the protectionist structure of the Chinese economy, one of the main features of Chinese economic organisation, which still influences the transitional economy, was a consciousness of responsibility to the Chinese community.

Prior to Deng Xiaoping's rise to power in 1978, no foreign businesses were entitled to operate in China at all. The first modern opening of the market to investment was implemented through the 1979 *Law on Chinese–Foreign Equity Joint Ventures* [34] that permitted foreigners to invest in limited liability companies provided that they invested at least 25 per cent of the registered capital.[35] The *Law on Chinese–Foreign Equity Joint Ventures* was administered so as to maximise the contribution from foreigners while limiting foreign control over the operation of the business. The dominant purpose of such market opening was to obtain money and expertise from the outside world. The encouragement of economic efficiencies through competition was probably a much less important objective. In such market opening, the state did not disavow its sense of responsibility to the community. One of the ways in which this sense of responsibility was manifested was in the way the new law placed great emphasis on the provision of sufficient capital by the foreign investor. Permission to create the business entity and to carry on the business was conditional upon Chinese government satisfaction that sufficient funds would be invested in the business. This attitude was also reflected in the *Company Law*, developed some years later, which also placed emphasis on a minimum paid-up capital and (until recent changes) did not permit companies to have nominal capital, like the $2 paid-up companies permitted in many other countries.

It remained difficult for foreigners to control their own operations. In 1980 *Interim Regulations on the Control of Resident Representative Offices* provided a means for foreign businesses to set up representative offices which were able to conduct 'business activities in the nature of those of a residence office'.[36] This inevitably led to some uncertainties about the permissible scope of business of such representative office. These uncertainties were removed when, in 1983, the State Administration for Industry and Commerce issued procedures which provided that resident offices of foreign offices could not engage in 'direct profit-making operations'.[37] No doubt, there were still some foreign representative offices which from time to time tested the boundaries of 'indirect profit-making operations'.

It was not until 1986 that China, through the provisions of the *Law on Foreign-Capital Enterprises* made it possible for foreigners to control 100 per cent of their Chinese-located business of direct profit-making operations.[38] However, foreign businesses could only have a wholly controlled business in China by establishing a subsidiary with adequate registered capital. Foreign businesses could not establish branches in China.

Until 1988, the only forms of foreign business permitted to operate in China were incorporated joint ventures and foreign subsidiaries, both subject to government approval of the foreign contribution of capital and of the business itself. However these forms did not address the interests of some foreign businesses that wanted to reduce their tax at home by offsetting losses on their business in China against profits at home. This was possibly part of the reason that, in 1988, China began to permit foreigners to create unincorporated joint ventures with Chinese enterprises under the *Law on Chinese–Foreign Contractual Joint Ventures*.[39] In fact, contractual joint ventures could be either incorporated or unincorporated.[40] In general, the same government controls over the foreign contribution of capital and the approval of the business applied to contractual joint ventures as to the other permissible business vehicles.

The day before the *Contractual Joint Ventures Law* was passed, the National People's Congress amended the Constitution to recognise the existence of the private economy as a complement to the public socialist economy.[41] However, five years after Constitutional recognition that the government had a role in protecting the rights of the private sector, China still had no general legislation relating to companies. In the intervening years, commerce with outsiders had increased, the private sector had grown and stock exchanges had been opened in Shanghai and Shenzhen.[42] China did not pass a general company law until December 1993.[43] The *Company Law* recognised that a foreign company could choose to establish a branch instead of a subsidiary to conduct business in China (Part IX, Article 199). Strict conditions applied. The foreign branch required government approval, which sometimes involved the satisfaction of conditions such as a minimum investment of funds, limiting such branches to their pre-approved scope of business activity and preventing them from removing assets from China (Company Law, Part IX). Sometime between the end of the bulk of the Uruguay Round negotiations in December 1993, and April 1994 when the parties signed the WTO Agreement in Marrakesh, China submitted the Schedule of Services Commitments that failed to win it Membership of the WTO. That schedule contained commitments to permit certain foreign businesses to establish branches to carry on business in China.[44] In July 1994, the Chinese *Company Law* came into force including the provision permitting branches of foreign companies to be approved. Unfortunately for foreign companies wishing to establish branches, the Chinese government overlooked the necessity of creating some regulations concerning how applications for approval of branches should be made and to whom they should be submitted.

In particular, it abstained from delegating to some part of the government the task of assessing such applications for the approval of branches. Some separate regulations had come into force earlier in 1994 to regulate the establishment of branches in the financial services sector.[45] Outside of the financial services sector, it remained impossible (in practice) to find a public servant who would approve the establishment of a branch. Inquiries of Chinese legal practitioners in July and August 2000 confirmed that, as late as that time, it remained impossible, in practice though not in law, for a foreign company to obtain authorisation to establish a branch to conduct business in China.

This effective limitation on branches provided a continued incentive for foreigners to use their ingenuity to devise ways to conduct as much as possible of their business through a representative office. Rules issued in 1995 by the Ministry of Foreign Trade and Economic Cooperation on their face reiterated that representative offices were limited to indirect business operations.[46] However, by specifying that indirect business operations included 'business liaison, product introduction, market surveys and research, and technological exchange', these rules may have given some additional security to those pushing the boundary between 'indirect' and 'direct' operations.

The opening of the stock exchanges was a catalyst for further changes as listed Chinese companies sought access to foreign funds and foreigners sought to take equity in listed Chinese businesses. With the *Company Law* in place, the Chinese government responded in August 1994 by permitting listed Chinese companies to list a limited proportion of capital on foreign exchanges that could be purchased by non-Chinese nationals.[47] In 1996, the reforms went further, permitting listed Chinese companies to create a non-voting class of shares that could be purchased by foreigners on Chinese stock exchanges.[48]

China has made enormous changes since 1978 at which time it had no legal infrastructure within which foreign service providers could conduct business in China. By 1995, when the negotiations for China's accession reconvened after the Uruguay Round, China had created a legal structure under which foreign businesses could participate in services, though always subject to government approval of the capital contribution and the scope of business.

Commercial presence under Chinese law

The Chinese Schedule to the GATS contains many entries that refer to the above mentioned legal means of having a commercial presence in China. To facilitate understanding of the commitments, we now add to the above outline of the transition in Chinese law regulating foreign businesses (whether relating to goods or services), by summarising the ways in which a foreign service provider might establish a commercial presence in China.[49]

It is proposed to deal in turn with the following types of business methods
- foreign companies having a representative office (not a separate legal entity)
- foreign companies having a branch office in China which is not a separate legal entity
- foreigners having a wholly-owned subsidiary incorporated in China
- foreigners having shares in a company incorporated under Chinese law
- foreigners joining with a Chinese entity in an unincorporated partnership or joint venture which is not a separate legal entity.

In general, foreigners cannot buy part or all of an existing Chinese business unless the transaction can be accommodated within one of the permitted categories of foreign investment set out hereunder.

Foreign companies having a representative office which is not a separate legal entity

Representative Offices of foreign businesses may not engage in a business of providing services. Foreign companies are not permitted to engage in production and business activities in China unless they establish a branch in accordance with the Chinese Company Law.[50] This restriction has led in practice to a distinction between representative offices which cannot engage in direct production or business activities and branches which can engage in direct production or business activities.

Foreign companies having a branch which is not a separate legal entity

Under the Company Law, it is theoretically possible to establish a branch in China. To do so, a foreign company must obtain approval from MOFTEC.[51] Then the foreign company must apply to the Company Registration Authority for registration and for a business licence for the branch (Company Law, Article 200). The company must appoint a representative or agent within the PRC to take charge of the branch (Company Law, Article 201). However, as pointed out above, in practice, in the past, it has not been possible for the establishment of a branch to be approved except in the particular sector of financial services where specific regulations are in force.

Foreigners having a wholly-owned subsidiary incorporated in China

Wholly foreign-owned subsidiaries are only permitted if they accord with the 1986 *Law on Foreign-Capital Enterprises* and the 1990 *Implementation Regulation of the PRC Wholly Foreign-Owned Enterprise Law*.[52] The law requires a two-step approval process (Foreign-Capital Enterprises Law, Article 6). First, the approval of MOFTEC (or other approved agency) is required. Second, an application must be made to the 'industry and commerce administration authorities' for registration and a business licence (Foreign-Capital Enterprises Law, Article 7). The guiding principle for the approval of a foreign capital enterprise is enunciated in Article 3,

> enterprises with foreign capital shall be established in such a manner as to help the development of China's national economy; they shall use advanced technology and equipment or market all or most of their products outside China.

Once approved, the foreign capital enterprise must make the investments that are specified in the terms of the approval of their establishment (Foreign-Capital Enterprises Law, Article 9). The law also requires that any major change in the enterprise must be approved by the examination authorities (Foreign-Capital Enterprises Law, Article 10). Without describing the scope of this provision, it seems clear that it would require approval for changes in shareholding and in the major business activity. Most importantly, a foreign investor would need approval to dispose of any or all of the shares in a wholly foreign-owned Chinese subsidiary company.

Foreign share-ownership in a company incorporated under Chinese law

Shares in unlisted companies

In general, foreigners cannot enter the market in a particular service sector by buying into an existing service business. Chinese law does not provide a general permission for foreigners to buy shares in an existing Chinese company. Such a transaction would require the existing company to be reconstructed as a Chinese Foreign Equity Joint Venture. Therefore, a foreign investment in a company providing services must take place in one of the two ways set out below.

Shares in listed companies

Foreigners may not purchase ordinary A class shares in listed Chinese companies. However, listed companies are permitted to create B class shares. Foreigners may purchase B class shares in companies that are listed on a Chinese stock exchange.[53] It is also possible for foreigners to purchase particular categories of shares of the limited number of Chinese companies that are listed on stock exchanges in other countries.[54]

Shares in Chinese–foreign equity joint ventures

Foreigners can join with Chinese nationals to provide services through the establishment of limited liability companies. Such companies and the investments in them must accord with the 1990 revision of the 1979 *Law of the People's Republic of China on Chinese–Foreign Equity Joint Ventures* and the 1986 *Implementation Regulation of the PRC Chinese–Foreign Equity Joint Venture Law.*[55]

As for other types of business entities, a two-step approval process applies. The relevant documents establishing the company and the business enterprise must be approved by MOFTEC. The most important prerequisite to approval is that the foreign investor must invest not less than 25 per cent of the registered capital of the company (Chinese–Foreign Equity JV Law, Article 4). The investment may be in the form of cash, in-kind or in industrial property rights but if the investment is contributed in the form of technology or equipment, then that technology or equipment must be advanced and must suit China's needs (Chinese–Foreign Equity JV Law, Article 5). Usually, the joint venture contracts must specify the duration of the joint venture.[56] After approval by MOFTEC, the equity joint venture must apply to the department in charge of industry and commerce for registration and for the issue of a business licence. The foreign investor cannot assign its shares without the consent of the Chinese investor (Chinese–Foreign Equity JV Law, Article 4).

Foreigners joining with a Chinese entity in an unincorporated partnership or joint venture which is not a separate legal entity

Foreigners can join with Chinese nationals to provide services through the establishment of Chinese–foreign contractual joint ventures (Fu 1998:287–8). Such contractual joint ventures and the investments in them must accord with the 1988 *Law of the People's Republic of China on Chinese–Foreign Contractual Joint Ventures*[57] and the 1995 *Implementation Regulation of the PRC Chinese–Foreign Contractual Joint Venture Law.*

As with the equity joint venture, a two-step approval process applies. The relevant documents establishing the joint venture must be approved by a government authority which may be MOFTEC but may be another department or local government authorised by the State Council (Chinese–Foreign Contractual JV Law, Article 5). The documents must set out the investments which each side shall make and generally the approval of the joint venture will be subject to the parties making the investment described in the contract. After approval of the contractual joint venture, the parties must apply to the administrative authorities for registration and for a business licence (Chinese–Foreign Contractual JV Law, Article 6), (Contractual joint ventures may also be established as separate legal entities as limited liability companies).

The content of China's GATS schedule

The Chinese Schedule of Specific Commitments is assessed by looking separately at

- the MFN Exclusions in Annex of Article II Exemptions
- the sectoral coverage of the vertical commitments
- the modes of supply covered by the commitments
- the cross-border commitments
- the commercial presence commitments focussing first on the horizontal limitations on the commercial presence commitments, and second, on the scope and range of the commercial presence commitments given in specific sectors and the limitations attached to them
- the presence of natural persons commitments including the horizontal limitations.

In assessing the content of China's Schedule we will make some comparisons with the schedules made by developed, developing and transition economy WTO Members.[58]

MFN exclusions in the Annex on Article II exemptions

China's Annex of Article II Exemptions lists include Maritime Transport, International Transport and Freight and Passengers. Presumably this means internal and international maritime transport of freight and passengers and all international transport by any other means of freight and passengers. It also refers to cargo sharing agreements.

Therefore, for all sectors other than maritime and international transport, China will be obliged to afford service providers from any WTO Member with treatment no less favourable than that it provides to service providers from any other country.

Legal implications for regulation of trade in services

Sectoral coverage of China's proposed commitments

The Uruguay Round negotiations dealt with 12 sectors (including one for 'other services') which were divided into 160 sub-sectors. In relation to these sector categories, China's draft Schedule includes at least one commitment in at least one sub-sector within the following sectors
- business services
- communications services
- construction and related engineering services
- distribution services
  education services
- environmental services
- financial services
- tourism and travel-related services
- transport services.

However, within these sectors, some sub-sectors are not subject to any commitment.
- In the area of Business Services, no commitment is made in respect of nursing or veterinary services, market research, or printing and publishing.
- In the area of communications services, no commitments are made in respect of telex or telegraph services.
- In the area of audiovisual services, no commitments are made in respect of radio and television transmission services.
- In the area of transport services, no commitments are given in respect of maintenance and repair of either ships, trains or road transport vehicles.

There are no commitments at all in the following two sectors
- health-related and social services
- recreational, cultural and sporting services.

In these last two sectors and in all of the sub-sectors in respect of which there are no proposed commitments, the Chinese government does not have any restraints imposed by the GATS on the level of access it permits foreigners to have to the Chinese market. The regulation of these areas of service provision is unbound. However, even in these sectors, China is still obliged by the MFN rule to provide service providers from any WTO Member with treatment no less favourable than that accorded to providers of such services from any other country; it is not entitled to discriminate between foreign providers, although it may still discriminate against them.

Of the 160 sub-sectors, China's Schedule includes at least some kind of commitment in 89 sub-sectors. This merely indicates that in respect of those service sectors, China is offering a commitment relating to at least one mode of service. Many of those commitments are qualified. The mere numeric count treats as equivalent sectors in which China qualifies that access commitment with limitations or derogations from national treatment, and sectors in which the market access commitments are not qualified at all.

Some idea of the scope of China's Schedule in comparison with other WTO Members' Schedules can be gleaned from statistics compiled by Altinger and Enders (1996) on the basis of the Schedules, as they were prior to the Fourth Protocol on Basic Telecoms and the Fifth Protocol on Financial Services. Their data also provides a simple count of sectors in which commitments have been made with respect to at least one mode of service without any qualitative assessment of the limitations or national treatment derogations. Altinger and Ender's (1996) count of the number of sub-sectors covered in the Schedules reveals the following information

- more than 100—Austria, EU Member states, Japan, Switzerland, United States
- between 81 and 100—Australia, Canada, Czech Republic, Hungary, Iceland, Norway, Slovak Republic, Sweden
- between 71 and 80—Finland, Hong Kong, Republic of Korea, Liechtenstein, New Zealand, South Africa, Thailand, Turkey
- between 61 and 70—Dominican Republic, Malaysia, Mexico
- between 51 and 60—Argentina, Poland, Singapore, Venezuela
- less than 50—all other developing countries.

These statistics could be augmented slightly to take account of additional sectors covered by the Fourth and Fifth Protocols.

Using this data, we can see that China has made commitments on about 10–15 less sectors than the average for industrialised country Members, and on a much greater number of sectors by a wide margin, than the average for developing country Members. China's Schedule covers about the same number of sectors as the advanced developing countries of Korea, Thailand and Turkey but more than all of the ASEAN Members other than Thailand and more than all of the Latin Amercian Members. Altinger and Enders (1996) calculate that on average the transition economies made commitments in about half of the sub-sectors. On this simple measure of coverage of sub-sectors, China's schedule is more similar to the schedules of transition economies than those of developing countries.

However, since this numeric count does not reveal much about the substance of the schedules, further investigation must be made of the content of the proposed commitments.

Legal implications for regulation of trade in services

Cross-border mode of supply

In general, the WTO Members' schedules demonstrate that, on average, WTO Members have tended to leave the cross-border mode of supply completely unbound in a higher proportion of sectors than they have left supply through the other three modes of supply completely unbound.[59] No doubt this arises partly because in respect of a number of service sectors, such as building and construction, the cross-border provision of the service is impossible in practice. However, developing countries have left cross-border supply completely unbound in a much larger number of sectors than developed or transition economies.[60] This reflects a tendency among developing countries (perhaps also present in developed countries to a lesser extent) to use their GATS commitments merely to reflect their existing regimes for attracting inward foreign direct investment rather than to liberalise the provision of the underlying service.

In China's Schedule, there are a number of service sub-sectors in which a commitment is offered on the commercial presence mode of service but where the regulation of cross-border provision of the service is unbound. This includes some services where cross-border supply of the service is not technically feasible, for example construction work for buildings and civil engineering. However, it also includes other service sectors where cross-border provision is feasible, such as

- cross-border advertising services direct to clients[61]
- all forms of cross-border education
- cross-border provision of life insurance
- cross-border provision of the key financial services of acceptance of deposits and lending
- cross-border provision of credit and debit card services
- cross-border retailing (except for mail order).

In the modes of supply for specific sub-sectors which are listed as unbound, none of the GATS rules on market access or national treatment apply. China is free to impose any regulation limiting the cross-border provision of those services, including any regulation which imposes less favourable treatment on foreign service providers than domestic providers. The MFN rule will still apply.

To assess whether exclusion of the cross-border mode in China's Schedule reflects the general developing country trend toward using the GATS reflect existing regimes for attracting inward foreign direct investment rather than to liberalise the provision of the underlying service, we can make a rough comparison of China's Schedule with statistics on other developing country schedules. Of the 89 sub-sectors upon which China's draft schedule includes some commitment, the cross-border mode of service provision is included for 59 sub-sectors or 66 per cent but is excluded from 30 sub-sectors or 34 per cent of them. Altinger and Enders (1996) data show that developed countries excluded the cross-border mode from 25 per cent of the sectors on which they made commitments, developing countries excluded it from 46 per cent and transition economies from 37 per cent. Therefore, China, as well as having made commitments in more subsectors than the average for developing countries, has also excluded the cross-border mode significantly less frequently than the other developing countries.

Again this mere numeric count abstracts from the content of the commitments. The numeric count of the number of sub-sectors for which cross-border provision remains unbound takes no account of the qualifications that China has placed upon its commitments on cross-border provision in other sub-sectors. The commitments in these sectors range from commitments to apply no restrictions at all through to commitments to permit foreigners to provide cross-border services provided they do so through Chinese business entities or in joint venture with Chinese business entities.

A closer examination of the particular commitments reveals that China's Schedule binds China not to maintain any restrictions on cross-border provision of some professional services including
- cross-border medical services
- cross-border accounting, auditing, bookkeeping and taxation services
- cross-border legal services excluding on Chinese law.

The Schedule also binds China not to maintain any restrictions on some other business services including
- cross-border software installation, implementation, consulting, programming or analysis services
- cross-border translation services
- cross-border distribution of videos, video games and sound recordings
- cross-border travel agency services.

On the other hand, China has only bound itself to permit cross-border architectural or engineering services that are provided through cooperation with Chinese professional organisations,[62] and to permit cross-border advertising services that are provided 'through advertising agents registered in China who have the right to provide foreign advertising services' (see Schedule CLII, item 1 F(a)). All of the commitments relating to telecommunications services only bind China to permit cross-border provision of the relevant service if it is provided through a joint venture which effectively means that China has only bound itself to permit the provision of the services through establishment of a commercial presence and, therefore, it has not bound itself to permit simple cross-border provision by foreigners at all (Schedule CLII, Category 2:17–20). In short, although the Chinese Draft Schedule indicates cross-border commitments in 59 sub-sectors, the actual number of sub-sectors in which there will be a significant liberalisation of cross-border supply will be smaller.

China's commercial presence commitments

China has made commitments in relation to provision of services through commercial presence in a range of sectors.

- Professional services including legal, accounting, taxation, architectural, engineering, medical; other business services including computer software installation and implementation services and data processing services; real estate services, equipment maintenance, some rental and leasing services, advertising, technical testing, offshore and onshore oilfield services, photographic services, packaging services, translation and interpreting services.
- Communication services including some international courier services; value-added telecommunications including email, voice mail and EDI, and basic telecommunications services including paging, mobile phone and domestic and international transmission of voice, packet switched data, circuit switched data and facsimile; distribution of videos and sound recordings and cinema theatre services.
- Construction and engineering services.
- Distribution services including wholesale and retail.
- Education services.
- Environmental services.
- Financial services including life insurance and non-life insurance; banking including borrowing, lending, leasing, credit card and payments services; advisory services and also in funds management and securities trading.
- Tourism including hotels and travel agencies.
- Transport including domestic rail and road freight, freight forwarding, aircraft maintenance, international maritime passenger and freight services, domestic waterway freight.

China's horizontal commitments on commercial presence

Limitations written in the horizontal section of the commitments describe limitations that apply to all of the particular sectors in which specific commitments are made. In general, most developed country Schedules of Commitments do not contain horizontal limitations on foreign service suppliers establishing a commercial presence through branches or subsidiaries though some do have horizontal limitations providing for an authorisation requirement.[63] However, most developing country Schedules do have some kind of horizontal entry relating to commercial presence, many containing a requirement as to authorisation, almost 20 requiring a particular form of legal entity and about 10 requiring joint ventures.[64]

The horizontal commitments part of China's Schedule contains a number of limitations. The description below sets out the horizontal entries relating to commercial presence in China's Schedule and then explains how they affect the operation of the obligations under the relevant provisions of the GATS relating to market access.

First, the horizontal commitments contain an undertaking not to make existing authorisations more restrictive. The undertaking provides

> the conditions of ownership, operation and scope of activities, as set out in the respective contractual or shareholder agreement or in a licence establishing or authorising the operation or supply of services by an existing foreign service supplier, will not be made more restrictive than they exist as of the date of China's accession to the WTO.

Since Article XVI:1 requires Members to treat service providers from other WTO Members no less favourably than provided in their Schedule, then with this commitment in its Schedule, Article XVI:1 prohibits the Chinese government from making any existing authorisation of service providers more restrictive than it was on 10 December 2001, the date of China's accession.

A number of other entries in China's horizontal commitments affect the operation of GATS Article XVI:2(e) which prohibits Members from maintaining measures which restrict or require specific types of legal entity or joint venture through which a service supplier may supply a service, in sectors where specific commitments are undertaken, unless those measures are specified in their schedule.

The first entry in the Schedule which affects the application of Article XVI:2(e) lists the permissible types of foreign invested enterprises.

> In China, foreign invested enterprises include foreign capital enterprises (also referred to as wholly foreign-owned enterprises and joint venture enterprises) and there are two types of joint venture enterprises: equity joint ventures and contractual joint ventures.

It is uncertain whether this paragraph has any legal effect of its own apart from being an introductory explanation to subsequent parts of the Schedule which refer to the various forms of foreign invested enterprises. If instead, the Schedule contained a horizontal entry which said that foreign invested enterprises may only be in the forms listed or that China was to be unbound in respect of foreign invested enterprises other than the forms listed, then the legal effect of such a paragraph would be that any Chinese law prohibiting foreigners from providing services through a commercial presence in other ways would not be a violation of Article XVI:2. For example, a law prohibiting foreign business enterprises from buying equity in Chinese businesses, whether incorporated or unincorporated, without going through one of the procedures for establishing one of the three permitted types of foreign invested enterprises would not be a violation of Article XVI:2. It is possible that the existing wording of this paragraph might be taken to have the same effect; that is, the effect of making China's regulation of other types of foreign capital enterprises unbound. A contrary argument might be stronger but this question of interpretation would have to be considered in the light of the WTO Appellate Body's enthusiasm in the past for the effectiveness principle of treaty interpretation, and its consequent inclination to interpret schedules so as to ensure that all words do have some legal effect (see *Canada Dairy* case, WT/DS103/AB/R and WT/DS113/AB/r, paras 125–39).

The other entries affecting GATS Article XVI:2(e) relate to particular types of establishments.

Representative offices. The Schedule makes a commitment that the establishment of representative offices is permitted but that except where specific sectoral commitments specify otherwise, representative offices may not conduct business.

Branches of foreign enterprises. The Schedule indicates that the establishment of branches of foreign enterprises is unbound except to the extent specifically bound in relation to specific sub-sectors.

Chinese–foreign equity joint ventures. The Schedule specifies that the proportion of foreign investment in an equity joint venture must be no less than 25 per cent of the registered capital of the joint venture.

These three entries in the Horizontal Commitments qualify the operation of GATS Article XVI:2(e). Taking into account these horizontal commitments in China's Schedule, Article XVI:2(e) obliges China in any sector in which China has undertaken market access commitments, not to maintain measures which restrict or require specific types of legal entity or joint venture through which a service supplier may supply a service except the following

- any specific restrictions that are set out in the relevant sectoral commitments
- any measure requiring that a representative office of a foreign enterprise shall not engage in any profit-making activities (except for some specific sectors)
- any measure restricting the establishment of branches of foreign enterprises
- a measure requiring the proportion of foreign investment in an equity joint venture shall be no less than 25 per cent of the registered capital of the joint venture.

The scheduling of the minimum 25 per cent foreign equity in joint ventures ensures that there will be no inconsistency between GATS Article XVI:2(e) and Article 4 of the 1990 *Law on Chinese–Foreign Equity Joint Ventures.*[65]

While the horizontal commitments do contain the requirement for minimum foreign equity in joint ventures, none of the horizontal commitments provide for maximum participation of foreign capital in joint ventures. Therefore, nothing in the horizontal commitments derogates from the obligation under GATS Article XVI:2(f) which prohibits Members from maintaining limitations on the participation of foreign capital in terms of maximum percentage or value, except to the extent scheduled. Therefore, in any sub-sector in which China gives a market access commitment on commercial presence, except to the extent to which that specific sectoral commitment is accompanied by qualifications relating to maximum participation of foreign capital, China would be in violation of Article XVI:2(f) if, in any particular instance, it maintained any measure which imposed a maximum limit on foreign capital in Chinese–foreign equity or contractual joint ventures. Since in effect any Chinese government requirement that a foreign service provider must operate through a joint venture rather than through a wholly-owned subsidiary or branch constitutes the imposition of a maximum limit on foreign equity participation, then in any sub-sector in which China makes a commercial presence commitment, China will be in violation of Article XVI:2(f) if it requires foreign service providers to operate through a joint venture unless the particular sectoral commitment refers to the joint venture requirement. As the subsequent analysis of specific commitments on commercial presence will show, such joint venture requirements have been listed in almost all of the commercial presence commitments in the vertical commitments part of China's Schedule.

China's specific commitments on commercial presence

The list of sectors in which commitments have been made hides the degree of variability and complexity in the different commitments. There is a broad range of types of commitments. Some commitments include no restrictions at all. Others include no restrictions at all but only after a phase-in period involving restrictions. The vast majority only commit China to permitting a foreign commercial presence in the form of a joint venture, or have some other specification as to the permitted legal entity. Some of these commit only to permitting an unspecified minority interest, others specify 49 per cent or 50 per cent interests, others majority interests or even 100 per cent wholly-owned subsidiaries. Some commitments permit wholly foreign businesses in the form of either branches or wholly-owned subsidiaries. Some limit the geographical area of the business and others limit the type of business or the type of customers. For most of the areas that were heavily negotiated, like distribution, telecommunications and financial services, the commitments will come into force in incremental steps over a phase-in period.

Rather than describing the commitments sector by sector, the following analysis gives an overview of the extent of the liberalisation undertaken, by describing the commitments in categories relating to the degree of liberalisation which will be achieved. Therefore, some examples of the various commitments China has made are sketched briefly below and set out in detail in Appendix 6.1. Commitments are divided into categories according to which China has agreed

- to impose no restrictions at all on commercial presence
- after a time limit, to impose no restrictions on commercial presence
- to permit wholly foreign-owned enterprises but only in the form of a wholly-owned subsidiary
- to permit wholly foreign-owned enterprises without limitation as to branch or subsidiary
- to permit wholly foreign-owned enterprises in the form of representative offices which can carry on profit-making activities
- to permit majority ownership of a joint venture
- to permit 50 per cent foreign ownership of a joint venture
- to permit specific levels of minority foreign ownership in a joint venture
- to permit commercial presence but subject to other types of limitations.

Many of the commitments are subject to elaborate phase-in commitments. Hereafter, only the end point of the liberalisation is discussed, though the phase-in arrangements are set out in Appendix 6.1. The time periods run from 10 December 2001.

In some areas, China commits to impose no restrictions at all on supply of service through a commercial presence. Such sectors include the installation of software, data processing and financial advisory services.

In other sectors China commits to move to a situation in which no restrictions would be imposed on supply through commercial presence, but only following a phase-in period. So, for example, there will be no restrictions in relation to

- distribution by commission agents or wholesale trade services (except for salt and tobacco) after five years
- retail distribution (except of tobacco) after five years
- franchising after three years.

In those sectors, in most cases, the commitments during the phase-in period consist of complicated incremental liberalisations. For example, in both retail and wholesale distribution, the initial commitments require joint ventures the number of which could be limited, and exclude dealing in certain products such as books, newspapers, magazines, pharmaceutical products, pesticides, mulching film, chemical fertilisers, processed oil and crude oil. China has agreed to remove the restrictions gradually.

In some sectors, China's proposed commitments would involve permitting commercial presence through a wholly-owned foreign enterprise in the form of a subsidiary (not a branch). Such commitments will apply in the sectors of

- architectural services and engineering services after five years
- taxation services and management consulting services after five years
- advertising services after four years
- maintenance and repair services after three years
- rental and leasing services after three years
- packaging services after three years
- technical testing and analysis after four years
- land-based international courier services after four years
- the hotel and restaurant sector after four years
- travel agencies and tour operators relating to foreigners and Chinese in China but not relating to Chinese travelling outside China after five years
- freight transport by road after three years and by rail after six years
- storage and warehousing services after three years.

Again, in a number of those sectors, the commitments are gradually introduced over a phase-in period.

Commercial presence by wholly foreign enterprises without limits as to the form of a branch or a subsidiary will be permitted according to different transitional periods ending after four years in relation to non-life insurance. Legal services will be permitted to operate in the form of a wholly foreign-owned enterprise through a representative office which will be able to conduct certain types of profit-making activities: practising in international and home country law, and providing 'information on the impact of the Chinese legal environment'.

The majority of China's commercial presence commitments specify some kind of joint venture requirement. Majority foreign ownership of the joint venture is to be permitted in

- services incidental to agriculture, forestry or fishing
- computer software implementation
- data processing
- real estate services
- scientific consulting
- photographic services
- convention services
- translation and interpreting
- construction and related engineering

- some education services
- some environmental services
- maritime cargo handling
- customs clearance
- container station and depot services.

Fifty per cent foreign ownership in joint ventures will be permitted in

- the field of life insurance after three years (in contract to non-life insurance in respect of which wholly foreign branches or subsidiaries are permitted)
- paging and various valued-added telecommunications businesses after two years.

Some others commitments require a joint venture arrangement but restrict foreign equity to a minority holding

- 49 per cent in mobile telecommunications joint ventures after three years
- 49 per cent in basic telecommunications including domestic and international transmission of voice and data after six years
- aircraft repair and maintenance services (subject to an economic needs test)
- 49 per cent in international maritime transport joint ventures.

In earlier versions of the Schedule, China had provided in respect of many sectors for supply through a joint venture without specifying the permissible extent of foreign equity. This was unsatisfactory. China would have been able to limit foreign equity to any chosen percentage or amount in these sectors without violating Article XVI:2(f). In the final schedule, each of these entries specify that majority foreign equity is permitted.

Finally, financial services are subject to a careful set of commitments. After a complicated phase-in that expires in December 2006, a foreign bank with more than US$20 billion in total assets may establish a branch and a foreign bank with more than US$10 billion in total assets may establish a subsidiary or a joint venture. Such institutions will be able to operate without geographical restriction, may do business in foreign currency and in local currency (subject to having operated for three years in China and being profit-making for two consecutive years).

The outcome: contestable markets in 2006 and beyond?

It is of course difficult to predict the actual economic liberalisation that will result from China's commitments under the GATS. It is clear from the analysis of China's Schedule that there are many sub-sectors in which the GATS will not remove some of the important barriers. In many sub-sectors, foreign suppliers will still face barriers precluding simple cross-border supply. In many more sub-sectors, foreign suppliers will still not be able to establish a commercial presence without having to become involved with a joint venture partner. The extent to which implementation of the GATS commitments in sub-sectors actually results in lower consumer prices will depend on whether such joint venture arrangements are actually implemented on a large enough scale.

Whether the theoretical legal opportunities to compete using a joint venture actually result in competitive markets will depend to some extent upon the way that the government sets and administers domestic regulations. Foreign suppliers will still have to find a Chinese partner who has approval to operate in the particular sector, and whether that constitutes a barrier will depend on how restrictive are the threshhold tests for Chinese people to engage in business in particular sectors. If only a few Chinese entities have permission to operate in a given sector then a commitment to permit Chinese–foreign joint ventures will not result in a large increase in competition in that sector. Of course, there will still be the need to have the joint venture approved but this part of the government decision-making process will be subject to the GATS rules on administration of domestic regulation which should ensure some minimum standards. Whether the theoretical legal opportunities actually result in enhanced competition will also depend on whether foreign suppliers want to enter the market on the terms given. In those sectors, where foreign suppliers are limited to position in a joint venture which they cannot control and ultimately cannot sell, then the incentive to enter the market is obviously less than it would be if the more liberal terms of entry applied.

Even in areas in which there are no joint venture requirements, the transformation of the legal opportunity to compete into real competition will still depend to some extent on whether domestic regulation obstructs the entry of foreign suppliers into the market. The GATS rules on licensing and administration should help but in the event of difficulties, the WTO dispute settlement process would not be able to provide quick solutions to such problems.

Two key areas will be banking and telecommunications. In the banking sector, foreign suppliers will be keen to implement technologies and practices used in other markets to try to win market share in a market accustomed to local branches and the use of cash. How successful they are will depend on how China regulates the use of such technologies and practices. If the regulation is restrictive, then it may take a long time before the presence of foreign suppliers has a significant impact on the efficiency of the market. In telecommunications, it is clear that restrictive conditions on the issue of licences could restrict competition. The abuse of market power and control over essential infrastructure might also hinder competition. Whether that is a problem will depend on the implementation and enforcement of appropriate competition laws in China.

Despite the possible problems, the implementation of the GATS commitments will still result in some extraordinary changes.

- The opening of distribution, road and rail transport, wholesaling and retailing to wholly foreign-owned companies seems certain to reduce prices not only for these services but in goods markets as well.
- The opening of life insurance to 50 per cent foreign-owned joint ventures together with the opening of the funds management industry to Chinese–foreign joint ventures will accelerate the ongoing transformation in the saving for and payment of retirement incomes.
- As the tourist industry adapts to having foreign participants who can supply local Chinese as well as foreigners, prices may fall causing an increase in the volume of foreigners and local Chinese wanting to travel in China.
- In the telecommunications sector, the minimum change is to a comfortable oligopoly of main carriers with competition among resellers resulting in modest price falls, but hopefully the increase in competition will be more dramatic than that.
- Similarly, in the banking sector, the minimum change is to a substantial increase in competition for business in the non-household sector but hopefully changes in business methods will facilitate a substantial increase across the whole sector.

The services negotiation has shown that some sectors of the Chinese service industries have a very significant capacity to lobby the government for the purposes of maintaining protection. Some of these have managed to limit the extent to which they will be exposed to foreign competitors. The most notable example is the telecommunications sector. Depending on the extent to which the GATS commitments actually achieve increases in competition, it is possible that the rent accruing to the existing producers in the more restricted markets will increase. In that event, we can expect some of the lobby groups that managed to avoid substantial liberalisation in the accession negotiation to lobby even more vigorously in the future to protect their position. In the such sectors as banking, telecommunications, maritime and international transport, and stockbroking, the Chinese government may find that further unilateral liberalisation is extremely difficult. It may only be through the pressure of further GATS negotiations that the Chinese government will be able to achieve further liberalisation.

It is quite staggering how far China has come since 1978 when it did not even have a legal framework for regulating businesses, let alone foreign businesses. The proposed commitments reflect the gradual development of that legal framework and reflect the Chinese socialist approach to regulating the economy. The restrictions in many areas and the use of incremental liberalisations are in some ways a continuation of the same techniques of experimental liberalisation which have been used since 1978 and which have previously been politically feasible—the technique of crossing the river by stepping on the stones. To some extent the government displays the same reluctance to give up of control over planning the economy. However, it is clear that the liberalisations to be implemented on WTO accession will mark a new phase that goes beyond previous economic reforms.

It is clear that the Chinese government has been pressured to increase the degree of liberalisation embodied in the offer. Importantly, one of the reasons for this is that the rest of the world has not stood still while China has been negotiating its accession. The post Uruguay Round GATS negotiations, particularly those culminating in the Fourth Protocol on Telecoms and the Fifth Protocol on Financial Services increased the entry price for China. This process is also indicative of what China will face in the future as WTO Members continue to negotiate liberalisations under the GATS.

China's commitments fall prey to some of the limitations that occur in a lot of countries including the tendency to avoid giving a cross-border commitment and the tendency to press foreign suppliers into joint venture arrangements. However, the general observation can still be made that China has given a level of commitments which vastly exceeds the commitments made by most developing countries.

There is the possibility that in some areas the commitments may not result in a significantly more competitive environment. However, there will still be many sectors where foreign participation will substantially increase competition. The time lags before the commitments result in actual increases in competition may vary from sector to sector and from region to region. As mentioned, it is desirable that further liberalisation occurs, particularly in the sectors that have escaped substantial liberalisation in the accession negotiation. With China in the WTO, it will be possible for the Chinese government to harness the pressures from services suppliers in other WTO Members to help it achieve that further liberalisation.

It is worth reflecting on the magnitude of the changes that accession to the GATS will bring to China. It is a magnitude of change that exceeds what any WTO Member was required to implement on their original implementation of the GATS. As the agreement is implemented it will pay all WTO Members to remember just how much China has changed in only twenty years and how much more the GATS will require it to change. If they lose sight of that and are too pugnacious in enforcing compliance then their efforts may backfire if the political climate in China swings away from economic liberalisation. On the other hand, if China's trading partners are firm but understanding of China's past and the great task ahead of China, then the Chinese government will be able to use the outside pressure to help continue the liberalisation process.

Appendix 6.1

China's specific commitments on commercial presence

This summary is based upon the authors' interpretation of the wording of Schedule CLII—The People's Republic of China, Part II—Schedule of Specific Commitments on Services, List of Article II MFN Exemptions to the *Protocol on the Accession of The People's Republic of China*, 10 November 2001, Doha, in force 10 December 2001 (Schedule CLII is published as an Addendum to the Report of the Working Party on the Accession of China, WT/ACC/CHN/49/Add.2, 1 October 2001) (hereinafter 'Schedule CLII').

The dates specified below are based on running the time period specified in the Schedule from 10 December 2001.

Sub-sectors with no scheduled restrictions on commercial presence. Consultancy on installation of software (though for commercial presence for implementation services, a joint venture is required).

Some data processing and tabulation services (though joint venture required for input processing).

Financial advisory services and giving financial information.

Accounting services—the Schedule does not provide for any limitation on the entity or maximum foreign equity but it provides that accountants must be licensed as Certified Public Accountants by Chinese authorities. An additional commitment provides 'Existing contractual joint venture accounting firms are not limited only to CPAs licensed by Chinese authorities'. This is a derogation from MFN but they have not included this in the Annex on Article 2 Exemptions. Another additional commitment provides, 'Foreign accounting firms are permitted to affiliate with Chinese firms and enter into contractual agreements with their affiliated firms in other WTO Members'.

Sub-sectors with no restrictions on commercial presence after a phase-in. Distribution—commission agents or wholesale trade services. No restrictions after 10 December 2006 (except for dealing in salt or tobacco). There is a complicated phase-in.

- Upon accession foreign invested are permitted to distribute their products manufactured in China.
- From 10 December 2002, foreigners will be able to establish joint ventures (with no assured level of foreign equity) to engage in business

as commercial agents or wholesalers but not for distribution of certain products: salt, tobacco, books, newspapers, magazines, pharmaceutical products, pesticides and mulching film, chemical fertilisers, processed oil and crude oil. At this stage there may be quantitative limits on the number of such joint ventures that can be approved and possible limitations on their geographic operation.

- From 10 December 2003, foreigners will be able to establish joint ventures wholesaling and agency businesses with majority foreign ownership, and China agrees to remove any limitations on geographic area of operations and also to remove any quantitative restriction on the number of joint ventures that may be approved. The same limitations as to products will continue.

- From 10 December 2004, China agrees to permit branches or wholly foreign-owned subsidiaries to operate in these businesses and to remove the restrictions on dealing in particular products except those on salt, tobacco, chemical fertilizers, processed oil and crude oil.

- From 10 December 2006, China agrees to remove the restrictions on dealing in fertilisers, processed oil and crude oil.

Some retail distribution (not including chain stores with more than 30 stores which sell certain listed products)—no restrictions after 10 December 2006 (except for selling tobacco). The wording is almost incomprehensible and there is a complicated phase-in.

- From accession, foreign invested enterprises will be able to distribute their own products manufactured in China. China agrees to permit foreigners to establish joint ventures (with no assured level of foreign ownership) to operate retailing businesses in the five special economic zones (Shenzhen, Zhuhai, Shantou, Xiamen and Hainain), in the six cities (Beijing, Shanghai, Tianjin, Guangzhou, Dalian and Qingdau) and in Zhenghou and Wuhan. China will retain the right to restrict the geographic area of operation of the businesses and to limit the number of such licences in most of those designated cities (no more that four in Beijing and Shanghai and no more than two in the other cities) and the right to prohibit such foreign invested joint ventures from engaging in retailing of certain products, including tobacco, books, newspapers, magazines, pharmaceutical products, pesticides, mulching films, processed oil or fertilizer.

- From 10 December 2002, China agrees to remove any prohibition on foreign invested joint ventures' retailing of books, newspapers and magazines.

- From 10 December 2003, China agrees to permit foreigners to have majority equity in joint ventures operating retail businesses (except non-branded chain stores with more than 30 outlets) and to permit additional joint ventures to be established in all provincial capitals and in Chongqing and Ningbo.

- From 10 December 2004, China agrees to permit foreigners to have wholly-owned subsidiaries in this sector (except in respect of certain chain stores), to remove any quantitative restrictions on the number of foreign invested enterprises that may be licensed to operate, to remove any limitations on the geographic area in which they may operate, and to remove any prohibition on retailing of particular products (for all except certain chain stores) except those on tobacco and fertilisers.
- From 10 December 2006, the restriction on chemical fertilisers will be removed.

For franchising, no restrictions after 10 December 2004.

Sub-sectors in which commercial presence will be permitted through a wholly foreign subsidiary. Commitments on some of these sub-sectors say 'None after [a date]' but then specify 'after which wholly owned subsidiaries will be permitted'. The insertion of the word 'None' on its own would have indicated no restrictions on the form of legal entity but the addition of the words giving permission for wholly owned subsidiaries may be taken to mean that branches will not be permitted. (For example, taxation services).

Architectural services and engineering services—wholly foreign-owned subsidiaries permitted after 10 December 2006; foreign majority ownership permitted from accession.

Taxation services, management consulting services—wholly-owned foreign subsidiaries permitted after 10 December 2006; foreign majority ownership permitted from accession.

Advertising services—wholly-owned foreign subsidiaries permitted after 10 December 2005; foreign majority ownership permitted after 1 January 2003; before that 49 per cent.

Maintenance and repair services—wholly-owned subsidiaries permitted after 10 December 2004, with majority ownership allowed after 10 December 2002.

Rental and leasing services—wholly-owned subsidiaries permitted after 1 December 2004, majority ownership allowed after 10 December 2002 (though this is complicated by a requirement that service suppliers will have global assets of US$5 million).

Technical testing and analysis services (excluding statutory freight inspection services)—permit wholly foreign-owned subsidiaries from 10 December 2005, with majority foreign ownership in a joint venture between 10 December 2003 and 10 December 2005, and less than majority interests in a joint venture between accession and 10 December 2003(There is a precondition that the joint venture company must have at least US$350,000 in registered capital, and that the foreign shareholder in the joint venture has been engaged in the business in their home country for more than 3 years).

Packaging—permit wholly foreign owned subsidiary after 10 December 2004 (from 10 December 2002, majority ownership, before that joint ventures).

Certain listed types of Construction and Related Engineering Services—wholly-owned subsidiaries permitted from 10 December 2004 (relates to four listed types of construction projects).

Courier (other than services reserved to Chinese postal service)—wholly-owned subsidiaries permitted after 10 December 2005, majority interest in joint venture after 10 December 2002, before that up to 49 per cent interest.

Certain listed types of Construction and Related Engineering Services—wholly-owned subsidiaries permitted from 10 December 2004 (relates to four listed types of construction projects).

Hotel and restaurant—wholly-owned subsidiaries permitted after 10 December 2005 but only after a phase-in period between accession and 10 December 2005 during which joint ventures with majority foreign ownership are permitted.

Certain Travel agency and tour operator services relating to foreigners and Chinese in China but not relating to Chinese travelling outside China (This schedule entry contains a few ambiguities but seems to allow the following): wholly foreign owned subsidiaries will be permitted from 10 December 2007 with no limit on the establishment of branches in China (There are conditions: the foreign investor must be mainly engaged in travel business and have annual world wide turnover exceeding US$40 million; and the foreign invested company must meet registered capital requirements applying to Chinese operators). The phase-in is complicated

- from accession, Joint Venture permitted in designated holiday resorts and in 4 named cities, with minimum registered capital of RMB 4 million
- from 10 December 2004, majority foreign ownership of a joint venture with minimum registered capital of RMB 2.5 million
- from 10 December 2007, permit wholly foreign owned subsidiaries, remove geographic restrictions removed and remove any limitations on the establishment of branches of the foreign invested operator.

Freight transport by rail will permit wholly-owned subsidiaries after 10 December 2007. The phase in is: from accession, joint ventures with 49 per cent ownership; from 10 December 2004, joint ventures with majority ownership, then from 10 December 2007, wholly-owned subsidiaries.

Freight transport by road will permit wholly-owned subsidiaries after 10 December 2004. The phase in is: from accession, joint ventures with 49 per cent; from 10 December 2002, joint ventures with majority ownership, then from 10 December 2004, wholly-owned subsidiaries.

Storage and warehousing will permit wholly-owned subsidiaries after 10 December 2004. The phase in is: from accession, joint ventures with 49 per cent foreign ownership, from 10 December 2002, joint ventures with majority ownership, and from 10 December 2004, wholly-owned subsidiaries.

Sub-sectors permitting commercial presence through wholly foreign-owned enterprises without limitation as to the form of a branch or a subsidiary. Non-Life insurance (which does not include health and pension insurance, reinsurance or brokerage)—after 10 December 2004, foreign non-life insurers may have a wholly-owned subsidiary or a branch providing the full range of non-life insurance services with no restriction on geographic location. The foreign investor must be a foreign insurance company with more than 30 years of establishment in a WTO Member, have had a representative office in China for 2 consecutive years and have total assets of more than US$5 billion. The phase in is complicated.

- From accession, may have a branch or a joint venture with 51 per cent foreign ownership, but only in Shanghai, Guangzhou, Dalian, Shenzen and Foshan; and limited to insurance of enterprises abroad or certain limited insurance services to foreign invested companies being property insurance, related liability insurance and credit insurance.
- From 10 December 2003, may have a branch, a joint venture or a wholly-owned subsidiary but only in the above-mentioned five cities and ten other cities. The business may provide the full range of non-life insurance services.
- From 10 December 2004, removal of limits on geographic location.

Sub-sectors in which supply through commercial presence is permitted through wholly foreign-owned enterprise in the form of a representative office only but with permission to carry on certain types of profit-making activities.

Legal services—From 10 December 2002, foreign law firms can establish representative offices which can engage in profit making legal services with limited business scope including home country and international law (There are also derogations from national treatment: a six month residency requirement and a bar on employing 'Chinese national registered lawyers outside of China'). Between accession and 10 December 2002, firms are limited to one office in one of nineteen listed cities.

Sub-sectors in which supply through commercial presence is permitted only through a joint venture but with majority foreign equity permitted. Services incidental to agriculture, forestry fishing: from accession, foreign majority ownership permitted.

Computer software implementation services: from accession, foreign majority ownership permitted.

Data processing and input preparation services: from accession, foreign majority ownership permitted.

Real estate services on a fee or contract basis: from accession, foreign majority ownership permitted.

Scientific consulting: from accession, foreign majority ownership permitted.

Photographic services: from accession, foreign majority ownership permitted.

Convention services.

Translation and interpretation (interpreting) services.

Construction and related engineering services (outside the scope of work which can be undertaken by wholly owned subsidiaries)—from accession, foreign majority ownership permitted.

Education: from accession, joint schools may be established in primary education, secondary education, higher education services, adult education services and other education services with foreign majority ownership permitted.

Environmental services (including sewage, solid waste disposal, exhaust gases, noise abatement, nature protection, sanitation, and other environmental services) only in form of joint ventures.

Maritime cargo handling services.

Customs clearance services for maritime transport.

Container station and depot services.

Sub-sectors in which supply through a commercial presence is permitted only through a joint venture with up to 50 per cent foreign equity. Various value-added communications services (including electronic mail, voice mail, on-line information an database retrieval, electronic data interchange and online information and data processing) and for paging services: from 10 December 2003, 50 per cent equity in joint ventures with no geographic restrictions. The phase-in is

- between accession and 10 December 2002, 30 per cent equity in joint venture which can operate in Beijing, Shanghai and Guangzhou
- between 10 December 2002 and 1 December 2003, permit 49 per cent equity in joint ventures which can operate in 17 Chinese cities
- from 10 December 2003, 50 per cent equity in joint ventures with no geographic restrictions.

For life insurance—from 10 December 2004, 50 per cent ownership in a licensed joint venture; preconditions for licenses are 30 years of establishment, have had a representative office in China for two consecutive years and have total assets of more than US$5 billion; permitted business includes individual life insurance and health insurance to foreigners and Chinese citizens, and group pension/annuities insurance to foreigners and Chinese; no geographic

restrictions. The phase-in is
- upon accession, 50 per cent joint ventures with licence subject to above conditions; limited to Shanghai, Guangzhou, Dalian, Shenzhen and Foshan; limited to individual (not group insurance) to foreigners and Chinese; (cannot provide group life insurance; cannot provide health insurance)
- from 10 December 2003, 50 per cent joint ventures, same limitations on scope of business, but expanded to an additional ten cities
- from 10 December 2004, 50 per cent joint ventures, removal of geographic restrictions;. Removal of restriction on providing health insurance and on providing group pension annuities insurance to foreigners and Chinese.

Sub-sectors in which supply through commercial presence is permitted only through a joint venture with minority foreign equity. Basic telecommunications—domestic and international transmission of voice, packet switched data, circuit switched data and fax: joint ventures with 49 per cent equity permitted from 10 December 2007. The phase-in is
- between 1 January 2004 and 1 January 2006, joint ventures with 25 per cent foreign equity, which may operate in and between three cities, with no limit on the number of joint ventures
- from 10 December 2006, joint ventures with 35 per cent equity operating in and between 17 cities
- from 10 December 2007, joint ventures with 49 per cent equity without geographic restrictions.

Basic telecommunications—mobile (voice and data) services: joint ventures with 49 per cent foreign equity will be permitted from 10 December 2006. The phase-in is
- between accession and 10 December 2002, joint ventures with 25 per cent foreign equity, which may operate in and between three cities, with no limit on the number of joint ventures
- from 10 December 2002, joint ventures with 35 per cent equity operating in and between 17 cities
- from 10 December 2004, joint ventures with 49 per cent equity
- from 10 December 2006, removal of geographic restrictions.

Construction and renovation of cinema theatre services limited to 49 per cent foreign equity. There is no commitment about the actual operation of the cinema.

Aircraft repair and maintenance—permits joint ventures but only with 'Chinese side shall hold controlling shares or be in a dominant position in the joint ventures' and says that granting of licences is subject to an economic needs test.

International maritime transport for freight or passengers—can have a joint venture only for operating ships under Chinese flag. Maximum foreign equity of 49 per cent (also chairman of board and general manager appointed by Chinese side of joint venture).

Maritime agency services—joint venture with up to 49 per cent foreign equity share.

Sub-sectors with various other restrictions. Joint venture hospitals with quantitative limitations in line with China's needs, with foreign majority ownership. National Treatment derogation specifies that the majority of doctors and medical personnel must be Chinese nationals.

Off-shore oilfield and geological services—required to be in the form of petroleum exploitation in cooperation with Chinese partners.

Onshore oil-field services—required to be in the form of petroleum exploitation in cooperation with China National Petroleum Corporation. The legal entity, its domicile and its bank accounts must be approved; the information acquired is the property of CNPC.

Video distribution (excluding motion pictures)—from accession, by contractual joint venture.

Banking services after 10 December 2006.

A foreign bank with more than US$20 billion in total assets may establish a branch.

A foreign bank with more than US$10 billion in total assets may establish a subsidiary or a joint venture.

No geographic restrictions.

Foreign banks may do business in foreign currency without restriction as to clients.

Foreign banks may obtain a license to do business in local currency, without restrictions as to clients, subject to having had three years business operation in China and being profit-making for two consecutive years.

The phase-in is complicated.

- Upon accession: Foreign financial institutions (same criteria for establishment) may do business in foreign currency without geographic restrictions and without restriction as to clients; foreign financial institutions may obtain licences to engage in local currency business if they have had 3 years business operation in China and been profitable for 2 consecutive years; those foreign financial institutions granted licences to do local currency business may be restricted to 4 named cities and to foreign customers.
- From 10 December 2002: those foreign financial institutions licensed to do local currency business may be restricted to 9 named cities.
- From 10 December 2003: those foreign financial institutions licensed

to engage in local currency business may provide services to Chinese enterprises but may be restricted to 13 named cities.

- From 10 December 2004: foreign financial institutions licensed to engage in local currency business may be restricted to do business in 16 named cities.
- From 10 December 2005: foreign financial institutions licensed to do business in local currency may be restricted to 20 named cities;.
- From 10 December 2006: foreign financial institutions licensed to do business in local currency will be permitted to provide services without geographic restrictions and to all Chinese clients.

Freight Forwarding Agency Services—the schedule says that there will be no restrictions after 10 December 2005 but provides that the commercial presence will be permitted through a wholly-owned subsidiary which implies that branches will not be permitted. In addition, for the wholly-owned subsidiaries, it specifies that the minimum registered capital is US$1 million and that the operation term is 20 years. A complicated phase-in applied prior to 10 December 2005.

Acknowledgments

The bulk of this chapter was written while Brett Williams was employed as Principal Research Officer, China and the WTO Project, The Australian National University Law Faculty until June 2001. Research on this paper was carried out under a grant from the Australian Research Council in cooperation with the Australian Department of Foreign Affairs and Trade.

Notes

1 World Bank, China fact sheet at http://www.worldbank.org giving a population at the end of 1998 of 1.239 million.
2 *Foreign Trade Law of the People's Republic of China.* Adopted at the Seventh Meeting of the Standing Committee of the Eighth National People's Congress, 12 May 1994, promulgated by Order No. 22 of the President of the PRC ,12 May 1994 and effective as of 1 July 1994.
3 These examples are extracted from Wang (1995:519) as examples of liberalisations that had occurred by September 1994.
4 The list of sectors is set out in WTO document MTN.GNS/W/120, 10 July 1991. A complete list of the sectors and sub-sectors is set out in Croome (1999:199–205). It seems that air reservations has been added to the 160 sub-sectors used during the Uruguay Round. Of course, there may be further creation of categories and sub-categories of sectors in the future.
5 A commitment relating to the supply of a service through the establishment of a commercial presence carries with it a commitment to allow related transfers of capital into its territory.

See the interpretative note to GATS, Article XVI:1.

6 GATS, Article XVI:2. The exception is given by the following words, 'unless otherwise specified in its Schedule'.

7 The phrase in Article XVI:2 which says, 'In sectors where market-access commitments are undertaken' must be interpreted in conjunction with the definition of the word 'sector'. in Article XXVIII (e) which provides that sector of a service means,

(i) with reference to a specific commitment, one or more, or all, sub-sectors of that service, as specified in a Member's Schedule

(ii) otherwise, the whole of that service sector, including all of its sub-sectors.

8 These additional rules are also set out in Altinger and Enders (1996:310–11).

9 See WTO, *Legal Instruments Embodying the Results of the Uruguay Round of Multilateral Trade Negotiations*, done Marrakesh, 15 April 1994, Annex 1b (GATS), Volume 28, 'China: Schedule of Specific Commitments:23, 211–53 ('China's 1994 Draft GATS Schedule').

10 The Uruguay Round negotiations made a distinction between basic and valued-added telecommunications services.

11 *Second Protocol to the GATS*, Geneva, 28 July 1995, in force on 1 September 1996.

12 See WTO, 'The Results of the Financial Services Negotiations under the General Agreement on Trade in Services (GATS)' downloaded from http://www.wto.org/wto/services/finance_background.htm on 17 April 2000. The United States, in particular, was unsatisfied with the result and broadened its MFN exemption in the financial services sector, wishing to maintain an approach based on reciprocity until more widespread and deeper liberalisation could be achieved in this sector.

13 *Third Protocol to the GATS*, done Geneva, 21 July 1995, in force 30 January 1996.

14 See WTO document WT/ACC/CHN/4, 4 December 1996 'Working Party on the Accession of China—Communication from China', containing a revised version of China's Schedule of Specific Commitments on Trade in Services, 21 November 1996 (China's 1996 Draft GATS Schedule). The document refers to its annexure as the attached revised version of China's Schedule of Specific Commitments on Trade in Services, 21 November 1996, reflecting the results of services negotiations held between China and WTO Members since January 1995. However, the document submitted by China is Headed 'China: Schedule of Specific Commitments (Revised version, October 1996)'. Despite references to different dates, all references are to the same document, WT/ACC/CHN/4.

15 *Fourth Protocol to the GATS*, Geneva, 15 February 1997, in force 5 February 1998 (Basic Telecoms Agreement). For a general description of the Basic Telecoms Agreement, see WTO, 1998a. 'WTO telecom talks produce landmark agreement', *Focus Newsletter*, 16(February):1–2; and WTO, 1998b. 'WTO telecoms accord enters into force' *Focus Newsletter*, 27:6.

16 See WTO *Focus*, No 27, February 1998, p6.

17 China's revised services offer contained in WT/ACC/CHN/12 was circulated on 20 November 1997 (China's 1997 Draft GATS Schedule).

18 See 'USTR says new Chinese services offer falls short of expectations', *Inside US Trade*, 15(45):1.'US official says China WTO negotiations could suffer from delay' *Inside US Trade,* 15(48):4–5; 'Kristoff says US to make decision on China WTO, MFN by March' *Inside US Trade,* 15(49):1, 23; 'US, China far apart on services; goods offer to come next year' *Inside US Trade,* 15(50):1, 18–19.

19 'The Results of the Financial Services negotiations under the GATS', downloaded on 18 April 2000 from the WTO website, http://www.wto.org/wto/services/finance_background.htm.

20 The 70 Members include the EC which submitted one schedule for the entire EC of 15 countries. See 'The Results of the Financial Services negotiations under the GATS' downloaded on 18 April 2000 from http://www.wto.org/wto/services/finance_background.htm.

21 Fifth Protocol to the GATS done Geneve 14 November 1997, in force generally 1 March 1999 (for Australia on 3 May 1999).

22 See 'Lang says WTO financial deal sets high standard for China, Russia', *Inside US Trade,* 16(2):8.

23 See USTR Press Release 99(34), 8 April 1999 (including the 17 page annexure). See also Australia Deputy Prime Minister and Minister for Trade, Media Release, 11 April 1999, 'US–China Trade Breakthrough'.

24 Eg, see Bhala, Raj, 'Enter the Dragon: An Essay on China's WTO Accession Saga' (2000) 15(6) *American University International Law Review* 1469–1538 at 1502–1503.

25 See Australia, Deputy Prime Minister and Minister for Trade, Media Release, 31 May 1999 'Major Trade Breakthrough with China–Australia reaches In-Principle Agreement On China's WTO Membership'; 'Australia reaches WTO Deal with China' *Financial Times* 14 July 1999. With Japan, see 'China and Japan reach outline deal on WTO entry' *Financial Times* 8 July 1999 (reporting a Japanese official saying the deal was substantially weaker than the deal offered by Zhu to Clinton in April) and 'Zhu says April WTO Concessions to US Still Valid, China and Japan Reach Deal' *China Online* 14 July 1999 www.chinaonline.com (reporting a Japanese official saying that Premier Zhu Rongji had said he would not withdraw the offer made in April 1999).

26 See USA, White House, Press Release 'Summary of US–China Bilateral WTO Agreement' 17 November 1999.

27 Canada, Department of Foreign Affairs and International Trade, News Release, 26 November 1999, No.256, 'Canada and China sign historic bilateral WTO agreement'.

28 US–PRC Bilateral Agreement, 15 November 1999 (which was published on CD Rom by China Online in March 2000) (for summaries and commentary, see the website of the United States–China Business Council http://www.uschina.org/public/wto/#bilat).

29 The European Union News Release No23/00, 19 May 2000 'EU–China Agreement on WTO'.

30 USTR, Press Release 01(38), 14 June 2001, 'USTR Releases Details on US–China Consensus on China's WTO Accession'.

31 *Protocol on the Accession of The People's Republic of China*, 10 November 2001, Doha, (published in Ministerial Decision of 10 November 2001, 'Accession of the People's Republic of China', WT/L/432 dated 23 December 2001). (available at http://www.wto.org/english/thewto_e/acc_e/completeacc_e.htm).

32 Schedule CLII—The People's Republic of China, Part II—Schedule of Specific Commitments on Services, List of Article II MFN Exemptions (published as an Addendum to the Report of the Working Party on the Accession of China, WT/ACC/CHN/49/Add.2, 1 October 2001) (hereinafter 'Schedule CLII').

33 For example, see the criticisms recorded in *Inside US Trade*, 5 December 2000, 15(49):5–6.

34 *Law of the PRC on Chinese–Foreign Equity Joint Ventures* (adopted at the second session of

the 5th National People's Congress on 1 July 1979).

35 *Law on Chinese–Foreign Equity Joint Ventures*, Article 4.

36 *Interim Regulations of the State Council of the PRC concerning the Control of Resident Representative Offices of Foreign Enterprises*, promulgated 30 October 1980 by the State Council. See Article 2.

37 *Procedures of the State Administration for Industry and Commerce of the PRC for the Registration and Administration of Resident Representative Offices of Foreign Enterprises*, promulgated 5 March 1983 by the State Council.

38 *Law of the PRC on Foreign Capital Enterprises* (adopted at the 4th Session of the 6th NPC, promulgated by Order No. 39 of the President of the PRC and effective 12 April 1986).

39 *Law of the PRC on Chinese–Foreign Contractual Joint Ventures (*adopted at the 1st Session of the 7th NPC of the PRC on 13 April 1988 and effective on the date of promulgation*).*

40 *Law on Chinese–Foreign Contractual Joint Ventures*, Article 2.

41 Amendment to the *Constitution of the PRC* (adopted at the 1st session of the 7th NPC on 12 April 1988).

42 In Shanghai in December 1990 and in Shenzhen in April 1991. See Hasenstab (1999:138).

43 *Company Law of the People's Republic of China (*adopted at the 5th Meeting of the Standing Committee of the 8th NPC on 29 December 1993 and promulgated by Order No. 16 of the President of the PRC on 29 December 1993 and effective as of 1 July 1994).

44 See China: Schedule of Specific Commitments, 15 April 1994 in Uruguay Round of Multilateral Trade Negotiations:Legal Instruments, 28:23211ff. See the commitments on insurance and banking permitting branches in some circumstances.

45 Administrative Regulations of Foreign Financial Institutions of PRC, promulgated by the State Council on 7 January 1994, in force 1 April 1994. See Zhipan (1996:186–204).

46 *Detailed Rules of the Ministry of Foreign Trade and Economic Cooperation for the Implementation of the Provisional Regulations governing the Examination, Approval and Administration of Resident Representative Offices of Foreign Enterprises*, promulgated 13 February 1995 by the Ministry of Foreign Trade and Economic Cooperation.

47 Special Regulations of the State Council Concerning Floating and Listing of Shares Overseas by Companies Limited by Shares, promulgated 4 August 1994 for H shares. See Xi-Qing (1996).

48 Regulations of the State Council concerning Foreign Investment Shares Listed Domestically by Companies Limited by Shares, promulgated 4 January 1996 for B shares. See Xi-Qing (1996).

49 Generally, on the types of business entities permitted under PRC law. See Fu (1998).

50 See the 1980 Interim Regulations, the 1983 SAIC Procedures and the 1995 MOFTEC Rules relating to Representative Offices referred to above, and see *Company Law of the People's Republic of China*, 1993, Article 199 provides that 'a foreign company may, in accordance with this Law, establish a branch within the territory of the People's Republic of China to engage in production and business activities'.

51 *Company Law of the PRC*, Article 200 requires the submission of an application to the authorities in charge in China.

52 *Law of the People's Republic of China on Foreign-Capital Enterprises* (adopted at the Fourth Session of the Sixth National People's Congress, promulgated by Order No. 39 of the President of the PRC and effective as of 12 April 1986).

53 See Gao (1996:15–16 and fn25) citing the *Regulations of the State Council Concerning*

Foreign Investment Shares Listed Domestically by Companies Limited by Shares, promulgated 4 January 1996 for B shares.

54 See Gao (1996:15–16 and fn25) citing the *Special Regulations of the State Council Special Regulations of the State Council concerning Floating and Listing of Shares Overseas by Companies Limited by Shares*, promulgated 4 August 1994 for H shares.

55 *Law of the People's Republic of China on Chinese–Foreign Equity Joint Ventures*. Adopted at the Second Session of the 5th National People's Congress on 1 July 1979 and revised in accordance with the Decision of the Law of the People's Republic of China on Chinese–Foreign Equity Joint Ventures adopted at the 3rd Session of the 7th National People's Congress on 4 April 1990.

56 *Law of the PRC on Chinese–Foreign Equity Joint Ventures*, Article 12. See also Fu (1998:287) which refers to Article 100 and Chapter 9 and 10 of the *Implementation Regulation on the PRC Equity Joint Venture Law*.

57 *Law of the People's Republic of China on Chinese–Foreign Contractual Joint Ventures* (adopted at the 1st Session of the 7th National People's Congress and promulgated by Order No. 4 of the President of the People's Republic of China on 13 April 1988, and effective as of the date of promulgation).

58 In general these comparisons are made upon the basis of the data collected in Altinger and Enders (1996). Their data are based on the schedules of the first 106 WTO Members (95 schedules including one schedule for the EC).

59 Altinger and Enders (1996:318) shows that on average WTO Members were unbound as to 34 per cent of sub-sectors for cross-border supply, but only 13 per cent for consumption abroad, 4 per cent for commercial presence and 6 per cent for presence of natural persons.

60 Altinger and Enders (1996:318) shows developing country Members remaining unbound as to cross-border supply on 45 per cent of commitments compared with 25 per cent for developed country Members.

61 In fact the commitment on advertising service (see entry 1F(a)) is not expressed to be unbound for cross-border advertising but is limited to business conducted through advertising agents registered in China which means that it is unbound with respect to advertising services conducted directly to clients.

62 Other than scheme design which can be provided on a cross-border basis: Schedule CLII, para 1 A(d) & (e):8.

63 See Altinger and Enders (1996), describing their classification of activities based on the list of 160 entries shown on the list used in the Uruguay Round, 'Services Sectoral Classification List' GATT document MTN.GNS/W/120. Table 6 lists 34 WTO Members' schedules which do not contain any horizontal restrictions on market access for commercial presence and lists 23 WTO Members' schedules which contain a horizontal limitation which require authorisations. The developed countries with horizontal limitations setting out authorisation requirements are Australia, Canada, Finland, France, Italy, Liechtenstein, New Zealand, Portugal and Spain.

64 See Altinger and Enders (1996:table 6) listing 18 Members with horizontal commitments specifying a particular legal entity and 9 with horizontal commitments requiring joint ventures.

65 See above: Article 4 requires a minimum of 25 per cent equity.

7

Income distribution in China

A macroeconometric approach

Jordan Shan

Rapid economic growth in China since the 1980s has attracted worldwide attention, but there also has been increased awareness in the 1990s about China's possible regional income inequality, before and after the reform era. There is growing literature on this issue, and the bulk of the literature is concerned with an empirical question: is there regional income inequality in China since the 1980s and what are the sources of this dispersion?

This chapter adds to this empirical literature by applying a VAR model which uses VAR techniques such as innovation accounting and Granger causality to examine the causal linkage, where appropriate, between macro factors and income disparity in China. Other various interrelationships among economic variables of interest in a VAR system are also investigated. In particular, this study uses GDP data recently released by China's Statistical Bureau to investigate how macroeconomic activity and policy can impact on income inequality in China. There has been relatively little recent work on the impact of macroeconomic activity on the level of inequality in China. Previously, Raiser (1998), Chen and Fleisher (1996), Sun and Chai (1998) and Sun (1998) mentioned the roles played by foreign direct investment (FDI) and exports in income disparity but their focus was not on the relationship between macroeconomic activity and income equality in China. Other scholars, while examining the sources of income dispersion, have concentrated on micro factors of income inequality and their studies are generally descriptive rather than using more rigorous econometric techniques.

By using a VAR model this study examines the possible causal linkages between the macro factors and income dispersion in China in a dynamic context. It will also consider feedback between income inequality and several other macro variables. The rest of the chapter then presents a brief review of the literature, followed by an analysis of China's possible income dispersion using some standard statistical measures, such as coefficient variation and Gini coefficients. The econometric model used in this chapter is presented, including empirical results.

A review

This section provides a brief review of the literature on China's income inequality and includes an analysis of income disparity for the period 1955–98 using conventional statistical indicators.

Economists' views on the various impacts of disparity on growth are inconclusive.[1] While it is not our intention in this chapter to judge whether there is a negative or positive relationship between economic growth and income disparity, it is important to note that this issue clearly has important policy implications, since income disparity exacerbates socio-political conflicts. Ultimately this will reduce growth (Benabou 1996 and Wu 1999). The Tiananmen incident in 1989 is an example of the importance and relevance of this disparity.

Therefore, we seek to address two questions: was there an income disparity in China before and after economic reform in the 1980s? If so, how do macroeconomic variables impact on this disparity?

This chapter concentrates on 1990s literature on Chinese income disparity. Table 7.1 presents some findings from previous studies. It is apparent that these economists were mainly concerned with whether or not there is income disparity or convergence in China. Their conclusions were mixed. While some economists presented evidence of reduced income disparity between the 1950s and 1990s others argued to the contrary (see for example, World Bank 1997; Wu 1999; Raiser 1998; Chen *et al.* 1996).

Some economists have looked into the causes of income inequality in China (for example, Hussain *et al.* 1994; Zhao and Li 1997; Khan and Riskin 1998; Tsui 1998). However, they all focused on micro variables such as non-farming and rental income, rural industrialisation levels, productivity and efficiency differences and urban-rural income gaps, and so on. The methodology used was index decomposition or other descriptive index numbers. No strong econometric method has been used in previous studies.

It is important to note that, as argued by Balke and Slottje (1994), macro variables could have an important impact on income disparity. Macroeconomic policy (such as fiscal spending, money supply and interest rates) and other macroeconomic variables (such as inflation, exports and inflation levels) will impact on income disparity. According to Balke and Slottje (1994), the role of government as a mechanism for redistribution and hence, the development of public policy, will inevitably influence the level of income inequality because of the impact of redistribution on regional economies. For instance, money supply and fiscal spending could have strong countercyclical effects. They may affect labour supply and GDP growth differently according to each region and hence have different effects on income disparity. This is particularly relevant in the Chinese case where the impact of money supply and fiscal policy on output and labour supply have been considerably different before and after the open-door policy. Similarly, macroeconomic variables such as exports and population and unemployment growth would also cause income disparity. In fact, Balke and Slottje (1994) and Blank and Blinder (1986) proposed that income inequality is a function of unemployment, inflation, fiscal spending and money supply. Other economists such as Blank (1989) also discussed the importance of including macroeconomic measures as sources of income disparity.

While these economists were primarily concerned with the cases of industrialised economies, their work sheds light on the debate regarding China. It is possible, for instance, that the Chinese fiscal system could have different redistributive effects on regional development and subsequently on income disparity in China. Without a doubt, fiscal spending is an important input in Chinese regional development, even after the de-centralisation of its fiscal system. Note that this chapter does not intend to investigate specific redistributive programs or the details of fiscal reform in China. We are interested in how overall fiscal spending influences the Chinese economy and how various macroeconomic factors interact to affect income dispersion, and vice versa. Macroeconomic variables such as FDI and exports could also contribute to income inequality in China. It is well know that FDI and exports have played an important role in Chinese economic development (Shan and Sun 1998; Sun and Chai 1998), but there are clear differences in FDI inflows and export performances in different Chinese provinces (see Sun 1998; Sun and Chai 1998). Thus, macroeconomic activities may have varying impacts on income disparity in China.

It is important to examine the relationship between income disparity, macroeconomic policy and macroeconomic activity in a dynamic way—that is, to look at how this relationship may have changed over time and how each macroeconomic activity influences income disparity in China. We also investigate fiscal spending dispersion and other dispersions such as money supply and inflation, and the relative contribution of these dispersions to income inequality in China between 1955–98.

Increasing income disparity in the 1990s

To measure income dispersion, we use the Gini coefficient, coefficient variation and Theil's Index.[2] Figure 7.1 plots these measurements between 1955–98. It shows clearly that there was an increase in income inequality in China in the late 1990s. All three measures show a similar pattern.

We also used 20 percentile and 80 percentile values, which measure the income levels for those income groups lower than 20 per cent and higher than 20 per cent within the population (Figure 7.2). Again there is evidence of income disparity in China after the reform policy, as the chart shows an increasing gap between mean income levels lower and higher than 20 per cent. This result supports the findings of Chen (1995) and Tsui (1998) but contrasts with the findings of Wu (1999) and Jian *et al.* (1996).

During the 1990s there was not only an increase in Chinese income dispersion but also major changes in macroeconomic performances and policies. During this decade, the opening of the Chinese financial system brought about a more market-orientated monetary policy. Similarly, China adopted a more expansionary fiscal policy combined with swifter decentralisation of its fiscal structure. The inflation rate fell in the late 1990s after high rates in the late 1980s and early 1990s. However, it had different lag effects in different regions. At the same time, the so-called reform of state-owned enterprises began in the late 1990s and has further increased the unemployment level in China. To what extent do these macroeconomic variables explain the increase in income disparity in China?

The model

We use a VAR model to examine the relationship between income disparity and macroeconomic activity in China. A VAR model is attractive because it need not impose any theoretical restrictions on the dynamic behaviour of the variables in the system and will let data speak with regard to the issue we wish to investigate. VAR analysis is common in the estimation and inference of macroeconomic relationships, despite its drawbacks in certain areas.[3] A VAR model is useful if there is no prior information and economic theories do not suggest a specific model. It is worth noting that a consensus is ineffective with a well-defined static theory of income distribution, let alone in terms of a dynamic theory.

According to Gujarati (1995:750) the centrepiece of VAR is innovation accounting. As mentioned earlier, innovation accounting includes both variance decomposition and impulse response function. Variance decomposition may be thought of in the following way. Suppose we wanted to use estimated VAR to forecast levels of income inequality in the future. The variance decomposition tells us how much of the forecast error variance in income inequality in each future forecast error period would be due to an innovation in the variable in question.

Furthermore, one has to keep in mind that there are possible feedbacks among several of the variables of interest. It is important to consider the

Table 7.1   Summary of selected studies on regional disparities in China

Authors	Sample	Methods	Main findings
Lyons 1991	1952–87 GVO consumption	CV	Disparity; (consumption);(output)
Knight and Song 1993	1987 counties	income functions	rural inequality among counties
Hussain, Lanjouw and Stern 1994	1986/household 5,000 (urban/rural each)	Gini ratio decomposition	low inequality/sources: urban non-wage and rural non-farming
Lee 1994	1984–90 NI	growth equation	disparity in export contribution
Chen 1995	1987–94 household data	Gini ratios	disparity
Hu, Wang and Kang 1995	1987–94 GDP	CV Descriptive analysis	disparity but large regional disparity by international standards
Wei and Wei 1995	1952–91 NI	Gini ratios/CV	Disparity 1987–91 but 1952–78
Chen and Warner 1996	1978–93	growth equation	regional convergence
Jian, Sachs and Fleisher 1996	1952–93 GDP	income dispersion	disparity & convergence
Chen and Ravallion 1996	1985–90 household data	rural poverty	less increase in poverty
Rozelle 1996	1983–92 household data	Gini ratio and sources	disparity and convergence. Source: rural industrialisation
Tsui 1996	post-reform	Gini/CV/GE sources	Disparity early 1980s and late 1980s
Lyons 1997	1990 Fujian	cross-tabulation	large disparity among countries
Zhao and Li 1997	1988 and 1995 household data	Gini ratio	disparity
Gundlach 1997	1979–89 output per worker	1979–89 output per worker	rate of convergence: 2.2%

124

Research Team 1997	1978–96	Gini ratio/descriptive analysis	disparity but low by international standards
Yang and Zhou 1999	Household survey and aggregate data 1978–97	production function	V-shaped process: disparity in 1978–85 but disparity after 1985. Source: labor productivity between urban and rural
Tong 1997	1978–91	data-envelopment analysis	Disparity source: industrial production efficiency across provinces deteriorated

Source: Wu, Y., 1999. *Income Disparity and Convergence in China's Regional Economies*, Paper from the Annual Meeting of the Association for Chinese Economic Studies (Australiasia), University of Melbourne, Australia:15–26, and author's additions.

Figure 7.1   Income disparity in China: index numbers

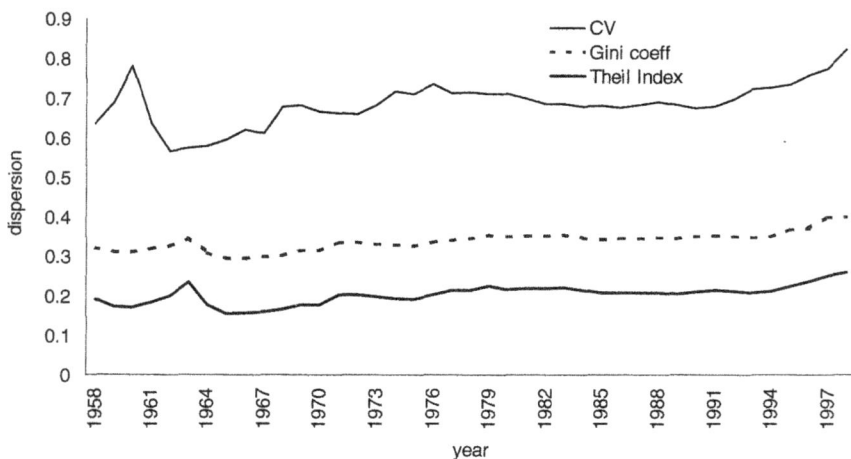

Figure 7.2   Income dispersion in China: mean and percentile values

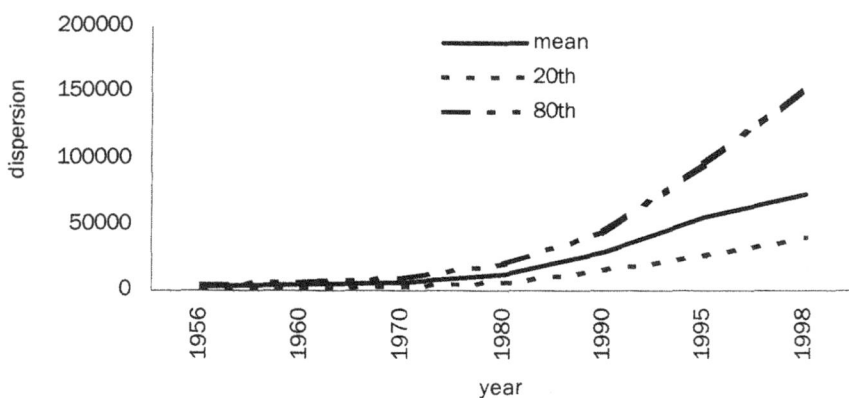

endogenous nature of a model like this one or it may be subject to a simultaneity bias. The use of a VAR model has been proven to generate more reliable estimates in an endogenous context (Gujarati 1995).

It must be acknowledged that the use of a VAR model is considered to be controversial within econometric literature. Concern is mainly focused on the choice of the lag length, the problem of being a-theoretic (it uses less prior information) and the difficulty of ensuring joint stationarity for all variables included in the VAR. If handled with care, however, 'they can be useful tools to examine the relationships among economic variables in a dynamic context' (Enders 1995:312).

We address these concerns by using AIC and SC to aid in choosing the lag length and, more importantly, to estimate the VAR with several lag structures to ensure that the results are robust.[4] As argued earlier, although the VAR may be considered a-theoretic, it is appropriate in a case in which no prior information or theories can be utilised. Furthermore, as Gujarati (1995:749–50) argues, a VAR model makes estimations simpler and the OLS estimation method can be used, provided all variables in the VAR are integrated in the same order.

The VAR used is

$$V_t = A_0 + \sum_{i=1}^{k} A_i V_{t-i} + \varepsilon_t \tag{7.1}$$

where $V_t = (CV_t, FP_t, MS_t, EXPORTS_t, FDI_t, CPI_t, UN_t)$

$\varepsilon_t = \left(\varepsilon_{gdp_t}, \varepsilon_{fp_t}, \varepsilon_{ms}, \varepsilon_{export}, \varepsilon_{fdi}, \varepsilon_{CPI_t}, \varepsilon_{un} \right)$

and A_1 to A_k are seven-by-seven matrices of coefficients; A_0 is an identity matrix; CV is the coefficient variation of per capita GDP of China; MS is money supply (M1); FP is fiscal spending; EX is exports; CPI is consumer price index (previous year = 100); FDI is total foreign direct investment and foreign loans actually utilised at the end of each year; UN is unemployment represented by the number of unemployed people in an urban area at the end of each year.[5]

The data

The VAR model is estimated using annual data in real terms (1985 prices) over the period 1955–98. In order to ensure stationarity of the data, all variables such as money supply (money), FDI, unemployment (UN), inflation level (CPI), exports (EX) and fiscal spending (FP) are in first differences of logarithms (growth rates).

Data is sourced from *The China Statistical Yearbook, Market Statistical Yearbook of China, Historical Data of GDP Statistics in China, Fifty Years of New China,* and *China Trade Union Statistics Yearbook,* as detailed in Appendix 7.1.

Empirical results

According to Enders (1995), the forecast error variance decomposition allows inference over the proportion of the movement in a time series, due to its own shocks versus shocks to other variables in the system. This breaks down the variance of the forecast error for each variable into components that can be attributed to each of the endogenous variables. On the other hand, impulse response function analysis traces the time path of various shocks on the variables contained in the VAR system. In other words, this approach determines how each endogenous variable responds over time to a shock in that variable and in every other endogenous variable. It traces the responses of the endogenous variables to such shocks. These two methods, which when combined are called innovation accounting, allow an intuitive insight into the dynamic relationships among the economic variables of interest in the VAR.

We can therefore use the variance decomposition method to break down the variance of the forecast error for the income dispersion, measured by coefficient variation (CV) into components that can be attributed to each of the endogenous variables. That is, money supply (money), FDI, unemployment (UN), inflation level (CPI), exports (EX), and fiscal spending (FP) in the VAR. If one variable (for instance, FDI) explains more in the variance of the forecast error for CV, then we would establish the hypothesis that FDI is the major source of income disparity in China.

At the same time, we can use the impulse response function to trace how the CV variable responds over time to a shock in another variable, and compared to its responses, to every other endogenous variable in the VAR. If the impulse response function shows a stronger and longer response of CV to a shock in FDI (for example), then we can establish that FDI is the most important source of income inequality in China.

The forecast error variance decomposition of unrestricted VAR (3) models consisting of the above variables were estimated using the Choleski decomposition method over a thirty-year forecast horizon (Table 7.2).[6]

As one would expect, innovations in income dispersion are explained by the preponderance of its own past values (26–30 per cent) over the different forecast horizons. It is followed by unemployment and fiscal spending (each around 25 per cent), exports and FDI (each around 10 per cent), and finally by inflation and money supply (each around 2 per cent).

In combining these results, we make further findings. Innovations in unemployment and fiscal spending together account for over 50 per cent of the forecast error variance at the various forecast horizons. The external factors (for instance exports and FDI) together account for around 20 per cent, while the monetary forces (for instance money supply and inflation level) together were below 5 per cent of the forecast error variance.

These results suggest that unemployment and fiscal spending are the most important forces in explaining the variations in China's income disparity between 1955–98. This indicates that fiscal policy plays an important role in the Chinese economy, while unemployment/population growth is a major constraint on income growth in China.

On the other hand, the monetary forces (that is, money supply and inflation level) play a less significant role in income inequality in China. This suggests that until the 1990s monetary policy was an unimportant and ineffective policy tool in promoting China's income growth. This is due perhaps to China's underdeveloped financial system, something that has gradually changed since the 1990s. The finding that fiscal spending and unemployment are more important than monetary factors is consistent with literature on income dispersion for industrialised economies (Balke and Slottje 1994; Blank 1989).

However, exports and FDI are not the most important elements influencing income disparity in China. This finding contradicts Sun and Chai (1998), and others who argue that FDI and exports can have different effects on regional development in China and hence, have different impacts on income distribution.

As a final note concerning variance decomposition results, one should pay attention to the values of the components of forecast errors over the entire forecast horizon. The results in Table 7.2 suggest that the proportion of each component (of forecast error variance) remain the same. As mentioned earlier, they are also robust to different lag structures.[7]

Empirical results based on dispersion variables

To investigate the source of income inequality further, we also used the dispersion variable for all variables discussed earlier. We used coefficient variation for money

Table 7.2   Variance decomposition for income dispersion (per cent)

| Horizon | CV | Forecast error attributed to | | | | | |
		FDI	Fiscal	Money	Inflation	Unemployment	Exports
1	41.4	7.8	21.4	0.9	1.4	21.5	5.6
2	30.0	7.0	23.6	1.8	1.4	27.5	8.7
3	27.4	7.8	24.6	1.7	1.3	27.2	10.0
4	26.4	8.5	24.8	1.9	1.5	26.3	10.5
5	26.2	9.1	24.5	2.0	2.0	25.9	10.3
6	26.1	9.1	24.4	2.0	2.1	25.8	10.5
7	26.0	9.1	24.4	2.0	2.1	25.8	10.7
8	26.0	9.1	24.3	2.0	2.1	25.8	10.6
9	26.0	9.2	24.3	2.0	2.1	25.8	10.6
10	25.9	9.2	24.3	2.0	2.1	25.7	10.7
15	26.3	9.1	23.9	2.1	2.5	25.3	10.8
20	25.0	8.7	22.9	2.0	4.4	24.6	12.4
30	22.0	8.5	22.1	1.9	6.2	24.3	14.9

supply, unemployment, inflation level, exports, FDI and fiscal spending. This means that each variable measured the dispersion of that variable over different provinces in China so that we could find the dispersion variable and the extent to which it influenced income dispersion (Table 7.3).[8]

These results confirm the findings reported in Table 7.2. That is, the dispersions in fiscal spending and unemployment explain most of the forecast error variance for overall income dispersion in China. Table 7.3 shows that dispersions in unemployment and fiscal spending together again account for over 50 per cent of the forecast error variance at the various forecast horizons, followed by the external variables (exports and FDI). Finally, the combined monetary forces (money supply and inflation level) were below 5 per cent of the forecast error variance.

This suggests that the macroeconomic reasons for China's income disparity over the 1955–98 period are dispersions in unemployment and fiscal spending among different provinces. Again this indicates that fiscal policy plays an important role in the Chinese economy, and that unemployment/population growth is a major constraint on income growth in China. On the other hand, the monetary forces (money supply and inflation level) play a less significant role in income inequality in China.

Impulse response function

We now proceed to impulse response function analysis. As suggested above, a graphic illustration of the impulse response function can provide an intuitive insight into the dynamic relationships that exist, because it presents the response of one variable to an unexpected shock in another over a certain time horizon (Figure 7.3).

Figure 7.3 illustrates the response of income dispersion (CV) to a shock in six other variables (money supply, FDI, inflation, fiscal spending, exports and unemployment). The response of income disparity (CV) to fiscal spending and unemployment has been most responsive (3–4 per cent changes for a 1 per cent shock in six other variables). This result confirms our earlier finding that both unemployment and fiscal finding are the two most influential factors in China's income dispersion.

Exports were found to be the third most important variable that explaining variations in income disparity in China (around 3 per cent change for a 1 per cent change in the six other variables). Figure 7.3 shows that FDI, money supply and inflation level have a much smaller effect on the income dispersion variable (CV) compared to unemployment and fiscal spending.

Finally, the response of CV to all other variables shows that CV reverts back to its original levels over about a seven-year time horizon.

Granger causality test

Another important aspect of VAR analysis is the Granger causality test. It states that X is said to Granger cause Y if past values of X can predict or precede the changes in Y. This study uses a Granger no-causality test developed by Toda and Yamamoto and extended and interpreted by Zapata and Rambaldi (1997).

We wish to find out if there is a Granger-type causal relationship between macroeconomic activities, macroeconomic policy and income inequality in China.

The results, reported in Table 7.4, indicate that there is Granger causality from unemployment and fiscal spending to income dispersion (both are significant at 95 per cent). However, the causal relationship between other variables and income disparity are weak (marginal at about 85 per cent). This finding is consistent with findings from the innovation accounting analysis.

Finally, the opposite causality (from income dispersion to macro variables) was not found or is only marginally significant. It suggests that innovations in income disparity do not have significant feedbacks on other macro variables in the VAR system. This was an interesting finding since there is also a debate as to whether or not income inequality hinders economic development. In passing, our findings do not support the view that income disparity will prevent further economic growth (Clarke 1995).

Table 7.3		Variance decomposition for income dispersion (per cent)					
			Forecast error attributed to				
Horizon	CV	FDI	Fiscal	Money	Inflation	Unemployment	Exports
1	40.3	8.9	21.9	0.7	1.7	22.0	5.1
2	28.9	8.1	24.1	1.6	1.7	28.0	8.2
3	26.2	8.9	25.1	1.5	1.6	27.7	9.5
4	25.3	9.6	25.3	1.7	1.8	26.8	10.0
5	25.1	10.2	25.0	1.8	2.3	26.4	9.8
6	25.0	10.2	24.9	1.8	2.4	26.3	10.0
7	24.9	10.1	24.9	1.4	2.4	26.4	10.2
8	24.9	10.2	24.8	1.8	2.3	26.3	10.1
9	24.9	10.3	24.8	1.7	2.5	26.1	10.2
10	24.8	10.3	24.8	1.8	2.4	26.2	10.2
15	25.2	10.2	24.4	1.9	2.8	25.8	10.3
20	23.9	9.8	23.4	1.8	4.7	25.1	11.9
30	20.9	9.6	22.6	1.7	6.5	24.8	14.4

Note: All variables are in coefficient variation form.

Conclusion

This study has investigated an issue that has drawn worldwide attention since the 1980s. How did macroeconomic activity and macroeconomic policy attribute to widening income disparity in China? This is an important question given that income inequality in China has increased in the 1990s, alongside vigorous economic growth. Unlike other scholars who have looked for micro factors, we have attempted to find an answer to this question by examining macro factors, such as inflation and unemployment, and macroeconomic policy such as fiscal spending and money supply.

Using a VAR approach, we have put China's income dispersion and other macro variables in a dynamic context to examine how they have interacted over a long time horizon. We found that unemployment and the dispersion of fiscal spending across different provinces played a prominent role in widening income inequality in China. On the other hand, monetary factors had a less significant role.

This finding provides strong empirical evidence for the view that macroeconomic forces have an important effect on income distribution, which is also consistent with findings based on industrialised economies (Balke and Slottje 1994). Both economists and policymakers should not lose sight of this fact.

A strong policy implication arising from this study is that a sound macroeconomic environment is crucial to income equality in China.

It is worth mentioning that the results reported here are not a substitute for, but a complement to, traditional microeconomic labour economics regarding income distribution. Future research might consider an approach that integrates

Figure 7.3   Responses of CV to other variables

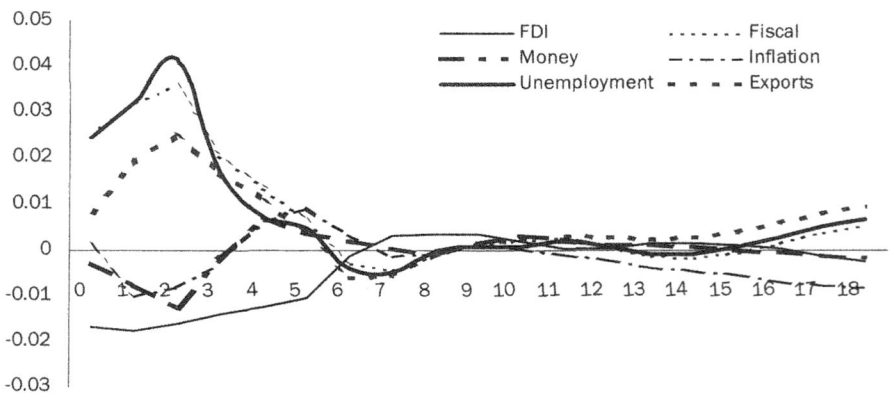

Table 7.4   **Income disparity and macro variables**

Causality pairs	p-values for both directions of the causality
CV, unemployment	0.085 *vs* 0.001
CV, fiscal spending	0.190 *vs* 0.006
CV, money	0.302 *vs* 0.199
CV, CPI	0.178 *vs* 0.098
CV, exports	0.201 *vs* 0.090
CV, FDI	0.101 *vs* 0.094

Note: The VAR order(s) for all causalities in this table are in optimal lag structures and was determined by AIC and SC. Variable definitions are explained in the text.

these two literatures and uses more rigorous econometric methodology and strong economic theory.

Appendix 7.1

The VAR model is estimated using annual data in real terms (1985 prices) over the period 1955–98. The data coverage for each series is cited from *China Statistical Yearbook 1998*, 'Explanatory Notes of Indicators', CD-Rom, Beijing. All data are in annual growth rates.

The data sources are as follows.

- GDP's CV: China Statistical Bureau, *China's GDP Data 1952–95*, Dongbei University of Economics and Finance Press, Dalian.
- The data for 1997 and 1998 are from China Statistical Bureau, 1999. *China Statistical Yearbook*, Beijing. The formula for CV is:
- Fiscal spending: China Statistical Bureau, 1998. *Market Statistical Yearbook of China*, Beijing:15. Data for 1998 was from China Statistical Bureau, 1999. *China Statistical Yearbook*, Beijing.
- Money supply: China Statistical Bureau, 1998. *Market Statistical Yearbook of China*, Beijing:22. Data for 1998 was from China Statistical Bureau, 1999. *China Statistical Yearbook*, Beijing.
- Inflation is CPI (previous year = 100). China Statistical Bureau, 1998. *Market Statistical Yearbook of China*, Beijing:273. Data for 1998 was from China Statistical Bureau, 1999. *China Statistical Yearbook*, Beijing.
- Exports: China Statistical Bureau, 1998. *Market Statistical Yearbook of China*, Beijing:328. Data for 1998 was from China Statistical Bureau, 1999. *China Statistical Yearbook*, Beijing.
- Unemployment: China Statistical Bureau, 1990. *China Statistical Yearbook*, Beijing:130; China Statistical Bureau, 1999. *China Trade Union Statistics Yearbook*, Beijing:60.

- FDI: includes all foreign capital (both FDI and foreign loans) which was the amount actually used.

The data for local provinces are from 18 provincial statistical yearbooks, including Tinjin, Beijing, Shanghai, Shandong, Hebei, Jilin, Jiangxi, Heilongjiang, Guizhou, Henan, Anhui, Guangdong, Shanxi, Liaoning, Jiangsu, Zhejiang, Hubei, Sichuan and NingXia. Due to the lack of data over the same range of variables, this sample provides a good approximation.

Notes

1 See Benabou (1996) for a comprehensive review.
2 The formulae for these indices are: coefficient variation = $\frac{1}{2}\Sigma(Y_i-Y)^2/n$ $/Y$.
   Theil Index = $\Sigma Y_i \log(Y_i/Y)/n\,Y$.
   Gini coefficient = $\Sigma\Sigma\frac{1}{2}(Y_i-Y_j)^2/2n^2/Y$.
   where Y_i is per capita income, Y is average per capita income and n is the sample size.
3 See Gujarati (1995) for a detailed discussion of advantages and disadvantages of using a VAR for macroeconomic analysis.
4 Our VAR estimation under different lag structures indicates no significantly different results and hence we present the results from VAR (3), which is an optimal lag length according to AIC and SC.
5 The data prior to 1982 was estimated by using the formula stated in *The China Statistical Yearbook*, 1999. The unemployment rate is 100 per cent urban unemployed persons/ non-rural population.
6 Optimal lag length was chosen according to AIC and SC.
7 Results for different lag structures are not reported but are available upon request from the author.
8 Due to the lack of data over the same range of variables, only 19 provinces were used in this study (Tinjin, Beijing, Shanghai, Shandong, Hebei, Jilin, Jiangxi, Heilongjiang, Guizhou, Henan, Anhui, Guangdong, Shanxi, Liaoning, Jiangsu, Zhejiang, Hubei, Sichuan and NingXia). But it is conceivable that this sample provides a good approximation.

8

Towards estimating agricultural production relations for China[1]

Peter Albersen, Günther Fischer, Michiel Keyzer and Laixiang Sun [2]

Fast economic growth has stimulated China's demand for food and feed grains. While the country has an impressive record in raising its agricultural production, it is not entirely clear to what degree China can, or should, maintain food self-sufficiency, and whether eventual imports should consist of meat or feed grains. The answer to these questions is not only important for China. It has strong implications for world markets at large. In its *World Food Prospects*, the International Food Policy Research Institute (IFPRI) (Pinstrup-Andersen *et al.* 1999) anticipates that net meat exports to East Asia will be 28-fold in 2020, primarily because the demand for meat in China is expected to double. The demand for maize as main feed grain will grow by 2.7 per cent per year.

Successful economic development, however, has itself created new room for choice and may render irrelevant any prediction that merely extrapolates past trends. Based on this recognition, the IIASA Land Use Change (LUC) Project has opted for an approach that seeks to identify alternative options for agricultural policy through a spatially explicit intertemporal model.[3] This model accounts for the main biophysical restrictions in various parts of the country, in conjunction with the main socio-economic factors that drive land-use and land-cover change (Fischer *et al.* 1996).

This chapter documents the specification of the input-output relationships for crop production and reports the estimation results. These relationships describe, for each of some 2040 counties in China in the year 1990, the crop output combinations that can, under the prevailing environmental conditions (such as climate, terrain, soils) be produced from given combinations of chemical and organic fertilisers, labour and traction power, and irrigated and rainfed land. The relationships are estimated separately for the eight economic regions distinguished in the LUC model.[4] In addition to these input-output relations for crop production, the LUC model also contains components for livestock production, consumer demand, land conversion and water development. These will be presented in separate reports.

Several examples exist in the literature of agricultural production functions which were estimated for China. The major interest was to generally assess the level of the total factor productivity and its change, to estimate the marginal productivity and output elasticities of the main production factors and to evaluate the specific contribution of rural reform to agricultural growth. On the basis of pooled data at the provincial level, Lin (1992) assesses the contributions of decollectivisation, price adjustments and other reforms to China's agricultural growth in the reform period. The study estimates that decollectivisation accounted for about half of the output growth during 1978–84. Wiemer (1994) uses micro-panel data from households and production teams in a rural township to analyse the pattern and change of rural resource allocation before and after the reform. Both studies applied a Cobb-Douglas form to specify an agricultural production function with four conventional inputs: land, labour, capital and chemical fertiliser (or intermediate inputs). Additional variables needed for the specific assessment purposes were incorporated into the exponential term of the Cobb-Douglas form.

Two recent studies by Carter and Zhang (1998) and Lindert (1999) incorporate climate and biophysical information as well as the conventional inputs. Carter and Zhang estimate a Cobb-Douglas model for grain productivity for the five major grain-producing regions in China with aridity indices using data between 1980–90. Lindert estimates the agricultural and grain productivity for both North and South China with a mixed translog and Cobb-Douglas specification using soil chemistry indices from soil profiles and input-output data at the county level. In both studies fertiliser input was limited to chemical fertiliser, although the manure aspect is implicitly incorporated by Lindert in an organic matter index.

Our aim to include the crop input-output relationships within the wider LUC welfare optimum model imposes various requirements.

First, an adequate representation of environmental conditions relevant to agricultural land use patterns should be reflected in the LUC model. To ensure this, the biophysical potentials as computed from an agro-ecological assessment were included in the crop production function in a form that fits meaningfully within the economy-wide model. The potentials enter through the vector of land resources and a maximal yield that serves as an asymptote to actual yields. The building bricks for the potential output calculation are potential yields at county level for different land types (irrigated and rainfed) and for major seasonal crops (such as winter and summer crops corresponding to relevant Asian monsoon seasons in China). These county-level potential yields were compiled in the LUC Project's land productivity assessment component, based on the experiences gained in site experiments employing detailed crop process models (Rosenzweig *et al.* 1998) and applying a China-specific implementation of the enhanced Agro-Ecological Zones (AEZ) methodology (Fischer *et al.* 2000). The AEZ assessment is a well-developed environmental approach. It provides an explicit geographic dimension for establishing spatial inventories and databases of land resources and crop production potential. The method is comprehensive in terms of the coverage of factors affecting agricultural production, such as components of climate, soil and terrain. It takes into account basic conditions in supply of water, energy, nutrients and physical support to plants. The AEZ method uses available information to the maximum. Moreover, it is also directly applicable to assessing changes in production potential in response to scenarios of climate change.

Second, the functions must satisfy global slope and curvature conditions (convexity for the output index and concavity for the input response function). These were imposed through respective restrictions on the relevant function parameters.

Third, the estimations must accommodate the limitations of the available information. For instance, no data was available on crop-specific inputs, such as fertiliser applied to wheat. This lack of information is not specific to China but is a fairly common situation in agricultural sector modelling, making it impossible to identify the parameters of separate crop-specific production functions. The usual approach is to represent the technology via a transformation function with multiple outputs jointly originating from a single production process with multiple inputs. Under the assumption of revenue maximisation this approach enables us to identify derived net output functions separately by commodity (Hasenkamp 1976; Hayami and Ruttan 1985). These functions use output and input prices and resource levels (land, labour, capital) as dependent variables. However, in the case of China two special difficulties impede the applicability of this approach. First, despite the decollectivisation in the 1980s, farm decision making has not yet become a fully family affair, and various rules and regulations are still in effect which do not find an expression in farm-gate prices and are not formally recorded. The data used in our study refers to the year 1990 when even more decisions were made at village government level than is the case now. Second, the only available output price data are (weighted average) state procurement prices for major crops at provincial and national levels and there are no published input price data available. To overcome these obstacles, the transformation function had to be estimated directly in its primal form. Yet, to investigate the degree to which the prevailing allocations could be interpreted as resulting from a profit maximisation model, we compute and compare the implicit prices that would support observed allocations under profit maximisation.

Transformation of the agricultural sector during 1979–99

In 1979, China initiated a dramatic reform of the institutional structure in its agricultural sector. From collective-based agriculture, changes were made towards a system in which the individual farm household became the basic decision-making unit with respect to inputs and most outputs. As a rule, the new family farms are small and fragmented and depend heavily on irrigation, which induces Chinese farmers to save land and capital and to opt for highly labour-intensive practices. What follows is a review of the main elements of this transformation process.

Institutional arrangement of China's family farms in the post-reform era

During the period 1979–83 collective farming was replaced by the household responsibility system (HRS). Under the HRS, individual households in a village are granted the right to use the farmland for 15–30 years, whereas the village community, via its government, retains other rights associated with the ownership of the land. This land tenure system constitutes a two-tier system with use rights vested in individual households and the ownership rights in the village community (Dong 1996; Kung 1995).

Unlike in the previous collective system, under the new land tenure system farm households are independent production and accounting units. Each household can independently organise its production and exercise control over outputs and production. Most importantly, control rights over residual benefits are assigned to individual households. A fraction of the crop is still sold to the state via state procurement requirements at prices below the free market level, and another fraction is delivered to the village government as payment for rent or taxes and as a contribution to the village welfare fund and accumulation fund. The remainder is left to the households for consumption, saving and possibly to sell in the free market. The right to use land also entails an obligation to contribute labour for the maintenance and construction of public infrastructure. The function of the village governments in the HRS includes the management of land contracts, the maintenance of irrigation systems and the provision of agricultural services such as large farm machinery, product processing, marketing and technological advice and assistance (Lin 1997; Wen 1993; World Bank 1985).

When the HRS was introduced, collectively owned land was initially contracted to each household in short leases of one to three years. In the distribution of land, the guiding principle was generally egalitarianism. Most villages have leased land to their member households strictly on the basis of family size rather than intra-household labour availability. Moreover, at the initial distribution, land was first classified into different grades. Thus, a typical farm household would contract 0.56 hectare of land fragmented into 9.7 tracts (Dong 1996; Lin 1997). Eventually the one to three-year contract was found to discourage investment in land improvement and soil fertility conservation. Further reforms were initiated and the duration of the contract was extended to 15–30 years. As a result, various models of the land tenure system have evolved in different regions as an adaptation to local needs and conditions.[5]

Pricing and marketing of agricultural products

During the establishment of the HRS, increasing emphasis was given to market mechanisms for guiding production decisions in the agricultural sector, although central planning was still deemed essential. The number of planned product categories and mandatory targets was reduced from 21 and 31 in 1978 to 16 and 20, respectively, in 1981, and reduced further to 13 in 1982. Moreover, restrictions on the interregional trade of agricultural products by private traders were gradually loosened. Cropping patterns that fit local conditions and exploited comparative advantages were encouraged. As a consequence, both cropping patterns and intensity changed substantially between 1978 and 1984. The sown acreage of cash crops increased from 9.6 per cent of the total in 1978 to 13.4 per cent in 1984, and the multiple-cropping index declined from 151 to 147 (Lin 1997:Table 3).

The second round of market reforms was initiated in 1985. The central government announced that the state would no longer set any mandatory production plans in agriculture and that the obligatory procurement quotas were to be replaced by purchasing contracts between the state and farmers (Central Committee of CCP 1985). Although the progress of this market reform has been slower and less smooth than expected, the market freedom enjoyed by Chinese farmers has significantly increased. In the early 1990s about two-thirds of China's marketable cereal production was purchased or sold in the form of free retails or wholesales at prices determined by market forces. The gap between market prices and quota prices has gradually narrowed although the pace has been slow and uneven. The production and marketing of vegetables, fruits and most cash crops have been fully liberalised since 1985.

Dependence on irrigation

About half of China's farmland has been under some form of irrigation since the 1980s.[6] The irrigated land produces about 70 per cent of grain output, most of cotton, cash crops and vegetables. Thus, heavy dependence on irrigation is another unique feature of China's agriculture. This contrasts sharply with the situation in other major agricultural world regions. For instance, in the United States only one-tenth of the grain output comes from irrigated land (Brown and Halweil 1998). While the major share of irrigation water has been delivered to the fields by gravity irrigation with the help of dams, reservoirs, canals and irrigation systems, an increasing proportion of irrigation water in China is being supplied by diesel and electric pumps. Machine-powered irrigation accounted for one-quarter of the total irrigated area in 1965, increasing to two-thirds in 1993 (SSB 1993: 349; Ministry of Water Conservation 1994). As a consequence, irrigation equipment has been accounting for a large fraction of the total power consumed by agricultural machinery since the 1980s.

Labour-intensive production

It is generally accepted that land is an extremely scarce factor in China's agriculture, capital is limited and labour is relatively abundant (Lindert 1999; Wang, 1998; Dazhong 1993). Although the percentage of the labour force engaged in agriculture has gradually fallen from 93.5 per cent in 1952 to 56.4 per cent in 1993, the total number of agricultural workers doubled during the same period due to rapid population growth (the population increased from 173 million in 1952 to 374 million in 1993). This was despite the impact of rapid expansion in the rural industrial sector which has created employment for more than 120 million rural workers since 1992. The growth in the absolute number of farm workers in the cropping sector persisted until 1984, and this trend persisted in 1993 for the agricultural sector as a whole (Lin 1992:Table 4; SSB 1997:94, 400). In 1990, the average family farm managed only 0.42 hectares of farmland but had 1.73 labourers engaging in agriculture (Ministry of Agriculture 1991).

Constrained by the unfavourable land–labour ratio, Chinese peasants have only been able to adopt labour-intensive, land-saving and yield-increasing technologies. These include the intensive use of organic and chemical fertilisers, irrigation development, the use of plastic film to cover fields, the rapid adoption of new crop varieties like hybrid rice, sophisticated cropping systems and high levels of multiple cropping. Most of the land-saving technologies increase the need for the application of nutrients and other farm inputs.

Organic fertiliser has always been central to traditional, small-scale Chinese farming. Farmers commonly use a wide variety of organic fertilisers, including night soil (that is, human excrements), animal manure, oil cakes, decomposed grasses and household wastes, river and lake sludge and various green manures. Night soil and animal manure have been the most important sources due to their high nutrient content and low cost.[7]

Chemical fertilisers have increasingly been used to improve crop yields owing to the rapid growth of domestic fertiliser production capacity and of fertiliser imports. Chemical fertiliser use in China has quadrupled since 1978. Since the early 1990s, China has emerged as the largest consumer, the second largest producer and as a major importer of chemical fertilisers in the world (FAO; SSB 1989–97). However, the average application of chemical fertiliser has remained modest, at 155 kilograms of nutrients per hectare in 1995, which is below the average level of East Asian developing countries and far below that in Japan and South Korea.[8] According to estimates of the World Bank (1997:16), fertiliser applied in 1995, with an estimated value of 125 billion yuan, was the major cash input in crop production. The rapidly increasing application of chemical fertiliser has been identified by many as a key factor contributing to the significant productivity growth in China's agricultural sector over the past three decades. Many studies suggest that the overall yield response to chemical fertiliser has been significant (Kueh 1984; McMillan *et al.* 1989; Halbrendt and Gempesaw 1990; Lin 1992), partly through mutual reinforcement between the increasing application of chemical fertiliser and the adoption of new crop varieties which are responsive to chemical fertilisers.

Two recent quantitative estimations suggest that chemical fertiliser application increased much faster than the use of organic fertiliser since the early 1970s and had become the dominant nutrient source by 1988 (Agricultural Academy of China 1995:Chapter 8) or 1982 (Wang *et al.* 1996). However, because of the low quality and inefficient methods of application of chemical fertiliser, about half the nitrogen applied to irrigated land is lost to evaporation (World Bank 1997:18), leaching and emissions and this leaves much room for efficiency gains.

Also of note is that organic fertiliser is more than merely a substitute for chemical macro-nutrients. With its high content of organic matter and a wide range of crop macro and micro-nutrients, organic fertiliser improves soil structure and fertility in the long run. Thus, it is believed that organic fertiliser should complement chemical fertiliser and improve its effectiveness. Organic fertiliser is also able to be applied to rainfed land without preconditions, whereas the application of chemical fertiliser is constrained by the necessity of a timely water supply. Finally, the traditionally careful use of organic fertilisers made the transition to chemical fertilisers relatively smooth and easy in China in the 1960s and 1970s (Stone and Desai 1989).

Crop-mix index and input response function

We follow Keyzer (1998) in our specification of the agricultural production relationships. We postulate a transformation function that is separable in outputs

141

and inputs, with a crop-mix index for outputs and a response function for inputs. The crop-mix index is in CES form and the input response is specified as a generalised version of the common Mitscherlich-Baule (MB) yield function, whose maximal attainable output is obtained from an agro-ecological zone assessment. The input response distinguishes two types of land: irrigated and rainfed. Their yield potentials and cropping practices differ significantly. However, as is usual in agricultural sector modelling, the data on inputs is not differentiated by type of land use or by crop, and since data on crop output is not land-use type specific, we cannot estimate a transformation function for each land-type or crop separately. Instead we must be satisfied with the estimation of a single transformation function applied for all crops and land-use types.

Let the subscript l denote observations (that is more than 2,000 counties in our case), Y a $l \times C$ vector of outputs, V a $l \times K$ vector of non-land inputs, and A a $l \times S$ vector of land uses with S different land quality types. The vector of natural conditions, including climate, soil and terrain characteristics, is denoted by x. We postulate a transformation function T(Y, -V, -A, x) that is taken to be quasi-convex, continuously differentiable, non-decreasing in (Y, -V, -A) and linear homogeneous in (V, A). The function T describes all possible input-output combinations. To ease estimation, separability is assumed between inputs and outputs

$$T(Y, -V, -A, x) = Q(Y) - G(V, A; x) \qquad (8.1)$$

where Q(Y) is the crop-mix index, and G(V, A; x) the input response function. Function Q(Y) is taken to be linear homogeneous, convex, non-decreasing and continuously differentiable, and G(V, A; x) is linear homogeneous, concave and non-decreasing in (V, A) and continuously differentiable. This implies that the transformation function T is convex and non-increasing in net outputs. The interpretation of this transformation function is as follows: under natural conditions x, the given input and land availabilities (V, A) make it possible to produce a quantity G of the aggregate production index Q, with any crop mix such that Q(Y) = G.

The input and output variables are measured in quantity terms and were compiled per county. As discussed earlier, the transformation function is estimated in primal form rather than in the dual form with separate crop-specific supply functions, for two reasons. First, profit maximisation may not be the relevant behavioural criterion for Chinese agriculture, and price data cannot capture the variability at county level since they are only available at provincial level and measured as a mix of procurement prices and free market prices. The estimation is cross-section over counties, in volumes per unit area (represented by the corresponding lower case characters).

That is $\quad q(y) = g(v, a; x) + \varepsilon \qquad (8.2)$

where ε denotes the error term, assumed to be independently and normally distributed.

Crop-mix output index

The crop-mix output index $Q(Y)$ is specified as a convex function with constant elasticity-of-substitution (CES)

$$Q(Y_\ell) = (\sum_c (\alpha_c Y_{\ell c})^{\alpha_0})^{1/\alpha_0}$$

(8.3)

where $\alpha_c \geq 0$ and $\alpha_0 > 1$. The curvature of the output function, or the (direct) elasticity of transformation between any two outputs, equals $1/(1 - \alpha_0)$. The restriction $\alpha_0 > 1$ guarantees the CES function to be convex.

The specification also needs to be flexible in order to account for differences in cropping patterns across counties (in case, say, in a county only ten of the sixteen crops are being grown. This could be incorporated in various ways. One way would be to drop the crops from the crop-mix index, while scaling up the coefficients for the remaining crops in Equation 8.3 through an additional parameter. In doing this however, we face the problem that in China the number of crop-mixes often outnumbers the observations and two to four crops often cover about two-thirds of the total production value. To deal with this problem we introduce a distinction between major and minor absent crops, and associate a limited number of scaling factors to the production function of a particular county, depending on the number and importance of the absent crops. Consequently, Equation 8.3 becomes

$$Q(Y_\ell) = (1 + \sum_m \mu_m M_{\ell m})(\sum_{c \in C_\ell} (\alpha_c Y_{\ell c})^{\alpha_0})^{1/\alpha_0}$$

(8.4)

where μ_m is an estimated scaling factor, $M_{\ell m}$ is a zero-one dummy that associates the county to a particular scaling factor and C_ℓ is the set for which $Y_{\ell c} > 0$. Each county has at most one non-zero crop-mix dummy.

Input response function

The input response function combines the information obtained from biophysical assessments with the statistical data available at county level. It is specified as

$$Q_\ell = f(V_\ell, H(A_\ell)) N(A_\ell, \bar{y}_\ell(x_\ell))$$

(8.5)

where $f(.)N(.)$ is a generalised Mitscherlich-Baule specification following Keyzer (1998), and $H(.)$ and $N(.)$ are the aggregate area and potential output index, respectively, which are specified as

$$H_\ell(A_\ell; \delta) = \sum_s \delta_s A_{\ell s}$$

(8.6)

$$N_\ell(A_\ell, \bar{y}_\ell(x_\ell); \delta) = H_\ell(A_\ell; \delta)\bar{y}_\ell(x_\ell)$$

(8.7)

with $\bar{y}_\ell(x_\ell)$ denoting the maximal attainable yield for given agro-ecological conditions x_ℓ. This potential yield $\bar{y}_\ell(x_\ell)$ is calculated as the maximal attainable production $\bar{Y}_\ell(x_\ell)$ divided by land index H_ℓ. Parameter δ_s is preset and was not estimated. The input response function f(.) in Equation 8.5 is specified in product form, to allow for different input groups. The functional form is

$$f(V_\ell, H(A_\ell)) = \prod_j f_j(V_\ell, H_\ell; \beta_j, \gamma, \rho_j)^{\theta_j}$$

(8.8)

with

$$f_j = 1 - \exp[-\beta_j - w_j(V_\ell, H(A_\ell; \delta); \gamma, \rho_j)]$$

(8.9)

where f_j is the jth component of a Mitscherlich-Baule (MB) yield function and its exponent $\theta_j > 0$ is such that $\sum_j \theta_j = 1$. This parameter θ_j avoids the increasing returns that would result from the standard MB-form with $\theta_j = 1$. In addition, a nested structure is assumed for inputs so as to ease the nonlinear estimation. In Equations 8.8 and 8.9, index j stands for two categories of inputs, power and nutrients. Power consists of labour and agricultural machinery. Nutrients include chemical and organic fertilisers. For both categories we assume a CES form, denoted by w_j.

$$w_j(V_\ell, H(A_\ell; \delta); \gamma, \rho_j) = \left(\sum_{k \in j} \gamma_k \left(\frac{V_{\ell k}}{H_\ell} \right)^{\rho_j} \right)^{1/\rho_j}$$

(8.10)

with $\gamma_k \geq 0$ and $\rho_j \leq 1$ ensuring concavity of w(.). Input response function (Equation 8.5) is linear homogeneous, globally concave and non-decreasing in (V,A) and continuously differentiable.

The biophysical diversity across China is reflected in the potential yield $\bar{y}_\ell(x_\ell)$ as will be explained later. However, cropping possibilities vary widely across China and also within the estimated regions, ranging from single cropping to triple rice cropping. The maximal attainable yield $\bar{y}_\ell(x_\ell)$ alone is not sufficient to capture this variability. To account for these differences, cropping system zone variables $Z_{\ell z}$ are introduced, where the subscript z indicates the cropping system zone. If for irrigated conditions a county is located in cropping system zone z, the value of the related variable is one or zero if this is not the case. Equation 8.5 then becomes

$$Q_\ell = Z_z f(V_\ell, H(A_\ell)) N(A_\ell, \bar{y}_\ell(x_\ell))$$

(8.11)

with

$$Z_z = \sum_z \zeta_z Z_{\ell z}$$

(8.12)

The outputs in Equation 8.4 and the potential production in Equation 8.5 are measured in different units. $Y_{\ell c}$ is given in metric tonnes of produce, while the potential is given as cereal equivalent in metric tonnes of economic dry matter. Harmonisation of the dimensions is restored via the crop and county specific parameter ratio $\alpha_c(1+\mu_m M_{\ell m})/\zeta_z Z_{\ell z}$.

Computing implicit prices for aggregation

The transformation function enters the land use change (LUC) model for China after an aggregation procedure from county to region. Our approach is to assume implicit profit maximisation at implicit prices. These are the prices that would support the observed crop and input allocations under profit maximisation. We interpret the gap between these prices and average market prices in the cities as processing margins, which we use in the aggregation procedure from county to region. Clearly, this procedure needs further empirical justification and we will show that the resulting margins have a meaningful interpretation. Despite the institutional peculiarities in China we can view the decisions concerning allocation as being based on profit maximisation at prices governed by institutionally determined wedges.

Assuming profit maximisation subject to the separable transformation function (Equation 8.1) ensures separability between output and input decisions. The farmer determines the crop-mix so as to maximise the revenue corresponding to a given value of the index Q, while choosing the level of inputs V and corresponding aggregate output Q so as to maximise his revenue, at given prices of V and Q.

Thus, the crop-mix problem of the revenue maximizing farmer with given output index $\overline{Q}_\ell$ is stated as

$$\max_{Y_{\ell c} \geq 0} \sum_{c \in C_\ell} p_{\ell c} Y_{\ell c}$$

$$s.t \qquad Q(Y_\ell) = \overline{Q}_\ell \tag{8.13}$$

with $p_{\ell c}$ as the price of crop c in county ℓ. The Lagrangean of this problem is

$$L = \sum_{c \in C_\ell} p_{\ell c} Y_{\ell c} - \overline{P}_\ell(Q(Y_\ell) - \overline{Q}_\ell) \tag{8.14}$$

where the Lagrangean multiplier is the county level price index $\overline{P}_\ell$ since the function $Q(Y_{\ell c})$ has constant returns to scale. The first order conditions of this problem determine the implicit (shadow) prices of crop $c \in C_1$

$$p_{\ell c} = \overline{P}_\ell \frac{\partial Q(Y_\ell)}{\partial Y_{\ell c}} = \frac{\overline{P}_\ell \overline{Q}_\ell}{Y_{\ell c}} \frac{(\alpha_c Y_{\ell c})^{\alpha_0}}{\sum_{c'} (\alpha_{c'} Y_{\ell c'})^{\alpha_0}} \tag{8.15}$$

For the base year the county level price index $\overline{P}_\ell$ has been calculated from provincial and national prices and county level production data (see Appendix 8.1). In simulation runs with endogenous crop prices $p_{\ell c}$ the index is calculated as

$$P_\ell = \frac{1}{(1 + \sum_m \mu_m M_{\ell m})} \left(\sum_{c \in C_\ell} \left(\frac{p_{\ell c}}{\alpha_c} \right)^\sigma \right)^{\frac{1}{\sigma}} \tag{8.16}$$

with $\sigma = \dfrac{\alpha_0}{\alpha_0 - 1}$.

The county specific relation between the base year price index and the obtained under the maximising producer assumption becomes

$$\overline{P}_\ell = P_\ell (1 + \varepsilon_\ell^p) = P_\ell (1 + \frac{\overline{P}_\ell - P_\ell}{P_\ell}) \tag{8.17}$$

In simulation runs the estimated price index can replace the 'observed' index.

Finally, for the input side the restricted profit maximisation problem becomes

$$\max_{V_{\ell k} \geq 0, A_{\ell s} \geq 0} \overline{P}_\ell G(V_\ell, A_\ell) - \sum_k p_{\ell k} V_{\ell k} - \sum_s p_{\ell s} A_{\ell s} \tag{8.18}$$

The first order condition with respect to input k of group j gives the marginal productivity

$$p_{\ell k} = \overline{P}_\ell \frac{\partial G(V_\ell, A_\ell)}{\partial V_{\ell k}} = \overline{P}_\ell \frac{\partial g(v_{\ell k})}{\partial v_{\ell k}} \tag{8.19}$$

with $v_{\ell k} = V_{\ell k} / H_\ell$ and

$$\frac{\partial g(v_{\ell k})}{\partial v_{\ell k}} = g_\ell \theta_j \frac{1 - f_{\ell j}}{f_{\ell j}} w_{\ell j}^{1 - \rho_j} \gamma_k v_{\ell k}^{\rho_j - 1} \tag{8.20}$$

For land-use type s the marginal productivity is

$$p_{\ell s} = \overline{P}_\ell \frac{\partial G(V_\ell, A_\ell)}{\partial A_{\ell s}} = \overline{P}_\ell \left(f_\ell \frac{\partial N(A_{\ell s})}{\partial A_{\ell s}} + N_\ell \frac{\partial f(V_\ell, A_{\ell s})}{\partial A_{\ell s}} \right)$$

$$= \overline{P}_\ell \delta_s g(v_\ell) \left(1 - \frac{\partial g(v_\ell)}{\partial v_\ell} \frac{v_\ell}{g(v_\ell)} \right) \tag{8.21}$$

where

$$\frac{\partial g(v_\ell)}{\partial v_\ell} \frac{v_\ell}{g(v_\ell)} = \sum_j \theta_j \frac{1 - f_{\ell j}}{f_{\ell j}} w_{\ell j} \tag{8.22}$$

and $f_{\ell j}$ and $w_{\ell j}$ are the same as defined by Equations 8.9 and 8.10.

Data—sources, adjustments and qualifications

Despite major improvements in the quality and availability of relevant statistics for China, various procedures had to be applied to scrutinise data, fill data gaps and define proxy variables.

Crop outputs and procurement prices

The total annual output of grain, cotton and oilseeds is available at county level (SSB and CDR 1996). The published data were matched with county administrative codes as used in the LUC Project's database of China. Also available are output data and sown areas of wheat, rice, maize, sorghum, millet, other starchy crops, potato and other root crops, soybean, oilseeds, cotton, sugar beet, sugarcane, fiber crops, tobacco, tea and fruit for 1989 but not for 1990. These data were compiled by the State Land Administration and provided to FAO. The year 1990 is representative of the average conditions of Chinese cropping agriculture during the period 1985–95. As the 1989 crop was fairly poor due to weather conditions, we use data for 1990 whenever possible. Consequently, we had to disaggregate the data for grains in 1990 on the basis of crop-pattern distribution available for 1989. According to Chinese statistics, the aggregate termed grains include wheat, rice, maize, sorghum, millet, other starchy crops, potato and other root crops and soybean (five kilograms of potato and other root crops are counted as one kilogram of grain; all other commodities have a conversion factor of unity). For sugarcane, fiber crops, tobacco, tea and fruits, the 1989 outputs had to be used.

Thus, crop outputs in 1990 were estimated as

$$q_c^{90} = G^{90} \cdot \frac{q_c^{89}}{G^{89}} \tag{8.23}$$

where G^t is total grain output in year t and q_c^t is crop-specific output measured in grain equivalent. In the case of vegetables, only estimates of sown areas at the county level for 1989 were available, and then there was no available output data for any year. The national average yield of 20.9 tonnes per hectare in 1989 was used to calculate vegetable output at county level (Xie and Keijing 1994:103).

Procurement prices at both provincial and national levels for wheat, rice, maize, sorghum, millet, soybean, oilseeds, cotton, sugarcane, fiber crops, tobacco, tea and fruit were extracted from *The Yearbook of Price Statistics of China 1992* (SSB 1992b:302–65). The procurement price for a crop is a quantity-share-weighted mean of quota prices, negotiated prices and free market prices. The procurement of commodities is not only done by government agencies, but also enterprises, social organisations and trade companies. There is no price data for Hainan province in this *Yearbook*. Prices in Guangdong were used as proxies for Hainan, in view of the fact that Hainan province had been a prefecture of Guangdong until 1988. No price data are available for the aggregate of other starchy crops. The price of maize is used as a proxy in each province following the information in the national price data for China listed in the FAO-AGROSTAT database. Again with reference to FAO-AGROSTAT, one-third of wheat price is used as a proxy for the price of potato and other root crops in each province.

Prices of vegetables were compiled from *Nationwide Data on Costs and Revenues of Agricultural Products 1991* (Eight Ministries and Bureaus 1991). The prices listed in this publication are the free market selling prices of major vegetables shown for selected major cities (typically the provincial capital city) in most of the provinces. Representative vegetables for each province were selected and the representative price for the vegetable category is the arithmetic mean of the various prices.

With the steps described in the previous paragraphs price data could be obtained for all of the major crops of each province. However, the price information for some minor crops was still missing and these are actually the main crops in some counties. To fill these gaps a corresponding price was used from one of the neighbouring provinces with similar production conditions. When no such province was available the national average price was used as a proxy.

In the compilation of the initial output index Q, the provincial prices were applied directly to the county level, ignoring all price differences across counties within each province.

Non-land and land inputs

Data on non-land inputs used in the broad agricultural sector at county level are available in the LUC Project for various years between 1985–94. They include agricultural labour force, total power of agricultural machinery, total number of large animals and the chemical fertiliser applied. We will only discuss the 1990 data since these were used in estimation. A data problem arises from the fact that in Chinese statistics, broad agriculture consists of farming, forestry, animal husbandry, fisheries and sideline production. We attribute non-land inputs to the crop sector based on the share of crop agriculture in broad agriculture. The total output value of broad agriculture is available at the county level. The availability of crop output enables us to calculate the total output value of cropping agriculture for each county by straight aggregation over crops valued at provincial prices. The resulting shares are applied to the agricultural labour force and the power of agricultural machinery.[9]

Two comments need to be made. First, the approach is questionable for counties where the share of cropping agriculture is minor or where agricultural workers or machinery are in fact used for non-agricultural activities. In some (sub) urban counties the number of agricultural workers per hectare of agricultural land is extremely high (more than ten). Machine power per hectare is likewise biased due to the fact that transport vehicles and other processing machineries are included in the statistics. Nonetheless these counties were initially included in the estimations. After the first round, some of the counties biased the estimation substantially and these observations were dropped. Secondly, prices are at the provincial level and consequently the variability at county level depends on quantities alone.

Whereas chemical fertiliser applied can safely be attributed to crop farming rather than to forests or pastures, organic fertiliser data can only be derived by imputation. We follow the approach in Wen (1993:Tables 4 and 5) and assume that

- one person produces 0.5 tonnes of night soil per year on average. In 1990, the utilisation rates of night soil in the rural and urban areas were 0.8 and 0.4, respectively. The nutrient content rate of night soil was 0.011, or 1.1 per cent
- a large animal produces 7.7 tonnes of manure per year on average. The utilisation rate is 0.8 and the nutrient content rate is 0.0102
- hog manure is assumed to be 2 tonnes per animal per year, with a utilisation rate of 0.8 and a nutrient content rate of 0.014.

No systematic data is available on other sources of organic fertiliser such as green fertiliser, oil cake, compost, and mud and pond manure. The resulting estimate of the national total at 17.5 million tonnes of organic fertiliser supply is six million tonnes lower than Wen's 1989 figure, but seven million tons higher than the corresponding 1991 figure given by the Agricultural Academy of China (1995:95). In some counties, where animal husbandry plays a key role, the manure of large animals may dominate in total organic fertiliser and animal manure is often used as fuel rather than as plant nutrient. Hence, to avoid unrealistically high estimates of organic fertiliser application in these counties, we impose a ceiling of 120 tonnes of raw organic fertiliser manageable per worker per year (Wiemer 1994), which is equivalent to about 1.2 tonnes of nutrient content.

For farmland, we use the county level data on total cultivated land areas and irrigated land compiled by China's State Land Administration (SLA). The national total of cultivated land areas obtained by summation over counties is some 135 million hectares, which is about 40 million hectares higher than the corresponding national figure published in the *Statistical Yearbook of China* (SSB 1991:314). However, this is still consistent with the figure recently compiled by the SLA based on a detailed land survey (see Fischer *et al.* 1998).[10] In addition to statistical data, the LUC Project database includes several digital coverages for China, including climate, land use, vegetation, altitude and soils. These were compiled, re-organised and edited jointly with the Chinese collaborators in the LUC Project to provide a basis for biophysical assessments of surface hydrology, vegetation distribution and for estimating potential yields of major crops.[11] Although these maps provide useful spatial information for land-use research, their scale is insufficient to derive accurate overlays of the actual farmland in 1990 with soil and terrain resources for differentiating land quality types among actual farmland. Hence, the land quality types (index s) applied at county level currently only distinguish irrigated and rainfed land.

In actual farming practice, the distinction between irrigated and rainfed land is not as strict as suggested by the statistical figures. In some areas, when rainfall is in time for cropping and is in adequate amounts, irrigation is unnecessary and the differentiation between irrigated and rainfed land becomes unimportant. Conversely, when the water shortage is severe, irrigation may be impossible despite existing irrigation facilities.

Potential yields

Biophysical reality enters the input-output relationships through a potential output index $N(A, \overline{y}(x)$ (Equation 8.7) and the cropping system zone index Z_l (Equation 8.12) and involves the estimation of potential production $\overline{Y}_{\ell,s}(x)$ by county and land-use type.

After conducting a detailed agro-ecological zones (AEZ) assessment across counties in China, the land suitability and potential yields were estimated for 27 major crops, differentiated into some 150 crop types. This evaluation was carried out both for irrigated and rainfed conditions using the methodology described in Fischer *et al.* (2000). To arrive at the potential yields to be used in the production function (Equation 8.5), a suitable aggregation had to be performed in three steps:
- classification of each 5x5 km grid-cell of the LUC land resources inventory for China into one of seven major multiple cropping zones
- classification of cereal crop types into eight crop groups according to crop cycle length and thermal crop requirements
- aggregation of results at 5x5 km grid-cells to county administrative units.

The calculations and aggregations were performed separately for both rainfed and irrigated conditions. As an example, the multiple cropping zones applicable under irrigation conditions are shown in Figure 8.1.

In zone one, thermal conditions allow for only one crop to be grown per year. The potential yields are determined by the highest simulated yield among all suitable cereal crop types under irrigated and rainfed conditions, respectively. In zone two, temperature profiles permit cultivation of two short-cycle crops or relay cropping systems. Examples include wheat and millet grown in sequence, or wheat or maize relay crops. Yields are calculated separately for crops adapted to cool and to moderately warm or warm conditions. Potential yields at county level are constructed from these pools according to the observed multi-cropping index (MCI). Zone three is a typical double-cropping zone with wheat or barley grown as a winter crop (including a dormancy period) and crops such as maize, soybean or sweet potato grown in the warm season. Potential annual yields are constructed from these two pools.

Zone four has double cropping similar to the previous zone, except that main summer crops such as rice or cotton demand more heat. Zone five is generally found south of the Yangtse, and permits limited triple cropping consisting of two rice crops and, for instance, green manure. The annual temperature profile is usually insufficient for growing three full crops. When the observed MCI does not exceed 2.0, the combination of the best suitable crops during the cooler and warmer seasons of the year defines the potential annual yield. The more the observed MCI exceeds 2.0, the less applicable are crop types with long growth cycles, because of the time limitations. When the MCI approaches 3.0, only crop types requiring 120 days or less are considered when calculating annual output. Zone six occurs in southern China and allows three sequential crops to be grown. A typical example is the cropping system with one crop of winter wheat and two rice crops grown in spring to autumn. In this case, only short-cycle crops can be considered.

Finally, zone seven delineates the most southern part of China where tropical conditions prevail and allows three crops to grow that are well adapted to warm conditions, such as rice. In our calculation, this condition is satisfied when the growing season is year-round and annual accumulated temperature (above 10°C) exceeds 7,000 degree-days. Only crop types requiring less than 120 days until harvest are considered when the MCI exceeds 3.0.

Table 8.1 shows the number of counties in each cropping system zone under irrigated conditions to be used in the estimation. If there are only very few counties in a cropping system zone of a particular region the observations have been added to the adjacent zone. Figure 8.2 summarises the results of the biophysical assessment weighted by actual shares of irrigated and rainfed cultivated land in each county.

Crop mix

Not all of the 16 crops considered are grown in each county or even in each region. To capture this aspect, scaling parameters were introduced into the crop-mix index function (Equation 8.4). Table 8.2 gives the shares of each

Figure 8.1 Multiple cropping zones under irrigated conditions

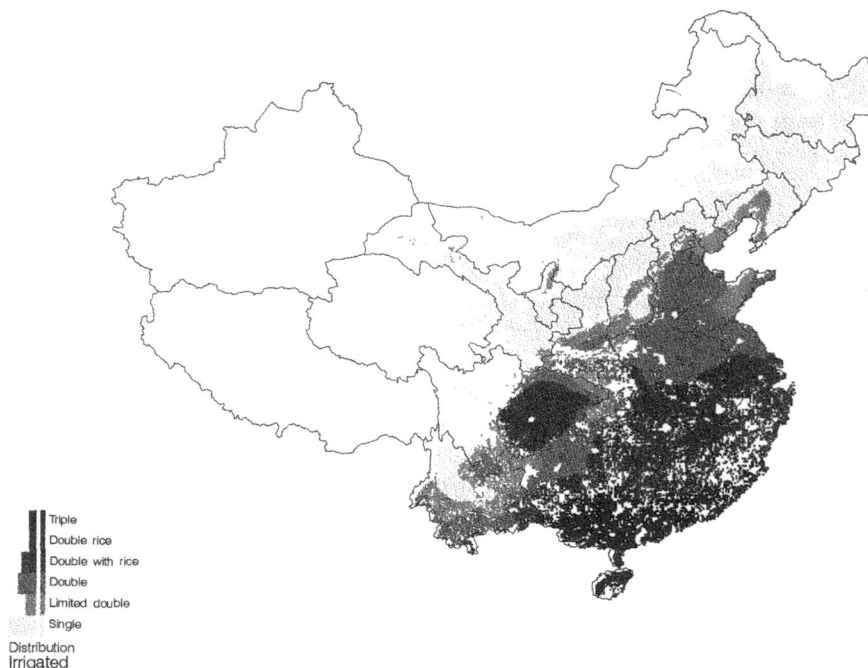

Triple
Double rice
Double with rice
Double
Limited double
Single
Distribution
Irrigated

Table 8.1 Number of counties per cropping system zone by region

	North	North East	East	Region Central	South	South West	North West/ Plateau
Single cropping	94	138	..	..	..	62	200
Limited double	111	21	..	10	..	64	48
Double cropping	287	..	73	14	..	102	22
Double with rice	..	..	115	171	18	90	..
Double rice	..	..	41	62	39	66	..
Triple cropping	..	..	..	..	116	..	..
Triple rice	..	..	..	..	78	..	..
Total	492	159	229	257	251	384	270

crop in total revenue and the number of counties where the crop is grown. The patterns clearly differ across regions. Rice, maize and wheat contribute most to revenue. However, fruit and vegetables are also important products in most regions.

Table 8.2 does not capture the broad variation of over 400 crop combinations, which enter the model through the crop (-mix) variables M_m. This definition is listed in Table 8.3. Guiding principles in the definition of crop-mix variables were: not to exceed a total of four crop-mix parameters, and to give missing major crops priority over the less important ones. Each county has, at most, one non-zero crop-mix dummy. Table 8.4 presents the results of these crop-mix definitions.

Data checking

Multiple checks were conducted in order to improve data reliability and consistency. This was done on the basis of checking various relative indicators such as the irrigation ratio, land per labourer, land per capita, output per sown hectare and each non-land input per hectare and per labourer. Occasionally, errors in the original publications could be corrected by comparison between data sources. In some cases missing or dubious data could be corrected by reference to data for other years. When data was missing or appeared to be highly implausible but could not be corrected by using other sources, the respective county was dropped from the estimation.

Eventually, of the total 2,378 administrative units contained in the LUC database, 2,042 counties could be retained in the study. That is, data were complete and were judged sufficiently reliable to be used for the output side as well as the input side of the estimation. Table 8.5 gives an account by region. Incomplete county level records eliminated 322 counties, and outliers mainly for labour and machinery figures eliminated another 14. These outliers were concentrated in the North, Plateau and North East regions. Only 20 counties on the Plateau located in Qinghai province qualified for inclusion in the estimation. Xizang (Tibet) had no acceptable data records at all. Consequently, it was decided to pool Qinghai with the North West region based on the similarity of the cropping zone pattern.

Results from estimation

Parameters of the model were estimated by Nonlinear Least Squares (NLS) separately for each region. The North West region and Plateau (a few counties in Qinghai province) were treated jointly because the number of valid

Figure 8.2   Annual potential production weighted average of irrigation and rain-fed potentials (tonnes/ha)

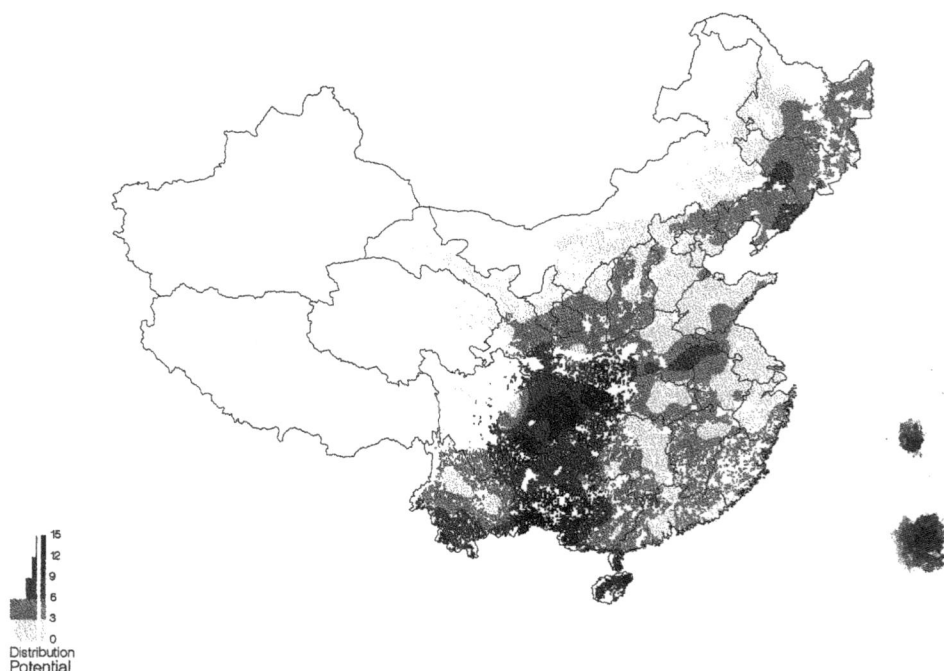

observations (20) was too low for a separate estimation of the Plateau region. The presentation of results proceeds as follows. We check whether the error term meets the statistical requirements, which permit us to consider NLS as a maximum likelihood estimator. Next, we discuss the estimation results of the input response function G. Coefficient values of the output index Q are then reported. Finally, we present and discuss the spatial distribution of calculated implicit (shadow) prices, and of the marginal productivity of input factors.

Analysis of error term

To test whether NLS amounts to maximum likelihood estimation, we check normality, homoscedasticity and independence of the error term. We apply two tests, one parametric and one non-parametric. First, we use the common Shapiro–Wilk test (Shapiro and Wilk 1965) to check whether for the sample

Table 8.2   Share of crop in total revenue and number of counties growing the crop

Crop	North %	North obs	North East %	North East obs	East %	East obs	Region Central %	Region Central obs	South %	South obs	South West %	South West obs	North West /Plateau %	North West /Plateau obs
Rice	32.0	467	6.7	116	14.4	227	4.5	219	0.9	155	9.5	380	36.2	268
Wheat	3.2	244	18.5	154	45.3	226	62.4	257	48.3	250	36.3	360	4.7	101
Maize	18.4	485	35.5	159	3.9	194	1.5	235	1.6	238	13.1	376	16.8	231
Sorghum	0.9	471	4.4	145	0.1	76	..	182	..	109	0.6	277	1.3	156
Millet	1.8	468	1.0	154	..	18	..	57	..	79	..	65	1.8	186
Other starchy	1.3	492	0.7	158	3.3	228	0.7	256	0.3	231	2.6	381	5.6	266
Root crops	2.2	492	1.4	145	1.4	216	1.0	256	1.9	250	3.1	379	2.4	250
Soybean	2.9	492	11.7	158	3.0	223	1.8	256	1.5	246	1.4	371	4.1	197
Oilseed	13.8	385	0.2	21	7.2	184	7.1	198	0.1	34	1.6	97	2.1	45
Cotton	6.2	490	2.5	156	6.4	228	5.4	257	4.2	251	6.4	373	8.6	270
Sugarcane	..	136	1.6	106	0.2	188	0.6	234	7.4	249	1.7	296	1.9	132
Fibre	0.3	265	2.3	120	0.8	190	0.8	234	0.1	157	0.4	295	..	91
Tobacco	1.6	272	1.7	136	0.3	96	1.4	209	1.6	192	4.5	362	1.4	150
Tea	..	33	..	141	1.4	148	1.2	233	1.3	207	1.3	303	..	20
Fruit	8.2	490	3.3	141	3.1	229	2.8	245	12.7	248	4.0	383	5.7	253
Vegetable	7.0	491	8.4	158	9.0	229	8.9	257	18.0	250	13.5	374	7.2	262
Number of counties	n.a.	492	n.a.	159	n.a.	229	n.a.	257	n.a.	252	n.a.	384	n.a.	270

Table 8.3   **Definition of crop-mix variables M_m (entries are crops missing)**

	Mix 1	Mix 2	Mix 3	Mix 4	No mix
North	Wheat	Maize, cotton, fruit	≥ 3 smaller crops	..	All other cases
North East	Maize, rice, soybean, vegetables	Wheat	≥ 3 smaller crops	..	All other cases
East	Rice, wheat	≥ 5 smaller crops	..	..	All other cases
Central	Rice, vegetables, cotton	≥ 3 smaller crops	..	..	All other cases
South	Rice, fruit, vegetables, sugarcane	≥ 3 smaller crops	..	..	All other cases
South West	1 of rice, vegetables, maize/wheat	2 or 3 of Wheat Rice, vegetables, maize	..	..	All other cases
North West	1 of wheat, maize, fruit, vegetables	2 or 3 of wheat, maize, fruit, vegetables	4 or 5 smaller crops	≥ 6 smaller crops	All other cases

Table 8.4   **County number corresponding to the crop-mix variables by region**

	North	North East	East	Region Central	South	South West	North West/ Plateau
None	130	88	200	159	123	163	87
Mix 1	25	7	5	59	7	14	36
Mix 2	87	42	25	39	121	13	8
Mix 3	250	22	..	..	..	194	101
Mix 4	..	..	..	..	..	..	38
Total	492	159	229	257	251	384	270

Table 8.5   **Observations per region**

	North	North East	East	Region Central	South	South West	North West/ Plateau	Total
All counties	510	184	244	275	272	402	491	2378
Missing data	13	25	15	18	21	18	212	322
Outliers (Labour, machinery)	5	0	0	0	0	0	9	14
For estimation	492	159	229	257	251	384	270	2042

as a whole, the errors are a random sample from the normal distribution. Second, we check whether errors might be spatially correlated, albeit locally. This is done by applying a spatial non-parametric (kernel density) regression (Bierens 1987; Keyzer and Sonneveld 1997), regressing the error term on longitude and latitude of the counties. For each county, the estimated value is calculated and the derivative with respect to longitude and latitude and the estimated probability of wrong sign for that derivative are calculated. Lack of spatial correlation finds expression in frequently changing signs of the derivatives and in a high average probability of the wrong sign of derivatives.

Table 8.6 presents the Shapiro–Wilk statistic. The normality test is passed at the 5 per cent level for all regions. The table also shows results from kernel density regression and indicates that no spatial dependency could be detected anywhere. On average, the probability of a wrong sign of the derivative in either direction is close enough to 0.5, implying that the error term could vary in any direction. Therefore, there is no need to correct for the spatial correlation of errors in the regression, and homoscedasticity and independence can be assumed.

We conclude that the model can be estimated by least squares. Appendix 8.1 describes an iterative numerical procedure to perform this estimation.

Input response

Next, we report on the coefficient values and their likelihood ratios, and on the elasticities of the input response equations, recalling that these were actually estimated simultaneously with the output mix equations. The likelihood ratio is used to check the robustness of the coefficients.

First, let us briefly recapitulate its main principles (see Gallant 1987; Davidson and MacKinnon 1993). We denote model parameters by ζ_1, ζ_2. Under our null hypothesis, H_0: $\zeta_1 = \overline{\zeta}_1$ and ζ_2 unrestricted, while under the alternative H_1: both ζ_1 and ζ_2 are unrestricted. With maximum likelihood estimation, the significance level of an estimated parameter ζ_1 can be determined by an F-test:

$$F(j,\ n-m) = \left(\frac{S(\overline{\zeta}_1, \tilde{\zeta}_2)}{S(\hat{\zeta}_1, \hat{\zeta}_2)} - 1 \right) \cdot \frac{n-m}{j}$$

where n, m and j are the number of observations, parameters and restrictions, respectively; $S(\hat{\zeta}_1, \hat{\zeta}_2)$ is the minimum residual sum of squares corresponding to maximisation of the unrestricted likelihood function. $S(\overline{\zeta}_1, \tilde{\zeta}_2)$ is the residual sum of squares for given reference value $\overline{\zeta}_1$ and free $\tilde{\zeta}_2$, corresponding to maximisation of the restricted likelihood function. Critical value for the region with smallest sample size (that is the North East region) $F(1,159)$ at 0.95 is 3.83.

Coefficient	North	North East	East	Region Central	South	South West	North West/ Plateau
Shapiro–Wilk's W	0.989	0.977	0.986	0.982	0.980	0.988	0.983
Probability < W	0.876	0.231	0.726	0.416	0.234	0.820	0.453

Spatial dependency using the mollifier method:
Probability of wrong sign of derivative:

Longitude	0.454	0.443	0.454	0.461	0.458	0.465	0.446
Latitude	0.441	0.418	0.455	0.457	0.452	0.448	0.423

Table 8.6   Tests on the error term

As a reference value we use 50 per cent of the original estimate ζ_1, as opposed to the usual reference value zero because the function form is given and all variables have to enter the welfare model eventually.[12] Hence, we need to assess the robustness of the estimated parameter value, rather than deciding whether the variable should be included at all.

Coefficients

Table 8.7 presents the estimated coefficients of the input response function index G, their corresponding likelihood ratios and the number of observations in each region. Clearly, for parameters with zero value no likelihood ratio can be calculated. Since $\Sigma_j \theta_j = 1$ no LR for $\theta_{Nutrient}$ is estimated. As the parameter $\delta_{Rainfed}$ is by definition equal to unity it has no LR value.

The area index H(A) is preset before estimation. The parameter $\delta_{Irrigated}$ converts irrigated land into rainfed equivalent. It is chosen on the interval between unity and the ratio of potential yield on irrigated land to potential yield on rainfed land and its significance was assessed. The estimation results for the North East region are generally slightly deviant on the input side. The quality of the input data and potential production in the North East is probably causing this result. Except for $\beta_{Nutrient}$ in the North East all parameters are significant at the 95 per cent level.

Not surprisingly, the input specific parameters γ show a large range of variability across regions, justifying estimation by region as opposed to a pooled estimation for China as a whole. For the Northern regions, including the North West/Plateau, North and North East, fertiliser substitution is at the lower bound and relatively inelastic (elasticity of substitution $\varepsilon_{Nutrient}$ = 3.33). Generally, the constants b of the input groups are small or zero. The upper bound for ρ_{Power} of -0.25 is in effect for five regions. The substitution elasticities for the power-related inputs range from 0.38 in the South West to 0.80 in most other regions.

Elasticities and marginal values

As a further description of the results from estimation, we present the output elasticities by input category, evaluated at the regional mean (Table 8.8) (see Appendix 8.3 for a specification of the analytical form of elasticities). Since the input response function G is linear homogeneous of degree one in (V, A), the elasticities of the inputs add to unity.

The results suggest a differentiation into three zones. First, the Southeast part of China, which includes the East, Central, South and to some extend South West regions, show a great similarity in elasticities for most inputs and input groups (Power, Nutrient and Land). The elasticity is highest for chemical fertiliser, followed by machinery and irrigated land, while labour has a small contribution to the output index. Second, we identify the North and North West/Plateau regions where the similarity between the elasticities manifests mainly in their pattern with respect to the non-land inputs and not so much in their levels. The levels of elasticities in the North region are comparable to the first zone. The picture is different in the remaining region, the North East, which has the highest elasticity for labour.

The elasticities of land-use types might wrongly convey the impression that investment in irrigation in the North East, South West and North West/Plateau is unprofitable. In fact the lower elasticities for irrigated land in some regions merely reflects the lower area under irrigation (see Appendix 8.2). For example, in the North East region rainfed agriculture is the dominant land-use type (78 per cent) and $\delta_{\text{Irrigated}}$ is 1.59, resulting in a ratio of rainfed over irrigated land of about 2.9. To assess the relative productivity of investment in irrigated and non-irrigated, a common area basis is needed. The two lines at the bottom of Table 8.8 measure the percentage increase in output if the land basis expands by 1 per cent of irrigated and non-irrigated land, respectively. Since $\delta_{\text{Irrigated}}$ exceeds δ_{Rainfed}, irrigation appears to be more productive.

Figures 8.3 and 8.4 map the county level elasticities for labour and machinery and seem to confirm the spatial pattern of the regional averages. The maps are computed on the basis of kernel density regression as in Keyzer and Sonneveld (1997). The histogram on the left of each panel shows the percentage shares of the coloured areas. A combined mask of estimated counties and agricultural areas as given by Figure 8.1 is applied.

As a further characterisation of the differences across regions, we calculate the marginal values (Table 8.9). These reflect the variability of implicit wages,

Table 8.7   Estimated coefficients for the input response function

Coefficient	North	North East	East	Region Central	South	South West	North West/ Plateau
ζ Single cropping	0.939 *33.8*	182.131 *136.6*	.. n.a.	.. n.a.	.. n.a.	3.050 *258.0*	40.205 *129.3*
ζ Limited double	0.892 *41.8*	169.202 *75.0*	.. *92.5*	5.150 n.a.	.. n.a.	2.217 *208.2*	32.751 *151.3*
ζ Double cropping	0.841 *43.6*	.. n.a.	5.983 *711.4*	4.353 *159.9*	.. n.a.	2.111 *275.5*	33.862 *154.9*
ζ Double with rice	.. n.a.	.. n.a.	5.768 *793.6*	3.502 *595.0*	2.806 *111.8*	1.891 *32.8*	.. n.a.
ζ Double rice	.. n.a.	.. n.a.	5.169 *636.0*	2.887 *2077.7*	2.553 *178.8*	1.742 *62.9*	.. n.a.
ζ Triple cropping	.. n.a.	.. n.a.	.. n.a.	.. n.a.	2.365 *30.5*	.. n.a.	.. n.a.
ζ Triple rice	.. n.a.	.. n.a.	.. n.a.	.. n.a.	2.595 *78.7*	.. n.a.	.. n.a.
θ Power	0.320 *376.6*	0.700* *772.9*	0.430 *4.8*	0.365 *115.4*	0.341 *160.2*	0.300* *210.7*	0.555 *22.7*
θ Nutrient	0.680	0.300	0.570	0.635	0.659	0.700	0.445
β Power	- n.a.	- n.a.	0.013 *20.8*	0.001 *68.7*	0.005 *122.7*	0.006 *33.9*	0.001 *16.8*
β Nutrient	- n.a.	0.031 *2.8*	0.005 *96.6*	- n.a.	- n.a.	0.013 *15.4*	0.003 *10.6*
ρ Power	-0.250* *43.4*	-0.250* *126.1*	-0.250* *15.5*	-0.250* *20.4*	-0.250* *24.1*	-1.630 *74.6*	-1.265 *48.9*
ρ Nutrient	0.700* *30.8*	0.700* *17773.5*	1.000* *16.8*	1.000* *3552.1*	1.000* *243.1*	1.000* *255.3*	0.700* *3.2*
γ Labour	0.161 *30.0*	2.062 *14.5*	0.464 *15.7*	0.389 *50.2*	0.291 *40.9*	3.010 *22.5*	7.856 *16.6*
γ Machine	0.807 *446.5*	2.141 *12.1*	1.024 *153.5*	1.779 *2264.7*	1.457 *817.3*	3.179 *34.9*	23.589 *22.6*
γ Chemicals	3.235 *38.0*	0.337 *10.8*	0.160 *549.5*	1.578 *826.3*	0.728 *174.4*	0.934 *12.8*	0.120 *12.5*
γ Organic	1.481 *37.8*	0.025 *11.2*	0.135 *97.3*	0.770 *75.5*	0.623 *28.3*	0.387 *37.8*	0.029 *13.8*
δ Irrigated [1]	2.110 *35.5*	1.590 *4.9*	1.000 *117.2*	1.000 *54.4*	1.000 *28.7*	1.000 *30.6*	2.210 *22.2*
δ Rainfed [1]	1.000	1.000	1.000	1.000	1.000	1.000	1.000
Observations	492	159	229	257	173	384	270

Notes: *parameter at bound; [1]preset value 4.9.
Figures in italics are likelihood ratios.

rental cost of machinery and price of chemical and organic fertilisers.

The marginal value of labour is high in the Northern regions and, as could be expected, low in densely populated areas of the Central and South regions where marginal returns to land are relatively high for both irrigated and rainfed land. Despite its dense population, the East region reflects—with the relatively high marginal value of labour—the attractiveness of the more industrialised area.

Output index

The coefficients of the output index function Q appear in Table 8.10. For the major staple crops (rice, wheat and maize) they generally come out very similarly across regions. Deviations are mainly due to the fact that certain crops are sometimes a major crop in one region but a minor crop in another. Wheat and maize are outliers in opposite directions in the South, where they contribute less than 1.0 and 1.6 per cent to total crop revenue, respectively. Wheat can only be grown in a few scattered areas in Fujian and Guangdong. The variation in estimates is most pronounced for the minor crops but estimates are stable for vegetables and (to a lesser extent) fruits, which are present in almost all counties and baskets of various kinds. The crop-mix correction factors m_m vary across regions and crop mixes. Most are negative as expected, especially those associated with a major crop. Other crop-mix parameters can be positive since some of the regional minor crops are a major crop at county level. The significance level for most parameters is well above 95 per cent.

Implicit prices

We are now ready to calculate implicit prices and compare these with the consumer prices in nearby urban centres. The difference between them measures an implicit trade and transportation margin. Clearly, this margin should increase with the distance to the main consuming areas. We show results for rice and wheat, the major staples, by means of a price map computed through kernel density regression.

Figure 8.5 displays the implicit price of rice for the main rice-producing provinces. Figure 8.6 shows the population density in 100 persons per km². It appears that the farm gate price of rice is in general higher in areas with a high population density. This holds especially for the relatively urbanised areas in the Southern provinces of Guandong, Guangxi and Hainan. The Red Basin area in Sichuan and the Dongbei Pingyuan Plains stretching from south to north in the three northeastern provinces also exhibit rising prices closer to consuming areas. Thus, the figures indicate that our (purely quantity-based) estimation results in a positive trade and transportation margin.

The implicit prices of the two other major crops, wheat and maize, for the relevant producing areas are shown in Figures 8.7 and 8.8, respectively. They

---

Figure 8.3   Elasticity for labour

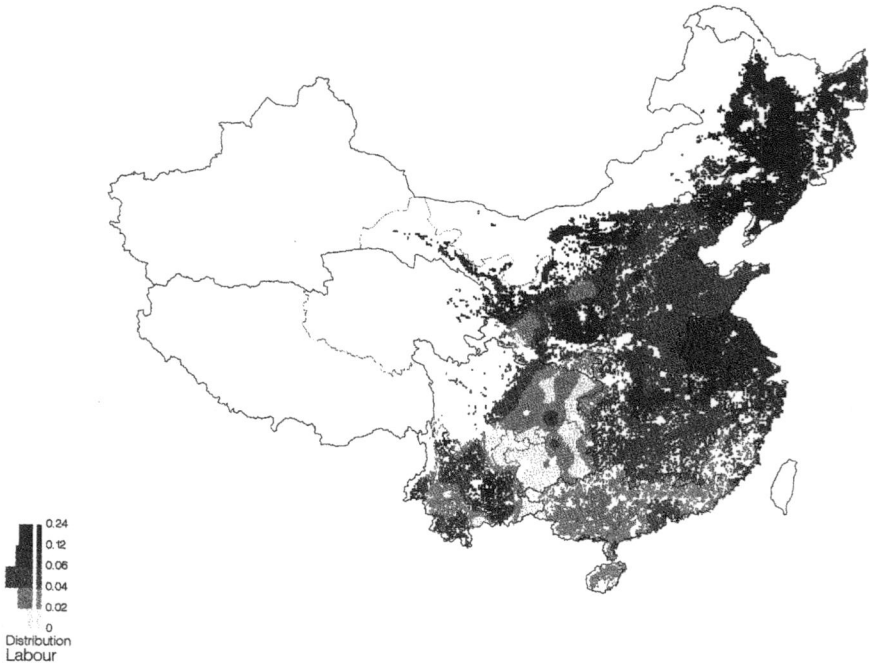

0.24
0.12
0.06
0.04
0.02
0
Distribution
Labour

---

also show that prices are rising as one nears densely populated areas. Wheat has an outlier in the South region, resulting in a high farm gate price. Note that there is no wheat in the plains of the North East where conditions are more favourable for maize, which is grown on more than 50 per cent of the area.

Table 8.11 compares observed farm gate prices and implicit prices at the regional level for rice, wheat and maize. The implicit prices are weighted with the county production. In the main producing regions, they are seen to fluctuate around the farm gate levels in the original statistics. As mentioned earlier, these recorded farm gate prices are a quantity-weighted mean of quota prices, negotiated prices and free market prices. They tend to lie below marginal productivity and hence below implicit free market prices.

We conclude that the differences between the observed market prices and the imputed farm gate prices leave positive margins that follow a plausible geographical pattern. This suggests that by keeping these margins exogenous to the farm model in a county, it becomes possible to reproduce the main properties of crop farming in China by means of a static profit maximising model.

Figure 8.4   Elasticity for machinery

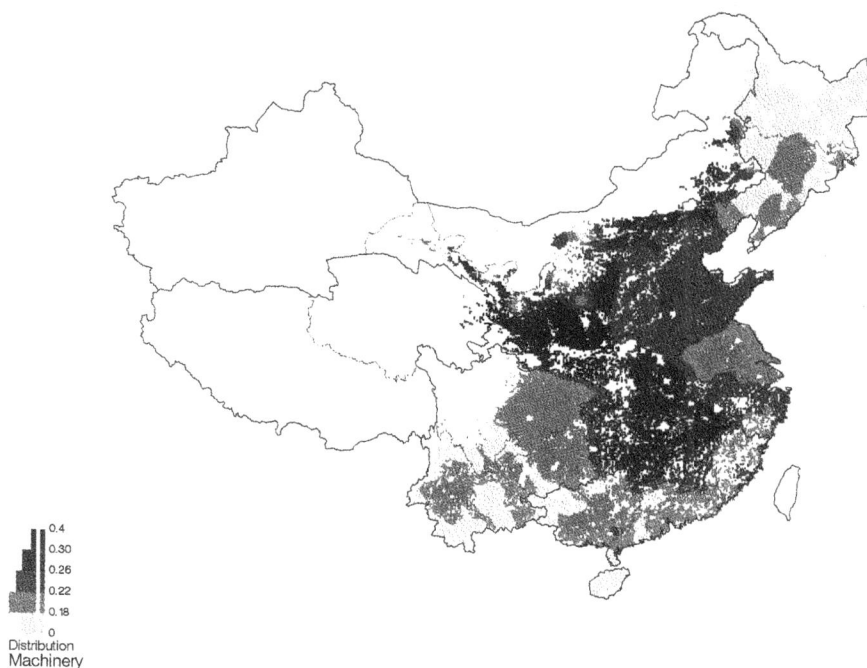

0.4
0.30
0.26
0.22
0.18
0
Distribution
Machinery

Table 8.8   Output elasticities of land and non-land inputs at the regional mean

Input	North	North East	East	Region Central	South	South West	North West/ Plateau
Labour	0.052	0.172	0.095	0.054	0.036	0.028	0.100
Machinery	0.248	0.160	0.216	0.279	0.202	0.211	0.331
Power	0.300	0.332	0.311	0.333	0.238	0.239	0.431
Chemical fertiliser	0.309	0.122	0.392	0.344	0.376	0.398	0.209
Organic fertiliser	0.084	0.005	0.121	0.102	0.184	0.192	0.042
Nutrient	0.393	0.127	0.513	0.446	0.560	0.590	0.251
Irrigated area	0.215	0.140	0.131	0.165	0.127	0.063	0.138
Rainfed area	0.092	0.401	0.045	0.056	0.075	0.108	0.180
Land	0.307	0.541	0.176	0.221	0.202	0.171	0.318

Elasticity of land-index H if change is attributed to:

Irrigated area	0.414	0.779	0.185	0.221	0.203	0.171	0.544
Rainfed area	0.196	0.490	0.185	0.221	0.203	0.171	0.246

163

Table 8.9   **Marginal values at the mean** (yuan)

Derivative $\partial G/\partial V$	North	North East	East	Region Central	South	South West	North West/ Plateau
Labour (person)	113.90	580.05	242.11	125.62	88.83	41.63	160.20
Machinery (kW)	429.76	348.17	614.77	1086.19	784.91	1056.26	573.56
Chemical fertiliser (kg)	4.72	1.61	5.76	6.20	5.62	8.23	2.96
Organic fertiliser (kg)	2.70	0.16	4.83	3.03	4.81	3.41	0.77
$\partial G/\partial A$							
Irrigated area farmland (ha)	1329.98	1190.84	862.63	1296.18	871.70	490.13	539.93
Rainfed area farmland (ha)	630.32	748.95	862.63	1296.18	871.70	490.13	244.31

Marginal productivity

Figures 8.9 and 8.10 present maps for the marginal productivity of labour and machinery. It appears that the marginal productivity of agricultural labour is usually higher in the neighbourhood of large urban areas: Hong Kong, Shanghai, Beijing, Tiajin and the delta of Liaoning. The figures also show that in the Southern regions (South West, Central and South) the marginal productivity is higher for machinery and lower for labour.

Figure 8.11 maps the marginal value of irrigated land, which by construction stands in fixed, region-specific proportion to the marginal productivity of rainfed land. Along the coastal zone and in the North East region, it follows the pattern of population density quite closely but inland the relationship is loose. Although marginal productivity is somewhat higher in the Red Basin area in Sichuan than in the surrounding mountainous area, its level lies substantially below comparable urban areas along the coast.

At the regional level, the average implicit costs (and returns) per labourer for land and wage are lowest in the Central and South West (Table 8.12). In the South West region, in 1990 an average labourer earned an income of 287 yuan. For the coastal regions South, East and North, the earnings for a crop labourer range between 631–813 yuan on average. This pattern is in line with the observed out-migration to the coastal provinces during the last decade. The marginal productivities of labour and land are highest in the northern provinces.

Table 8.10 **Estimated coefficients for the output function**

Coefficient	North	North East	East	Region Central	South	South West	North West/ Plateau
$\alpha_0{}^1$	1.500 *46.6*	1.500 *25.4*	1.500 *29.9*	1.500 *35.6*	1.500 *35.1*	1.500 *74.4*	1.500 *42.7*
α_{Rice}	0.780 *36.4*	0.727 *1.3*	0.892 *199.8*	0.752 *281.8*	0.712 *111.4*	0.839 *93.2*	0.890 *18.3*
α_{Wheat}	1.171 *163.7*	0.881 *5.0*	1.099 *21.0*	1.374 *32.3*	5.425 *33.1*	1.035 *28.5*	1.024 *17.0*
α_{Maize}	1.433 *38.4*	0.668 *11.1*	3.863 *14.5*	10.922 *23.5*	13.532 *23.0*	0.030* *31.9*	0.030* *16.5*
$\alpha_{Sorghum}$	2.095 *43.7*	0.168 *5.0*	0.030* *14.5*	0.030* *17.3*	49.332 *20.5*	0.030* *30.3*	0.793 *16.9*
α_{Millet}	0.720 *48.7*	0.586 *9.4*	0.934 *16.0*	0.806 *17.7*	2.346 *39.6*	1.205 *68.5*	0.672 *19.7*
$\alpha_{Other\ starchy}$	0.944 *30.9*	3.588 *6.9*	0.714 *14.2*	2.592 *16.5*	0.030* *18.8*	0.592 *33.3*	0.159 *17.6*
$\alpha_{Root\ crops}$	0.383 *30.2*	0.030* *5.9*	0.534 *14.7*	0.724 *16.5*	0.030* *19.9*	0.841 *33.1*	0.959 *16.2*
$\alpha_{Soybean}$	2.624 *33.7*	1.231 *3.9*	3.467 *15.3*	6.385 *17.8*	0.030* *20.1*	0.030* *30.0*	0.030* *16.9*
$\alpha_{Oilseed}$	1.324 *28.2*	0.503 *5.4*	3.300 *17.7*	4.417 *23.9*	7.972 *31.3*	2.361 *29.1*	0.526 *17.0*
α_{Cotton}	6.796 *46.8*	35.730 *5.5*	10.066 *17.6*	9.360 *22.0*	6.079 *22.7*	18.836 *33.3*	11.477 *22.0*
$\alpha_{Sugarcane}$	1.043 *35.9*	0.030* *5.0*	0.536 *14.7*	0.342 *15.8*	0.201 *24.1*	0.212 *49.6*	0.563 *20.7*
α_{Fibre}	4.802 *34.6*	0.030* *5.0*	2.889 *13.7*	2.577 *15.3*	13.924 *21.8*	11.246 *24.2*	39.267 *16.3*
$\alpha_{Tobacco}$	3.203 *31.5*	8.088 *7.3*	0.030* *14.3*	7.062 *32.8*	6.844 *23.4*	4.713 *45.5*	1.391 *18.3*
α_{Tea}	31.912 *32.8*	.. *n.a.*	10.469 *17.7*	12.199 *17.0*	17.698 *24.6*	11.082 *31.7*	0.030* *17.2*
α_{Fruit}	1.674 *30.1*	1.241 *7.3*	1.427 *15.3*	2.504 *24.1*	1.901 *21.5*	2.206 *28.9*	1.885 *15.3*
$\alpha_{Vegetables}$	0.346 *42.1*	0.267 *7.9*	0.364 *26.9*	0.484 *29.9*	0.347 *18.9*	0.461 *64.2*	0.335 *19.4*
$\mu_{Mix\ 1}$	-0.182 *41.6*	-0.182 *7.7*	-0.076 *12.5*	-0.014 *14.1*	0.121 *20.8*	-0.215 *35.1*	-0.376 *34.4*
$\mu_{Mix\ 2}$	-0.083 *41.8*	0.203 *10.9*	-0.119 *29.8*	-0.043 *20.8*	0.054 *24.0*	-0.031 *30.7*	-0.022 *16.6*
$\mu_{Mix\ 3}$	-0.014 *32.3*	0.021 *5.0*	.. *n.a.*	.. *n.a.*	.. *n.a.*	-0.034 *35.7*	-0.043 *21.3*
$\mu_{Mix\ 4}$	.. *n.a.*	.. *n.a.*	.. *n.a.*	.. *n.a.*	.. *n.a.*	.. *n.a.*	0.019 *17.6*

Notes: *parameter at bound; [1]preset value.

Figure 8.5   **Shadow price of rice** (yuan/kg)

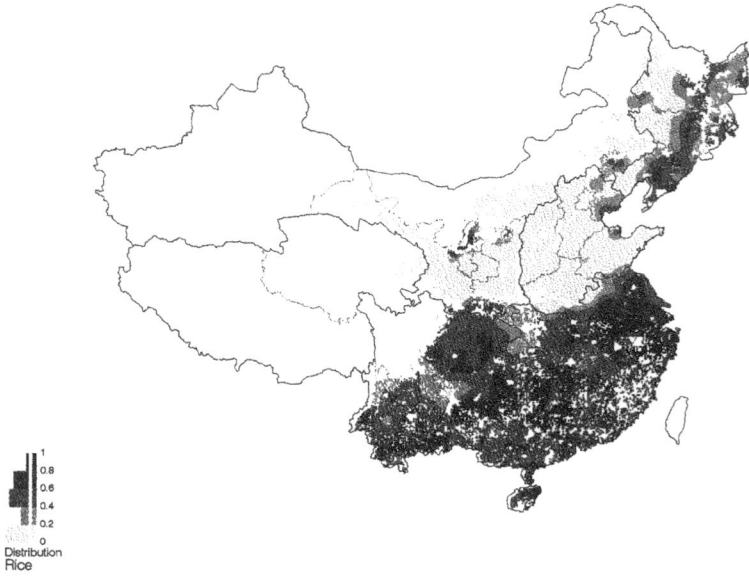

Figure 8.6   **Population density** (persons/km²)

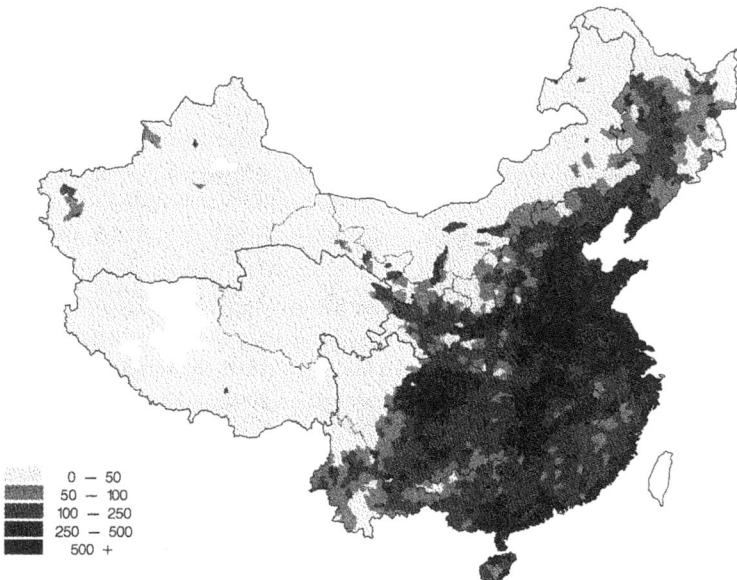

Figure 8.7   Shadow price of wheat (yuan/kg)

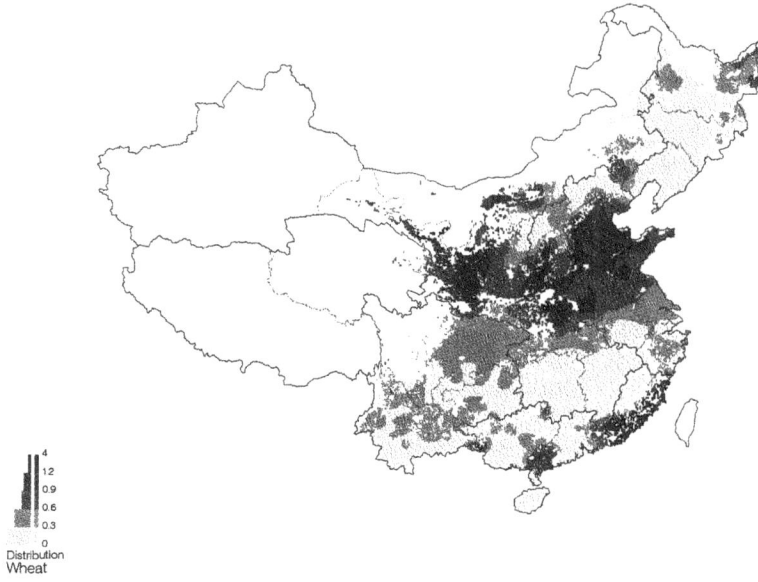

4
1.2
0.9
0.6
0.3
0
Distribution
Wheat

Figure 8.8   Shadow price of maize (yuan/kg)

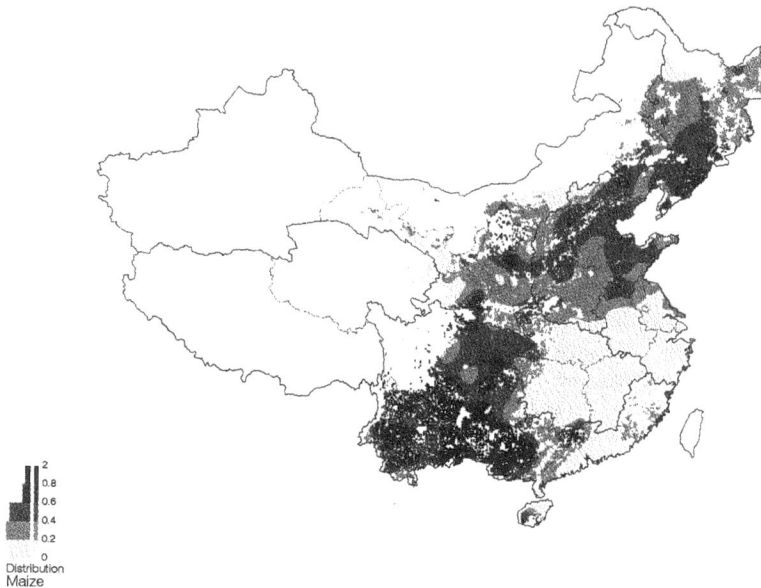

2
0.8
0.6
0.4
0.2
0
Distribution
Maize

Figure 8.9   Marginal productivity of labour (yuan/person)

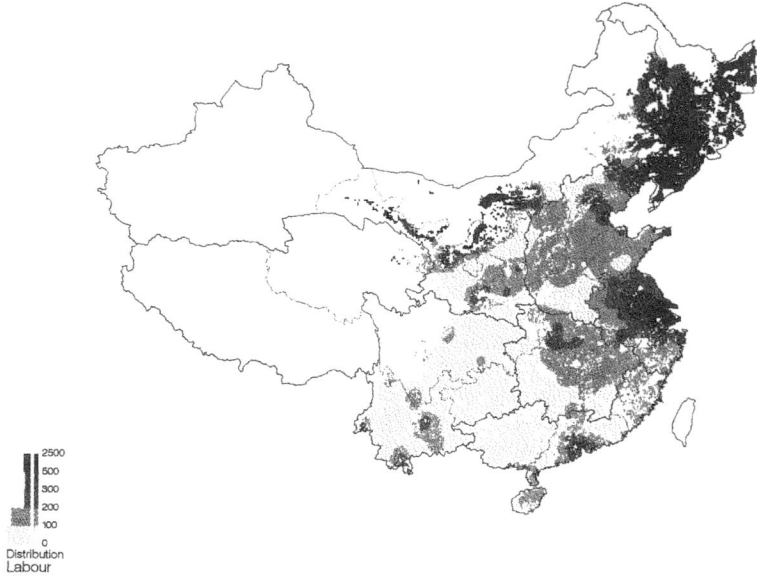

Figure 8.10   Marginal productivity of machinery (1000 yuan/10kW)

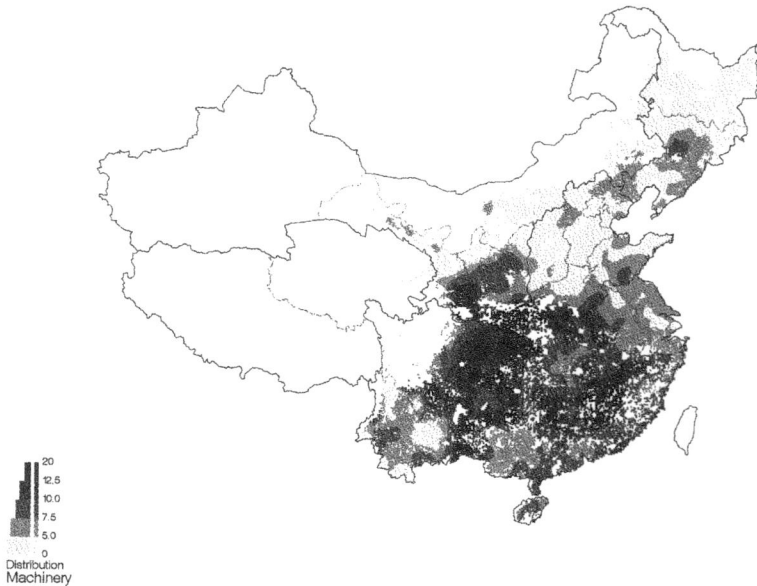

Figure 8.11   Marginal productivity of irrigated land (yuan/ha)

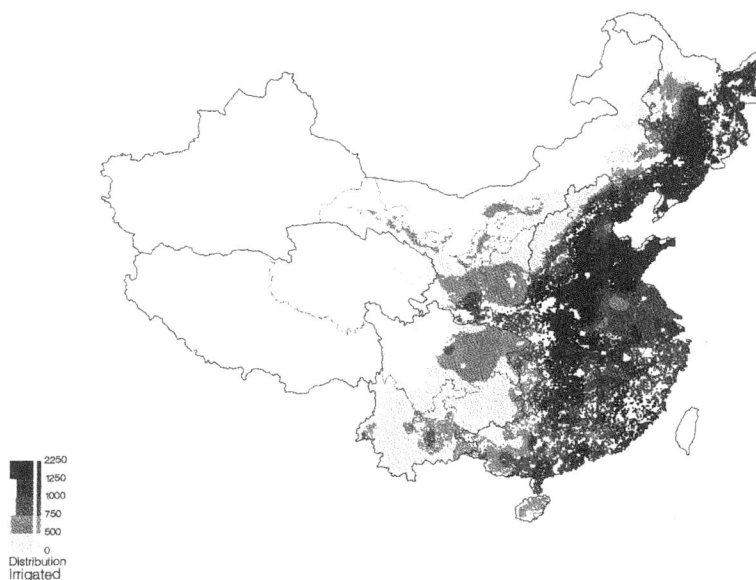

2250
1250
1000
750
500
0
Distribution
Irrigated

Table 8.11   Price comparison of original and shadow prices for the major crops

Region	Rice Original	Shadow	Wheat Original	Shadow	Maize Original	Shadow
North	..	..	0.66	1.00	0.53	0.42
North East	0.64	0.52	..	..	0.39	0.43
East	0.65	0.75	0.57	0.68	0.56	0.41
Central	0.60	0.59	0.58	0.73	..	..
South	0.62	0.64	..	..	..	..
South West	0.55	0.59	0.57	0.42	0.55	0.67
North West/Plateau	0.71	0.61	0.64	0.84	0.46	0.39

Note: Shadow prices using Equation 9.13 (regional average is weighted with production).
Source: Original prices are from SSB, Survey Team of Urban Socio-Economy, 1992b.
Yearbook of Price Statistics of China, 1992, China Statistical Publishing House, Beijing, (in Chinese).

Table 8.12   Input cost (yuan/labourer)

	North	North East	Region East	Central	South	South West	North West/ Plateau
Chemical fertiliser	631	425	947	683	897	498	350
Organic fertiliser	176	16	301	213	456	249	66
Machinery	531	547	517	562	487	257	496
Wage and land	813	2321	673	580	631	287	666
Total costs	2151	3309	2438	2038	2471	1291	1578

Conclusion

This chapter has reported on the specification and estimation of a spatially explicit transformation function for crop production in China, and indicates that the implicit prices associated with this function seem compatible with static profit maximisation at county level, at prices that correct for the distance from the main consuming areas. The next step is to conduct scenario simulations with such a profit-maximising model, after the inclusion of a livestock production and feed demand equation. We will then confront these with consumer demand and balance of payment restrictions. The final step will be to incorporate investment into irrigation and solve an intertemporal welfare model.

Appendix 8.1

Description of the estimation procedure and calculation of partial derivatives for the Taylor expansion approach

The transformation function described in the crop-mix output index of the input response function, can be written in more compact form as

$$Q_l(Y, M; \alpha_0, \alpha, \mu) = C_l G_l(V, A, \bar{y}(x), \theta, \rho, \beta, \gamma, \delta)$$

where Greek symbols refer to parameters that should be estimated or fixed. On the output side Q_l is a combination of a sum of crop-mix constants and a CES

$$Q_\ell = \left(1 + \sum_m \mu_m M_{\ell m}\right)\left(\sum_c (\alpha_c Y_{\ell c})^{\alpha_0}\right)^{1/\alpha_0}$$

(A8.1)

and on the input side C_l is the sum of cropping zone constants

$$C_\ell = \sum_z \zeta_z Z_{\ell z}$$

while G_l is the generalised Mitscherlich-Baule function

$$G_\ell = \prod_j f(V_\ell, A_\ell; \beta, \gamma; \delta, \rho)^{\theta_j} N(A_\ell, \bar{y}_\ell(x); \delta)$$

(A8.2)

with

$$f_{\ell j} = 1 - \exp(-\beta_j - w(V_\ell/H_\ell))$$

$$w_{\ell j} = \left(\sum_{k \in j} \gamma_k (V_{k\ell}/H_\ell)^{\rho_j} \right)^{1/\rho_j}$$

$$H_\ell = \sum_s \delta_s A_{\ell s} \quad \text{and}$$

$$N_\ell = H_\ell \bar{y}_\ell$$

Index l stands for counties, m for crop-mix, c for crops, z for multiple cropping zones, s for land-use types, j for input groups and k for inputs. Estimation is performed by each of seven regions.

Numerical implementation of the estimation procedure

As the estimation problem to be solved is highly nonlinear and non-convex in parameters, and relatively large and complex in parameters, it cannot be solved by invoking a standard numerical optimisation procedure. Therefore, it was necessary to develop an iterative procedure, which operates in five steps.

1. Generation of the initial quantities $\tilde{q}_\ell = \tilde{Q}_\ell/H_\ell$ as data for the separate estimation of the input and the output function. Calculation of $\bar{y}_\ell = \bar{Y}_\ell / H_\ell$.

2. Iterative estimation of parameters of the input function $\tilde{q}_\ell = C_\ell \cdot G_\ell / H_\ell + \varepsilon_1$ by linear regression using a first-order Taylor expansion of the function, which is adjusted until convergence. This provides good initial estimates for Step 3.

3. Further estimation of the parameters of the input function in the original nonlinear form.

4. Estimation of parameters of the output function $\tilde{q}_\ell = Q_\ell / H_\ell + \varepsilon_2$ in the nonlinear form, for fixed substitution parameter α_0.

5. Update the quantity index $\tilde{q}_\ell$ and go to Step 3 until convergence.

Thus, Steps 1 and 2 constitute the initialisation and Steps 3 to 5, the actual estimation. We note that a free nonlinear regression would do without separate data for the quantity index. Attempts to relax this restriction causes convergence problems in the estimation. It should be added that since the estimation problem is non-convex, only a stationary point could be obtained which appears to be a local optimum. The robustness of this estimate was tested by checking convergence to the optimal value after shocks and also by

171

assessing the resulting change in the other parameters in the calculation of the likelihood ratios (which performs new rounds of least squares, while iteratively setting parameters at half their originally estimated value). We conclude with some additional remarks on the various steps.

Step 1: The initial county-level output index $\tilde{Q}_\ell$ is calculated based on the available provincial prices P_{rc}, the national prices P_c and the county-level crop outputs. The provincial crop output Y_{rc} is the sum of the county level outputs $Y_{\ell c}$. A provincial output price index P_r^i is calculated as

$$P_r^i = \frac{\sum_c P_{rc} Y_{rc}}{\sum_c P_c Y_{rc}}$$

to measure the departure of the provincial price level from the national price level. This provincial level price index, together with provincial level output prices, is applied to all counties l in province r, yielding a country-level output index $\tilde{Q}_\ell$.

$$\tilde{Q}_\ell = \sum_c Y_{\ell c} P_{\ell c} / P_\ell^i$$

Step 2. The Taylor expansion uses two matrices e and e_p of dimension $z \times \psi$. Let subscript p denote the results of the previous iteration. Using the definitions of Equations A8.1 and A8.2, the sum of squared disturbances $e_\ell(z; \psi)$ can be written as

$$e_\ell(z; \psi) = \quad Q_\ell - C_\ell(Z_{\ell z}; \zeta_z) G(V_{\ell j}, A_{\ell s}, \bar{y}_{ls}; \theta_j, \beta_j, \rho_j, \gamma_k) / H_\ell \quad \text{(A8.3)}$$

and the derivatives are

a) partial derivative with respect to ζ_z

$$\frac{\partial e_\ell}{\partial \zeta_z} = -Z_{\ell z} G_\ell / H_\ell \quad \text{(A8.4)}$$

b) partial derivative with respect to θ_j

$$\frac{\partial e_\ell}{\partial \theta_j} = -\log f_{\ell j} C_\ell G_\ell / H_\ell \quad \text{(A8.5)}$$

c) partial derivative with respect to β_j

$$\frac{\partial e_\ell}{\partial \beta_j} = -\theta_j \frac{1 - f_{\ell j}}{f_{\ell j}} C_\ell G_\ell / H_\ell \quad \text{(A8.6)}$$

d) partial derivative with respect to ρ_j

$$\frac{\partial e_\ell}{\partial \rho_j} = \frac{-\theta_j w_{\ell j}}{\rho_j} \frac{1 - f_{\ell j}}{f_{\ell j}} \left(\frac{\log w_{\ell j}^{\rho_j}}{\rho_j} - \frac{\sum_{k \in j} (\gamma_k v_{\ell k}^{\rho_j} \log v_{\ell k})}{w_{\ell j}^{\rho_j}} \right) C_\ell G_\ell / H_\ell \quad \text{(A8.7)}$$

with $v_{\ell k} = V_{\ell k} / H_\ell$

e) partial derivative with respect to $\gamma_k, k \in j$

$$\frac{\partial e_\ell}{\partial \gamma_j} = -\theta_j \frac{1-f_{\ell j}}{f_{\ell j}} \frac{1}{\rho_j} w_{\ell j}^{1-\rho_j} v_{\ell j}^{\rho_j} C_\ell G_\ell / H_\ell \qquad (A8.8)$$

Step 3. To avoid parameters drifting away in the course of the estimation, the parameters ζ, θ, ρ and η are estimated keeping the others fixed, and next the parameters β and γ are estimated keeping ζ, θ, ρ and η fixed. The parameters are updated until convergence is reached. The update procedure of the parameters and convergence level are the same as in Step 2.

Step 4. The parameter α_0 is estimated by scanning over the interval [1.5, 2].

Step 5. Convergence is reached when two full rounds lead to less than 0.1 per cent change of the sum of squares of $\left(\hat{Q}_\ell / H_\ell - \hat{C}_\ell \hat{G}_\ell / H_\ell \right)$

The entire estimation procedure was implemented in GAMS* (Brooke *et al.* 1992). The databases for estimation of the output and input response functions were stored and managed as MS-Excel worksheets. The statistical software package SAS was used to transfer the basic data into GAMS format, with a proper declaration and initialisation of sets in GAMS syntax. The resulting database in GAMS format was stored with the save option 's = ..\data', so that it can be used by the different parts of the GAMS programs independently using the restart option 'r = ..\data'.

Appendix 8.2

Output elasticities of input k and land input s and of crop c

Output elasticity with respect to input $V_{\ell k}$

$$\frac{\partial G_\ell}{\partial V_{\ell k}} \frac{V_{\ell k}}{G_\ell} = \frac{1-f_{\ell j}}{f_{\ell j}} \theta_j \gamma_k w_{\ell j}^{1-\rho_j} \left(\frac{V_{\ell k}}{H_\ell} \right)^{\rho_j} \qquad (A8.9)$$

Output elasticity with respect to land input of type $A_{\ell s}$

$$\frac{\partial G_\ell}{\partial A_{\ell s}} \frac{A_{\ell s}}{G_\ell} = \frac{\delta_s A_{\ell s}}{H_\ell} \left(1 - \sum_j \left(\theta_j \frac{1-f_{\ell j}}{f_{\ell j}} w_{\ell j} \right) \right) \qquad (A8.10)$$

Output elasticity with respect to crop $Y_{\ell c}$

$$\frac{\partial Q_\ell}{\partial Y_{\ell c}} \frac{Y_{\ell c}}{Q_\ell} = \frac{(\alpha_c Y_{\ell c})^{\alpha_0}}{\sum_c (\alpha_c Y_{\ell c})^{\alpha_0}} \qquad (A8.11)$$

Notes

1 In this chapter the results emerging in the first stage of the estimation are presented. The full results and an extended analysis will be published soon in IIASA's peer-reviewed

Research Report Series, under the title 'Estimation of Agricultural Production Relations in the LUC Model for China'. The research of the LUC project is a multidisciplinary and collaborative effort. It has involved researchers at IIASA and in various collaborating institutions in China, Europe, Japan, Russia and the United States. For the work presented in this paper, the authors are grateful to the researchers who have developed and significantly contributed to the various themes: Silvia Prieler and Harrij T. van Velthuizen (IIASA, LUC) contributed to the AEZ modeling. Li Xiubin, Liu Yanhua, Zhao Mingcha (Institute of Geography, Chinese Academy of Sciences, Beijing) and Zheng Zenyuan (State Land Administration, Beijing) greatly supported the provision, adequate interpretation and compilation of data. Liu Jiyuan (Institute of Geographical Sciences and Natural Resources, Chinese Academy of Sciences, Beijing) kindly provided mapped data defining the spatial distribution of cultivated land.

2   All authors provided some specific contributions to the writing of this report. Günther Fischer and Laixiang Sun compiled the database. Günther Fischer developed the agro-ecological assessment model for China and estimated the biophysical potentials. Laixiang Sun and Peter Albersen estimated the input response function. Peter Albersen also estimated the output function, performed the final, joint estimation of the output and input components and computed the implicit prices. Michiel Keyzer provided general guidance and gave technical advice.

3   IIASA and SOW-VU cooperated in the construction of the LUC model.

4   The eight LUC economic regions are: north including Beijing, Tianjin, Hebei, Henan, Shandong and Shanxi; north-east including Liaoning, Jilin and Heilongjiang; east including Shanghai, Jiangsu, Zhejiang and Anhui; central including Jiangxi, Hubei and Hunan; south including Fujian, Guangdong, Guangxi and Hainan; south-west including Sichuan, Guizhou and Yunnan; north-west including Nei Mongol, Shaanxi, Gansu, Ningxia and Xinjiang; and plateau including Tibet and Qinghai.

5   For more information on various innovative models of land tenure see Dong (1996), Fahlbeck and Huang (1997), Wang (1993), Rural Sample Survey Office (1994), Chen and Han (1994) and Lin (1995).

6   There are two sets of farmland data in China. Most widely used is the data set published by State Statistical Bureau (SSB) in the *Statistical Yearbook of China*. Another data set was compiled by the State Land Administration (SLA), based on a land survey in the 1980s. SSB has noticed that its figures for cultivated areas may underestimate the actual extent. According to SSB, the area of cultivated and irrigated land in 1990 was only 95.7 and 47.4 million hectares, respectively, whereas the corresponding figures from SLA were 132.7 and 63.5 million hectares. Thus the irrigation share is similar on average but the differences between the estimates at province and national level are quite large (SSB 1994:329, 335; Fischer *et al.* 1998).

7   We note that econometric studies may underrate the role played by organic fertiliser because relevant statistical data are often lacking and where available they exhibit high correlation with total labour input.

8   This rate is calculated on the basis of the State Land Administration's (SLA) figure of the total farmland area, which was about 132 million hectares in 1995. SLA's farmland figure is based on a detailed land survey conducted from 1985–95, and is consistent with estimates derived from satellite imagery (see also Fischer *et al.* 1998).

9   We used the total number of large animals as a proxy for draught animals. However, due to the poor performance of this proxy in all estimations, we finally had to drop it from the estimation.

10 Personal communications with Chinese officials suggest that the farmland data compiled by SLA based on detailed surveys will eventually replace the unrealistic estimates published in the *Statistical Yearbook of China*. Except where specifically mentioned, the data in this subsection are derived from various publications of China's State Statistical Bureau.

11 For detailed documentation and references regarding the compilation and editing of these land use and soil maps, see http://www.iiasa.ac.at/Research/LUC/

12 The alternative values against which the estimated values are tested, read: $\theta_{Power} = 0.5$; $\zeta_z = 1$; $m_m = 0$; $\rho_{Power} = -1.5$; $\rho_{Nutrient} = 0.7$ or 1; and $\alpha_0 = 2$. For $\delta_{Irrigated} = 1$, the ratio between the potential yield on irrigated land to the potential yield on rainfed land is used as the alternative and in the other cases if $\delta_{Irrigated} = 1$ is the hypothesis, leading to the values $\delta_{Irrigated} = 1.00, 1.00, 1.05, 1.04, 1.03, 1.16$ and 1.00, respectively, for the various regions.

9

Determinants of household grain stocks

Does price matter?

Guanghua Wan

China is the largest grain producer and consumer in the world. This fact underlies the enormous interest in the production and consumption of grains in China. In particular, the publications of Lester Brown (1995) led to worldwide comments, speculation and policy debate on the Chinese grain sector (Huang *et al.* 1996; Ministry of Agriculture 1996). It is estimated that some 60-70 per cent of annual output or 270-315 MMT of grains are held as household stocks in rural China. Needless to say, this volume and its changes could have profound implications on the design and implementation of domestic policies, such as price stabilisation and income-support schemes. For example, government retreat to a grain trade monopoly in China did not achieve expected outcomes in 1996–97. The stockpiling of state grain storage did not push up market prices because of the substantial grain stocks held by households and a general lack of understanding of farmers' grain storage behaviour.

Furthermore, household grain stocks also affect the demand for food imports and thus represent an essential ingredient of trade policymaking for the Chinese government and its trading partners (USDA 1994; OECD 1995b). To a large extent, national food security hinges on the volume and spatial distribution of grain stocks in rural China.

Despite the importance of grain stocks in China, little published work has appeared in the literature with exceptions of Zhong (1995) and Park (1996). This is a direct result of scarce or unavailable data.

Relying on household survey data compiled by the China Center for Agricultural Policy, the objective of this chapter is to identify determinants of household grain stocks in China. In particular, three sets of hypotheses are tested, each of which corresponds to a different motive of grain storage by

Chinese farmers. Motives include price speculation, food security considerations and the minimisation of market transaction costs. To test these hypotheses, an adaptive-expectation and partial-adjustment model will be developed and applied to cross-sectional time-series data from China.

A commodity storage model

General commodity storage theory, which usually assumes that markets are operational and efficient, suggests that private storage can be explained by speculative behaviour (Williams and Wright 1991). Based on this theory, the desired level of grain stocks to be carried over to the next period, which is equivalent to the planned or desired stock level at the end of the current period, can be expressed as a function of expected price, formed for the next period

$$S^*_t = f(P^*_{t+1}) + u_t \tag{9.1}$$

where t indexes time period, S^*_t denotes desired level of grain stocks at the end of period t, and P^*_{t+1} indicates the price which is expected to prevail in period t+1.

It is important to note that the stock level at the end of the present period S^*_t does not depend on the expectation for this period's price P^*_t which was formed in the previous period. This is because at the present time, actual price P_t is already observed or being realised. Consequently, information contained in P^*_t becomes obsolete in period t except in forming future expectations. Decision making at time t will be based on the current price P_t and newly formed expectation on price for the next period P^*_{t+1}. This is why P^*_{t+1} rather than P^*_t appears on the right-hand side of Equation 9.1. It can be shown that under adaptive expectations the same model (such as Equations 9.7 or 9.13) can be obtained with or without inclusion of P_t in Equation 9.1. To reiterate, current (actual or planned) stock depends on current expectation for next period's price P^*_{t+1}, not previous expectation for this period's price P^*_t.

Postulating that f is of a linear form, Equation 9.1 can be specified as

$$S^*_t = a_0 + a_1 P^*_{t+1} + u_t \tag{9.2}$$

Although Equation 9.1 is consistent with standard storage theory and is intuitively appealing, neither the planned stock S^* nor expected price P^* are directly observable.

Taking advantage of the classic work of Nerlove (1958), price formation is assumed to follow the well known adaptive expectation process:

$$P^*_{t+1} = P^*_t + r (P_t - P^*_t) \tag{9.3}$$

where P_t indicates realised price in period t. Clearly, $P_t - P^*_t$ represents errors in the previous expectation. According to Equation 9.3, the current expectation for next period price is equal to the previous expectation for this period price plus an expectation-error-correction term. Put another way, speculators adjust their expectations over time based on the degree of accuracy or inaccuracy of their previous expectation. In the absence of expectation of any form, it should be held that $P^*_{t+1} = P_t$ in Equation 9.3. This corresponds to $r = 1$. Otherwise, a proportion of the past expectation error is factored into the present adjustment in expectation, that is, $0 \leq r \leq 1$. The value of r is clearly case-dependent and is determined by empirical data. It is noted that the absence of adaptive expectation ($r = 1$) can be treated as a hypothesis and can be tested.

On the other hand, storage level is assumed to follow the partial adjustment process such that

$$S_t = S_{t-1} + k (S^*_t - S_{t-1}) \tag{9.4}$$

That is, realised changes in the level of stocks ($S_t - S_{t-1}$) is a fraction of desired/planned changes ($S^*_t - S_{t-1}$). Complete realisation of desired changes is assumed not to take place because of certain costs or constraints, such as bad harvests, changed financial situation, various shocks to the market, and so on. Again, the fraction k ($0 \leq k \leq 1$) is case-dependent and is to be determined by data. Of course, complete realisation implies absence of partial adjustment. In this case, $k = 1$ in Equation 9.4 or $S_t = S^*_t$.

It is useful to point out that both adaptive-expectation and partial-adjustment processes bring dynamics into the storage model. Alternatives to these dynamic specifications, such as rational expectations, are available in the literature. However, all are hypotheses themselves and there is no conclusive theoretical or empirical evidence to justify a preference for one over another. Adaptive expectations and partial adjustment are adopted in this chapter because of their popularity and will be tested later in the chapter.

To obtain an estimable version of Equation 9.2, manipulations of both Equations 9.3 and 9.4 are necessary. Starting from Equation 9.4, it is easy to solve for S^*_t and equating the resultant expression with the right hand side of Equation 9.2:

$$1/k \, S_t + (1-1/k) \, S_{t-1} = a_0 + a_1 \, P^*_{t+1} + u_t$$

or

$$S_t = (1-k) \, S_{t-1} + ka_0 + ka_1 \, P^*_{t+1} + ku_t \tag{9.5}$$

Using L to denote the lag operator, Equation 9.3 can be written as (see Judge *et al.* 1985)

$$(1 - (1-r)L) \, P^*_{t+1} = r \, P_t \tag{9.6}$$

Defining $b = 1 - r$ and multiplying Equation 9.6 by $(1 - bL)^{-1}$ yields

$$P^*_{t+1} = r (1 - bL)^{-1} P_t$$

Substituting the above for P^*_{t+1} in Equation 9.5 produces

$$S_t = (1-k) \, S_{t-1} + ka_0 + ka_1 \, r (1 - bL)^{-1} P_t + ku_t \tag{9.7}$$

Multiplying both sides of Equation 9.7 by $(1-bL)$ gives

$$S_t(1 - bL) = ka_1 \, r \, P_t + (1- bL) \, [(1-k) \, S_{t-1} + ka_0 + ku_t]$$

or

$$S_t - b \, S_{t-1} = (1-k) \, S_{t-1} + ka_0 + ka_1 \, r \, P_t + ku_t - b(1-k) \, S_{t-2} - bka_0 - bku_{t-1}$$

This is equivalent to

$$S_t = (1-k+b)S_{t-1} + b(k-1) \, S_{t-2} + (1-b) \, k \, a_0 + ka_1 \, r \, P_t + ku_t - bku_{t-1}$$
$$= \gamma_1 + \gamma_2 S_{t-1} + \gamma_3 S_{t-2} + \gamma_4 P_t + kV_t \qquad (9.8)$$

where $\gamma_1 = (1-b) \, k \, a_0 = r \, k \, a_0$, $\gamma_2 = 1-k+b = 2 - r - k$, $\gamma_3 = b(k-1) = (1-r)(k-1)$, $\gamma_4 = k \, a_1 r$ and $V_t = u_t - bu_{t-1}$ is the new disturbance term. After obtaining estimates of γ_2 and γ_3, it is possible to solve for estimates of r and k as $r = 1 - 0.5(\gamma_2 \pm \tau)$ and $k = 1 + 0.5(-\gamma_2 \pm \tau)$, where $\tau = (\gamma_2^2 + 4 \, \gamma_3)^{0.5}$. Estimates of αs can then be recovered. These estimates are not unique unless $\tau = 0$.

Clearly, Equation 9.8 incorporates both adaptive expectations and partial adjustment. Absence of adaptive expectations (only partial adjustment prevails) is implied by $r = 1$ or $b = 0$. In this case, Equation 9.8 reduces to

$$S_t = (1-k) \, S_{t-1} + ka_0 + ka_1 \, P_t + ku_t$$
$$= \delta_0 + \delta_1 P_t + \delta_2 S_{t-1} + ku_t \qquad (9.9)$$

where the definitions of new notations are self-explanatory. Conversely, the absence of partial adjustment (only adaptive expectations prevails) is implied by $k = 1$. In this case, Equation 9.8 reduces to

$$S_t = b \, S_{t-1} + r \, a_0 + a_1 r \, P_t + u_t - bu_{t-1}$$
$$= \beta_0{}^* + \beta_1 P_t + \beta_2 S_{t-1} + V_t \qquad (9.10)$$

It is not difficult to show that if neither adaptive expectations nor partial adjustment exists, Equation 9.8 simply reduces to

$$S_t = a_0 + a_1 \, P_t + u_t \qquad (9.11)$$

Therefore, fitting Equations 9.8–9.11 to a set of data enables construction of appropriate statistics to test various hypotheses. If Equation 9.11 is rejected in favour of Equation 9.8, either or both of adaptive expectations and partial adjustment should be maintained. Otherwise, none of these dynamic specifications are acceptable.

Conditional on the rejection of Equation 9.11, the hypothesis of $\gamma_3 = 0$ can then be tested. By definition, $\gamma_3 = (1-r)(k-1)$. Thus, rejecting $\gamma_3 = 0$ means $k \neq 1$ as well as $r \neq 1$. Thus, both dynamic specifications were prevalent. It is important to note that once Equation 9.11 is rejected $k = 1$ and $r = 1$ cannot occur simultaneously. As a consequence, accepting $\gamma_3 = 0$ implies mutual exclusion of the two forms of dynamic specifications.

When $\gamma_3 = 0$ is concluded, it is necessary to distinguish partial adjustment of Equation 9.9 from adaptive expectations of Equation 9.10. In theory, this can be accomplished by testing $r = 1$ or $k = 1$. However, $r = 1 - 0.5(\gamma_2 \pm \gamma_2)$ and $k = 1 + 0.5(-\gamma_2 \pm \gamma_2)$ under $\gamma_3 = 0$. In this case, it is not possible to distinguish r from k. This lack of distinction is also evident if, ignoring the stochastic terms, Equations 9.9 and 9.10 are compared. However, Equations 9.9 and 9.10 do differ in the structure of the disturbance term. This difference provides a way of testing partial adjustment against adaptive expectations under alternative assumptions for u_t. In particular, if u_t is a white noise, V_t and kV_t would be MA(1) while ku_t remains a white noise. If u_t is AR(p), V_t and kV_t would be MA(p+1) while ku_t remains AR(p), where p denotes the order of autocorrelation or moving average.

It is useful to point out that what distribution and properties u_t really possesses is unknown and subject to numerous speculations. However, as mentioned by Rao and Miller (1971:169), it is often inevitable for one to take chances in econometrics. In other words, some maintained hypotheses would have to be introduced, particularly those relating to disturbance terms. A most common practice is to assume AR(1) for u_t. If AR(1) is accepted for the error terms in Equations 9.9 or 9.10, partial adjustment rather than adaptive expectations should be adopted. This, in turn, implies that r =1 and k = 1 - γ_2.

Grain storage motives in China and construction of the empirical model

The model specified in the preceding section is based on speculative theory. Assumptions underlying Equation 9.8 are unlikely to be consistent with situations in less developed countries (LDCs) (Renkow 1990). Observations from China indicate that significant price fluctuations co-exist with consistently rising household grain stocks in China. Such a phenomenon calls for alternative explanations of determinants of grain stock levels in China, beyond those of Williams and Wright (1991).

Motives for grain storage other than speculation

In a recent contribution, Park (1996) proposed that consumption smoothing is a dominant factor underlying the storage behaviour of Chinese farmers. In more concrete terms, households hold grain stocks for two reasons that are associated with inefficient or incomplete markets (Park 1996). These include attaining a convenience yield or the minimisation of transaction cost and food security. When transactions costs for selling and buying grains are high, farmers may decide to store enough grain to meet their own consumption requirements before the next harvest. The benefit of holding their own grain for consumption purposes is called the convenience yield and is equal to the costs saved if all grains had to be sold after harvest from production and bought back later for consumption needs.

Also, farmers may store grain for food security reasons, such as to insure households against rising prices. Although both monetary savings and storage are forms of intertemporal income transfer, only storage can provide food security by shielding the household from price risks. This is particularly so in a country like China where markets are absent or localised and production or yield risk is often reinforced by price risks.

To account for the motive of transactions cost minimisation in our study, a variable indicating market development is clearly needed. Grain purchase from the free market can be used but its absolute value may not be a good indicator as small purchases may be due to small consumption demands for raw grain in better-off or more developed areas. Consequently, the ratio of grain purchase to total grain consumption is utilised to indicate market development. It is conceivable that when the ratio approaches zero, consumption is completely drawn from their own production or storage, indicating absence of grain market. On the other hand, if the ratio approaches one, all consumption needs are satisfied from the market, indicating a high level of marketisation of grain production.

In considering food security the inclusion of insurance substitutes in the empirical model are required. These are represented by household savings, wealth status and off-farm income. Household savings and off-farm income are liquid assets and they can be used to purchase grain for consumption if needed. It is important to point out that whatever variables are used as indicators of insurance substitutes, they must not be directly and positively correlated with grain production. Under normal circumstances, those with substantial savings or high non-farm income are expected to hold less grain for two reasons. First, high-income families usually feel less threatened by grain shortages and subsequently stock less. Second, wealthier individuals are less risk averse. Non-liquid wealth may not be easily converted to cash in rural China. However, the level of wealth will affect decisionmakers' attitudes towards risk. Thus, it is relevant to include household wealth in the model. The best indicator of household wealth status is the value of housing. The wealth variable is expected to have a negative coefficient.

Given the above arguments, it is obvious that some stocks, say S_p, could be used for price speculation and the rest, say S_o, are attributable to other motives and other factors. Consequently, it is useful to rename S_t in the earlier discussions as S_p and then set $S_t = S_p + S_o$. Defining $S_o = g(X) + u^*$, where X is a vector of additional variables, the gain storage model for China can be written as

$$S_t = S_p + S_o$$
$$= \gamma_1 + \gamma_2 S_{t-1} + \gamma_3 S_{t-2} + \gamma_4 P_t + g(X) + V_t^* \qquad (9.12)$$

As argued earlier, some of the variables in X are related to food security and transactions cost minimisation motives. Others in X are control variables to be discussed below. The new disturbance term V^* is assumed to possess the same properties as V.

Control variables

In the complete absence of markets, all three motives discussed above become irrelevant. In this case, storage may simply represent a passive response to grain output shocks. That is, fluctuations in grain production will simply translate into stock changes, so stock level will be highly correlated with output. Even under efficient but localised markets, as output increases, given the inelastic demand of basic food items, prices will drop, sales will be down and stock levels will rise. On the other hand, when output is low, prices will be high and farmers will tend to draw their supplies from stocks. It is necessary to account for cross-region differences in production capacity. For that purpose, a per capita output variable will be included in the model.

In a country as large as China, the amount of grain held by a household will depend on the length of time until the next grain harvest. For example, in regions where spring sowing is possible, the stocks required would be less for consumption needs than otherwise. Obviously, this is related to cropping patterns, which differ from region to region in China. In the south, multiple cropping is common so households may only store enough grain for six months' consumption needs, while nine to twelve-month stocks are needed in the north. A variable controlling for this effect is the multiple cropping index, which would be negatively related to stock levels.

Livestock activities are expected to affect storage levels as well, since they can transform extra grain into cash income or alternative food substitutes. Meanwhile, some farmers will not consume the locally produced staple crop in one of the seasons. This happens in areas where maize is grown mainly for feed. Therefore, even though there are more than one cropping seasons within a year, these farmers may hold just as much for various motives as a household with only one cropping season. To control for these, a variable indicating the scope of household livestock activities is included. It is worth noting that grain output and livestock activities differ substantially over time and across regions in China.

In the area north of the Yangtze River (the rice and wheat regions of Jiangsu, Anhui, Hubei and Sichuan) where tastes and preferences favour rice, almost all wheat is marketed. In other words, households in these regions would hold one year of grain for its convenience yield or food security, despite high levels of multi-cropping. Dummy variables (DJ, DA, DH and DS) will be incorporated to control for this pattern of consumption preference.

Another dummy variable, DD, is needed to account for the infamous reintroduction of the grain trade monopoly in 1996. A time trend variable, T, is included to capture factors such as economic reforms, changing macroeconomic environment such as more liberalised policies, gradually changing ideology, the learning-by-doing of market instruments, the increasing availability of information and improved infrastructure.

Because price speculation is conditional on market development, it is useful to include the interactive variable MP, defined as MxP, into the model. Inclusion of this variable is justified because it may help to confirm that speculation effects are stronger in more developed areas.

The empirical model

Assuming g also takes a linear form, the standard storage model is to be extended by augmenting Equation 9.8 by g(X), where (time index is dropped when there is no confusion)

$$g(X) = \delta_4 M + \delta_5 I + \delta_6 W + \delta_7 Q + \delta_8 HH + \delta_9 MCI + \delta_{10} L + \delta_{11} DJ$$
$$+ \delta_{12} DA + \delta_{13} DH + \delta_{14} DS + \delta_{15} DD + \delta_{16} T + \delta_{17} MP + u^*$$

Given the above discussions and specification of g(X), the extended model becomes

$$S_t = \gamma_1 + \gamma_2 S_{t-1} + \gamma_3 S_{t-2} + \gamma_4 P_t + \delta_4 M + \delta_5 I + \delta_6 W + \delta_7 Q + \delta_8 HH +$$
$$\delta_9 MCI + \delta_{10} L + \delta_{11} DJ + \delta_{12} DA + \delta_{13} DH + \delta_{14} DS + \delta_{15} DD +$$
$$\delta_{16} T + \delta_{17} MP + V^*_t \qquad (9.13)$$

In Equation 9.13, M indicates market development (as defined earlier), I indicates insurance substitutes (defined as per capita net income from all sources other than farming plus per capita savings), W indicates wealth status (defined as per capita housing value), Q indicates production capacity (defined as per capita grain output), HH indicates household size (defined as number of family members). Household size (HH) is expected to have a negative impact on S as dictated by economies of scale in food demand or requirement. MCI indicates cropping pattern (defined as the multi-cropping index), L indicates livestock activity (defined as output value from livestock) and a group of dummy variables are as defined earlier.

Corresponding to the standard storage model, and dependent on the absence or presence of dynamics, the extended model may take the form of either Equations 9.13 or 9.14–9.16 as follows (disturbance terms are omitted). Absence of adaptive expectations produces

$$S_t = a_0^* + \delta_1 P_t + \delta_2 S_{t-1} + g(X) \qquad (9.14)$$

Absence of partial adjustment produces

$$St = \beta_0^* + \beta_1 P_t + \beta_2 S_{t-1} + g(X) \qquad (9.15)$$

If neither adaptive expectations nor partial adjustment exists, the extended model becomes

$$S_t = a_0 + a_1 P_t + g(X) \qquad (9.16)$$

It is noted that parameters in Equations 9.13–9.16 have the same symbols as in Equations 9.8–9.11. However, they are not equivalent. The same notations are used for easy exposition.

Hypotheses and hypotheses testing

Having specified the model, it is appropriate to consider the hypotheses and their testing. The three sets of motives for household grain storage lead to three sets of hypotheses.

- H_1: absence of price speculation

    As the expected price of grain rises (and it is expected to continue to rise), households will not store more grain. In the absence of price speculation, $a_1 = 0$ in Equation 9.1 and this is equivalent to $\gamma_4 = 0$ in Equations 9.8 or 9.13. However, $\gamma_4 = 0$ is only a necessary but not sufficient condition for accepting H_1. This is because $\gamma_4 = ka_1 r$ and k and/or r could be zero empirically, although in theory they are assumed to lie between zero and unity. Therefore, when $\gamma_4 = 0$ is accepted, it is necessary to recover the estimate of a_1 and test its significance.

- H_2: transactions cost minimisation
  In areas where markets are poor, transactions costs would be high and there is a greater motive to hold grain for its convenience yield. As the market develops, transactions costs are likely to decline and people may become more reliant on markets to provide food. As a consequence, stock levels are likely to fall. To test this motive, it is necessary to derive the marginal effect of market development on stock levels as $\delta_4 + \delta_{17}P$ and simply test $\delta_4 + \delta_{17}P = 0$ at the sample mean of P against $\delta_4 + \delta_{17}P < 0$.

- H_3: food security consideration
  By and large, farmers are risk averse (Anderson $et\ al.$ 1977). Poorer farmers will be more risk averse and thus will hold more grain for food security. It is postulated that the higher the non-farming income and savings, the less the farmer fears food insecurity. One would expect $\delta_5 < 0$ and $\delta_6 < 0$. Absence of food security motive is given by $\delta_5 = \delta_6 = 0$.

Data issues and preliminary analysis

It is common knowledge that Chinese data are often incomplete. This is particularly the case with market information. As price data are only available for 1987–97, this study is confined to that time span as far as empirical modelling is concerned. Currently there are 31 provinces and autonomous regions in China. However, price data for Xizhang (Tibet) and Xinjiang are incomplete. Chongqing became an autonomous city in 1996, so data for Chongqing will be merged with Sichuan. Similarly, data for Hainan will be merged with Guangdong. Thus, 26 provinces or regions are covered in this study.

Through the efforts of the China Center for Agricultural Policy, data on the required variables are compiled from various sources. With the exception of prices, most observations are available at the provincial level on a yearly basis from 1982 onwards. The free market price data are available separately on a monthly basis for rice, wheat, maize and soybean. However, the seasonality of agricultural production and trading dictates that prices for some months are non-existent. To obtain a yearly price indicator, a weighted average of monthly prices should be computed with trading volumes as the weights. Unfortunately, the absence of monthly volume data precludes such a possibility. As a consequence, a simple arithmetic average is used to convert monthly prices to yearly prices for each commodity. This is also the practice of statistical bureaus in China.

After the above conversion, there are still some price observations missing for some individual commodities and particular regions/years. Initially, it was thought that neighbouring prices could be used as proxies. However, it was found that prices in neighbouring regions do not always have similar values. This is understandable given the fragmented nature of markets in China. Price levels depend on transportation costs and local supply, demand and marketing conditions. Regional protection and trade blockages occur in China which also lead to price differences in different regions. Neighbouring regions, however, share similar price trends. This discovery prompts us to use extrapolation to fill in the small number of missing values for rice and wheat.

Across commodities, it was found that observed prices for different commodities display remarkably similar trends. When price levels are converted into price indices, the indices for rice, wheat and maize are almost equivalent in many cases. Clearly this is because prices for these products are highly correlated. Without such equivalence, aggregating prices across all products is necessary in order to obtain an overall grain price indicator. This would require trading volumes for various commodities that are only available for some years and only for rice and wheat. Under such equivalence, however, weighted averages based on major food items will be sufficient. Thus, a price index based on the prices of rice and wheat will be constructed and used as the regional grain price indicator. This was the practice undertaken by Renkow (1990) and Saha and Stroud (1994:528), who used the price of a major crop to represent the general grain price.

China's staple foods are rice and wheat and these are the grains farmers normally hold as stocks. Most southern regions grow rice while most northern regions grow wheat. However, there are many regions that grow and trade both. This is why the general grain price will be obtained as the weighted average of rice and wheat prices. The weights are based on the trading volumes of rice and wheat, averaged over the period 1987–97 for individual regions. The average is used because of the lack of complete time-series data on trading volumes.

It is noted that speculation can only occur in response to prices on the free market. Procurement prices are of little (if any) relevance in this context, as they are set once a year well before harvest and are known to not be subject to speculation. Although procurement prices are associated with the delivery quota, promises regarding both the price and quota have often proven to be empty. Only a small portion of grain produced is subject to government procurement where procurement prices may have relevance.

Observations on household stocks and other variables are available from various publications of the State Statistical Bureau (SSB, various years). Plots of the year-end stock data indicate that there is a general increasing trend in grain stock levels. This trend relates well to increases in grain outputs. Such a relationship is consistent with the fact that grain production in China is largely subsistent. The development of the market and increases in income may weaken this relationship. However, it will take time for farmers to learn how to use the market and change their ideology.

Preliminary data analysis reveals that substantial increases in stock levels occurred in 1994 and 1997 respectively, following increased outputs in 1993 and 1996. Similarly, an apparent drop occurred in 1996 for many regions. The drop clearly correlates with decreases in the production outputs in 1995. Drops in 1991 are likely to be a result of the substantially increased state purchase price even though grain output increased in 1990. On the other hand, 1985, 1988,1992, and 1994–95 saw drops in output which had little impact on stock levels, except in the last case.

There is clearly an asymmetric pattern relating output and stock levels. This asymmetry is attributable to two major factors. First, risk-sharing may have played a role. That is, farmers dispose of less grains in years of adverse harvest in order to maintain stock levels. Second, the lack of market development implies that isolated markets cannot be relied on for grain disposal. In years of adverse harvest, price may be high but food security can take prevalence over profit motives. Conversely, in years of good harvest more disposals are hindered by the absence of an efficient market. Even if the market is present and efficient, no profit exists for grain disposal.

Nevertheless, one would expect a convergence in the stock levels as the national economy moves towards integration and the farming sector becomes more commercialised. However, this is not clearly evident, as the cross-region differences in stock levels seem to have been maintained over years. One possible explanation lies in the habit of storing grains. As with other habits, it takes time for farmers to change their ideology and traditional practices even if markets are fully developed, let alone when the markets are largely isolated as in rural China.

Substantial inflation and deflation have occurred in China since the 1980s. Subsequently, it is important to deflate those observations in value terms. The regional consumer price indices (CPIs) compiled by Wan (2001) are to be used for this purpose.

Model estimation and selection

Given the availability of cross-sectional data, three approaches can be used to estimate the model. The first is the random effects or error components approach

(Wan and Anderson 1990; Wan *et al.* 1992 for applications to China). The second is the so-called fixed effects or dummy variable approach (Fan 1991; Wan and Chen 2001). The third is the Kmenta procedure (Kmenta 1971). For applications to China, see Wan (1996a and 1996b).

There are no clear-cut conclusions as to which is the superior approach. Applied researchers choose an approach according to the research problem at hand and their individual preferences. The Kmenta procedure is used in this chapter, primarily because it accounts for both autocorrelations over time for each region and heteroscedasticity across regions. Meanwhile, this approach enables distinction between the partial adjustment and adaptive expectations, as discussed elsewhere in this chapter. The Kmenta procedure also converges to the maximum likelihood upon iterations.

Subsequently, Equation 9.13 was fitted to the Chinese data using the Kmenta procedure. Three versions of Equation 9.13 were obtained: (1) no autocorrelation was assumed at all. That is, the coefficient of autocorrelation $\rho = 0$ for all regions; (2) the same autocorrelation was assumed (that is, AR(1) with an identical ρ for all regions); and (3) different ρ for different regions. Heteroscedasticity is always permitted.

By convention, it is necessary to devise a sequence of tests to aid model selection. Towards this end, a four-stage testing procedure is developed as shown in Figure 9.1. Since there exists no a priori knowledge on the error structure and hypothesis testing could be affected by the assumptions on the error structure, all tests are to be carried out under each of the three versions of Equation 9.13. Hopefully, this will help minimise the possibility of incorrect testing due to mis-specification of the disturbance term.

This procedure starts with testing the applicability of equation extensions proposed in this chapter. This is followed by testing the presence or absence of dynamics in the model. At the third stage, the specific form of dynamics (that is, partial adjustment and adaptive expectations co-exist or are mutually exclusive) is tested.

Finally, tests are used to choose between adaptive expectations and partial adjustment. It is noted that while jointly testing γ_2 and γ_3 is needed in assessing the presence or absence of dynamics (stage 2), the significance of parameter γ_2 becomes irrelevant at stage 3. Nevertheless, unless both dynamics are supported by data, $\gamma_3 = (1-r)(k-1) = 0$ must be true (either $r = 1$ and/or $k = 1$). On the other hand, as long as one form of dynamics exists, then $k \neq 1 (r = 1)$ or $r \neq 1$ $(k = 1)$. If this is the case, $0 \leq k-1+r \leq 1$ and $\gamma_2 = 1 - (k-1+r)$ must be between zero and one.

The first two stages can be accomplished by using Wald's Chi-square test. The test statistic is tabulated in Table 9.1. As indicated on the top panel of Table 9.1, in all cases the standard model is rejected. A major implication is that in LDCs, and particularly in China, the standard storage theory and models are not applicable without modification. In other words, motives other than price speculation are important in explaining farmers' storage behaviour. The existence of partial adjustment and/or adaptive expectations behaviour is confirmed by the Chi-square values in the middle panel of Table 9.1. This is so at any level of significance and under all specifications of the error structure. Thus, dynamic forces play a role in determining household grain stocks in China.

The attempt to identify the actual form of dynamics proves to be difficult as t-tests (see bottom panel of Table 9.1) produce conflicting results depending on the structure of the error term. Under the most restrictive and the most general specifications, however, $\gamma_3 = 0$ cannot be rejected at the 5 per cent significance level. Further, the findings from stage 4 (Table 9.2) indicate that the most general specification (autocorrelation differs from region to region) is most preferred. Therefore, it is concluded that the empirical data do not support simultaneous existence of partial adjustment and adaptive expectations: only one dynamic specification is consistent with the observed behaviour.

Which dynamic specification is consistent with the data, partial adjustment or adaptive expectations? To address this question, it is necessary and sufficient to verify the structure of the disturbance term. In general, any test on the structure of the error term is necessary but insufficient for obtaining conclusive answers to the question. In this particular context, however, the test or tests would be sufficient simply because earlier tests have made it clear that the two dynamic specifications are mutually exclusive. Of course, it is impossible to exhaust all possible error structures for u. Attention has been confined to three possibilities: white noise, identical AR(1) and differing AR(1).

The relevant test statistic is essentially equivalent to a generalised likelihood ratio, as outlined in Mood *et al.* (1974:Section 5.1). If all regions have the same variance, an F-test rather than a Chi-square test should be used. The former possesses small sample properties while the latter is only valid

---

Table 9.1   Model selection tests

	Error structure					
H_0	$u_{it} = \rho_i u_{it-1} + v_{it}$		$u_{it} = \rho u_{it-1} + v_{it}$		$u_{it} = v_{it}$	
	Chi-square value					
All $\delta s = 0$	311.648	(-)	196.778	(-)	242.313	(-)
$\gamma_2 = \gamma_3 = 0$	119.331	(-)	141.074	(-)	163.784	(-)
	t-ratio					
$\gamma_3 = 0$	1.243	(0.214)	2.94	(0.003)	1.692	(0.091)

Note: Figures in parentheses are levels of significance.

Figure 9.1   Model selection procedure

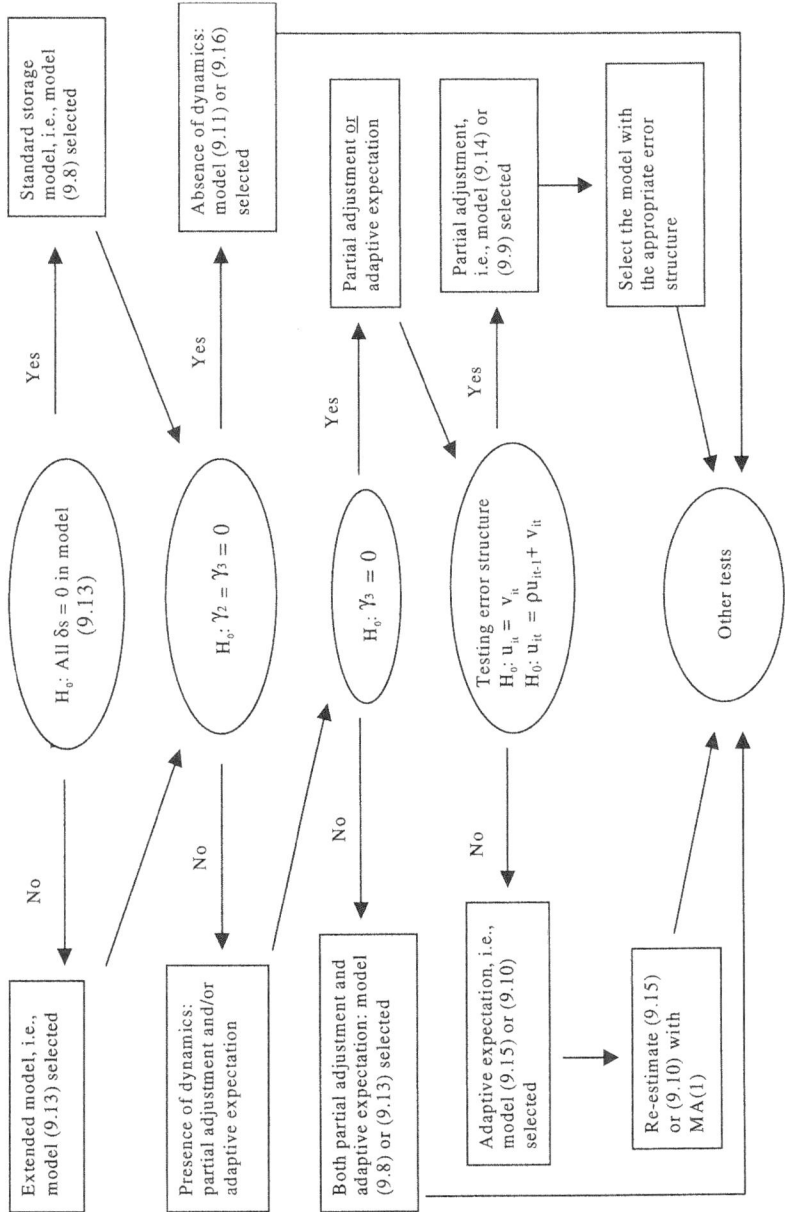

asymptotically. Given the large sample size and the generality of the heteroscedasticity specification in the Kmenta procedure, the Chi-square test will be applied where possible.

Following Wan (1996b), the test statistic is simply -2 (ln λ_R - ln λ_U). The subscripts R and U stand for restricted and unrestricted models respectively and λs denote the relevant likelihood values. Given that there are 26 regions in the panel data, the degrees of freedom can easily be worked out (Table 9.2).

Absence of autocorrelation is rejected in favour of identical autocorrelation, which is in turn rejected in favour of different autocorrelation for different regions (Table 9.2). Further, AR(1) is accepted whether γ_3 = 0 or not. As discussed earlier, the acceptance of AR structure implies the acceptance of partial adjustment. Although heteroscedasticity is not tested, given the substantial differences in stock levels and vastly diverse socio-economic conditions across regions, it would be unreasonable to assume homoscedasticity.

In short, the model finally selected is the one with proposed augmentation, heteroscedasticity and differing ρ for different regions. Because both dynamics do not prevail simultaneously, γ_3 must be set to zero in the final model. Further, acceptance of partial adjustment and rejection of adaptive expectations imply k = 1 - γ_2 and r = 1 or b = 0.

Results and discussions

Estimation results based on the most preferred model are presented in Table 9.3. Judging from the Buse's R^2, the model fits the data well. Most of the parameters are significantly different from zero except the wealth variable, which was included to account for the possible impacts of risk attitudes on stock levels. The signs of the estimates are all consistent with expectations, although one might argue for a negative coefficient for the variable of market development.

The marginal impact of market development on household stocks is given by 4.845 - 0.072 P, which would be less than zero as long as P is greater than 67.3. The sample average of the price variable is 57.25. Thus, market development does not help reduce household stocks. A formal statistical test produced a Wald χ^2-value of 2.14 which indicates that the market variable is not significant in explaining household storage decisions. Given this finding, the hypothesis of transactions cost minimisation is rejected. This rejection is unsurprising given that the level of household grain stocks has been consistently increasing despite the noticeable development of rural markets since the 1980s. From a theoretical perspective, the convenience yield concept is closely related to the opportunity cost of labour. When the opportunity cost is virtually zero (as in most rural areas of China), convenience yield will be negligible. This is probably why the hypothesis of transactions cost minimisation is rejected.

Table 9.2 **Model selection tests: testing error structure** (cf. Figure 10.1)

	Chi-square value $\gamma_3 \neq 0$	$\gamma_3 = 0$	Degrees of freedom	Critical value (test size = 5%)
$H_0: u_{lt} = v_{lt}$				
	19.257	24.400	1	13.84
$H_1: u_{lt} = \rho u_{lt-1} + v_{lt}$				
$H_0: u_{lt} = \rho u_{lt-1} + v_{l}$				
	43.264	46.416	25	37.70
$H_1: u_{lt} = \rho_l u_{lt-1} + v_{lt}$				

Table 9.3 **Estimation results**

Variable	Estimate	Asymptotic T-ratio	Level of significance
St_{-1}	0.456	11.530	-
P	0.920	2.041	0.041
M	4.845	2.604	0.009
I	-0.080	-3.833	-
Q	0.392	14.070	-
HH	-33.136	-4.615	-
MCI	-78.748	-8.150	-
L	0.256	2.190	0.028
W	-6.862	-0.140	0.888
P*M	-0.072	-2.287	0.022
Time trend	4.860	4.854	-
Dummies			
DA	-21.795	-0.952	0.341
DJ	-34.724	-3.537	-
DH	-53.463	-5.747	-
DS	-17.875	-1.769	0.077
DD	-78.442	-9.662	-
Constant	219.400	3.967	-

Buse $R^2 = 0.947$ Buse Raw-moment $R^2 = 0.993$

This rejection also means that food security and price speculation dominate the motives of grain storage in rural China.

Food security motives are related to income and wealth variables. Both are associated with negative coefficient estimates that signal the acceptance of the hypothesis of food security consideration. The coefficient of the income variable is significant while the wealth variable is insignificant. This insignificance is perhaps unsurprising given the level of data aggregation. Household-level data are better in assessing the impact of diminishing risk aversion in general.

To analyse the price effect, the marginal impact of the price variable is needed. This is given by 0.92 - 0.072 M. Since M $\leq$ 1 by definition, increases in (expected) prices lead to increases in storage levels. To confirm the speculative motive, it is useful to recover the estimate of α_1 and compute its standard error. Referring to the definitions below Equation 9.8 and given that r = 1 and k = 1 - γ_2, it is easy to find that $\alpha_1 = \gamma_4/(1 - \gamma_2)$. Its asymptotic variance can be obtained as Var(γ_4)/k^2 + Var(γ_2) (γ_4 /k^2)^2 - 2 Cov (γ_2, γ_4) /k^3. The estimate of the parameter is 1.69 and that of the standard error is 0.93. This value is positive and statistically significant, implying the existence of speculative motive. In fact, more market-developed areas are associated with smaller responsiveness to price changes. This may imply the localised nature of markets in less developed areas.

The estimates of k, α_1 and α_0 are found to be 0.544, 1.69 and 403.31 respectively. The positive signs and magnitudes of these estimates are not inconsistent with a priori expectations. It is interesting to note that the estimated value of k is 0.544 which lies in the range (0, 1). The significance of γ_2 implies the significance of k, which in turn provides further support for the dynamic specification of partial adjustment.

As expected, most of the control variables are significant. In particular, local production capacity is positively related to stock levels. This implies that to a large extent, supply shocks are absorbed by grain storage. The estimated coefficient suggests that about 0.4 kg of grain would be stored following every 1kg increase in production. Similarly, multiple cropping exerts quite a large and significant negative impact on household stocks.

Summary

To answer the question posed in the title of the chapter, price does matter. That is, rural farmers in China do engage in speculative activities. In fact, the more developed the grain markets, the more active the speculative activities, thus the smaller the marginal price impact. A secondary finding is that households in rural China tend to adjust their stock levels based on partial adjustment dynamics, not adaptive expectations. Food security but not transactions cost consideration affects farmers' grain storage behaviour as well.

Alternative frameworks including system approaches are not adopted due to the lack of data and associated assumptions of complete product and factor markets. The ad hoc specification used here is a direct result of the unavailability of data, which prevents us from modelling household behaviour in an optimising and system framework. The maintained hypothesis of optimisation may not be compatible with reality in China given the subsistence nature and backward product and factor markets (see Rabin 1998 for inadequacy of existing utility theory). The optimising model comes with further costs. For example, the linear production function is often assumed to simplify the system model and make the model empirically estimable (Saha 1994; Park 1996).

Saha and Stroud (1994) proposed a model where consumption, storage and labour supply are estimated jointly as SUR. However, it is well known that SUR with identical regressors, as in Saha and Stroud (1994) can be estimated separately. In other words, our focus on the storage equation is unlikely to suffer from system equation bias.

Acknowledgments

This report is prepared under the support of the China Center for Agricultural Policy. I wish to thank Professor Jikun Huang (Director), Professor Linxiu Zhang (Deputy Director) and Professor Scott Rozelle of University of California for various inputs into the research.

10

Part-time farming trends in China

Zhang Yue Zhou, Daniel A. Sumner and Hyunok Lee

Since the Chinese government instituted a strict policy restricting rural labour movement in the early 1960s, a huge labour force has been retained in agriculture. Currently, the labour force that is in excess of farming requirements is estimated in the order of over 200 million. To sustain China's economic development, it is argued that this labour force needs to be absorbed into non-farming activities (Zhou *et al.* 1992; Johnson 1999).

Broadly, there are two major paths through which labour can be shifted out of farming activities: leaving the farm completely and moving to other industries; or remaining farm-based and where possible engaging in non-farming activities. The latter has often been referred to as part-time farming. While any large-scale relocation of farm labour may not be expected in the near future, there is already an emerging trend towards part-time farming.

Hence, an understanding of the development of part-time farming in China would be invaluable for both academic inquiry and policy formulation. Unfortunately, despite the fact that there is a rich literature that addresses the agricultural labour issue in general, studies that examine the part-time farming issue in China remain scarce. A few such examples include Yang and Cai (1991), Tian and Shi (1991), Ye (1992), and Zhang *et al.* (1996).

Yang and Cai (1991) suggest a model of decision making on part-time farming behaviour and examine factors that affect part-time farming behaviour using macro-level data. Tian and Shi (1991) offer a broad discussion on the social and economic background of part-time transfer of agricultural labour and the relationships between part-time transfer, industrialisation, urbanisation and agricultural development. They point out that part-time transfer can be used as a practical choice for transferring agricultural labour in China.

Using cross-sectional farm survey data, Zhang *et al.* (1996) describe the part-time farming situation and the impact of part-time farming on farm households in ten provinces in 1994. Using 1986 survey data, Wan (1995) assesses rural-rural, rural-urban and urban-rural migration in China. Rozelle *et al.* (1999) examine rural-urban migration using cross-sectional data collected in 1996 from eight provinces in China.

Few have attempted to empirically assess the historical trend of part-time farming in China. This study, using ten-year farm-level survey data, examines the development of part-time farming in China. The two key research questions we attempt to answer are how part-time farming evolves over time and whether part-time farming may be related to regional economic development.

Factors affecting part-time farming

Part-time farming can be found in many countries (see Jussaume 1991; Loyns and Kraut 1992; Tweeten *et al.* 1993; Ali 1995; Weiss 1997). Part-time farming is an important way for farmers to divert family labour to non-farming activities. There are some major factors that affect the allocation of on-farm and off-farm labour.[1]

Technical change

Capital input using technical change will substitute capital with labour. The output effect induced by the increase in the marginal product of labour input would positively affect the demand for labour but with a quasi-fixed input (in this case, land) the negative substitution effect will be greater. As a result, part-time transfer will take place when farmers try to utilise their labour best but cannot completely leave their farm due to farming needs.

Land system

In countries where land is equally distributed and land transfer is restricted, part-time farming will evolve.

Relative return

It is common that farming has a relatively lower return, as often observed in disparity of rural and urban incomes. The desire to obtain a higher return and maximise family income is an important force driving farmers to engage in non-farming activities.

Traditional land ideology

In some countries, farmers are so attached to their land that they do not want to give it up. Some perceive their land as security or family insurance where social security programs are lacking. This leads them to hold onto their land even if their non-farming income is very high.

Urbanisation and industrialisation

Rapid urbanisation and industrialisation mean a higher capacity to absorb agricultural labour.

Dual social structure

Where rural and urban areas are separated by administrative forces, there is little chance for agricultural labour to leave farming completely and be engaged in urban industrial activities. It can only take part in non-farming activities within rural areas.

In China, all of the above factors play a role in inducing the development of part-time farming, and indeed, there is already a trend towards part-time farming. While this trend has important implications in government policy formation, this issue has received little attention. This study attempts to fill this gap by using farm-level survey data to assess the status of part-time farming in China.

Conceptual considerations and data

What is part-time farming?

Part-time farming refers to 'the practice whereby a farm worker or farm family earns income from both agricultural and non-agricultural employment or self-employment' (Jussaume 1991:3). Part-time farming is not unique to modern times or to developed nations. 'It is an option that agriculturally dependent households around the world have exercised for generations. Only the recognition of the importance of part-time farming is new' (Jussaume 1991:3). While there is consensus about the notion of part-time farming, the technical definition differs slightly by country. This chapter adopts the classification of part-time farming that has been used in Japan. The Organisation for Economic Cooperation and Development (OECD) also adopts Japan's classification of part-time farming (Krasovec 1982, cited in Jussaume 1991:48).

In Japan part-time farming is defined as 'very small farms and any farm in which one or more household members are engaged in jobs other than farming' (OECD 1995:14–15). More detailed classification includes (OECD 1995:11)[2]

- Part-time farm household. Farming household which has one or more household members engaged in jobs other than farming and where they have been employed for 30 days or more, or engaged in their own non-farm business from which they have earned 100,000 yen in 1990 (70,000 yen in 1980) or more, during a year.
- Part-time farm household Type I: Farm household where less than 50 per cent of income was earned from non-farm jobs.

- Part-time farm household Type II: Farm household where more than 50 per cent of income was earned from non-farm jobs.
- Full-time farm household: Farm household which has no household member engaged in non-farm employment.

Data

Farm-level survey data are regularly collected by the Research Centre for Rural Economy (RCRE) of the Ministry of Agriculture in China. The survey first began in 1986 and was carried out annually except in 1992 and 1994. In each village, some 100 households were surveyed. The survey instruments have evolved over the years. Those used for 1986–91 were the same (with 312 variables) but they were expanded for the 1993 survey (with 394 variables) and further expanded for the 1995–97 surveys (with 439 variables). Data used in this study cover the period 1986–97.

For this study, three provinces representing the different stages of economic development are selected. They include Guangdong, which represents the most developed; Hubei, which represents medium development; and Yunnan, which represents the least developed. Three villages are then selected again from each province according to the level of economic development as measured by per capita income. Brief background information on the selected provinces and villages is presented in Table A10.1 (see Appendix 10.1).

In the farm household surveys by the RCRE, there are nine categories of major family business activities: (1) cropping, (2) forestry, (3) animal husbandry, (4) fishery, (5) industry, (6) construction, (7) transportation, (8) tertiary services, and (9) others. Since the rural economic reforms, farms have been allowed to diversify their farm activities in any of these categories.

In this study, activities belonging to categories 1–4 are considered as farming and the rest as non-farming (categories 5–9).[3] Detailed data on labour-days used for each of the nine business activities are available from the household survey. To ensure the accuracy of data, we used a number of variables to cross-check the data. Whenever doubt arose about observation, that observation was eliminated.

Empirical results

Figure 10.1 shows the historical trend of part-time farming for the data combining all three provinces. Three observations stand out. First, for the period under examination, part-time farming (both Type I and Type II) is significant, at close to 50 per cent. Second, the majority of part-time farming households are Type II. Third, part-time farming peaked in 1993 and then began to slow.

The part-time farming trend broken down at the provincial level is shown in Figure 10.2. As expected, Guangdong province shows the highest part-timing farming trend, consistent with its economic development. This is also the region where the post 1993 downturn of part-time farming did not occur. Further, while the bulk of part-time farm households are Type II, the share of Type I part-time farm households has been steadily declining, reaching 2 per cent in 1997. In the economically least-developed Yunnan province, part-time farming development fluctuates most and has declined sharply (from 50 per cent in 1993 to 32 per cent in 1997). It also has a higher proportion of Type I part-time farm households. In the economically medium-developed Hubei province, the part-time farming level is below that of Yunnan, the economically least-developed region. This is due to the fact that one of the villages included in the analysis for Yunnan (Village 1) is in a wealthy area with a very high part-time farming level (Table 10.1).

When we examine the data at the village-level (Table 10.1), it is observed that in general, in economically more developed areas, such as all three villages in Guangdong province and in Yunnan's Village 1, part-time farming is taking place at a much higher level (50 per cent or higher) and is increasing. On the other hand, the level of part-time farming in medium or less-developed areas is accordingly lower. This indicates that the level of local economic development is an important factor for the emergence of part-time farming in a region. It is interesting to note that the poorest village (Village 2 in Yunnan) once had a very high part-time farming level (65 per cent in 1993) but dropped sharply

Figure 10.1   Part-time farming trends in China (all three provinces)

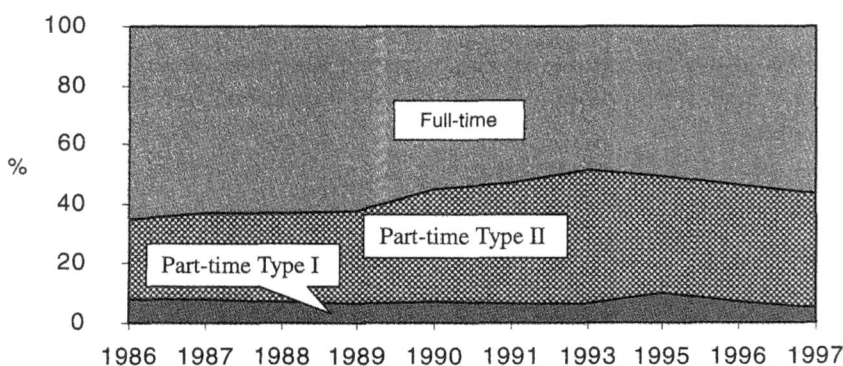

Source: Calculated from the survey data.

Part-time farming trends in China

Figure 10.2   Part-time farming trends at the provincial level

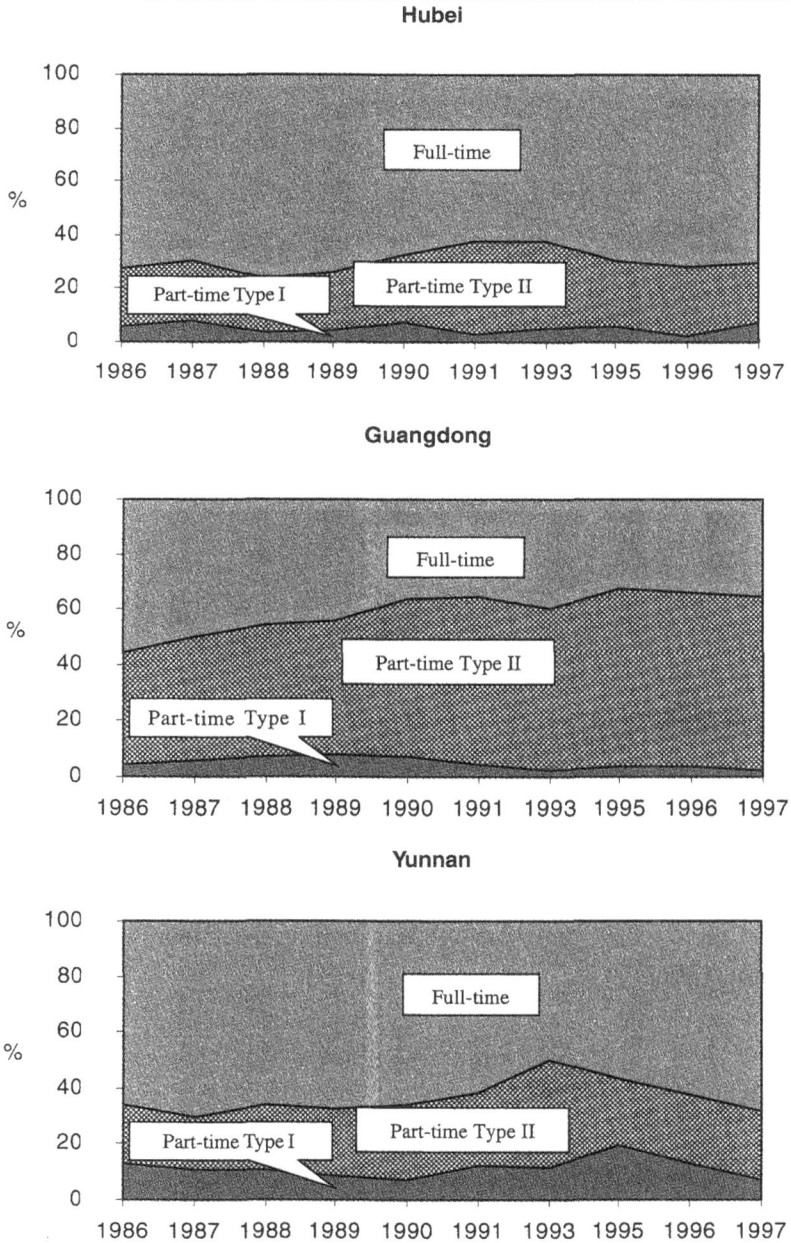

Hubei

Guangdong

Yunnan

Source: Calculated from the survey data.

Table 10.1   Part-time farming trends in China at the village level (1986–97)

	1986	1987	1988	1989	1990	1991	1993	1995	1996	1997
Hubei province, Village 1										
Full-time	82	83	76	77	..	73	57	62	78	75
Part-time	18	17	24	23	..	27	43	38	22	25
Type I	4	1	4	1	..	1	-	4	2	6
Type II	14	16	20	22	..	26	43	35	20	19
Hubei province, Village 2										
Full-time	44	41	58	50	49	27	45	69	63	56
Part-time	56	59	42	50	51	73	55	31	37	44
Type I	12	13	4	10	12	4	12	5	2	8
Type II	45	46	38	40	39	69	43	26	36	36
Hubei province, Village 3										
Full-time	93	84	92	92	89	89	85	79	78	82
Part-time	7	16	8	8	11	11	15	21	22	18
Type I	2	10	3	2	2	3	3	8	2	6
Type II	5	6	6	7	9	8	12	13	20	12
Guangdong province, Village 1										
Full-time	70	63	54	49	40	42	51	51	50	51
Part-time	30	38	46	51	60	58	49	49	50	49
Type I	8	10	17	10	11	9	-	-	1	1
Type II	23	27	29	41	49	49	49	49	49	48
Guangdong province, Village 2										
Full-time	42	35	40	45	41	39	45	34	35	46
Part-time	58	65	60	55	59	61	55	66	65	54
Type I	3	2	2	4	4	1	3	4	7	3
Type II	55	63	57	51	55	60	52	62	58	51
Guangdong province, Village 3										
Full-time	58	54	43	38	28	26	24	13	16	10
Part-time	42	46	57	62	72	74	76	87	84	90
Type I	2	5	3	9	6	2	3	7	4	2
Type II	39	41	53	53	66	72	73	80	80	87
Yunnan province, Village 1										
Full-time	50	57	41	49	46	48	38	41	43	35
Part-time	50	43	59	51	54	53	62	59	57	65
Type I	7	6	6	4	4	1	-	-	1	4
Type II	43	37	53	47	51	51	62	59	56	61
Yunnan province, Village 2										
Full-time	79	85	78	73	67	55	35	49	61	83
Part-time	21	15	22	27	33	45	65	51	39	17
Type I	14	10	14	11	11	26	22	41	31	14
Type II	7	5	8	16	21	19	43	10	8	3
Yunnan province, Village 3										
Full-time	65	67	74	75	84	80	76	78	80	84
Part-time	35	33	26	25	16	20	24	22	20	16
Type I	17	15	13	9	7	8	13	14	4	4
Type II	17	18	14	16	10	12	11	8	15	12

Source: Calculated from the farm survey data.

in recent years (17 per cent in 1997). This phenomenon may have been dictated by the availability of non-farm employment. It is possible that many farmers from this poor village look for employment opportunities outside farming. Therefore, their non-farm activities also fluctuate with outside opportunities. This is consistent with the situation that prevailed in China during that time period.

In the early 1990s, there were increased numbers of farmers who travelled around the country to look for employment opportunities and there were abundant reports about this trend (see for example, Chen and Xu 1993; Zhu 1993; Wang 1994; Research Group 1995). As reflected in the results from this study (Figure 10.1), part-time farming level increased and peaked in 1993. Then, as urban economic reforms went further, employment for urban dwellers became a problem. Many city governments imposed restrictions on employment for rural labourers (Cai and Chan 2000). Soon many of the rural labourers had to return to their land and part-time farming declined (Figure 10.1). The reverse may also be true; reduced restrictions on farmers' employment in urban areas would result in increases in part-time farming. It is likely that government policy has an important bearing on the rise and fall of part-time farming, particularly in the case of Village 2 of Yunnan.

In addition to the level of local economic development and government policy, there are a number of other factors that affect the development of part-time farming, such as per capita arable land (Figure 10.3). The average landholding over the three-provinces is about one mu (1/15 hectare).

Figure 10.3   Per capita arable land (mu)

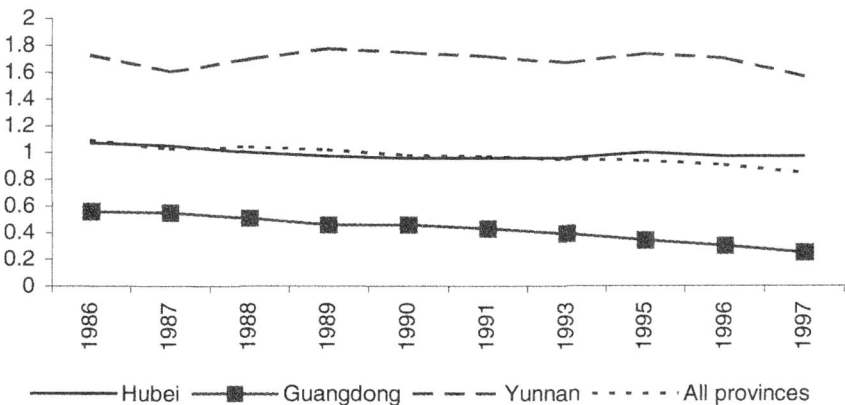

Source: Calculated from the survey data.

Guangdong's higher level of part-time farming is in part related to the low per capita arable land. Figure 10.3 shows that per capita arable land has declined over time; faster in more developed regions. If this trend continues, we will observe growth of part-time farming.

Figure 10.4 presents the ratio of non-farm earnings to farm earnings per labour-day. In all provinces and years studied, non-farm earnings have been higher than farm earnings. This encourages employment away from the farm. Note that this ratio was greatest in 1993 and the part-time farming level peaked during the same year (Figure 10.1). Johnson (1999) noted that '[t]he margin between the return to farm and nonfarm labour must be large enough to induce a rapid transfer to nonfarm jobs'. The results from this study tend to support Johnson's proposition. Figure 10.4 indicates that while the provinces differ in ratio by some margin these differences became pronounced in 1993. It is interesting to note that these differences are more distinct at the village level (Table A10.2). However, comparing Table A10.2 with the part-time trend at the village level (Table 10.1), it is not clear that higher part-time farming is always related to higher income ratios.

Besides these exogenous factors such as earning ratios, part-time farm decisions are also affected by the individual's qualification (suitability) and transactions costs. Whether an individual can start up his non-farming activities,

Figure 10.4   Ratio of per labour-day income between non-farming and farming employment

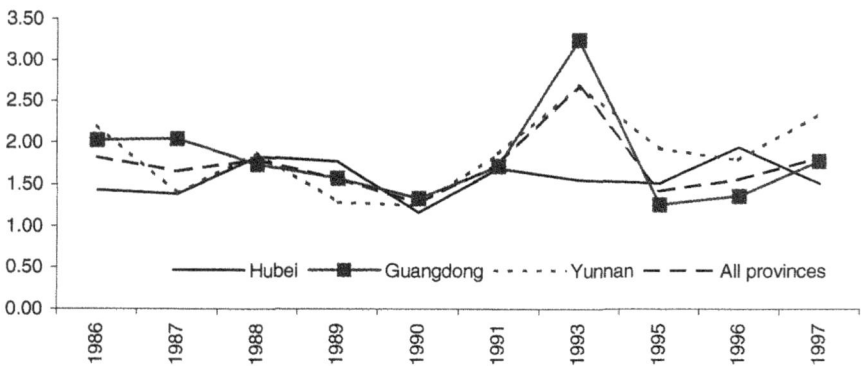

Source: Calculated from the survey data.

Figure 10.5   Per family expenditure on cultural items (yuan/year)

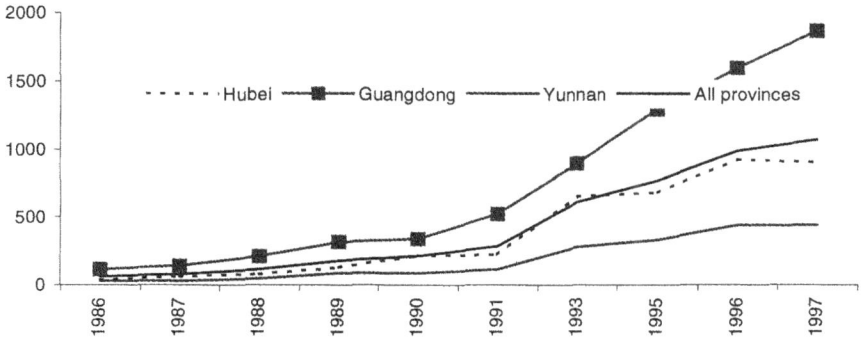

Source: Calculated from the survey data.

Figure 10.6   Number of radios/recorders owned per family

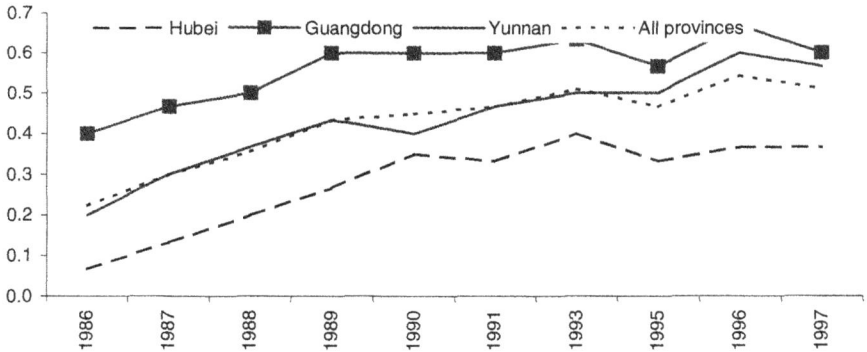

Source: Calculated from the survey data.

Figure 10.7   Number of TVs owned per family

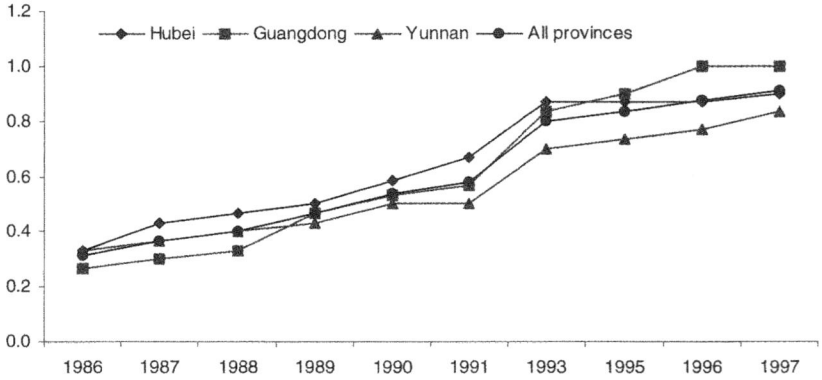

Source: calculated from the survey data.

Figure 10.8   Percentage of illiterate or semi-illiterate rural labourers

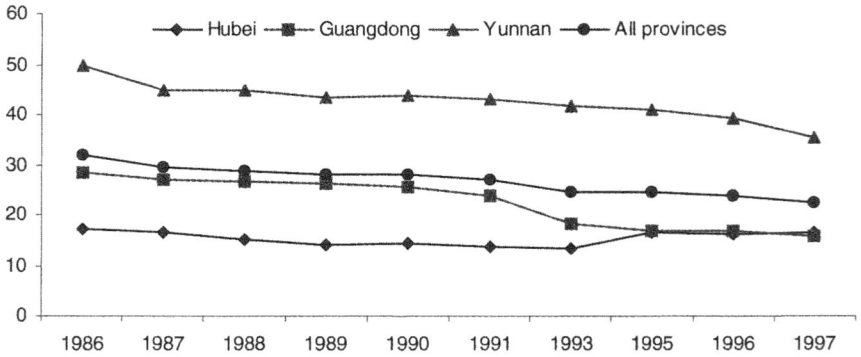

Source: Calculated from the survey data.

Table 10.2   **Education of rural labourers at the village level (1986–97)**

Province	Village	1986	1987	1988	1989	1990	1991	1993	1995	1996	1997
Illiterate and semi-illiterate rural labourers (%)											
Hubei	1	12	10	11	9	10	11	11	8	6	10
	2	25	25	22	22	20	20	12	18	18	16
	3	15	14	12	11	13	10	17	23	24	23
Guangdong	1	10	10	11	13	13	11	5	4	3	3
	2	40	38	37	36	34	34	24	25	29	28
	3	35	33	32	30	30	27	26	21	18	16
Yunnan	1	16	14	11	14	12	11	10	13	9	9
	2	90	92	89	87	88	87	85	84	85	81
	3	43	29	35	30	32	31	30	26	24	16
Rural labourers who completed primary school (%)											
Hubei	1	47	48	44	47	45	43	42	43	47	47
	2	32	31	31	33	32	33	30	34	30	32
	3	44	43	45	43	47	51	45	39	35	38
Guangdong	1	65	66	65	63	61	58	61	60	56	52
	2	33	35	36	37	36	36	39	41	37	40
	3	34	37	39	40	38	38	39	41	42	43
Yunnan	1	56	55	55	53	56	56	49	46	49	47
	2	9	7	10	10	10	10	14	13	13	17
	3	35	47	45	48	47	46	45	50	50	58
Rural labourers who completed junior high school (%)											
Hubei	1	31	32	33	32	33	33	41	43	41	37
	2	32	33	35	33	37	36	49	40	43	41
	3	34	37	36	40	37	35	33	33	36	35
Guangdong	1	21	22	22	22	24	26	28	29	35	37
	2	23	24	24	25	25	26	30	28	28	26
	3	25	25	23	24	26	28	29	30	32	30
Yunnan	1	27	27	30	29	27	28	37	36	33	35
	2	1	1	2	2	2	3	1	2	2	2
	3	20	23	18	20	19	21	23	23	25	24
Rural labourers who completed senior high school or above (%)											
Hubei	1	10	9	12	12	13	13	6	6	6	6
	2	11	11	12	12	11	11	9	8	8	11
	3	7	6	6	6	3	3	5	5	4	4
Guangdong	1	3	1	2	3	3	5	7	7	7	8
	2	4	4	3	3	4	4	7	5	6	6
	3	6	6	6	7	6	7	7	8	8	12
Yunnan	1	1	3	4	5	5	5	3	5	8	8
	2	..	..	..	..	..	..	..	..	..	..
	3	2	2	2	2	2	2	2	1	1	2

Source: Calculated from the farm survey data.

whether he knows which non-farming activities to work on, and can market his non-farm products (or equivalently, if looking for a job elsewhere, whether he goes beyond the village to look for a job, knows where to look for a job, and is offered a job), depends on his education level, labouring skills and ability to obtain information. Figures 10.5–10.8 show that in Guangdong, there is a higher family expenditure on media items, radios, recorders and TVs with a lower percentage of rural labourers who are illiterate or semi-illiterate. The percentage of rural labourers who completed senior high school or above is also highest (Table 10.2). This indicates that rural labourers in Guangdong are likely to be better informed about the opportunities of local non-farm work, which is consistent with high part-time farming in Guangdong.

Besides TVs and radios, telephones and computers play an important role in obtaining information. Ownership of telephones by rural households was not recorded in the survey until 1993 and the ownership of computers was not recorded until 1997. As expected, the ownership of telephones and computers is higher in more economically affluent provinces. Village 3 in Guangdong has a high level of computer ownership (Table 10.3). Interestingly, it is in this village that the part-time farming level has increased most (Table 10.1).

It is noted that in Village 2 of Yunnan, the percentage of illiterate and semi-illiterate rural labourers is very high (92 per cent in 1987 and 81 per cent in 1997) and the proportion who completed junior high school or above is very low (2 per cent in 1997) (Table 10.2). Yet the part-time farming level

Table 10.3   Possession of telephones and computers at the village level

	Hubei			Guangdong			Yunnan		
	Vil 1	Vil 2	Vil 3	Vil 1	Vil 2	Vil 3	Vil 1	Vil 2	Vil 3
Telephone 1993									
No. of households	60	60	60	100	100	100	100	100	100
No. of telephones	1	..	..	31	2	11	15	..	..
Average per household	0.02	..	..	0.31	0.02	0.11	0.15	..	..
1997									
No. of households	60	60	60	100	80	100	100	100	100
No. of telephones	18	9	5	97	7	33	54	..	..
Average per household	0.30	0.15	0.08	0.97	0.09	0.33	0.54	..	..
Computer 1997									
No. of households	60	60	60	100	80	100	100	100	100
No. of computers	..	..	..	3	..	20	..	..	..
Average per household	..	..	..	0.03	..	0.20	..	..	..

Source: Calculated from the farm survey data.

was relatively higher, especially since the early 1990s (Table 10.1). It reached 65 per cent in 1993 but dropped sharply to 17 per cent in 1997. Table A10.3 shows that non-farm earnings by part-time households from this village are much lower compared to other villages.

It is likely that for farmers to take part in non-farm activities, they must have the internal desire, the intellectual and financial abilities, and there must be external opportunities for them to do so. This indicates that farmers' intellectual and financial abilities are crucial. These enable farmers to gather and digest information, to have the courage to look for non-farming job opportunities and to have the minimal labouring skills to be engaged or employed in non-farm work. Local economic development status, conditions of infrastructure, availability of markets for non-farm products, and government policies are important external factors. Not all of these external factors were addressed in this study due to the lack of data. Nonetheless, local economic development and the policy environment are two important factors affecting part-time farming development.

Concluding remarks

In this chapter we have assessed the status of part-time farming in China using farm-level survey data. Our findings indicate that part-time farming is significant in the regions of China examined. Overall, part-time farming was increasing over the period 1986–97. It peaked in 1993 but has slowed since then. Part-time farm households now account for more than 40 per cent of total farm households in the studied regions.

It seems that the level of local economic development is a major factor in the development of part-time farming in a region. In economically more-developed regions, part-timing farming is developing fast and is at a much higher level. In economically less-developed regions, part-time farming development is relatively slow and its growth inconsistent.

Government policy also has an important bearing on the development of part-time farming in China. With reduced restrictions on farmers' employment in non-farming activities or in urban areas, part-time farming increases; otherwise, many farm labourers have to return to or stay on their land. Other major factors that affect the development of part-time farming in China include the very small per capita arable land, income differences between farming and non-farming employment, farmers' education level and labouring skills and their ability to obtain and digest information.

The development of part-time farming in our data for China seems to have halted since the mid 1990s, especially in the poor areas. It has been widely recognised that this phenomenon is related to the sluggish market in recent years. However, following other countries' examples, there will be a further shift in the labour force from farming to non-farming. How to make this shift is an important area that calls for further investigation. Given the relatively more important role of public policy in China, this transition can be significantly aided by prudent policy planning.

Future policy can be directed towards carrying out needed institutional reforms, especially removing restrictions on rural employment in the urban areas. Carefully conceived policy measures are needed to increase the opportunities of non-farm employment for rural people within the rural areas. Such policy measures will help China to alleviate or avoid over-concentration of industrialisation and population and other associated social problems as occurred in Japan in the 1970s and in Korea in the 1980s. The availability and improvement of basic infrastructure in rural areas (such as roads, water, electricity and telecommunication facilities) is also essential.

Part-time farming is a complex issue. This present study is only a modest attempt to address a very small number of questions. Many more questions remain to be explored.

- To what extent has traditional land ideology affected the development of part-time farming in China?
- How fast is China's part-time farming likely to develop in the near future?
- How has part-time farming affected farmers' income in China?
- How has part-time farming development affected the life of rural people and rural community development?
- How has part-time farming affected agricultural production and how will it affect agricultural production in the future?
- What are the likely impacts of part-time farming on the preservation of rural traditions and institutions?
- What are the key institutional reforms that are needed to facilitate the development of part-time farming in China?

Jussaume (1991:xiv) notes that, '[a] great deal about part-time farming remains unknown to the scientific community'. This is especially true for China. This fact encourages an increase in research attention on the trends and development of part-time farming. This is an issue that China will have to face as it will affect China's long-term sustainable economic development.

Appendix 10.1

Table A10.1	Per capita rural income at the provincial, city/county and village level, 1997

Province	City/county	Village	Brief description of the region
Hubei (¥2,102)	Hanyang (¥3,189)	Village 1 (¥3,304)	A relatively developed region within the province with good transportation
	Hanchuan (¥2,424)	Village 2 (¥2,938)	Similar to Hanyang but slightly less developed
	Changyang (¥1,636)	Village 3 (¥1,784)	A hilly area with a less developed economy and market
Guangdong (¥3,468)	Dongguan (¥5,021)	Village 1 (¥10,667)	Highly industrialised area close to Guangzhou and Hong Kong
	Dianbai (n.a.)	Village 2 (¥2,411)	Relatively less developed area within Guangdong province
	Wuchuan (n.a.)	Village 3 (¥2,948)	Similar to Dianbai but in a coastal area
Yunnan (¥1,375)	Yuxi (¥3,248)	Village 1 (¥6,442)	A wealthier area with much injection from a highly developed tobacco industry
	Lanchang (¥578)	Village 2 (¥719)	Very remote and mountainous area, one of the poorest regions
	Dali (¥2,279)	Village 3 (¥2,114)	Very remote and mountainous area, one of the poorer regions with tourist resources

Notes: National level per capita income of rural population in 1997 was ¥2090. At the city/county level, there are no systematic data available for per capita income of rural population. Village level per capita income was calculated from the village sample survey data.
Sources: Ministry of Agriculture, 1997. *China's Agricultural Statistics*, China Agricultural Press, Beijing:433; Hubei Statistical Bureau, 1999. *Hubei Rural Statistical Yearbook 1999*, China Statistical Press, Beijing:391–92; Yunnan Statistical Bureau, 1998. *Yunnan Statistical Yearbook 1998*, China Statistical Press, Beijing:489–90; State Statistical Bureau, 1998. *China Statistical Yearbook*, China Statistical Press, Beijing:346.

Table A10.2   Ratio of per labour-day income between non-farming and farming employment

	Hubei			Guangdong			Yunnan		
Year	Vil 1	Vil 2	Vil 3	Vil 1	Vil 2	Vil 3	Vil 1	Vil 2	Vil 3
Per labour-day income from farming employment (yuan)									
1986	5	5	3	5	4	7	2	1	2
1987	6	6	3	6	5	6	5	1	3
1988	7	6	3	9	7	8	8	1	3
1989	8	7	3	7	10	9	10	2	2
1990	7	8	4	15	10	8	11	2	3
1991	6	7	3	15	10	7	10	2	3
1993	7	8	5	13	17	11	9	3	4
1995	19	15	7	70	18	18	16	5	8
1996	14	14	6	66	16	18	22	4	8
1997	18	13	8	44	14	14	16	4	9
Per labour-day income from non-farming employment (yuan)									
1986	9	5	4	7	18	7	5	3	3
1987	14	5	2	7	19	8	7	2	3
1988	17	6	6	10	24	8	8	6	8
1989	18	7	7	18	15	8	6	6	6
1990	15	7	7	19	16	9	11	5	4
1991	12	7	8	28	18	9	17	6	5
1993	17	7	7	72	37	24	26	11	6
1995	32	17	13	60	49	24	29	8	19
1996	32	18	16	66	50	20	40	7	14
1997	20	26	13	66	41	21	46	3	19
Ratio of per labour-day income between non-farming and farming employment									
1986	1.8	1.0	1.5	1.4	4.3	1.1	2.3	3.3	1.5
1987	2.2	0.9	0.6	1.2	3.9	1.4	1.4	1.8	1.2
1988	2.6	1.0	2.0	1.1	3.5	1.0	1.1	4.0	3.0
1989	2.3	1.0	2.3	2.6	1.5	0.9	0.6	3.0	3.0
1990	2.1	0.9	1.8	1.3	1.6	1.1	1.0	2.5	1.3
1991	2.0	1.0	2.7	1.9	1.8	1.3	1.7	3.0	1.7
1993	2.4	0.9	1.4	5.5	2.2	2.2	2.9	3.7	1.5
1995	1.7	1.1	1.9	0.9	2.7	1.3	1.8	1.6	2.4
1996	2.3	1.3	2.7	1.0	3.1	1.1	1.8	1.8	1.8
1997	1.1	2.0	1.6	1.5	2.9	1.5	2.9	0.8	2.1

Source: Calculated from the farm survey data.

Table A10.3 Share of farming income and non-farming income

I. Part-time farm households (yuan)

Province	Village	Net Income and % out of total income	1986	1987	1988	1989	1990	1991	1993	1995	1996	1997
Hubei	1	Farming	878	1,579	2,178	1,907	..	1,218	852	3,315	1,352	3,284
		%	24	29	25	22	..	17	9	18	8	27
		Non-farming	2,766	3,873	6,632	6,667	..	5,931	8,192	14,773	15,349	8,714
		%	76	71	76	77	..	83	90	82	92	73
Hubei	2	Farming	1,012	984	1,157	1,455	1,555	1,098	2,480	3,222	3,309	2,654
		%	31	31	29	31	35	24	34	27	26	18
		Non-farming	2,281	2,223	2,892	3,209	2,925	3,548	4,848	8,506	9,514	12,335
		%	69	70	72	68	66	76	66	73	75	82
Hubei	3	Farming	1,050	1,383	973	1,259	1,442	1,144	2,056	2,874	2,420	3,390
		%	37	41	24	25	36	26	34	37	28	37
		Non-farming	1,812	1,985	3,042	3,786	2,529	3,235	4,056	4,948	6,175	5,666
		%	64	59	75	75	64	74	66	63	72	63
Guangdong	1	Farming	2,080	2,384	3,792	2,902	4,588	4,529	1,879	3,000	6,669	5,923
		%	34	28	32	17	24	16	3	5	9	7
		Non-farming	4,123	5,986	7,937	14,474	14,698	22,939	52,251	53,201	69,977	74,386
		%	66	72	68	83	77	83	96	95	91	92
Guangdong	2	Farming	745	816	1,136	1,429	1,678	1,679	2,864	5,074	4,397	3,098
		%	6	6	8	15	15	14	15	21	19	17
		Non-farming	11,001	12,616	12,899	8,054	9,660	10,460	15,716	18,915	18,285	15,018
		%	93	94	91	85	85	86	84	79	81	83
Guangdong	3	Farming	991	1,077	1,286	1,763	1,548	1,544	798	2,463	2,027	1,448
		%	22	17	17	21	16	15	3	11	9	8
		Non-farming	3,572	5,399	6,235	6,513	8,067	8,906	23,031	20,071	19,594	17,111
		%	78	83	83	79	84	86	96	89	90	92
Yunnan	1	Farming	420	778	904	1,140	1,249	953	672	932	1,266	1,792
		%	11	17	15	17	14	9	4	4	4	6
		Non-farming	3,318	3,816	5,070	5,526	7,391	9,555	17,734	21,592	28,947	30,729
		%	89	83	85	83	85	90	96	96	96	95

Province	Village		1986	1987	1988	1989	1990	1991	1993	1995	1996	1997
Yunnan	2	Farming	613	404	635	1,104	869	926	890	1,920	1,823	2,583
		%	54	57	47	41	39	42	29	60	59	56
		Non-farming	523	301	720	1,605	1,376	1,293	2,233	1,282	1,286	2,062
		%	46	43	53	59	61	58	72	40	41	44
Yunnan	3	Farming	1,278	1,402	1,610	1,355	2,025	1,724	2,810	4,973	3,307	4,470
		%	50	49	46	38	47	29	32	47	17	25
		Non-farming	1,291	1,482	1,919	2,221	2,305	4,253	5,899	5,630	16,733	13,427
		%	51	51	55	63	54	71	68	53	84	75

II. Full-time households (yuan)

Province	Village	Net income and % out of total income	1986	1987	1988	1989	1990	1991	1993	1995	1996	1997
Hubei	1	Farming	1,403	1,486	1,802	2,049	..	1,590	1,423	3,774	3,299	3,601
		%	40	34	36	37		30	24	39	34	30
		Non-farming	2,101	2,920	3,252	3,465	..	3,705	4,520	5,997	6,463	8,280
		%	60	66	64	63		70	76	61	67	70
Hubei	2	Farming	856	935	1,135	1,212	1,477	1,194	2,267	3,303	3,201	3,724
		%	35	36	34	37	35	44	38	23	29	35
		Non-farming	1,566	1,637	2,221	2,055	2,785	1,520	3,678	10,873	7,757	6,811
		%	65	64	66	63	65	56	62	76	70	64
Hubei	3	Farming	1,372	1,523	1,273	1,379	1,597	1,474	2,184	3,090	2,453	3,107
		%	70	65	50	52	59	56	59	54	50	55
		Non-farming	601	826	1,291	1,248	1,124	1,167	1,501	2,581	2,439	2,514
		%	30	36	51	47	42	44	41	45	50	44
Guangdong	1	Farming	2,793	3,326	4,853	3,502	4,266	4,354	2,020	6,681	3,283	2,463
		%	47	46	48	28	25	27	9	15	7	5
		Non-farming	3,174	3,849	5,271	9,157	13,036	12,045	20,371	38,726	45,621	50,215
		%	53	54	52	72	76	73	91	86	94	95
Guangdong	2	Farming	462	728	924	1,722	2,159	2,118	3,035	6,035	6,463	4,832
		%	4	5	5	8	16	13	26	42	27	29
		Non-farming	11,030	13,009	19,166	19,867	11,198	14,322	8,733	8,472	17,506	11,644
		%	96	95	95	92	84	87	75	58	73	70
Guangdong	3	Farming	1,029	1,022	1,626	1,927	1,778	1,705	3,227	3,935	3,576	1,415
		%	23	16	20	20	19	16	20	27	21	8

Part-time farming trends in China

Yunnan 1	Non-farming	3,356	5,254	6,465	7,727	7,433	8,769	12,836	10,651	13,208	16,023
	%	77	83	80	80	81	84	80	73	78	92
	Farming	759	916	1,504	1,976	1,317	1,332	905	1,533	2,023	1,569
	%	25	21	26	30	21	18	10	8	9	7
	Non-farming	2,275	3,383	4,175	4,673	4,851	5,966	7,741	17,072	20,749	22,291
	%	75	79	74	71	78	82	89	92	91	93
Yunnan 2	Farming	561	744	944	876	933	1,082	1,055	2,343	2,240	2,500
	%	75	76	75	64	65	69	59	72	70	73
	Non-farming	187	235	318	498	493	482	723	910	982	916
	%	25	24	25	37	35	30	41	28	31	27
Yunnan 3	Farming	1,037	1,656	1,903	1,766	1,998	2,220	2,646	4,147	4,416	3,898
	%	64	69	67	58	63	61	53	57	44	46
	Non-farming	580	743	947	1,280	1,159	1,416	2,363	3,154	5,710	4,493
	%	36	31	34	42	37	39	47	43	57	54

Source: Calculated from the farm survey data.

Acknowledgments

Part of the research work for this study was carried out while Zhang-Yue Zhou was on sabbatical leave at The Department of Agricultural and Resource Economics of The University of California. The authors wish to thank a number of individuals who helped with this study, especially De-Wen Wang of The Ministry of Agriculture in China, Wei-Ming Tian of The China Agricultural University, and Xiao-Hui Zhang of The Research Centre for Rural Economy. We also thank Ji-Hong Li for her assistance in data analysis and Marjorie Wilson for her editorial assistance.

Notes

1 The discussion on factors affecting part-time farming is partly based on Tian and Shi (1991).
2 For more details about the evolution of the definition of part-time farming, see Institute of Developing Economies (1969).
3 In 1996, one further category was added: no family business operations. Currently, the number of families without any business operations is small.

11

Is China abundant in unskilled labour?

The departure from the HOV Theorem and the implications

Ding Jianping

Being a populous country, China will exert a significant impact on international markets with its labour-intensive goods. If measured by absolute quantity (amount of labour), no country in the world can rival China. As advocated by the Heckscher-Ohlim-Vanek (HOV) Theorem, countries tend to export goods that are intensive in the factor with which they are abundantly supplied. Constrained by the availability of data on natural resources and physical capital, we are only able to examine human capital stock, although the former features in China's exports.[1] Similar to other developing countries, China has experienced the natural-resource exporting stage for a long period. Only after economic reform did China begin to leap the ladder of labour-intensive exports, with which many other developing countries are still struggling. Nevertheless, does China really export its abundance as suggested by the size of its population? What implications can be induced from the HOV Theorem? We endeavour to answer these questions empirically.

There is a large amount of literature and empirical studies on factor content among industrialised countries, however few relate to developing countries. Bowen et al. (1987) include countries and regions like Brazil, Hong Kong, Korea, Mexico and the Philippines, leaving China untouched. Bowen and Sveikauskas (1992) extend their factor content study by adding Burma and Egypt, but with more focus on industrialised countries. Wood (1991) analyses the factor content of North–South trade by using broad data without reference to individual countries. Maskus et al. (1994) group all developing countries together and compare their trade with the United Kingdom and the United States. The United Kingdom is revealed as being specialised in capital-intensive activities in relation to developing countries. However, the result for the United States is against conventional wisdom in that professional and skilled non-manual labours are ranked lower in the determination of the US net exports with developing countries. This chapter is the first attempt to use the input–output table of developing countries (China) as the benchmark to study factor content, instead of the single input–output table for the United States, used predominantly in previous studies.

After broad analysis of physical and human capital, recent studies have shifted attention to the detailed composition of human capital stock, since the future of international competition will be based around scientific and technological aspects. Webster (1993) emphasises the importance of education in his study, by advocating that human capital is an important determinant of a country's specialisation in the processes of international trade. Maskus *et al.* (1994) began human capital stock studies with an empirical analysis of the United States and the United Kingdom. Shortly after that, Engelbrecht (1996) did the same with an empirical test on West Germany.

This chapter is based on the categorisation of different occupations by educational attainment in the empirical analysis, and finds that labour content, when correctly classified, will reveal the ranking of abundance. Moreover, it is easy to be misled in cases of disproportion of consumption, where a shortage of other relevant factors such as physical capital and arable land will prevent an accurate measurement of labour content. Finally, an extremely uneven distribution of the occupations across sectors will overvalue one factor while undervaluing the other.

HOV Theorem and Maskus' methodology

Before presenting the HOV model, the following symbols should be specified. Matrices and vectors are indicated by capital letters, the country or the world by right lowercase letters, the factor number by left uppercase letters. The notations are listed as follows:

$T_i = n \times 1$ vector of the net exports by country i

$F_i = m \times 1$ vector of factor endowments of country i, and $F_w = \Sigma_i F_i$

$A_i = m \times n$ matrix of factor input requirements where the element a_{jk} indicates the amount of factor j used to produce one unit of commodity k in country i. Relaxation of the assumption from $m = n$ to $m \leq n$ is adopted in this chapter[2]

$Q_i = n \times 1$ vector of commodities produced in country i

$C_i = n \times 1$ vector of commodities consumed in country i

$Y_i = GNP$ of country i, and $Y_w = \Sigma_i Y_i$

B_i = trade balance of country i.

Then the identities can be established between outputs, inputs and factor intensities

$$F_i \equiv A_i Q_i \qquad (11.1)$$

Similarly, trade is related to outputs and consumption by the following identities

$$T_i \equiv Q_i - C_i \qquad (11.2)$$

With the above identities introduced, we restate the HOV Theorem. It assumes (1) a competitive equilibrium with commodity price equalisation, (2) constant returns to scale production functions with nonreversible factor intensities for all goods, (3) identical technologies in all countries, (4) identical and homothetic preferences for all countries. Incomplete specialisation is included in (5), which is not specified in the Hechscher-Ohlin theorem. This assumes that China produces all the goods under the trade. Therefore, the input–output matrix A is the same for all countries. That is, $A_i = A$, and endowments and trade are related by the set of equations

$$AT_i = F_i - \alpha_i F_w \qquad (11.3)$$

where α_i $i = 1, ..., I$ is a set of positive scalars; that is, $\alpha_i = (Y_i - B_i)/Y_w$ with subscript i indicating individual country i.

From the assumptions mentioned, we obtain identical input–output coefficients. As all countries face the same prices (1), the identical homothetic preference (3) implies that equal proportions of all commodities will be consumed.

$$C_i = \alpha_i Q_w \quad (Q_w = C_w) \qquad (11.4)$$

By summarising the relations among the above identities, we find that Equations 11.1, 11.2 and 11.4 imply Equation 11.3:

$$AT_i = A(Q_i - C_i) = F_i - \alpha_i AQ_w = F_i - \alpha_i F_w \qquad (11.5)$$

As long as A and are provided, the most direct way to estimate the factor abundance is to compute, the net export in factor services, which theoretically is equal to the excess supply of factors $(AT_i = F_i - \alpha_i F_w)$. Since the matrix A is not square, it cannot be inverted. Consequently, trade has a degree of indeterminateness equal to $n - m$. However, any given net export of factor services $F_i - \alpha_i F_w$ can still be achieved in many different bundles of net exports T_i. In empirical study, only identical matrices A for different countries are required, not equal numbers of factors and commodities.

Markusen *et al.* (1995) explicitly demonstrate the factor-ranking relationship for the case of m factors and n goods, with $n \geq m$. The ranking of factor abundance and scarcity for country i by virtue of its share of world endowments of each stands logically as follows

$$\frac{^1F_i}{^1F_w} > \frac{^2F_i}{^2F_w} > \cdots > \frac{^jF_i}{^jF_w} > \alpha_i > \frac{^{j+1}F_i}{^{j+1}F_w} > \cdots > \frac{^mF_i}{^mF_w} \qquad (11.6)$$

Under the HOV Theorem, country i's share lies somewhere in the middle of this chain. For the sake of empirical estimation based on a country's data, the ranking of factors indicated by Equation 11.6 is usually carried out in the following steps.

We start by rewriting Equation 11.5 in order to make a comparison in the form of Equation 11.6.

$$F_i = AT_i + \alpha_i F_w \tag{11.7}$$

$$\frac{F_i}{F_w} = \frac{AT_i}{F_w} + \alpha_i = \alpha_i \left(\frac{AT_i}{\alpha_i F_w} + 1 \right) = \alpha_i \left(\frac{AT_i}{F_i - AT_i} + 1 \right) = \alpha_i \left(\frac{F_i}{F_i - AT_i} \right) \tag{11.8}$$

For simplicity, let us assume that there are only two factors, and Factor 1 is relatively more abundant than Factor 2.

$$\frac{{}^1F_i}{{}^1F_w} > \frac{{}^2F_i}{{}^2F_w} \quad \text{or} \quad \frac{{}^1F_i}{{}^1F_i - {}^1AT_i} > \frac{{}^2F_i}{{}^2F_i - {}^2AT_i} \tag{11.9}$$

This is subject to $({}^jF_i - {}^jAT_i) > 0$. Multiplying both sides of Equation 11.9 by $({}^1F_i - {}^1AT_i)({}^2F_i - {}^2AT_i)$ yields

$${}^1F_i({}^2F_i - {}^2AT_i) > {}^2F_i({}^1F_i - {}^1AT_i) \quad \text{or} \quad {}^1F_i \times {}^2F_i - {}^1F_i \times {}^2AT_i > {}^2F_i \times {}^1F_i - {}^2F_i \times {}^1AT_i \tag{11.10}$$

$$-{}^1F_i \times {}^2AT_i > -{}^2F_i \times {}^1AT_i \tag{11.11}$$

We can infer from Equations 11.1 and 11.2 that the following equation is also valid:

$$F_i = AQ_i = A(T_i + C_i) \tag{11.12}$$

To simplify the notations, we redefine $AT_i = F_i^T$ and $AC_i = F_i^C$. Thus Equation 11.12 becomes

$${}^jF_i = {}^jF_i^T + {}^jF_i^C \quad j = 1, 2 \tag{11.13}$$

Replacing Equation 11.11 by Equation 11.13, we arrive at

$$-({}^1F_i^T + {}^1F_i^C) \times {}^2F_i^T > -({}^2F_i^T + {}^2F_i^C) \times {}^1F_i^T \quad \text{or} \quad -{}^1F_i^C \times {}^2F_i^T > -{}^2F_i^C \times {}^1F_i^T \tag{11.14}$$

Dividing both sides of Equation 11.14 by $-{}^1F_i^C \times {}^2F_i^C$ yields

$$\frac{{}^1F_i^T}{{}^1F_i^C} > \frac{{}^2F_i^T}{{}^2F_i^C} \tag{11.15}$$

where, ${}^jF_i^T$ and ${}^jF_i^C$ are total (direct plus indirect) factor requirements of net exports and consumption of factor j. This applies to any pair of factors (pair-wise comparison); that is, ratios of net export requirements to consumption can be used to establish factor abundance rankings. Consumption implies the proportion relative to the world because of the identical homothetic tastes assumption. Rankings of Equation 11.15 are valid for an arbitrary number of factors, given the validity of the HOV Theorem under fairly general circumstances. Similar to Equation 11.6, Equation 11.15 is also a chain of factor comparison in a multi-factor case.

$$\frac{^1F_i^T}{^1F_i^C} > \frac{^2F_i^T}{^2F_i^C} > \cdots > \frac{^jF_i^T}{^jF_i^C} > 0 > \frac{^{j+1}F_i^T}{^{j+1}F_i^C} > \cdots > \frac{^mF_i^T}{^mF_i^C} \qquad (11.16)$$

It also follows that country i's net exports of the service of any factor $^jF_i^T$ ($^jF_i^T = {^jAT_i}$) are positive if its abundance ranking for that factor lies above the consumption share, and its net exports are negative if its ranking lies below that share. Thus, a country exports the services of its abundant factors and imports the services of its scarce factors when factor abundance is measured relative to a global standard.

To determine the human capital stock required to produce this trade flow with China's coefficients, we multiply n-item trade vector T by a $m\times n$ matrix A, in which the elements a_{jk} ($j = 1, 2, \ldots, m$; $k = 1, 2, \ldots, n$) represent an average of China's direct requirements of labour for m occupation (in the form of wage share) to export one unit. This applies regardless of whether or not China's endowment j exceeds world endowment j. The ranking will be dramatically altered if the content of consumption acts as a denominator.

Selecting matrix A and grouping human capital

This chapter distinguishes itself by adopting China's matrix A, unlike a majority of the previous studies, which were based on that of the United States (Leamer 1992; Maskus *et al.* 1994 and many others). Webster (1993) and Engelbrecht (1996) apply matrices of their own countries (the United Kingdom and Germany) to the factor-content studies. Although both industrialised countries, the United Kingdom and Germany have separate technical requirements and demonstrate different results. This allows for meaningful examinations of factor-content studies. Selecting China's matrix A is also to this endeavour. It may have more implications since China is a developing country. Wong (1995:111) lists several advantages of using domestic coefficients.[3] Theoretically, all the assumptions made above are taken for granted because all the data used are from a single country. Empirically, it is easier to identify different inputs (occupations and physical capital in this chapter) with relative codes in an input–output table. Furthermore, using the technologies of a country's trading partner proves to be very difficult in practice.

According to the statistics of China's occupational classification, the employed fall into eight categories. Although the definition for each occupation is specified in detail by Feng and Zhu (1994), it is also based on industrial classification, and career transfer within the same skill category is not addressed. Is it credible to regard these categories as eight factors of production? Can we take it for granted that machine assemblers and precision instrument workers are similar to wood, bamboo, flax, rattan and straw processing workers, despite the fact that these two kinds of workers have attained different levels of education? Webster (1993:152) studies this problem of disaggregation and aggregation of factor inputs, 'On the one hand, unwarranted disaggregation violates the theoretical basis of the model, and on the other hand, excessive aggregation risks overlooking important sources of international specialisation'. Let us assume that no arbitrary barrier exists which prevents a career change at the same level of educational attainment. Obviously, China's official occupational classification disregards this point. Career by industrial sector is not a type of production factor. As a factor, it should be relatively stable. This requires special training either at university level or in vocational schools. It is unrealistic to expect a graduate of literature to apply for a position in a chemical laboratory. However, it is possible to ask a farmer to engage in fishing. Basic education (primary, middle and high school) is suitable for a broad range of carriers. The longer the vocational training required, the higher the cost incurred to the individual, and therefore the more unlikely for him to move to other trades. The lower the educational attainment, the more likely is movement between occupations. Due to the temporary mobility of workers between sectors and the chance of fluctuation, a benchmark must be set. Since workers with low educational attainment are considered mobile, we classify the occupations in line with high educational attainment (that is, university, college and vocational school graduates) and aggregate 63 occupations into six groups.

- Group 1. Farmers and other agricultural manual labour covers those people with primary school education or no education at all, engaged in manual work in the fields.
- Group 2. Named resource-related workers and others includes the low-educated service workers and those who relate closely to natural resources. In fact, the resource matters in their export performance, that is, the less resources the fewer workers.
- Group 3. Termed manufacturing manual workers, though with relatively higher education than the previous two groups, this group still conducts hand operations (physical labour) in most cases.
- Group 4. Entitled manufacturing technical workers, this group consists mostly of graduates with majors in natural science.
- Group 5. Managerial and administrative workers; predominantly social science graduates.
- Group 6. Labelled 'scientific intellectuals', this group has the highest educational attainment.

As a factor of production (group as a whole), it should be identified by its special characteristics, both in education attainment and in export performance. Analysis of variance (ANOVA) is the test used to verify the above classifications.

Thus, if within-category variations are statistically insignificant in relation to between-category variations we can conclude that the level of aggregation employed does not ignore important effects (Webster 1993:152). The results of the ANOVA test by occupational and educational classifications are presented in Table 11.2. The F-ratio demonstrates whether the variation between categories is larger or smaller than within categories. The results indicate that the skill aggregation (six groups) survives both tests and is significant.

Empirical results of human capital rankings

After the aggregation of 63 occupations into six groups in line with educational attainments, and after the application of Maskus' methodology, the skill ranking of China's net exports is obtained. We have demonstrated, as expected according to the HOV Theorem, that China is abundant in unskilled workers in its net exports generally, but not in absolute terms.

We are unable to access data for the occupations and input–output tables over a long period.[4] Nevertheless, let us assume approximation to reality of factor intensity and technical coefficients, with 1992 as a benchmark. This can be justified by the composition of China's population with 70 per cent or nearly 80 per cent in the rural areas between the 1950s and 1990s (estimation period).

General framework of China's human capital stock

We intend to reveal which occupational group is the most abundant within the category of low educational attainment, and similarly, which is the scarcest within the high category. Adding physical capital data (building and machinery) only serves to verify the rankings. Meanwhile, an attempt is made to find

Table 11.1   Groups of human capital embodied in China's net exports, 1992

Occupation	Group	Average educational attainment
Farmers and other agricultural manual labour	G1	0.06321
Resource-related workers and others	G2	0.14432
Manufacturing manual workers	G3	0.18105
Manufacturing technical workers	G4	0.27722
Managerial, administrative and others	G5	0.50949
Scientific intellectuals	G6	0.85235

Note: Average educational attainment is the ratio of those with university, college and vocational school attainments, to the total group.
Sources: State Statistical Bureau (SSB), 1990. *Tabulation on the 1990 Population Census of People's Republic of China* Volume 2, Population Census Office, State Council and Department of Population Statistics, China.

departures from the HOV, due to some constraints arising from the scarcity of arable land, physical capital and disproportion of consumption.

The groups within the category of low educational attainment are as follows.

Group 1. Farmers and other agricultural manual labour. On average, this group is ranked fourth. Chinese farmers have been sustaining 20 per cent of the world's population with only 7 per cent of the world's arable land. In accordance with the HOV Theorem, Chinese farmers should be regarded as an abundant factor since their share in the labour force (72 per cent) exceeds the world average (49 per cent) (World Bank 1996). Markusen *et al.* (1995) list disproportion of consumption as one of the explanations of Leontief's Paradox, which violates the assumption of identical and homogeneous preferences. Neither individuals nor countries actually have identical budget shares. The proportion spent on food varies from the low ratio in the United States to the high ratio in India. The budget shares depend on the income level, though differences in tastes probably explain some special phenomena. For example, the Japanese devote a high share to education and seafood. The Chinese have a strong preference for food consumption, amounting to 61 per cent of total household expenditure, which nearly doubles the world average (32.44 per cent) (World Bank 1993). Countries with labour shares equal to GNP shares, or equivalently with per capita incomes equal to world per capita income, will have trade in conformance with the HOV equations. Countries that have an abundance of labour will tend to import the commodities

Table 11.2   Analysis of variance (ANOVA) of China's human capital classification

Source of variation	Sum of squares	Degrees of freedom	Mean square error	F-ratio	Prob>F
I. According to educational attainment					
Between groups	2.81973804	5	0.5639476	43.86	.
Within groups	0.73293897	57	0.0128586		
Total	3.55267701	62	0.0573012		
II. According to net export performance					
Between groups	0.08489215	5	0.0169784	2.04	0.0867
Within groups	0.47462360	57	0.0083267		
Total	0.55951575	62	0.0090244		

Notes: Total number of observations is 63; since there is only one observation of labourers not elsewhere classified in educational attainment, we classify it as the subtotal of staff and personnel because of similar educational attainment; F-ratio indicates numerator and denominator as follows: F = variance explained by education (or occupation)/unexplained variance; educational attainment refers the ratio of those gradates from university, college and vocational school, to the total group; net export performance is the ratio of net exports to consumption.

consumed by the poor, and vice versa. The continuing growth of population in absolute numbers keeps per capita income lower and the consumption ratio almost unchanged in China. Though absolute agricultural output is the highest in the world, after consumption, it is lower than the world average (Table 11.4). Furthermore, arable land appears to be a major constraint. The growth of the manufacturing industry, expansion of residential buildings and infrastructure are encroaching on the limited arable land; the growth of China's industry is at the expense of agriculture because both compete for physical capital and land. In addition, land erosion is worsening (sandy desert and saline-alkali soil is becoming common, and desert increases by 2,100 square kilometers annually).

Of great concern is the low educational attainment of this group. Twenty-three per cent of the farmers are semi-illiterate and 45 per cent of them have only a primary school education. On average, the ratio of one technician to hundreds of farmers makes dissemination of advanced knowledge almost impossible. During the period 1985–90, Chinese scientists invented 396 new farm products. Only 30 per cent of them were applied. This suggests that the contribution of science to the growth of agriculture is only 30 per cent in China in comparison with 70–80 per cent in industrialised countries. One explanation for this is that Chinese choose labour-intensive techniques because of low wages, and not because they are unaware of the capital-intensive techniques used in the United States. Given the trend towards capital intensity in global agriculture, demand for highly educated farmers will increase and China will struggle to stay abreast of developments.

Group 2. Resource-related workers and others, this group is ranked second. The ever-growing domestic consumption of limited natural resources and the fledgling service industry make it impossible for this group to rank higher. During the Cultural Revolution, China had few commodities to export, except natural resources. This situation lasted until the initial stage of economic reform in 1980. Since the 1990s, China has become first in the world in coal and fifth in world crude petroleum production. However, economic development

Table 11.3   Ranking of China's human capital stock embodied in its net exports

Occupation	Group	Ranking	Ratio of net exports to consumption
Farmers and other agricultural manual labour	G1	4	0.01004
Resource-related workers and others	G2	2	0.04250
Manufacturing manual workers	G3	1	0.11874
Manufacturing technical workers	G4	5	-0.00246
Managerial, administrative and others	G5	3	0.02616
Scientific intellectuals	G6	6	-0.00382

accelerates demand as well. Being tied to natural resources, Group 2 will descend the ladder in the years to come, with growing domestic consumption of natural resources.

Group 3. Manufacturing manual workers, this group has been ranked first. Their role increased after economic reforms began, and with the growth of trade. Especially after 1987, China jumped to the top position in exporting textiles and apparel, reaching 14 per cent world share. Group 3 is regarded as an abundant factor even after taking into account the share of consumption. There are almost no constraints on its supply. This group requires only primary and middle school educational attainment (compulsory for every child in China), few physical capital inputs (sewing machines, forging machines and mills), low consumption share, and resource dependency. Unlike the agricultural sector, the application of machinery in production seems difficult since most goods produced by this group are specially ordered on customer demand.

It is common for middle school education to play a crucial export role at the initial stages of a country's development. This is true of Group 3, where more than half have graduated from middle school. This occurred in Japan in the early 1950s and other newly industrialised Asian countries in the late 1960s. Moreover, the number of middle school graduates in China is approximate to the world average (World Bank 1996). Group 3 is regarded as an inexhaustible factor. After China's accession to the World Trade Organization (WTO), the tariff against the exports of this group will be reduced (bringing the situation closer to the assumption of HOV: absence of impediments to trade), and Group 3 is expected to maintain its first ranking.

The groups within the category of high educational attainment are: Group 4, manufacturing technical workers, and Group 6, scientific intellectuals. These groups have been regarded as the most scarce in China with no improvement

Table 11.4   Ranking of China's agricultural output in the world, 1949–94

	1949	1957	1965	1978	1980	1985	1992	1993	1994
Cereal	..	3	2	2	1	2	1	1	1
Meat*	3	2	3	3	3	2	1	1	1
Cotton	4	2	2	3	2	1	1	1	1
Peanuts	2	2	3	2	2	2	2	2	1
Rape seed	2	2	2	2	2	1	1	1	1
Sugarcane	..	3	..	9	9	4	3	3	3
Tea	3	3	3	2	2	2	2	2	2

Note: *refers to the ranking of pork, beef, and mutton during 1949–92, and all meat in 1993.
Source: State Statistical Bureau, 1995. *China Statistical Yearbook*, China Statistical Publishing House, Beijing.

seen in rankings. This can be interpreted as either fewer graduates of natural sciences (chemistry, physics and others) or by a serious shortage of physical capital. Capital is indispensable for scientific research projects. Suspension of university enrolment during the Cultural Revolution has interrupted the development of this group, and human capital investment is a lengthy process. Crop failures tend to improve the rankings of technical workers and scientists due to an uneven distribution of these groups between the industries. Although more than 70 per cent of the population is engaged in farming, scientific intellectuals are highly represented in manufacturing sectors. As a result, the more farm products that are exported, the lower the rank of scientific intellectuals, and vice versa. Such structure produces a misleading result during crop failures. Previous empirical studies attribute such misleading results to trade deficits; that is, when a country is running a large trade deficit its statistics are unlikely to reveal the truth. This happened during the oil shock and big famine, where large import expenditures skewed the figures.

Group 5. Managerial and administrative personnel and supervisor, this group ranked third. It requires a relatively high educational attainment, but not significant levels of physical capital. Comparatively speaking, it is easier to transfer to the social sciences (this group) than to the natural sciences because the latter requires a prolonged systematic education. Even distribution of this group across the sectors makes its ranking very stable.

As stated by Keesing (1965) and Webster (1993), skills and higher educational attainment are a big advantage in international competition. The skill content of the workforce is a reflection of past governments' educational policy. The endless political movements in the 1960s and 1970s weakened China's international competitiveness. Moreover, the relatively small educational expenditure by both state and household (lower than the world average) is a cause for concern.

Inclusion of physical capital and problems of sector aggregation

Any multi-factor, multi-good case can be regarded as a two-factor, two-good model by aggregation. In order to verify the ranking of physical capital, the original commodity input–output matrix must be sorted out to fit the data of physical capital stock. The sources of China's physical capital stocks are listed in Table 11.5.

Using the data from Wang *et al.* (1998) and adapting the agricultural sector from Chow (1993), we aggregate a 42-commodity matrix (may be regarded as 42 sectors) into a 16-sector matrix. To some extent, the aggregation destroys the useful information entailed in those aggregated commodities. The empirical

Table 11.5   Incorporation of physical capital into the ranking

Author and publication	Time span	Sectors
Chow (1993)[1]	1952–85	Agriculture Construction Transportation Commerce
Wang et al. (1998)[2]	1979–95	Food Beverages Tobacco Textiles Apparel Leather, fur and their products Sawmill and wood processing Paper products and printing industry Chemical products Rubber and plastic products Non-ferrous metals and materials Metal products Machinery and transport equipment Electric machinery and instruments Other manufacturing industrial sectors

Notes: [1]Chow, G., 1993. 'Capital formation and economic industry growth in China', *The Quarterly Journal of Economics*, 108(3):809–42; [2]Wang, Y., Ren, R. and Liu, X. 1998. *Estimation of physical capital stock in China's manufacturing sectors*, Institute of Management working paper, Beijing Aviation and Spaceflight University.

Table 11.6   Summary of rankings of China's human capital stock

Group	Benchmark: year 1992	Average rankings across years 1955–96	Re-ranking after inclusion of physical capital
G1	4	4.2	5
G2	2	2.2	2
G3	1	1.4	1
G4	5	5.0	6
G5	3	3.0	3
G6	6	5.2	4
K		5.6	7

Notes: G1: farmers and other agricultural manual labour; G2: resource-related workers; G3: manufacturing manual workers; G4: manufacturing technical workers; G5: managerial, administrative and others; G6: scientific intellectuals; K: physical capital; calculations are based on Equation 11.16.
Source: Import and export data for 1955, 1964 and 1980 are from internal sources at the Institute of Economic Research, Hitotsubashi University, Tokyo, Japan; 1992 is directly from the Input–output Table 1992; 1996 is derived from *Customs Statistics Yearbook 1996* edited by General Administration of Customs, PRC; G1 and G6 are from the same source as Table 11.1; K is estimated in this section.

results are presented in Table 11.6.

Aggregation does not significantly change the human capital rankings. The conclusions thus reached are as follows.

1 The most scarce factor in China is physical capital (K). This is consistent with the conventional wisdom that it is unlikely for a low-income developing country to be rich in machinery and infrastructure. However, among the human capital stocks, the fact that manufacturing technical workers (Group 4) are ranked lower than scientific intellectuals (Group 6) is misleading due to the aggregation problems.

2 The most abundant factor is manufacturing manual workers (Group 3) with relative low educational attainment. Aggregation of sectors does not affect the ranking of this group.

3 The ranking of farmers (Group 1) is worsened after aggregation, for unknown reasons. The aggregation of several sectors (agriculture, forestry, livestock production, fishing and others) into one sector seems justifiable.

The more sectors there are, the more information will be retained. Aggregation of sectors will destroy much of the information indispensable to the accurate measurement of China's human capital stock. The present study deals exclusively with ranking of human capital based on two assumptions.

The first assumption is that the rankings of physical capital and human capital are relatively stable. Keesing (1965), Webster (1993), Markusen *et al.* (1995), and Engelbrecht (1996) narrow down their analyses to human capital ranking exclusively.

The second assumption is that the ranking of human capital will not alter as long as sectors in the input–output table remain unchanged. If detailed data concerning physical capital becomes available, accurate measurement of all factors will be possible.

We assume that machines are instantaneously producible by labour and are completely consumed in the production process. Then, in fact, output is an instantaneous function of labour alone. The tradition of writing capital as the input instead of machines is a reminder that it takes time to produce machinery and that machinery is only partially consumed in the production process.

Conclusion

China has a large supply of cheap labour relative to other factors. Therefore, China will tend to produce relatively more goods that use its abundant factors intensively. This is confirmed in this empirical study. The main findings of this chapter indicate that China is neither rich in all of its low-educated (unskilled) labour, nor poor in its entire high-educated profession due to many constraints. Special attention should be paid to the subgroups within the low-educated category. Nine-hundred million farmers are not ranked as China's first abundance (*Population Yearbook of China* 1994:390). Thus, absolute large numbers are not an abundant factor after taking consumption ratio into account.

The most abundant factor in China is manufacturing manual workers, with low educational attainment because of fewer constraints (physical capital, land and natural resources). Special orders from customers make it difficult to further modernise these sectors. In the absence of serious impediments to trade from its trading partners (after China's accession to the WTO), there is room for further expansion of this group.

The per capita income level (which affects consumption behaviour) and limited arable land are regarded as departures from the HOV assumption in the measurement of Chinese farmers. It is undeniable that the Chinese have a strong preference for food consumption. However, this will not alter the empirical result greatly. Low income (wage) will also retard the application of advanced technology to agricultural sectors because more labour will be employed instead of machinery. To some extent, the rapid growth of the manufacturing industry leaves less room for development of agriculture because both place demands on land and capital.

The findings of this chapter concur with the conventional wisdom that China is lacking in skilled workers, especially manufacturing technical workers and scientific intellectuals. The scarcity of these high-educated groups is not only due to the physical capital constraint, but also to the suspension of higher education during the political turmoil of the 1960s and 1970s. The difference can be seen between the natural and social sciences; for example, there are fewer manufacturing technicians and more administrative personnel. A developing country has the potential to be rich in managerial and administrative personnel.

Finally, adding a factor such as physical capital does not alter the rankings of human capital so long as *n* remains unchanged. Therefore, any aggregation of commodities or sectors will affect the rankings to some extent because relevant information is lost. China is in dire need of physical capital, which serves as a premise for China's technicians and intellectuals to climb the ranking.

Further studies on capital stock and natural resources are essential as adequate data becomes available. Meanwhile, bilateral testing of factors based on unified input–output and occupational codes will reveal more findings.

Appendix 11.1

Specialisation of skills with different trading partners

It is possible to rank the endowment of any country by computing its share of each endowment in the global supply. However, it is more difficult to rank factors in bilateral trade. Wong (1995) compares this case to $'F_i + F_r = F_w'$ (where i is home country; r is the rest of the world; w is the whole world), and assumes that it is similar to Equation 11.16. Markusen *et al.* (1994) bypass this issue by discussing international specialisation. With the same approach, this appendix addresses the probability of specialisation in occupations (skills) bilaterally.

The results give little enlightenment to educational attainment or occupational specialisation, but rather seem to serve as proxies of the relative endowment of natural resources between China and its trading partners. For example, the average arable land per country in the world is 11 per cent. China's ratio is 10 per cent; whereas, the ratio of the United States is 20 per cent, France 35 per cent and Thailand 41 per cent.[5] This phenomenon also arises in Maskus *et al.* (1995) when they interpret the advantage of US farmers, who serve as a proxy for the large land endowment in US bilateral trade. Keesing (1965:288) argues, 'In measurements of total trade, natural resources tend to dominate trade patterns and obscure the role of labour skills'.

The highly educated category ranks lower (or in negative signs); any specialisation seems impossible. This matches the HOV theorem in that China is not only lower than the world average in educational attainment, but also lower than most of the Asian developing countries. Only in comparison with Thailand are China's scientific intellectuals found to be plentiful. It is misleading to regard China as having a higher educational attainment ratio than that of Thailand. All statistics compiled by the United Nations Educational, Scientific and Cultural Organisation (UNESCO) confirm that it is not the case. That is, China has a lower ratio in all aspects. This phenomenon is also due to the uneven distribution of the group among the sectors.

However, it cannot be inferred that the ranking of the highly educated groups will rise simply by the provision of sufficient physical capital. China made a large purchase of facilities and equipment from abroad in an attempt to modernise its industry over a very short time, and was not very successful. Educational investment is a cumulative process.

Appendix 11.2

Data compilation and aggregation

Data relevant to matrix A.

1 Department of National Economic Accounting, State Statistical Bureau of Peoples Republic of China, 1996. *Input–output Table of China 1992*, China Statistical Publishing House. The book provides information for 118 commodities (118×118 matrix).

2 The Population Census Office under the State Council and Department of Population Statistics, State Statistical Bureau, PRC, 1994. *Tabulation on the 1990 Population Census of the People's Republic of China, Volume 2*, China Statistical Publishing House. The book lists Table 6–26 and Table 6–27:728–59, providing all the data required for the empirical test. Detailed information on human capital stock in China is available by occupation (309 professions), by education (seven levels) and by industry (75 sectors). As a direct input, labour statistics contain 64 aggregate occupational employment classifications (which can be further subdivided into 309 occupations with seven levels of educational attainment).

Matching of the census data to the input–output table proves to be a demanding task. However, according to the industrial classification description of China's input–output table 1992:378–95, the allocation is carried out with little effort. There is no wage data by occupation, and we substitute for it by using sector average wages originating from the *Yearbook of Labor Statistics of China, 1993* (195–300). In China, the wage variance can be disregarded due to the equal distribution of income in the past.

Data on imports and exports.

1 The trade data before China's economic reform in 1955, 1964 and shortly after the reform 1980 originate from internal sources processed by *Asian Historical Statistics Project* under the Institute of Economic Research, Hitotsubashi University, Tokyo, Japan. All the import and export data are precise (1955 and 1964 are in China's unique classifications, 1980 is in SITC, and 1996 is in HS classification), which makes it possible to find the respective commodity category in China's input–output table.

2 Net exports (1992) are derived directly from China's input–output table (1992) compiled by Department of National Economic Accounting, State Statistical Bureau of People's Republic of China, 1996. *Input–Output Table of China 1992*, China Statistical Publishing House, Beijing.

Table A11.1 China's human capital embodied in its bilateral trades

I.	Indonesia		Thailand		Malaysia		Korea, Rep. of		Singapore		Australia		Britain	
Y	670		1,840		2,790		6,790		15,730		17,260		17,790	
T	2.0247		1.3187		1.4749		5.0253		3.2653		2.3309		1.9356	
	Ratio	R	Ratio	R	Ratio	R	Ratio	R	Ratio	R	Ratio	R	Ratio	R
G1	0.00075	1	-0.00011	6	0.00184	1	0.00639	1	0.00137	2	-0.00092	2	0.00031	3
G2	-0.00112	3	0.00039	4	-0.00146	6	0.00310	2	0.00096	3	-0.00263	6	0.00080	2
G3	-0.00428	6	0.00051	2	-0.00116	5	0.00059	3	0.00172	1	-0.00028	1	0.00095	1
G4	-0.00131	4	0.00026	5	-0.00033	3	-0.00166	6	0.00070	5	-0.00171	3	-0.00081	5
G5	-0.00174	5	0.00047	3	-0.00064	4	0.00002	4	0.00091	4	-0.00204	5	-0.00027	4
G6	-0.00066	2	0.00052	1	-0.00032	2	-0.00055	5	0.00063	6	-0.00188	4	-0.00115	6

II.	Italy		Netherlands		Canada		France		Germany		United States		Japan	
Y	20,460		20,480		20,710		22,260		23,030		23,240		28,190	
T	2.8420		1.7077		2.5785		2.2580		6.4600		17.4863		25.3492	
	Ratio	R	Ratio	R	Ratio	R	Ratio	R	Ratio	R	Ratio	R	Ratio	R
G1	0.00099	1	0.00194	1	-0.00944	6	-0.00167	4	0.00065	1	-0.00489	4	0.01062	2
G2	0.00014	3	0.00111	2	-0.00153	4	0.00023	2	0.00048	3	0.00095	2	0.00517	3
G3	0.00079	2	0.00110	3	0.00006	1	0.00033	1	0.00062	2	0.01493	1	0.01087	1
G4	-0.00203	5	0.00085	4	-0.00203	5	-0.00182	5	-0.00475	5	-0.00798	5	-0.01345	5
G5	-0.00133	4	0.00041	5	-0.00147	2	-0.00103	3	-0.00305	4	-0.00233	3	-0.00525	4
G6	-0.00256	6	0.00023	6	-0.00150	3	-0.00190	6	-0.00612	6	-0.00826	6	-0.01474	6

Notes: Y is current GNP per capita in respective countries (US$); data are from World Bank (1994); T is counterpart country's share in China's total trade (per cent); all bilateral trade data are from General Administration of Customs, PRC, 1993; R refers to ranking.

Sources: World Bank, 1994. *World Tables 1994*, The Johns Hopkins University Press; General Administration of Customs, PRC, 1993. *Customs Statistics Yearbook 1992 III*, China Statistical Publishing House, Beijing.

3 Data for 1996 originate from *China's Customs Statistics Yearbook, 1996*, edited and published by General Administration of Customs, People's Republic of China.

4 The data for bilateral trade with 14 countries are taken from *China's Customs Statistics Yearbook, 1992*, edited and published by General Administration of Customs, People's Republic of China. However, in order to make use of all available information, the selected countries for factor content comparison are China's major trading partners, ranging from developing to industrialised countries. The transaction volume with these countries is about 76 per cent of China's total trade excluding Hong Kong, Macao and Taiwan.

Acknowledgments

I received useful comments and suggestions from Professors Kyoji Fukao, Juro Teranishi, Hiroshi Tsubouchi, Makoto Ikema, Jota Ishikawa, Ximing Yue and Ippei Yamazawa from Hitotsubashi University, Tokyo. *Changing Global Comparative Advantage: Evidence from Asia and the Pacific* by Ligang Song gave me an insight into the unsettled issue of the chapter. However, any errors are solely mine.

Notes

1 Refer to the empirical results of human capital rankings in this chapter for primary estimation of physical capital within sixteen commodities.

2 Generally speaking, HOV uses an even model, which is true to studying trade in goods, requiring inversion of the technology matrix. This condition is not necessary for a factor-content study adopted by Maskus (1985), Trefler (1995), and Davis *et al.* (1997), all of whom use an uneven model. The detailed explanation is also given by Markusen *et al.* (1995).

3 This may be regarded as using domestic matrix *A*.

4 China began publishing its input–output table in 1987, but using neither MPS nor SNA. In 1992, China moved towards an SNA-type national accounting system and this made international comparisons possible.

5 Canada is an exception, and was below the world average in 1993. Data originate from The World Bank, 1996. *World Development Report 1996*:208–9.

12

Regional development in China

The role of FDI, exports and spillover effects

Qing Zhang

This chapter develops a model of provincial growth in China taking into account the differing policy treatment of China's regions, the contribution of foreign direct investment (FDI) and exports to provincial growth, and the spillover effects on different regions.

The motivation for studying the growth of China needs little embellishment. The opening of China's markets in 1978 created the almost unprecedented prospect of new market and investment opportunities for the rest of the world.[1] Until the East Asian currency crisis, China had fulfilled its growth potential by recording growth outcomes that made China the fastest growing economy in the world. The East Asian crisis and China's response to it, including the resistance of the Chinese government to devaluation, slowed China's overall growth rate but China made it through the crisis and has continued with the fastest growth in East Asia

Research on the subject of export-led growth has increased steadily since 1970, and empirical studies in particular provide conflicting evidence. The studies by Voivodas (1973), Michaely (1977), Balassa (1978), Tyler (1981), Kavoussi (1984) and Feder (1982) support the export-led growth hypothesis. The export-led growth hypothesis has been a widely accepted explanation in the development literature after the success stories of several newly industrialised countries (NICs). Some empirical investigations, however, fail to find any positive impact of exports on economic development. The reasons for these different results have been discussed in a number of recent studies (Kohli and Singh 1987; Boulding 1992; Greenaway and Sapsford 1994; Poon 1995; Yaghmaian and Ghorashi 1995). These authors argue that the relationship between exports and economic growth depends on the level of development and the economic structure of a country. Export expansion may not impact on economic growth effectively at a low level of development, but the contribution of exports to economic growth will be of great significance when economic development progresses. Most of the studies mentioned above are conducted using multi-country samples. A few studies have examined the case for the NICs (Chen and Tang 1990; Dutt and Ghosh 1996). Consensus has not been reached on the impact of export expansion on economic growth in the context of China, a nation which is reforming its centrally planned economy.

This study is based on provincial rather than national data. The preference for provincial data is driven by two considerations: the limited nature of Chinese national data, and the diverse experience of the Chinese provinces in relation to the receipt of FDI and export growth. In terms of the former, reliable national data about FDI and exports tends to only be available from 1980 onward, and is then usually recorded on an annual basis. FDI and export data are accessible for the provinces and cities of China over the same period so that time series and cross-section data can be pooled as a resource for panel data regression modeling. Panel data sets have sufficient degrees of freedom to allow for reliable inferences to be drawn. This procedure is applied in the formal study cited here.

The development experiences of the Chinese provinces vary so greatly that an aggregate study of economic growth for China as a whole would be devoid of any meaning. An aggregate study, including FDI and exports in China, simply misses the basic point: that the distribution of inward FDI across China's provinces is unevenly distributed. Analysts of the Chinese economy generally concur with the view that the provinces of China are at present an appropriate basis for Chinese macro studies at present. Sun and Chai (1998) and Kam Ki Tang (1998) have undertaken two recent studies that support this view. The adoption of Zhang and Felmingham's (1999) grouping of the Chinese provinces is also appropriate. These authors group the individual provinces functionally. The groupings that apply are the high FDI provinces (HFDI), the medium FDI group (MFDI) and the low FDI grouping (LFDI).[2] This choice was based on functional characteristics, namely the differing policy treatment of the three regions and the concentration of inward FDI in the HFDI provinces. Zhang and Felmingham's study indicates that this grouping should be preserved.

The grouping of provinces by location and function dictates that this study takes into account the potential spillover effects of growth in one region or province on growth in others. This is a most important policy consideration as any policy that encourages inward FDI in one region will potentially impact on other regions, provided spillover effects are evident. This study extends the models developed by Feder (1982) to allow for interregional spillovers.

A model of export expansion, growth and spillover effects

The most commonly applied approach for empirical investigations of exports and economic development in the PRC is based on the neoclassical aggregate production function (NAPF), adding the indicator of export performance on the right-hand side of the NAPF equation to explain the possibility of export-led economic growth.

The model used in this study is an extended version of Feder's (1982) model. The advantage of Feder's model is that it allows for the separate measurement of a sector externality effect and a factor productivity effect, both of which are associated with export expansion. Feder's model is augmented with the addition of FDI as an independent variable in this study. This involves the disaggregation of total investment into FDI and domestic investment leading to the inclusion of a third relative marginal productive condition in Equation 12.8.

First, the economy is assumed to consist of two sectors: the export and the non-export sectors. So overall output (GDP) is the summation of the output from each sector.

Let Y = GDP, N = output of the non-export sector, and X = output of the export sector. Thus,

$$Y = N + X \tag{12.1}$$

It is assumed that there are two kinds of capital stock in each sector: foreign capital (K^*) and domestic capital (K^-). The production functions for sector X and N are specified as the functions of the factors allocated to each sector with an externality from sector X to N.

$$N = F(K^-_n, K^*_n, L_n, X) \tag{12.2}$$
$$X = G(K^-_x, K^*_x, L_x) \tag{12.3}$$

where K^-_n, K^-_x are domestic capital stock in N and X sectors, respectively, K^*_n, K^*_x are foreign capital stock in N and X sectors, respectively, and L_n, L_x are labour force in N and X sectors, respectively.

The assumptions here are that the domestic capital stock and FDI are used in both sectors and the total labour force is distributed across both the export and non-export sectors. So $K^- = K^-_n + K^-_x$, $K^* = K^*_n + K^*_x$, $L = L_n + L_x$.

Let the dot notation symbolise the time change of the specified variables.

$$\dot{Y} = \dot{N} + \dot{X} \tag{12.4}$$

Taking total differentials of Equations 12.2 and 12.3 with respect to time, and letting I^- and I^* represent the change of domestic capital and FDI ($\dot{K}^-, \dot{K}^*$), respectively, yields

$$\dot{N} = F_k I^-_n + F_k^* I^*_n + F_L \dot{L}_n + F_x \dot{X} \tag{12.5}$$

$$\dot{X} = G_k I^-_x + G_k^* I^*_x + G_L \dot{L}_x \tag{12.6}$$

In Equation 12.5, F refers to the marginal productivity with subscripts K^-, K^*, L standing for the input of domestic capital, FDI and labour in the non-export sector. In Equation 12.6, G refers to the marginal productivity with subscripts K^-, K^*, L representing the input of domestic capital, FDI and labour in the export sector.

Substituting Equations 12.5 and 12.6 into Equation 12.4 yields

$$\dot{Y} = F_k^- \dot{I}_n^- + F_k^* \dot{I}_n^* + F_L \dot{L}_n + F_x \dot{X} + G_k^- \dot{I}_x^- + G_k^* \dot{I}_x^* + G_L \dot{L}_x \quad (12.7)$$

A specific transformation is required if aggregate data is applied to estimate the sectoral marginal productivities. Suppose the respective marginal products in each sector are not the same, regardless of the source of the capital stock.

$$(G_k^- / F_k^-) = (G_L / F_L) = (G_k^* / F_k^*) = 1 + \delta \quad (12.8)$$

Equation 12.8 then shows that the ratios of marginal productivity of FDI, domestic capital and labour in sector X and N differ by δ. The underlying argument is that marginal factor productivities are likely to be lower in the non-export sector. One major reason is that export firms are located in a highly competitive sector of the economy. Competition encourages innovation, adaptability and the efficient management of a firm's resources (Feder 1982). The various regulations and constraints such as credit and foreign exchange rationing (Balassa 1978) are another reason for the differences between sectoral marginal factor productivities. Export companies are disciplined through competition in the international markets. Consequently, the export sector is forced to be more efficient than sheltered domestic industries and so productivity is forced up in this sector.

To advance the model further, G_k^*, G_k^- and G_L of Equation 12.8 are substituted into Equation 12.7 to yield

$$\dot{Y} = F_k^- (\dot{I}_n^- + \dot{I}_x^-) + F_k^* (\dot{I}_n^* + \dot{I}_x^*) + F_L (\dot{L}_n + \dot{L}_x) + F_x \dot{X}$$
$$+ \delta (F_k^- \dot{I}_x^- + F_k^* \dot{I}_x^* + F_L \dot{L}_x) \quad (12.9)$$

Using Equation 12.8 in Equation 12.9 yields

$$\dot{Y} = F_k^- \dot{I}^- + F_k^* \dot{I}^* + F_L \dot{L} + F_x \dot{X} + (\delta / 1 + \delta)(G_k^- \dot{I}_x^- + G_k^* \dot{I}_x^* + G_L \dot{L}_x) \quad (12.10)$$

Since the last three variables involve sectoral data, which are not available yet, we substitute Equation 12.6 into Equation 12.10 and simplify to obtain

$$\dot{Y} = F_k^- \dot{I}^- + F_k^* \dot{I}^* + F_L \dot{L} + [Fx + (\delta / 1 + \delta)] X \quad (12.11)$$

Note that the partial derivative of F with respect to X, (F_x), captures the sector-externality effect of export expansion and measures the positive externality of the export sector on the non-export sector. The symbol δ indicates the productivity differentials between the export and the non-export sectors—or the factor productivity effect—which measures the gain due to the higher productivity of factors in the export sector.

Now, let $F_k^- = \alpha_1$, $F_k^* = \alpha_2$, $F_L = \alpha_3$, $\gamma = [Fx + (\delta / 1 + \delta)]$, then Equation 12.11 can be simplified as

$$\dot{Y} = \alpha_1 \dot{I} + \alpha_2 \dot{I}^* + \alpha_3 \dot{L} + \gamma \dot{X} \qquad (12.12)$$

Equation 12.12 forms the basis of our estimation: α_1 measures the marginal productivity of domestic capital in the non-export sector, while α_2 measures the marginal productivity of foreign capital in the non-export sector. It is expected that both α_1 and α_2 will be positive, while α_3 refers to the labour growth for Chinese total labour forces and γ represents the parameter for the export variable ($\dot{x}$). It includes both a sector-externality effect (F_x) and the productivity differential (δ). Both should be positive and significantly different from zero since the hypothesis suggests that marginal productivities in the export sector are higher and that exports generate beneficial externalities to the non-export sector. If marginal productivities are equalised across sectors ($\delta = 0$) and if there are no inter-sector externalities ($F_x = 0$) then Equation 12.12 will reduce to the transformed neoclassical production formulation of the sources of growth model with foreign capital stock.[3] In fact, it is appropriate to identify the role of sector-externality and factor-productivity effects separately; γ can be decomposed at this stage on the assumption that exports affect the production of non-exports with constant elasticity (θ). The production function for the non-export sector will be

$$N = F(K_n, K^*_n, L_n, X) = X^\theta \Psi (K_n, K^*_n, L_n) \qquad (12.13)$$

Now the partial derivative of F with respect of X is given by

$$F_x = \partial N / \partial X = \theta (N/X) \qquad (12.14)$$

Because of Equation 12.1,

$$F_x = \theta (Y\text{-}X)/X \qquad (12.15)$$

Substituting Equation 12.15 into Equation 12.11 and after some manipulation, Equation 12.11 can be rewritten as

$$\dot{Y} = \alpha_1 \dot{I} + \alpha_2 \dot{I}^* + \alpha_3 \dot{L} + \theta (Y\text{-}X)(\dot{X}/X) + (\delta/1 + \delta) \dot{X} \qquad (12.16)$$

So Equation 12.16 is the basis of estimation allowing for the separate measurement of δ.

Data and methodology

Data and definition of variables

The data for 29 Chinese provinces, municipalities and autonomous regions (referred to as provinces) in China over the period 1984–98 are utilised in this study. Chongqin is a municipal city in China but is excluded from this study since it was only established in 1997. Because it was a part of Sichuan province prior to achieving its city status, we treat it as part of Sichuan province in order to keep the data consistent. Tibet is not included in this study since at this point in time, it has no FDI.

The data on Chinese provincial GDP, CPI, domestic investment, FDI, population and exports are taken from the various sources.[4] The GDP deflators for China and United States for the period 1983–98 are obtained from the DX data file (2000), WBWT: Data Table 2 and Data Table 3, respectively. The exchange rate for Chinese yuan RMB in terms of US dollars for the year 1995 is used in this study (IMF 2000).

By and large, Chinese statistics are internally consistent and accurate enough for empirical work (Chow 1993). One concern regarding data is the limited time series. Since panel data sets are employed in this research, the limited sample data restrictions need to be overcome. The models for this study can not only be applied to the whole sample consisting of 435 observations but also to the three regions defined later in this section. The panel of the HFDI, the MFDI and the LFDI provinces when combined with 15 time-series observations produces data sets of the following size: the HFDI region (120 observations), the MFDI region (195 observations) and the LFDI region (120 observations). The panel data constitutes a sufficiently large data set for the current study.

The variables are defined in the following way.

- Y is the first difference of real provincial GDP (billion yuan RMB) in China for the period 1984–98. The year 1995 is specified as the base year. It is calculated as follows. The current values of GDP for each province are first converted into real values using 1995 constant prices for each province. Then $\dot{Y}_t = GDP_t - GDP_{t-1}$, where GDP_t, GDP_{t-1} are the real GDP for the two consecutive years respectively.
- I is the change in domestically financed capital stock (billion yuan RMB) in each province for the period 1984–98 in real terms, with 1995 as the base year. The current domestically financed total fixed asset investment is converted into real terms using the GDP deflator as a proxy for the total fixed asset investment deflator, because total fixed investment deflators are only available from 1992 for the Chinese provinces.
- I^* refers to the change in foreign capital stock which is specified as real Chinese provincial inward FDI (billion yuan RMB). The initial FDI data are nominal data measured in millions of US dollars. This variable is obtained as follows. First, the current values of FDI are deflated using the US GDP deflator (1995 = 100). Then the real values of FDI in millions of US dollars for each province are transferred to the real values measured in billion yuan RMB. The exchange rate of yuan RMB with respect to US dollars in 1995 is employed here to exclude the effect of inflation and the instability of the exchange rate.
- L is the first difference of the total labour force in each province of China for the period 1984–98. It is calculated as $\dot{L} = L_t - L_{t-1}$, where

L_t is the labour force in the current year and L_{t-1} stands for the labour force in the previous year. We use the supply side of labour force data because the analysis adopts a supply side description of changes in aggregate output and also because the unemployment data for provinces is incomplete. Provincial population growth is used as a proxy for total labour force growth in each province on the assumption that the participation rate remains the same.

- $\dot{X}$ refers to the first difference of real exports for the period 1984–98. Export data are originally expressed in millions of US dollars at current values. So first, the real values of exports for the provinces are found by dividing the current exports by the US GDP deflator (1995 = 100). Then exports are expressed in real billions of yuan RMB using the exchange rate of yuan RMB to US dollars in 1995. This is an attempt to avoid the effect of inflation and the instability of the exchange rate. Then, $\dot{X} = \mathrm{Exp}_t - \mathrm{Exp}_{t-1}$, where Exp_t, Exp_{t-1} are real exports in consecutive years.

Methodology

The major part of this study is focused on investigating the roles of exports and FDI in regional economic growth and identifying the likely interregional spillover effects. The first step is to divide China into regions according to their stage of development. The three classifications chosen here are suggested by Zhang and Felmingham (1999) and conform to policy directions of the Chinese government.

The 29 provinces in the PRC were divided into three groups depending on the average value of FDI received by each province over the period 1983–98. The high FDI group (HFDI) had received no less than US$500 million on average. The provinces qualifying as HFDI are Beijing, Tianjin, Liaoning Shanghai, Jiangsu, Zhejiang, Fujian, Shandong and Guangdong. The medium group (MFDI) received an average annual FDI in the range of US$100–500 million, and include Hebei, Jilin, Heilongjiang, Anhui, Jiangxi, Henan, Hubei, Hunan, Guangxi, Hainan, Sichuan and Shanxi. Provinces receiving less than US$100 million comprised Shaanxi, Inner Mongolia, Guizhuzo, Yunnan, Xinjiang, Gansu, Qinghai and Ningxia. These are defined as the low FDI group (LFDI). The HFDI, MFDI and LFDI groups coincide with the Eastern, the Central and the Western geographical regions of China.

Three models are estimated in this study. Estimation of the first model, based on Equation 12.12, examines the contribution of export expansion to economic growth for China as a whole and the three regions (the HFDI, MFDI and LFDI regions), respectively. Estimation of the second model based on Equation 12.16 allows identification of differences in the nature as well as the magnitude of the contribution of export expansion to growth among the three regions of China. The econometric forms of Equations 12.12 and 12.16 are written as

$$\dot{Y} = \alpha_1 \dot{I}^- + \alpha_2 I^* + \alpha_3 \dot{L} + \gamma \dot{X} + \varepsilon_1. \qquad (12.17)$$
$$Y = \alpha_1 \dot{I}^- + \alpha_2 I^* + \alpha_3 L + \theta (Y-X)(\dot{X}/X) + (\delta/1+\delta)\dot{X} + \varepsilon_1 (12.18)$$

Both models, Equations 12.17 and 12.18, capture the contribution of export expansion to growth through two channels: sector-externality and factor-productivity effects. The second model is differentiated from the first in that it allows for the separate identification of these two effects. The sector-externality effect measures the positive externality of the export sector on the non-export sector. The factor-productivity effect measures the gain due to the higher productivity of factors in the export sector.

The third model applied in this study is designed to test the spillover effects from the HFDI region to the MFDI and LFDI regions and from the MFDI to the LFDI region. This model is based on the fact that the degree of economic development differs substantially across the three regions of China. Trade and FDI are heavily concentrated in the coastal region. The Chinese government has strongly encouraged the HFDI region to establish close links with the rest of the world. Subsequently, the East is the richest region, followed by the MFDI region. The LFDI region is backward with a low degree of openness. Our assumption is that there are positive spillover effects from the richer to the poorer regions.

The growth pole theory forms the theoretical basis for Model 12.3. Regional development theories and policies have largely focused on the dynamic interactive process between the relatively developed regions, termed the core, and the less developed regions, termed the periphery. The industrialised regions refer to the main economic centres or areas while the less industrialised regions refer to countryside or far inland areas. According to Hirschman (1958), the development process is a chain of disequilibria. Uneven growth between different regions is inevitable and occurs frequently. The different regions interact through input–output linkages and other relationships. The input demand effects and output supply effects are important interactive effects between different regions.[5] Both backward and forward linkage effects are realised through input and output flows, including labour migration and trade in intermediate and final products. In addition to input–output relations, interregional capital flows, technological transmission, consumer market demand and income remittances are important mechanisms through which interactive impacts between regions are achieved.

A number of studies have shown that there are positive and negative transmission effects (Richardson 1976; Gaile 1980; Wilber and Francis 1986; Hughes and Holland 1994; Barkely, Henry and Bao 1996). The positive impacts are known as the spread effect, which refers to the diffusion of growth from advanced to backward regions. The spread effect tends to promote economic development and increase income per capita in the backward areas and eventually leads to a convergence of interregional development. Backwash effects, on the contrary, are the unfavourable effects on the poor regions, of interregional interdependence. These include the migration of educated, skilled and technical workers and the flows of capital from poor to rich regions, and unfavourable changes in the terms of trade between primary and manufactured products. This seems likely to impede economic development in backward regions.

The third model is formulated to test interregional spillovers in the context of China. For this purpose, the following equations are applied.

$$\dot{Y}_M = \alpha_{11}\dot{I}_M + \alpha_{12}I^*_M + \alpha_{13}\dot{L}_M + \gamma_{11}\dot{X}_M + \beta_{11}\dot{Y}_H + \varepsilon_{11} \quad (12.19)$$

$$\dot{Y}_L = \alpha_{21}\dot{I}_L + \alpha_{22}I^*_L + \alpha_{23}\dot{L}_L + \gamma_{21}\dot{X}_L + \beta_{21}\dot{Y}_H + \varepsilon_{21} \quad (12.20)$$

$$\dot{Y}_L = \alpha_{31}\dot{I}_L + \alpha_{32}I^*_L + \alpha_{33}\dot{L}_L + \gamma_{31}\dot{X}_L + \beta_{31}\dot{Y}_M + \varepsilon_{31} \quad (12.21)$$

In Equations 12.19, 12.20 and 12.21, $\dot{Y}$, $\dot{I}$, I^*, $\dot{L}$ and $\dot{X}$ are, respectively, the change of GDP, domestic investment, FDI, the growth of the labour force and the change in exports. All variables are in real terms expressed in billions of yuan RMB, except for labour which is measured in number of workers. Subscripts H, M and L with respect to the variables stand for the HFDI, MFDI and LFDI regions. $\dot{Y}_H$, $\dot{Y}_M$ in Equations 12.19, 12.20 and 12.21 are the average first differences of GDP in the HFDI and MFDI regions, respectively, used as an indicator of interregional spillover effects. Our assumption here is that the spillover from the HFDI region is evenly distributed to the MFDI and the LFDI regions, but that feedback from the MFDI and the LFDI provinces to the HFDI region is negligible. If the coefficients of $\dot{Y}_H$, $\dot{Y}_M$ (β_{11}, β_{21}, β_{31}) in Equations 12.19, 12.20 and 12.21 are positive and significant, then we can conclude that there is spillover from the HFDI to the MFDI and LFDI regions, or from the MFDI region to the LFDI region. In addition, we try the change of exports ($\dot{X}$) and FDI (I^*) as indicators of interregional spillover effects.

The regional level panel data used overcome a number of problems encountered with either cross-section or time-series data alone. The advantages of panel data are varied and include an increased number of observations, more variability and information and the possibility of treating two dimensions (cross-section and time-series) separately.

All the regressions are performed using Limdep software. The estimation results of fixed effect and random effect models are obtained for panel data. Test results from the fixed effect model may raise questions about the endogeneity of export expansion or the variable as a determinant of GDP growth. This problem may be solved by a further step where the models are estimated by simultaneous methods.

Results and interpretation

The results obtained from the estimation of Equation 12.12 are reported in Table 12.1 for the entire sample of 29 provinces as well as the sub-samples for the three regions. A preliminary test for the correlation between variable FDI and X is also performed and it is found that the correlation coefficient is 0.5120 with t-test of 12.48 for the whole sample and 0.4647 (5.70), 0.1511 (2.12), -0.2115(2.35), for the HFDI, the MFDI and the LFDI, respectively (t-ratio in brackets).[6] These correlation coefficients are all significant at the five per cent level, but the correlation coefficients are not high enough to be of concern regarding the reliability of results.

The study uses panel data so that both random effect and fixed effect models are estimated. The random effects model is rejected in favour of the fixed effect model for the whole sample by the Hausman test $\chi^2(3) = 21.45$, $\chi^2(4) = 19.36$ for the Neoclassical model and Model 12.1 (Equation 12.17), respectively. However, for the sake of simplicity, only the results from estimation of the fixed effect model are presented here for the whole sample.[7] The results from within estimates (fixed effects) and random effects are listed in Appendix 12.1. Fixed effect models are rejected in favour of the random effect models for all three regions since the Hausman test (χ^2) with four degrees of freedom are 7.45, 2.04, 1.58 for the HFDI, the MFDI and the LFDI groups, respectively. The results from the fixed effect model for the three regions are also listed in Appendix 12.1.

The results listed in columns two and three are the two specifications of the regression equation for the whole sample. Column two contains the results from the modified conventional Neoclassical model (including the FDI in the equation) assuming $\gamma=0$ in our Equation 12.17. It investigates GDP growth based on domestic investment, FDI, and the growth of labour only. The test results for Model 12.1 are presented in column three. The coefficients of domestic investment, FDI and the growth of labour are positive and significant in both columns (columns two and three). These results indicate not only that the domestically-financed investment and growth of labour are the major factors in explaining Chinese economic growth, but also that the role of inward FDI cannot be ignored. This is supported by the fact that inward FDI in China grew on average at 35 per cent per annum, increasing from US$1,258 million to US$45,463 million between 1984 and 1998. FDI accounted for 10.3 per cent and 9.1 per cent of the total domestic capital formation in China in 1997 and 1998, respectively (SSB 1998 and 1999).

The adjusted R^2 is higher in Model 12.1 than in the modified Neoclassical

Table 12.1 **Regression results for Model 12.1,** panel data

Dependent variable $\dot{Y}$: $\dot{Y} = \alpha_1\dot{I} + \alpha_2\dot{I}^* + \alpha_3\dot{L} + \gamma\dot{X} + \mathcal{E}_1$ (12.17)

Variable (parameter)	Whole sample	HFDI region	MFDI region	LFDI region	
1	2	3	4	5	6
	Neoclassical model (Fixed effect)	Equ. 12.17 (Fixed effect)	Equ. 12.17 Random effect model	Equ. 12.17 Random effect model	Equ. 12.17 Random effect model
$\dot{I}$ (α_1)	0.222 (10.932)*	0.225 (11.056)*	0.175 (3.834)*	0.165 (2.795)*	0.059 (0.059)*
$\dot{I}^*$ (α_2)	0.245 (3.956)*	0.197 (2.850)*	0.267 (2.132)*	0.906 (2.488)*	1.422 (4.113)*
$\dot{L}$ (α_3)	0.465 (5.449)*	0.442 (5.112)*	0.394* (2.833)	0.101 (0.445)	-0.090 (-0.250)
$\dot{X}$ (γ)	.. ..	0.073 (1.659)**	0.071 (1.443)	-0.143 (-0.504)	-0.290 (-1.541)
constant	-3.446 (-0.389)	-3.343 (-0.378)	24.570 (0.770)	28.350 (0.940)	85.703 (0.420)
(Adj) R²	0.570	0.577	0.625	0.462	0.898
No. of obs	435	435	135	180	120
Hausman test	$\chi^2(3)=21.45^*$	$\chi^2(4)=19.36^*$	$\chi^2(4)=7.45$	$\chi^2(4)=2.04$	$\chi^2(4)=1.58$

Notes: T-ratio is in brackets.
* and ** represent 5% and 10% significant level respectively.

model, indicating that the explanatory power of Model 12.1 improves when export growth is modelled as an explanation for GDP growth for China as a whole. The coefficient of $\dot{X}$ (γ), which picks up both the sector externality effect and the factor-productivity effect, is positive and significant at the ten per cent level in Model 12.1. These findings support the existence of the combined effects of export growth and also confirm the important role of exports in the economic development of China.[8]

The test results reveal different stories for the HFDI, the MFDI and the LFDI regions. For each region, domestic investment and FDI are significantly different from zero, supporting the Neoclassical view that economic growth is influenced by capital formation. In relation to labour, the coefficient of growth of labour (α_3) is positive and significant in the HFDI region in particular. This implies that the labour surplus was not the prevalent explanation in the coastal provinces. On the other hand, the coefficient of labour growth is positive in the MFDI region and negative in the LFDI region. However, both the coefficients of labour are insignificant. One explanation is that there is high or disguised unemployment in these inland regions, especially in the countryside. Another explanation involves the strong trend of migration from the MFDI and the LFDI region to the HFDI region since the early 1980s. It is estimated that in 1997 12.9 million labourers migrated from the countryside to the provincial cities, while 5.9 million and 2.9 million labourers migrated from the inland regions to the coastal areas. The absorption of these unemployed labourers into the eastern economy has tended to contribute to lower unemployment and the higher growth of the inland regions (Sun 2000).

Columns four, five and six of Table 12.1 show that the coefficients of $\dot{X}$ vary across the three regions. The coefficient of export growth is positive and the t-ratio is higher than 1 only in the HFDI region. The coefficient of $\dot{X}$ (γ) is -0.143, which is not significant for the MFDI region. These estimates indicate that the relationship between exports and GDP growth does not seem to be particularly strong in the East if the relationship is examined in the context of each region separately. However, export expansion is not related to economic growth for the MFDI region. The statistical results from column six of Table 12.1 show that export growth has a negative impact on GDP growth in the LFDI region. This may be due to the lack of available infrastructure in that region, a problem exacerbated by the diversion of resources away from the non-export sector in that region.

These findings indicate that there are substantial differences in the relationship between exports and growth among regions. This is also supported by Lee's (1994) study of much earlier data.

The results from Equation 12.18 for the separate effects of sectoral externality and factor productivity are reported on Table 12.2. The fixed effect model (between group) estimation results are listed in column two of for the whole sample. The Hausman test has $\chi^2 = 18.92$ with five degrees of freedom suggesting that the fixed effect model estimators are consistent and efficient. But for all regional tests, the Hausman test results of $\chi^2(5) = 7.14$, $\chi^2(5) = 2.60$, and $\chi^2(5) = 0.54$ for the three regions are insignificant, resulting in a clear rejection of the null hypothesis of the fixed effect against the random effect model. The results from within estimates of the fixed effect model and the random effect model for the whole sample and the fixed effect estimators for regional estimation are listed in Appendix 12.2.

The results in column two of Table 12.2 for Equation 12.18 suggest that the marginal productivities of domestically-financed capital, FDI and the marginal productivity of labour are positive and statistically significant. These findings confirm the results obtained in Table 12.1. The differential marginal productivity parameter δ is 0.0622 ($\delta/1+\delta = 0.0586$), indicating that factors used in the export sector are 6.22 per cent more productive than those used in the non-export sector. But this parameter is not significant. No conclusion can be drawn from the observation that marginal productivity is higher in the export sector than the non-export sector for the whole sample. The parameter θ representing the externality effect of the export sector on the non-export sector is 0.015, with t-ratio not significant. This suggests that there is no positive impact of the export sector on the non-export sector for China as a whole.

The regional estimation results in columns three, four and five of Table 12.2 indicate that the marginal productivity of foreign capital is both positive and significantly different from zero for all three regions. The results also indicate that marginal productivity of domestically-financed capital is significantly different from zero in the HFDI and the MFDI regions. The statistical results for FDI both from Table 12.1 and Table 12.2 confirm that economic growth is largely dependent on FDI whether it is examined in the context of China as a whole or for the three individual regions. The highest coefficient of FDI is in the LFDI region, implying that the marginal productivity of FDI in the non-export sector is highest in that region. This reveals that the growth of the west relies substantially on capital formation and (most likely) capital expenditure on infrastructure.

In the HFDI region, the differential marginal productivity parameter δ is positive but not significant $((\delta/1+\delta) = 0.0246)$, suggesting that there is no difference between marginal productivity in the export and the non-export sectors. This can be explained by the more advanced industrial structure and the greater openness of the coastal economy. Openness in trade is increasingly being viewed as an important mechanism for steady economic growth in less industrialised countries.[9] China's economy has opened up significantly since 1979. The volume of exports and imports as a percentage of GDP increased from 8 per cent in 1979 to 34 per cent in 1998 (SSB 1980 and 1998). It is noted that the openness of the Chinese economy is biased towards the coastal area. However, the externality effect of exports on the non-export sector represented by θ (0.0754) is positive and significant, implying that the externality from the export to the non-export sector does exist for the Coastal provinces. This may be explained by the emergence of more foreign invested enterprises (FIEs) along the coast. Their involvement in the export sector may have impacted on the non-export sector in the East. This argument will be investigated in a further study.

The statistical results in column four of Table 12.2 show that there is neither a factor productivity difference nor an externality effect from the export to the non-export sector for the MFDI region.

The results for the LFDI region are reported in column five of Table 12.2. The finding is that marginal productivity is higher in the non-export sector, as indicated by the negative and significant sign of δ $((\delta/1+\delta) = -0.073)$.

Table 12.2   Regression results for Model 12.2, panel data

Dependent variable $\dot{Y}$: $\dot{Y} = \alpha_1 \dot{I} + \alpha_2 I^* + \alpha_3 \dot{L} + \theta (Y\text{-}X)(\dot{X}/X) + (\delta/1+\delta)\dot{X} + \varepsilon_2$

(12.18)

Variable (parameter)	Whole sample	HFDI region	MFDI region	LFDI region
1	2	3	4	5
	Equation 12.18 Fixed effect	Equation 12.18 Random effect	Equation 12.18 Random effect	Equation 12.18 Random effect
$\dot{I}$ (α_1)	0.223 (10.921)*	0.159 (3.46)*	0.181 (3.342)*	0.061 (1.667)**
I^* (α_2)	0.205 (2.957)*	0.297 (2.38)*	0.877 (2.425)*	1.731 (4.331)*
$\dot{L}$ (α_3)	0.437 (5.067)*	0.367 (2.658)*	0.185 (0.845)	-0.019 (-0.990)
$\dot{X}$ $(\delta/1+\delta)$	0.059 (1.282)	0.025 (0.370)	-0.239 (-0.890)	-0.073 (-2.659)*
NGX (θ)	0.015 (1.364)	0.075 (2.002)*	0.009 (0.560)	0.029 (1.293)
constant	-4.411 (-0.520)	20.480 (0.662)	17.268 (0.663)	29.640 (0.322)
(Adj) R²	0.572	0.641	0.463	0.898
No. of obs	435	135	180	120
Hausman Test	$\chi^2(5)=18.92$	$\chi^2(5)=7.14$	$\chi^2(5)=1.17$	$\chi^2(5)=0.54$

Notes: T-ratio is in the bracket
* and ** represent 5% and 10% significant level respectively.

Comparatively speaking, the LFDI region is backward and markets are largely domestically-oriented with a low degree of openness. The substantial gap in technology applied to the export and the non-export sector partly explains the deficiency of the export sector in the LFDI group. The test results from Model 12.2 confirm the argument that a certain level of development is necessary before the export sector positively impacts on the non-export sector and overall economic growth.

These findings are consistent with the theoretical hypothesis that the impact of export expansion and FDI on economic growth varies according to regional economic characteristics, including the level of development, economic structure and policy orientations. To a large extent, the differential impact of exports and FDI account for divergent growth performance across different regions. On the other hand, the level of development and the structural characteristics and policy orientation shape the direction and the extent of the impact of export expansion and FDI. This study therefore confirms that export expansion and economic growth are two interactive processes of economic development. Simultaneous modelling will confirm or deny this absolutely, but it is a matter for further analysis.

The results from the Model 12.3 developed are listed in Table 12.3. Columns two and three contain the test results of spillover effects from the HFDI region to the MFDI and the LFDI regions. Column four shows the results of the spread from the MFDI to the LFDI region. It is noted that the parameters (β_1, β_2, β_3) are significantly different from zero.

These estimates support the rejection of the hypothesis that there are no spillover effects from the HFDI to the MFDI and the LFDI regions, or from the MFDI to the LFDI region, when the output in the HFDI and the MFDI region (Y_H, Y_M) are used as indicators of interregional spillover effects.

The interregional growth transmission between the HFDI and the MFDI region and between the HFDI and the LFDI can be explained as follows: the eastern region is traditionally more advanced. This is reflected in its industrial structure. It is widely agreed that primary industry comprises a large share of GDP and total employment when the economy is at an early stage of its development (see Richardson 1976; Sun and Dilip 1997; Sun 2000). However, secondary and tertiary industries tend to become more important and account for a larger share of GDP as the economy develops. Industrial structure and the stage of development vary across regions in China. Some basic statistical data supports this view. Table 12.4 provides the share of industries as a percentage of GDP for the three regions in 1997 and 1998. It is found that the share of primary industry in GDP in the HFDI was 13.27 per cent and 12.64 per cent in 1997 and 1998, respectively. These statistics were higher in the MFDI and the LFDI regions, where the primary industry share was 22.64 per cent and 21.37 per cent for the MFDI region, and 25.57 per cent and 24.62 per cent for the LFDI, in 1997 and 1998, respectively. On the contrary, the share of the secondary and tertiary industries as a percentage of GDP were higher in the HFDI region than was the case in the other two regions.

Since the 1980s, the coastal region has been identified as the growth core of the national economy. The regional development policies pursued there have favoured the HFDI region where a series of special preferential policies have been applied. These include tax concessions for the enterprises located in the SEZs and coastal open area, more autonomy in foreign trade and FDI, and a relatively large share of tax income retained by the local government. At the same time, market-oriented economic reforms and the opening of the Chinese market to foreign trade and FDI have progressed far more broadly and deeply in the HFDI region than in the inland regions. More developed markets have contributed to productivity growth and the overall improvement in economic

Table 12.3   **Regression results for Model 12.3** (interregional spillover effects)

Variables	Equation 12.19 Spillover from HFDI to MFDI (Random effect model)	Equation 12.20 Spillover from HFDI to LFDI (Fixed effect model)	Equation 12.21 Spillover from MFDI to LFDI (Fixed effect model)
1	2	3	4
I⁻ (α_{i1})	0.101 (1.658)**	0.118 (4.084)*	0.136 (4.957)*
I* (α_{i2})	0.262 (0.649)	0.536 (2.028)*	0.532 (1.992)*
$\dot{L}$ (α_{i3})	0.329 (1.415)	0.391 (2.810)*	0.326 (2.406)*
$\dot{X}$ (γ_i)	-0.079 (-0.290)	-0.127 (-0.547)	-0.124 (-0.532)
$\dot{Y}$ (β_i)	0.355 (3.937)*	0.073 (3.104)*	0.124 (2.920)*
constant	-22.810 (-0.656)	-8.463 (-1.270)	-7.883 (-1.174)
(Adj) R^2	0.505	0.824	0.823
No. of obs	180	120	120
Hausman test	$\chi^2(5)=2.11$	$\chi^2(5)=20.04$	$\chi^2(5)=18.60$

Notes: T-ratio is in bracket
*and** represent 5% and 10% significant level respectively.

efficiency of the HFDI region. More importantly, the Chinese central government has committed a large amount of capital in the HFDI provinces to improve infrastructure, especially the transportation system and telecommunication facilities. These incentives have provided a better investment environment, attracting FDI to this region. It is widely recognised that the HFDI area is more open than the MFDI and LFDI regions.[10]

Input–output linkages are important reasons behind interregional spillover effects. Input demand, also termed the backward linkage effect, can stimulate growth in the production of intermediate products and materials. With regard to the spatial distribution pattern of Chinese industries, the LFDI and MFDI regions are largely oriented towards primary industries, such as agriculture, mining and forestry, while manufacturing and services dominate in the east. Coastal economic growth, since the opening of the Chinese economy, has created a strong demand for raw materials and intermediate products from the inland regions, transmitting a growth stimulus from the HFDI provinces to the MFDI and LFDI regions. Further government policies have encouraged the use of domestic resources in producing exports.

The measure of the spillover effects $ß_1$ (0.3551) from the HFDI to the MFDI is higher than $ß_2$ (0.073) which represents the spillover effects from the HFDI to the LFDI. This suggests that the dimension of spillover effects from the HFDI to the MFDI provinces is larger than the spillover to the LFDI. This can be explained by the spatial location and the degree of similarity of the economic structures in the HFDI and the MFDI regions. The MFDI region is more open and more closely linked with the eastern economy in comparison with the LFDI provinces. As described, $\dot{X}$ and FDI are also employed in the model instead of $\dot{Y}$ as indicators for spillover effects, but the test results fail to show the presence of interregional spillover effects. A reasonable explanation is that output in the export sector and the activities involving the FIEs in the HFDI regions are not significant enough to impact on the economic development of other regions, although the previous analysis shows FDI and exports are the major factors in coastal economic growth.

Conclusion

China has experienced remarkable economic growth since the 1980s. Economic reform, export expansion, FDI, SEZs and joint ventures have all affected the three main regions of China. The empirical study in this chapter analysed the impact of exports and FDI on regional economic growth. In addition, the interregional spillover effect model was applied, based on growth pole theory, to investigate the transmission of growth from the comparatively rich HFDI region to the MFDI and the LFDI, and from the MFDI to the LFDI regions.

Three models were developed. The first two investigated the effects of export growth, FDI, domestic investment and labour growth on economic growth in the context of China as a whole as well as the three individual regions. FDI was found to be significant in all cases and all three models established that the contribution of FDI to overall economic growth is critical. Another finding was that exports have a positive and significant impact on Chinese economic growth. The positive externality from the export to the non-export sector was evident in the HFDI region. These findings indicate that the contribution of export growth to overall economic growth is important.

When the study focuses on the regional development of the three areas, it is clear that the role of export expansion varies across all three regions. Export growth significantly contributed to economic growth on the coast, while its impact was insignificant in the MFDI region and negative or marginally significant in the LFDI region. These results indicate that the role of exports in economic development depends largely on the individual situation of each region. The level of development and industrial structure, the policy orientation

Table 12.4   Industrial structure of the HFDI, MFDI and LFDI regions

	Primary industry (% of GDP)		Secondary industry (% of GDP)		Tertiary industry (% of GDP)	
	1997	1998	1997	1998	1997	1998
HFDI region	13.27	12.64	48.94	48.41	37.68	38.95
MFDI region	22.64	21.37	46.34	46.27	31.09	32.28
LFDI region	25.57	24.62	41.78	41.82	32.69	33.55

Source: SSB, 1998 and 1999. *Statistical Yearbook of China*, China Statistical Publishing House, Beijing.

and the degree of openness are quite different among the three regions. Without attaining a certain level of development and openness, exports are unlikely to change economic growth effectively and will fail to act as a driving force in economic growth.

The spillover test results clearly indicate that economic growth in the HFDI does spread to the MFDI and the LFDI regions. This positive growth transmission spreads from the comparatively rich coastal region to the inland regions through input–output linkage effects and the absorption of disguised unemployment. This result has important implications for policy. If the HFDI region plays the role of a growth core, the policies applied in the HFDI region will not only promote productivity and facilitate growth in that region, but will also increase economic development in inland regions. At the same time, more open policies should apply to the inland regions at this stage of their development. Policies promoting export performance and attracting FDI are required. The open door policy should extend as far as possible to the inland regions, where there is huge growth potential. The inland regions should have at the very least, similar development policies and incentives as those applying to the high FDI recipients. Regional discrimination policy should be eliminated. In addition, the central government should improve infrastructure in the MFDI and LFDI regions so as to help them achieve a minimum level of development within the shortest period of time. These measures promise to lessen the gap between different regions in respect of their rate of economic development, and to facilitate its spread from the coastal to the inland regions.

Appendix 12.1

Table A12.1 Regression results for Model 12.1, panel data for China as a whole

Dependent variable $\dot{Y}: \dot{Y} = \alpha_1 \dot{I} + \alpha_2 \dot{I} + \alpha_3 \dot{L} + \gamma \dot{X} + \varepsilon_1$ (12.17)

Variable (param.)	Whole Sample Neoclassical model		Equation 12.18		HFDI Region Fixed effect		MFDI Region Fixed effect		LFDI Region Fixed effect	
	Fixed (within)	Random	Fixed (within)	Random	Between	Within	Between	Within	Between	Within
1	2	3	4	5	6	7	8	9	10	11
$\dot{I}$ (α_1)	0.167 (5.240)*	0.215 (10.000)*	0.169 (5.293)*	0.217 (9.946)*	0.213 (5.712)*	0.158 (3.097)*	0.217 (5.323)*	0.916 (1.060)	0.159 (7.584)*	0.033 (0.914)
$\dot{I}$ (α_2)	0.265 (2.860)*	0.253 (3.920)*	0.247 (2.600)*	0.210 (2.930)*	0.182 (1.645)*	0.254 (1.819)*	0.625 (2.211)*	1.350 (1.959)*	0.750 (3.664)*	2.303 (2.943)*
$\dot{L}$ (α_3)	-2.000 (-1.180)	0.437 (5.120)	-0.194 (-1.140)	0.410 (4.710)	0.521 (3.854)	-0.247 (-0.880)	0.261 (1.422)	-0.062 (-0.203)	0.266 (2.474)*	0.032 (0.187)
$\dot{X}$ (θ)	..	..	0.039 (0.830)	0.072 (1.596)	0.076 (1.183)	0.046 (0.732)	-0.099 (-0.361)	-0.173 (-0.542)	-0.172 (-0.921)	-0.153 (-0.705)
constant	..	0.131 (0.010)	..	0.375 (0.030)	6.175 (0.313)	..	5.478 (0.320)	..	3.574 (0.817)	..
(Adj) R²	0.602	0.572	0.608	0.575	0.612	0.671	0.450	0.443	0.898	0.898
No. of obs	435	435	435	435	135	135	180	180	120	120

Notes: T-ratio is in bracket

* and ** represent 5% and 10% significant level respectively.

Appendix 12.2

Table A12.2 Regression results for Equation 12.6, panel data

Dependent variable $Y_i = \alpha_1 \dot{Y}_i + \alpha_2 \dot{L}_i + \alpha_3 \dot{L} + \theta (Y-X)(\dot{X}/X) + (\delta/1+\delta)\dot{X} + \varepsilon_2$ (12.18)

Variable (parameter)	Whole Sample		HFDI region		MFDI region		LFDI region	
	Fixed Within	Random	Fixed effect Between	Within	Fixed effect Between	Within	Fixed effect Between	Within
Ï (α_1)	0.171 (5.316)	0.216 (9.761)	0.185 (4.799)	0.147 (2.862)	0.214 (5.170)	0.095 (1.096)	0.145 (5.520)	0.042 (0.918)
Ï (α_2)	0.246 (2.594)	0.217 (3.011)	0.237 (2.139)	0.277 (1.982)	0.692 (2.231)	1.340 (1.925)	1.232 (4.178)	2.368 (2.435)
$\dot{L}$ (α_3)	-0.188 (-1.108)	0.405 (4.639)	0.468 (3.474)	-0.224 (-0.800)	0.283 (1.502)	-0.053 (-0.173)	0.254 (1.909)	0.031 (0.149)
X ($\delta/1+\delta$)	0.031 (0.636)	0.059 (1.251)	0.025 (0.384)	0.011 (0.157)	-0.200 (-0.598)	-0.298 (-0.729)	-0.659 (-2.392)	-0.619 (-1.959)
NGX (θ)	0.008 (0.737)	0.014 (1.291)	0.091 (2.410)	0.058 (1.502)	0.008 (0.531)	0.008 (0.492)	0.033 (3.222)	0.291 (2.836)
constant	..	-0.721 (-0.072)	4.602 (0.218)	..	3.001 (0.169)	..	3.267 (0.604)	..
(Adj) R²	0.602	0.577	0.626	0.673	0.447	0.441	0.824	0.828
No. of obs	435	435	135	135	180	180	120	120

Notes: T-ratio is in bracket.

Notes

1   This indicates China's spectacular growth.
2   See details in methodology for grouping method.
3   $\dot{Y} = \alpha_1 I + \alpha_2 I^* + \alpha_3 L$
4   The data on Chinese provincial GDP, CPI, domestic investment, FDI, population and exports from 1985 to 1995 are taken from *China's Regional Economy after Seventeen Years of Reform and Opening up*, published by the China Statistical Publishing House in 1996. The above-mentioned data for 1983, 1984 and 1996–98 are drawn from *The Statistical Yearbook of China* for various years, published by the China Statistical Publishing House.
5   The input demand effects and output supply effects are also known as the backward linkage effects and forward linkage effects, respectively.
6   $T = r / \sqrt{(1 - r^2) / (n - 2)}$ distributed according to the t-distribution.
7   For the fixed effect model, there are two sets of results. One is constrained least squares regression (between estimation) and the other is the least squares dummy variable model (within estimation). The former is estimated by simple OLS assuming all individual specific constants are equal. The latter is estimated by partitioned OLS with individual specific constant terms (no overall constant).
8   Refers to a sector externality and factor productivity effects.
9   Openness is defined as the ratio of the sum of exports and imports to GDP.
10 The eastern region (HFDI) is found to have the highest degree of openness in several studies (Lee 1994; Sun and Dilip 1997; Sun 2000.)

13

Decentralisation, economic growth and the local provision of public goods

Yu Chen

Decentralisation is a widespread phenomenon in many countries, especially in developing countries and transitional economies. Whatever its origin, decentralisation impacts greatly on important aspects of economic development such as the mobility and allocation of resources, the provision of local public goods, macroeconomic stability, incentives and efficiency, equity, and so on. While decentralisation is widespread in developing and transitional economies, theories of decentralisation are mostly, if not exclusively, based on the experiences of developed countries. Therefore, assumptions such as the existence of adequate institutions may not be satisfied in developing and transitional economies. This should make us cautious when applying traditional decentralisation theories to developing and transitional economies, and we should be aware of the possibility of obtaining contradictory or insignificant results when we empirically estimate the effects of decentralisation in these economies. We do not have enough empirical knowledge of decentralisation to enable us to make definitive recommendations as to what, when, or how, to decentralise. Much discussion on decentralisation is a curious combination of strong theoretical beliefs and weak empirical evidence (World Bank 1999).

Sometimes the complexity of decentralisation is ignored by decision-makers who are pressed to establish reform measures. Analysing the effects of decentralisation policies is significant because in the short run it helps to identify pragmatic approaches for compensating weak institutions in developing and transitional economies, and in the long run helps to reflect on appropriate key institutions for successful decentralisation. From this perspective we look at decentralisation in the transitional economy of China and hope to glean some useful results and implications for future reforms.

China began its economic reforms in 1978 and has become one of the world's fastest growing economies. The third plenum of the Eleventh Party Congress in December 1978 changed the national objective from a battle of classes to one of economic development. During the third plenum of the Twelfth Party Congress in 1984 the ideology became the development of a planned merchandise economy. Since 1994, the transformation of China into a market-oriented economy has become the main reform objective. Whatever the principal domain concerned, a shared characteristic of economic reform in China has been the decentralisation of economic decision-making power in order to create incentives for economic development. Decentralisation has various transmitting canals which are translated into various systems in different domains of the economy, such as the household responsibility system in the rural areas, the floating salary system in state-owned enterprises (SOEs), and fiscal contracting systems between different levels of the government. As the fiscal system is an integral part of any economy and has important implications for other aspects of the economy, this chapter focuses on fiscal decentralisation.

Decentralisation in China

The idea of decentralisation is not new to such a vast country as China. During the late 1950s and early 1970s there were waves of decentralisation (Qian 1999). During these periods, about 24,000 People's Communes were established under Mao's initiative. Each commune combined industry, agriculture, military and trade. The whole country was divided into seven cooperative regions, each of which was instructed to industrialise quickly. A number of centrally-owned enterprises were delegated to local governments, who were responsible for the local allocation of production factors, including investment and labour.

These measures can only be strictly classified as decentralisation because the measures were administrative, limited within the public sector, and aimed only at improving the central government's supervision at local levels.[1] Only since 1979 has decentralisation accompanied by economic liberalisation been aimed at facilitating market-oriented reforms, concerning both the state and the non-state sector. Subsequently, these moves can be classified as decentralisation in a broad sense.[2]

Fiscal decentralisation

Before 1979, the fiscal system was centralised despite waves of decentralisation in the late 1950s and early 1970s. Local governments and SOEs transmitted all their revenues and profits to the central government, and the central government determined expenditure plans for local governments and SOEs. Local governments were only local agents of the central government that supervised SOEs and had little managerial autonomy over local economic development. In 1980 a major fiscal reform took place, changing from a centralised to a contracting system, and changing accordingly the inter-governmental relationship. Fiscal revenues in each province were divided into fixed central revenue, transferred totally to the central government; fixed local revenue, belonging to the local government; and shared revenue, subject to sharing with the central government according to a fiscal contract negotiated individually with the central government on an annual basis. There were six basic types of sharing schemes including

- fixed sharing, where a fixed proportion was remitted to the centre
- incremental sharing, where a certain proportion was retained by the province up to a quota, then a higher proportion was retained in excess of the quota
- sharing up to a limit, where revenue was shared up to a certain amount; above this amount all revenue was retained by the province
- lump-sum remittance
- lump-sum remittance with growth, where the lump-sum amount remitted to the centre increased at a contracted rate annually
- lump-sum subsidies by the centre (Bahl and Wallich 1992; Wong 1991).

The intention of such fiscal contracting is to induce a strong positive relationship between local revenues and local economic prosperity, providing incentives for local governments to foster local economic development (Montinola *et al.* 1996).

Another important aspect of fiscal decentralisation in China is the expansion of extra-budgetary funds of local governments. These funds, composed principally of surtaxes, fees of utilisation, SOE profits and depreciation, reached 80 per cent of total budgetary funds in 1990. Unlike budgetary revenues, these funds are neither subject to sharing with, nor to supervision by the central government. They are assigned to specific utilisation by local governments without having to obtain the central government's approval. These funds are especially valuable to local governments who have found ways to convert budgetary funds into extra-budgetary funds (Shah 1998).

The increasing role of local governments

A direct consequence of fiscal decentralisation is the increasing role of local governments in the provision of local public goods and in the local economy.

Before 1979, investment in infrastructure was considered non-productive. Thus, the central government gave little attention to infrastructure construction and maintenance, and local governments had limited authority to procure investment funds for constructing and maintaining local infrastructure. When economic reforms began, the insufficiency of infrastructure became evident and constituted a bottle-neck of economic development. Decentralisation policies gave local governments the responsibility for urban construction, which comprised housing, road, water and power systems. As better infrastructure improves the productivity of enterprises, and local governments are responsible for local economic performance, local governments have the incentive to improve local infrastructure (Qian 1999).

Not only do Chinese local governments play the basic role of providing public services such as education, health, culture, policing and infrastructure, but they are also direct actors in local economies. They are responsible for the fixed investment in public enterprises and supervise nearly three quarters of industrial enterprises in terms of production. They also give out licenses, make policies concerning the non-state sector, coordinate urban development, and can facilitate the creation of new enterprises and even conciliate conflicts between enterprises. One of the most important mechanisms at the disposal of local governments, is their control of resource allocation through their influence on the nomination of managers and the allocation of employees in state-organised enterprises, and through their considerable control of the allocation of public investment and bank credit.

Township and village enterprises (TVEs) are a good example of local governments' close relationship with local enterprises and their direct involvement in productive activities. As some authors point out, the autonomy of TVEs is great, but is mainly limited to daily operation decisions. Main decisions, such as those concerning investment and finance, are made by township and village governments. The latter transform their bureaucratic relations into business networks and take charge of many important links of the production chain (Oi 1996).

Decentralisation in itself is not the goal of reforms. The essential question to ask is whether the substantial decentralised economic power of local governments is of net benefit to the economy. Before seeking an answer to this question through empirical estimation, let us first look at some theoretical arguments.

Economic theories of decentralisation

Theories in favour of decentralisation

A large body of theory in favour of decentralisation are based on the conception of public goods.[3] Given the consideration that information transmission is costly, decentralisation may permit better decision-making on the provision of local public goods because local governments are better informed about local conditions and preferences (Hayek 1945). Decentralisation may also allow residents across regions to group themselves together and choose the menu of public goods that suits the group members best (Tiebout 1956). Given the assumption that the decision on the quantity of public goods to be produced by a jurisdiction is independent from decisions of other jurisdictions, and that there are no economies of scale, 'it is always easier for the sub-national groups to produce the goods in Pareto optimal quantities than for the central government (or at least as easy)' (Oates 1972). In the presence of externalities, local governments are better positioned to take charge of those public goods having local externalities.[4]

The aforementioned theories take for granted that governments want to provide public goods as efficiently as possible. A second body of theory highlights the incentives and competition created by decentralisation, and seeks to answer the question of why governments want to provide public goods as efficiently as possible. According to these theories, decentralisation gives the responsibility of the provision of public goods and the development of local economy to local governments. Those who do well are praised in public and are more likely to be promoted to higher positions. Their fiscal revenues also increase as production value grows in their localities. Decentralisation thus creates both moral and material incentives for local governments to improve the provision of local public goods and to promote economic growth in their localities.

Given the important role of local governments in promoting local economic development and the, at least partial, mobility of production factors, local governments compete with one another to attract production factors to their localities, and to provide necessary infrastructure and facilities to local enterprises for the utilisation of these factors. They may also initiate and encourage experiments on new production and commercialisation methods within their localities. Successful outcomes can be diffused into other localities and the whole economy can thus benefit. Failures can be limited within a region and do not affect other regions (Qian and Xu 1993).

One of the theories of particular relevance to China is that developed by Montinola, Qian and Weingast (1996), who elaborated on Chinese-style federalism. This theory says that when a set of conditions are met, federalism—whose fundamental feature is decentralisation—is market-preserving and induces competition among jurisdictions.[5] This competition provides a number of salutary effects, including hardened budgetary constraints for local governments and incentives for local governments to promote local economic development through the increased provision of infrastructure, utilities and market access.

A third body of theory is based on the consideration of soft budgetary constraints (SBCs). SBCs exist when enterprises or any other economic agents can be bailed out of financial difficulty, as is often the case in the public sector and in a centralised system. Economic agents with soft budgetary constraints tend to be less responsible for their decision-making and they are less efficient in their management than those with hard budgetary constraints (Kornai 1980). Decentralisation demands local governments and enterprises be responsible for balancing their budgets. In this way, hard budgetary constraints force them to be more efficient (Raiser 1996).

Theories against decentralisation

The theory of fiscal federalism can be criticised on the grounds that where developing countries are concerned, the theory's explicit or implicit assumptions are unlikely to be met. The federalism theory assumes that the main difference between various localities or regions is their preferences or tastes. In reality, in most developing countries, the main difference is income, and the main concern is to satisfy basic needs rather than reveal the fine difference in preferences across the country. This theory also assumes that the residents of each locality can express their preferences through voting, which is not often the case in developing countries. Another assumption is that elected officials will satisfy the revealed preferences of local residents. In reality, officials may lack adequate resources to do so. They may also lack incentives, especially if they are elected on political, personal or tribal considerations. On the other hand, it is not always the case that goods or services provided by the central government are uniform rather than geared to the different needs of different regions. Higher-level government officials may be quite able to differentiate the services they provide (Prud'homme 1994). Furthermore, the production costs of public goods are assumed to be the same at the central and local levels, but where economies of scale exist, the central government may well be more cost-efficient than local governments.[6]

A substantial body of literature concerning redistribution, regional protectionism and macroeconomic stability issues warns against decentralisation. In terms of redistribution, decentralised redistribution is likely to be unfair across regions and self-defeating (Prud'homme 1994)[7]. When redistribution is actually considered a national public good that the central government should be responsible for, the central government should dispose of sufficient revenue in order to be able to redistribute income effectively. Decentralisation tends to increase local governments' revenue share and reduce that of the central government, thus reducing the latter's ability to redistribute income effectively.

In terms of regional protectionism, the competition between local governments to attract production factors and to sell local products can result in regional protectionism such as commercial barriers, unequal treatment of local enterprises and enterprises of other jurisdictions. Competition of this kind is called destructive competition (Prud'homme 1994).

In terms of macroeconomic management, which is classified as a national public good, if the central government is to use fiscal policies for macroeconomic management, its share of revenues must be sufficiently large in relation to both GNP and total governmental revenues.[8] However, decentralisation risks reducing the importance of the central government's revenue and thus weakens its macroeconomic management ability. Furthermore, it is possible that the fiscal policies of local governments run counter to those of the central government (Prud'homme 1994).[9] This opposition is a source of economic instability.

Econometric analysis of the effects of decentralisation in China

The theories presented in the previous section provide no clear-cut opinions on the effects of decentralisation, and so we turn to an empirical estimation of the effects of decentralisation in this section. We restrict ourselves to the domain of fiscal decentralisation for lack of detailed data on enterprises and on government–enterprise interactions. The important role played by local governments also justifies a concrete empirical analysis.

Literature review

As noted in the introduction, analyses of the impact of decentralisation are often characterised by strong theoretical beliefs and weak empirical evidence. For example, a study of twenty-three developing countries for the period 1974–91 (Woller and Phillips 1998) failed to find a significant relationship between decentralisation and economic growth. On the other hand, although decentralisation theories are largely based on public goods, few studies really deal with the impact of decentralisation on public goods. In addressing this gap, we provide an estimation of the effect of decentralisation on the provision of local public goods in China.

There are four notable studies, whose results are mixed, on the impact of decentralisation on economic growth in China (Zou and Zhang 1995; Lin *et al.* 1997 and 1998; Qian *et al.* 1999). We estimate that the ambiguity principally comes from the following two processes.

Indicator of decentralisation. In cross-sectional studies, one indicator of decentralisation is the ratio of the expenditure of local governments over that of the central government. This measures the relative importance of local governments in terms of expenditure. In cross-provincial studies, the counterpart would be the ratio of the expenditure of each provincial government to the expenditure of the central government in each province. But this data is unavailable for China. Zou and Zhang (1995) used the ratio of the expenditure of each provincial government to the total expenditure of the central government as an indicator of decentralisation. In our view, this is not a reliable indicator of decentralisation because different provinces share a common denominator. Thus, the degree of decentralisation in each province depends on the size of its expenditure: the more it spends, the more decentralised it is. Government expenditures, however, also depend on the size of the population, the state of economic development of the province and other factors (Lin *et al.* 1998).

In our study, we use the marginal fiscal revenue retention rate as an indicator of decentralisation as stated in Bahl and Wallich (1992) and Lin *et al.* (1997 and 1998). This ratio reflects the marginal percentage of an increase in fiscal revenue in each province that the provincial government can retain. For example, if a province remits a certain percentage of its fiscal revenues to the centre, the remaining percentage will be its marginal fiscal revenue retention rate; if it remits a lump-sum amount of revenue, or receives a subsidy, its marginal fiscal revenue retention rate will be 100 per cent.

Control variables. Lin *et al.* (1997 and 1998) have twice studied the impact of fiscal decentralisation on economic development in China, with contradictory results. They recognised the importance of including different reform variables in the growth equation, but they did not include any variable of openness. In the work of Qian *et al.* (1999), the growth equation has only labour force and tax rate as control variables. These are insufficient to explain growth.

In our study, we try to include as many reform variables as possible. Indeed, decentralisation may influence the economy both directly and indirectly through its effects on other growth variables. We shall see what the effect of decentralisation is after controlling for other growth variables.

Empirical results

In looking at the estimation of the impact of decentralisation on the local provision of public goods, we adopt a model based on a study by the World Bank (Estache and Sarbajit 1995).[10] In general the level of infrastructure can be explained by the density of the population, GDP per capita, budgetary expenditures (including infrastructure investment), urbanisation and decentralisation (Estache and Sarbajit 1995). In China, due to its special importance, the extra-budgetary expenditure should also be included. Another variable, the household responsibility system, which has been the most important source of rural growth, could also be an explanatory variable because it raised the demand for infrastructure to transport products and people between the countryside and cities.

Our data are a panel that covers 29 Chinese provinces between 1979 and 1993. After testing for specific effects (tests of Breusch and Pagan) and fixed effects (Hausman test), a fixed-effects model is retained to account for unobservable characteristics or circumstances in each province such as technological differences in building infrastructure.[11]

Table 13.1 reports the results of decentralisation and provision of local infrastructure in China (see Table A13.1 for the description of these variables). As expected, DENPOP is significantly positive, reflecting the congestion phenomenon of infrastructure: more people need more infrastructure. GDP is significantly positive, reflecting the fact that a more developed economy creates a greater need for infrastructure, and can also afford more infrastructure. HRS is significantly positive; and URB is positive but not significant. Its effects have probably been captured by HRS since urbanisation is principally a phenomenon resulting from rural growth.

The variables of interest are the last three. EXD is significantly positive (at ten per cent confidence), while BUD is significantly negative, implying opposing effects of the expansion of provincial budgetary and non-budgetary expenditures on provincial infrastructure. In fact, expenditure responsibility has been less decentralised than revenue responsibility, and is still subject to control by the central government, which often prioritises national rather than local infrastructure, and tends to limit local expenditure on local infrastructure in order to spare scarce resources (Wang 1996). In this case, local governments turn to extra-budgetary funds to satisfy local infrastructure needs. This is a phenomenon of unaccomplished decentralisation. One can expect that when decentralisation deepens, local governments will assume greater expenditure responsibilities, and extra-budgetary funds will be included in regular budgetary funds, conforming to international practice. DC is significantly positive, confirming the view that decentralisation allows and encourages local

Table 13.1 Decentralisation and provision of local infrastructure in China, 1979–93

Dependent variable: INFRA

Explanatory variables	Coefficient	(t-student)
DENPOP	0.0047	(5.487)
GDP	0.0002	(7.299)
HRS	0.3223	(2.166)
URB	0.0848	(1.208)
EXD	0.0955	(1.73)
BUD	-0.169	(-4.074)
DC	0.010	(2.642)

Notes: R^2 (within) is 0.7841; The number of observations is 254.

governments to be more involved in local infrastructure provision.

The growth equation we have adopted to estimate the impact of decentralisation on provincial economic growth is based on previous studies on decentralisation in China (Zou and Zhang 1995; Lin *et al.* 1997, 1998; Qian *et al.* 1999):

$$gGDP_{it} = \gamma GDP_{it-1} + \beta X_{it} + \delta DC_{it} + \alpha_i + \eta_t + \varepsilon_{it}$$

where gGDP is the growth rate of real GDP, GDP(-1) is initial GDP, X is a vector of control variables susceptible to influence growth, DC is a vector of variables of decentralisation, α_i controls for possible unobservable provincial characteristics, and η_t for temporal effects. Here *X* includes, on the one hand, variables of investment and labour, and on the other, variables of tax rate, openness, agricultural reform and non-state sector development, which capture the effects of different reforms. The data are also a panel that covers twenty-nine Chinese provinces over the period 1979–93.[12] After testing for specific effects (tests of Breusch and Pagan) and fixed effects (Hausman test), a pooled model is retained.

The variables EXR, EXD and DC all have a negative sign, implying that fiscal decentralisation, as measured by the expansion of extra-budgetary funds and the marginal fiscal revenue retention rate, had negative effects on GDP growth in Chinese provinces during 1979–93 (Table 13.2).[13]

We provide several possible explanations of this result based on both theories and considerations of the actual situation in China, while being conscious of the multi-faceted nature of the transmission of the impact of decentralisation on the economy.

In the analytical framework of market-preserving federalism (Montinola *et al.* 1996) concerning the competition between local governments, it is beneficial only if local governments do not erect trade barriers and if the entire nation becomes a common market (Condition 3). One can, however, discover much regional protectionism among Chinese provinces. Provincial governments effectively reduce competition for local enterprises through their intervention in intra and inter-regional trade (Wong 1987). Concerning local governments' budget constraints (Condition 4), if revenue-sharing among governments is limited by the fiscal contracting system, borrowing by governments is not as constrained. Governments at the provincial, municipal and county levels gained great influence over credit decisions through the regional branches of the central bank and specialised banks. These banks were subordinate to both the banking hierarchy and to local governments. The latter gained more weight as reforms proceeded and were directly involved in the formulation of credit plans and able to impose loans on specialised banks (Qian *et al.* 1999). Furthermore, although the larger part of centrally controlled enterprises have been decentralised to local governments, they are still under government control. When they are in financial difficulty, they can still rely on local governments

Table 13.2   Decentralisation and provincial economic growth in China, 1979–93

Dependent variable: gGDP

Explanatory variable	(1) coefficient	(t-student)	(2) coefficient	(t-student)
GDP_1	-0.4188	(-4.385)	-0.4124	(-4.343)
TAX	-0.2647	(-2.394)	-0.2759	(-2.492)
INV	0.2768	(2.036)	0.2796	(2.063)
LABOUR	0.3237	(3.216)	0.3209	(3.197)
GPOP	-0.1419	(-2.654)	-0.1425	(-2.669)
OPEN	0.1654	(3.014)	0.1649	(3.010)
FDI	0.038	(2.038)	0.0374	(2.056)
HRS	2.0687	(2.104)	2.012	(2.057)
NSOE	0.7144	(2.868)	0.6909	(2.795)
YEAR89–90	-0.6208	(-8.108)	-0.6149	(-8.031)
EXR	-0.1196	(-4.423)	..	..
EXD	..	..	-0.1228	(-4.497)
DC	-0.4103	(-4.638)	-0.4163	(-4.708)
Observations	236	..	236	..
Adjusted R^2	0.5585	..	0.5597	..

to bail them out. While these essential economic production units still face soft budget constraints, their productivity remains low, limiting economic growth. The institutionalisation and durability of decentralisation (Condition 5) has not yet been achieved. The necessary conditions for market-preserving federalism to take full shape and to have the favourable effects on economic growth as predicted are still to be met in China.

Under the fiscal contracting system, local governments effectively controlled tax collection efforts by offering varying degrees of tax concessions, and found ways to convert budgetary funds into extra-budgetary funds. Thus, while it is common in industrialised countries that the proportion of government revenue in GDP increases as the country's economy grows and then stabilises having attained a certain level (Chen 1996), in China the evolution of the proportion of government revenues in GDP displays an inverse tendency.[14]

On the expenditure side, however, the central government has failed to achieve corresponding reductions in expenditure responsibilities so that the government deficit increased over the same period.

The shortage of financial resources affected the central government's macroeconomic management ability as well as its capacity to provide national public goods. The lack of the central government's effective macroeconomic control and the monetary expansion initiated as local governments gained further autonomy thanks to fiscal decentralisation have caused periods of double-digit inflation in the late 1980s and early 1990s (Fan 1995). The lack of funds for national infrastructure investment exacerbated the bottleneck in the economy (Shah 1998).

Table 13.3   Share of government revenues in GDP in China

Year	1979	1981	1983	1985	1987	1989	1991	1993	1995
%	28.4	24.2	23	22.4	18.4	15.8	14.6	12.6	10.7

Source: SSB, 1999. *China Statistical Yearbook 1999*, China Statistical Publishing House, Beijing.

Table 13.4   Government deficit in China (100 million yuan)

Year	1979	1981	1983	1985	1987	1989	1991	1993	1995
Deficit	-135.4	37.4	-42.6	0.57	-62.4	-158.9	-237.1	-293.4	-574.5

Source: SSB, 1999. *China Statistical Yearbook 1999*, China Statistical Publishing House, Beijing.

The way in which the fiscal contracts between the central and provincial governments were determined depended on individual negotiations instead of on institutional or legal grounds. The considerable amount of bargaining involved suggests a central government whose actions are severely constrained by the provinces (Zhang 1999).

The substantial power of local governments in capital allocation can delay the development of a national capital market and affect the efficiency of capital allocation. Despite a promising start, non-state investment societies have not developed into serious competitors with state banks, due in part to local governments' intervention and administrative barriers (Wong 1987).

The direct involvement of governments in economic activities may be risky and problematic. While government officials are not trained to be entrepreneurs their entrepreneurial capacity in the allocation of resources and credit may be overestimated thanks to their bureaucratic power and authority. And it may be problematic because local governments undertaking entrepreneurial activities is not consistent with the objective of constructing a market economy, where governments should intervene only indirectly as providers of public goods and as macroeconomic regulators. In fact, the excessive role played by local governments in China may become the bottleneck of a true or complete decentralisation, which implies that economic decision power should belong to enterprises. 'Putting local governments out of business and keeping them within their own business is very crucial in the process of transition from plan to market' (Bird and Wallich 1993).

Despite the positive effects of decentralisation, its negative effects have come to compromise them. Our study, however, is at the provincial level; studies at lower levels may show opposite results. For example, Lin *et al.* (1997) studied the impact of decentralisation on growth at the town and village level and found a positive relationship between decentralisation and growth. Perhaps this justly implies that decentralisation should be deepened to lower levels to have positive effects on economic growth.

Conclusion

During the period 1979–93, fiscal decentralisation, as measured by extra-budgetary funds and the marginal fiscal revenue retention rate of each province in China, had a positive impact on the provision of local public goods, as represented by infrastructure, and a negative impact on provincial economic growth.

The negative impact of decentralisation on provincial economic growth in China may be due to an inappropriate degree, or a badly adapted form, of decentralisation. In terms of intergovernmental relationship, decentralisation has perhaps gone too far for the central government to take effective control of the macroeconomic situation of the country. However, in terms of the government–enterprise relationship, decentralisation may not have gone far enough for enterprises to have true autonomy or hard budget constraints. Enterprise must be emphasised in the process of decentralisation, while the close link between local governments and enterprises must be broken so that enterprises can react on their own to market signals, and so that local governments restrain themselves from direct involvement in productive activities and act only as regulators of the economy and providers of public goods. Concurrent with reducing the role of local governments in the allocation of resources, it is essential to develop factor markets so that the market can fulfil its function of allocating resources.

Indeed, the contractual system of sharing fiscal revenues between the central and local governments should be viewed as an intermediate step in fiscal reform, which was itself a product of gradual reform. This was also an outcome of compromising reformist forces and the pressures coming from different interest groups that had benefited under the previous regime. This system was reformed in 1994, with three main objectives: re-addressing the two ratios, the ratio of budgetary revenue to GDP and the ratio of the central government's revenue to total governmental revenues; constructing a new intergovernmental relationship through the separation of central and local tax collections; and, establishing a more effective and more uniform system of taxation. This reform did not significantly change the ratio of budgetary revenues to GDP (10.7 per cent in 1995, 10.9 per cent in 1996, 11.6 per cent in 1997; *China Statistical Yearbook 1998*). The ratio of the central government's revenue to total governmental revenue, however, increased noticeably (22 per cent in 1993, 55.7 per cent in 1994, 52 per cent in 1995, 49.4 per cent in 1996, and 48.9 per cent in 1997; *China Statistical Yearbook 1998*). The reforms of 1994 have established separate tax collection agencies for the collection of central and local taxes, respectively. A more equitable and more uniform fiscal system has been established, imposing the same tax rate on enterprises with different property rights, favourable to a more equitable competitive environment for all enterprises. An interesting task for future studies would be to find another reliable indicator of decentralisation after 1993 and to estimate the effect of decentralisation since then.

Appendix 13.1

Table A13.1	Description of variables with dependant variable INFRA (in logarithm form)

Dependent variable

INFRA: the density of infrastructures, measured by the length of rails and roads divided by the area of the province.

Explanatory variables

DENPOP: the density of the population, measured by the number of persons divided by the area

GDP: real GDP divided by the population

HRS: the variable for the household responsibility system, measured by the percentage of agricultural households that have adopted this system

URB: urbanisation, measured by the percentage of the non-agricultural population to the total population

EXD: extra-budgetary expenditure divided by GDP

EXPEND: budgetary expenditure divided by GDP

DC: the marginal fiscal revenue retention rate of each province

Table A13.2   Description of variables with dependant variable gGDP
(in logarithm form)

Dependent variable

gGDP: real GDP growth rate

Explanatory variables

GDP_1:   real GDP of the previous year
TAX: taxes divided by GDP
INV: total fixed investment divided by GDP
LABOUR: total number of employees
GPOP: the growth rate of the population
OPEN: the sum of imports and exports divided by GDP
FDI: foreign direct investment divided by GDP
HRS: the variable for the household responsibility system, measured by the
               percentage of agricultural households that have adopted this system
NSOE: the share of non-state enterprises in industrial production
1989–90:   dummy for years 1989 and 1990
EXD: extra-budgetary expenditure divided by GDP
EXR: extra-budgetary revenue divided by GDP
DC: the marginal fiscal revenue retention rate of each province

Appendix 13.2

Explanation for the signs of variables in Table 13.2

Variable	Sign	Explanation
GDP_1	Negative	Conditional convergence: poorer provinces grow more rapidly than richer provinces, all other things equal (Barro 1996)
TAX	Negative	Excessive tax rate discourages economic agents; governments can channel tax revenues to non-productive activities (Zou and Zhang 1995; Lin and Liu 1998)
INV	Positive	Essential positive growth factor (Levine and Renelt 1992; Barro 1996)
LABOUR	Positive	Essential positive growth factor (Barro 1996)
GPOP	Negative	Growth of population can entail a reduction of resources per capita
OPEN	Positive	Openness attracts advanced technology, managerial skills and international competition (Lucas 1988; Grossman and Helpman 1991; Balassa 1993)
FDI	Positive	FDI adds to domestic investment and brings about technological progress in the recipient country (Blomstrom 1991; Coe and Helpman 1995; Démurger 1997)
HRS	Positive	Successful rural reform, improving rural productivity (Lin and Liu 1998)
NSOE	Positive	The development of non-state enterprises—notably township and village enterprises—contributes to product and productivity growth (Qian 1999)
1989–90	Negative	Political events troubled economic growth process.

Notes

1 In a broad sense, decentralisation implies eliminating restrictions and decentralising decision-making power to individual and private activities. In a strict sense, however, decentralisation can only mean giving autonomy to lower levels of government and to public enterprises and banks; that is, decentralisation within the public sector (Fan 1995).

2 Under the strict definition of decentralisation, eliminating restrictions on the private sector is referred to as economic liberalisation. Economic liberalisation is represented by reforms in the price system and the emergence and rapid development of the non-state sector. Before 1979, product prices were fixed by the central government; not long after the beginning of reforms, this planned price system was replaced by a dual price system, planned and market prices coexisting; with the advancement of the reforms, market prices became increasingly predominant. Before 1979, all enterprises were publicly owned; since 1979, enterprises with other forms of ownership have emerged and developed rapidly.

3 A public good is characterised by the non-exclusivity and non-rivalry of its consumption. It can be consumed simultaneously by several or many consumers without its disposable quantity being diminished; consumers who pay a certain price for it cannot exclude each other in its utilisation (Greff 1994).

4 Externalities are defined as the variations of utility of an agent engendered by the action of another agent without resulting in any compensatory movement on the market (Greff 1994).

5 These conditions are a hierarchy of governments with a delineated scope of authority; that sub-national governments have primary authority over the local economy; that national government has the authority to police the common (national) market and to ensure the mobility of goods and factors across sub-national jurisdictions; that both revenue-sharing among governments and borrowing by governments are limited so that all governments face hard budget constraints; and that the allocation of authority and responsibility has an institutionalised degree of durability so that it cannot be altered by the national government either unilaterally or under pressure from sub-national governments.

6 There are reasons to believe that central bureaucracies are more likely to operate near the technical production frontier: the central government is likely to attract better qualified people—not necessarily because of higher salaries but because of better careers or distinguishing positions. The central government is more likely to be able to afford large investments in research and development for new technologies (Prud'homme 1994).

7 If a jurisdiction adopts policies that impose high taxes on rich people and give more benefits to poor people, rich people tend to leave for jurisdictions where tax policies are more favorable for them. Poor people in other jurisdictions tend to move into this jurisdiction. This generous jurisdiction will soon be unable to sustain its policies.

8 Local governments have few or no incentives to provide it because a local government that would provide such a good would have to take charge of all the costs of its production but would receive only a small benefit.

9 In practice, local governments may want to increase expenditures or raise taxes while the central government is trying to reduce spending or cut taxes.

10 In this study, the dependent variable was the expenditure of infrastructure in each country. In the case of China, a portion of infrastructure expenditure comes from extra-budgetary funds, for which we have no detailed category data. The portion of infrastructure

expenditure financed by public bank lending is not shown in the public finance data either. Here, our dependent variable of infrastructure is the density of rails and roads.

11 See Appendix 13.1 for a description of the variables.

12 See Appendix 13.1 for a description of the variables.

13 See Appendix 13.2 for an explanation of the signs of GDP_1, TAX, INV, LABOUR, GPOP, OPEN, FDI, HRS, NSOE and 1989–90.

14 For example, the evolution of the proportion of government revenues in GDP in the United States is as follows

Share of government revenues in GDP in the United States.

year	1902	1920	1940	1950	1960	1970	1980
per cent	7.8	12.6	17.7	23.1	29.7	32.9	34.0

14

The determinants of economic growth

Evidence from a panel of Chinese provinces

Yanrui Wu

A recent resurgence of interest in economic growth has led to blossoming literature.[1] Among the many approaches proposed, cross-country growth regressions have been widely applied to examine the role of various structural and policy indicators in economic growth. The findings in this large and growing literature often conflict and are yet to be sorted out. For example, Levine and Renelt (1992) carried out a sensitivity analysis of the determinants of the average annual growth rate of GDP per capita for a sample of 101 countries during the period 1960–89. According to their extreme bounds analysis, among many, only three variables (investment, international trade and initial income) are found to possess a fairly robust predictive power. Recently, Sala-i-Martin (1997) presented a more optimistic study which shows that a substantial number of variables are strongly related to growth. This finding is supported by Ley and Steel (1999).

One of the common features of the existing studies is their reliance on cross-section statistics. The main drawback associated with cross-country analyses is the presence of heterogeneity in data aggregation, economic structure and institutional framework among the countries considered.[2] By focusing on a panel of Chinese provinces, this study may overcome the problems associated with heterogeneity in the existing literature and hence shed further light on the determinants of economic growth. China has undertaken two decades of economic reform and has achieved impressive growth. This study presents a timely assessment of China's economic performance over the past two decades. The next section describes the analytical framework and data issues. The estimation results and analysis of the empirical findings are then presented. This is followed by an investigation of the robustness of the empirical results, with summary remarks presented in the final section.

Analytical and data issues

In the growth literature, a set of variables have been identified as being related to growth.[3] The standard analytical framework is based on the following growth regression

$$Y = \alpha X + \beta Z + \varepsilon \qquad (14.1)$$

where Y is the average annual growth rate of GDP per capita, X a set of variables or the so-called conditioning variables which are always included in the regression, and Z is a subset of variables, chosen from a pool of variables, which are assumed or identified to be important explanatory variables to growth. The choice of X-variables is based on either past empirical studies or economic theory. For example, Levine and Renelt (1992) selected the initial income, the initial secondary school enrolment rate, the average annual rate of population growth and the investment share of GDP as the X-variables. Sala-i-Martin (1997) chose the level of income, life expectancy and primary school enrolment rate in the initial year by assuming that these variables were good *a priori*.

As this chapter focuses on a single country, the number of variables to be considered is relatively small. For instance, the political and institutional factors are not relevant in the case of a single country. As a result, this study investigates the influence of several key economic and policy indicators, such as physical capital stock, human capital, economic reform, infrastructure, the initial income, openness, labour productivity and foreign capital. Some stylised facts about these variables are detailed in the following sections. It is noted that Equation 14.1 implies causality from X and Z to Y. This causal relationship should be tested. However this is beyond the scope of this study.

To capture the impact of foreign investment in China, capital stock is divided into domestic and foreign components. The Chinese government agencies have only published information on capital formation or the incremental capital which was available for all regions over the period 1952–97. As a result, the value of capital stock is estimated according to the following formula

$$K(t) = \Delta K(t) + (1 - \delta)K(t - 1) \qquad (14.2)$$

where $K(t)$ is the capital stock at time t for each region, δ is the rate of depreciation, and $\Delta K(t)$ is the incremental capital at time t. $\Delta K(t)$ is available for the period 1952–97 for all regions. The data series for $\Delta K(t)$ are backcasted to the year 1900. Accordingly, Equation 14.2 is expanded to

$$K(t) = \Sigma_0^{t-1901} (1 - \delta)^k \Delta K(t - k) + (1 - \delta)^{t-1990} K(1900) \qquad (14.3)$$

Equation 14.3 implies that, given the value of capital stock in 1900 and an appropriate rate of depreciation, a capital stock series for each region can be derived. It is assumed that the rate of depreciation is four per cent and K (1900) equals zero.[4] In addition, in the empirical analyses, capital stock and GDP are deflated by region-specific price indexes and expressed in 1990 constant prices.

Capital stock derived according to Equation 14.3 covers capital accumulation from both domestic and foreign investment. The value of domestic capital stock is the total value of capital stock net of the value of foreign capital stock. The latter is derived by applying a formula similar to Equation 14.3, with the initial year being 1981. China started receiving foreign capital in 1979. At the beginning, foreign direct investment (FDI) was small in scale and concentrated mainly in two southern provinces, Guangdong and Fujian. It slowly spread to other regions in the early 1980s. As a result of this development process, FDI figures by region are only available for the period 1982–97. To estimate foreign capital stock series for the regions, it is assumed that foreign capital was zero in 1981 and that the rate of depreciation is four per cent.[5]

Summary statistics of the estimated capital stock and other variables are reported in Table 14.1. The western and central regions have lagged behind coastal China. Their relatively slow economic growth matches their poor performance in many other areas, such as capital formation, foreign investment, openness, infrastructure development and human capital. This relationship should be captured by the growth regressions to be conducted in the following sections.

Determinants of China's regional growth

The empirical analysis begins with a baseline model which is employed to investigate the impact of physical capital accumulation and the initial income on regional growth. For the purposes of comparison, the empirical analyses focus on two periods: 1982–90 and 1991–97. The point of division is largely dictated by the availability of statistics. For example, many Chinese regions began receiving FDI in 1982, and population censuses were conducted in 1982 and 1990, respectively.[6] In addition, it is interesting to compare regional growth in the 1980s and 1990s.

Capital accumulation and initial conditions

Capital accumulation has often played a key role in economic growth (Young 1995). The average growth rate of capital stock is used in the estimations in this chapter. It is expected to be positively correlated with the rate of economic growth. The initial income is regarded as an important factor underlying growth.[7] It is argued that less developed economies may be able to take the advantage of backwardness and hence enjoy faster growth (Abramovitz 1986). The initial income variable in the empirical models takes the value of GDP per capita in the first year of the time period considered, and its coefficient is expected to have a negative sign. Equation 14.1 is applied to cross-section data of twenty-eight Chinese provinces (Table 14.2). The results from the baseline model (Model 1) are reported in column 2. The estimates of all coefficients have the appropriate sign and are statistically significant at the various levels shown.

As expected, the growth of physical capital stock (domestic) has made a significant contribution to economic growth over the periods considered. The initial level of income is found to be negatively related to economic growth. This relationship is significant at a given level of confidence. Thus, it may be concluded that there is evidence of conditional convergence among the Chinese regions over the past two decades. The rate of convergence is about 1.5 per cent per annum according to the baseline regressions. The coefficients of the two regional dummies have shown that the western regions grew relatively fast in the 1980s but lagged behind both the coastal and central regions in the 1990s. Thus, the estimated convergence as indicated by the sign of the initial income took place mainly within the regions. This finding is consistent with observations from regional disparity studies (Wu 2000).

Other factors such as infrastructure, labour productivity conditions, foreign capital, economic reform, openness and human capital have also played important roles in China's growth over time. However, these variables cannot enter the regressions simultaneously due to the existence of multicollinearity. For example, the coefficient of correlation between the variables representing infrastructure and economic reform and that between foreign capital and openness are relatively high (Table 14.3). As a result, various optional models are estimated.

Infrastructure and labour productivity

The level of infrastructure development can be proxied by several indicators, such as the length of roads and number of telephones.[8] However, the use of the length of roads is likely to be biased against regions where rail is the dominant means of transportation. As a result, this study focuses on the number of telephones. Due to the fact that the large and relatively more developed regions always have more telephones, the growth rate of the number of telephones per head is used to reflect the change in infrastructure among the regions. The use of growth rate rather than level is also consistent with the case of other variables. It is clear from Table 14.1 that the regions led by Guangdong and Fujian have achieved substantial growth in infrastructure during 1982–97.

Table 14.1   Summary statistics of selected variables

Regions	Y	GDP	K	PRO	INF	FK	REF	HK	OPEN
Coastal regions									
Beijing	1087	10.5	13.0	17.3	15.1	3.1	50.6	73.5	17.8
Tianjin	741	9.6	9.8	17.4	20.5	3.3	77.6	61.1	25.8
Hebei	325	12.0	10.2	19.1	18.9	0.7	76.8	48.2	5.0
Liaoning	569	9.7	9.3	17.9	18.2	2.0	68.6	58.7	11.8
Shanghai	1307	10.0	12.7	16.3	20.1	3.9	70.8	74.1	28.6
Jiangsu	441	13.5	12.4	20.5	23.8	2.6	82.3	47.9	10.2
Zhejiang	477	13.8	13.4	20.7	25.4	1.3	90.6	44.2	14.5
Fujian	385	14.2	11.2	22.8	27.8	8.6	88.8	39.0	24.3
Shandong	399	12.7	11.2	19.9	21.3	1.7	74.8	43.3	9.5
Guangdong	531	14.5	9.9	21.8	29.8	11.0	87.3	47.7	66.4
Guangxi	228	10.5	7.9	18.1	20.9	2.2	72.1	38.1	6.6
Sub-mean	*590*	*11.9*	*11.0*	*19.3*	*22.0*	*3.7*	*76.4*	*52.4*	*20.1*
Central regions									
Shanxi	302	10.0	8.7	16.3	13.6	0.2	68.0	53.8	6.6
Inner Mongolia	309	10.4	10.1	17.9	15.6	0.3	56.8	48.1	4.7
Jilin	353	10.6	9.5	18.4	19.0	0.9	40.5	55.1	12.1
Heilongjiang	435	7.8	9.2	18.0	19.4	0.7	45.7	55.2	16.9
Anhui	218	11.4	11.0	17.4	21.2	0.7	80.2	41.5	4.2
Jiangxi	228	11.0	8.9	16.7	17.5	0.8	59.0	42.7	4.7
Henan	226	11.2	9.9	18.2	19.7	0.5	72.4	49.5	3.0
Hubei	317	11.1	9.7	18.8	20.0	0.9	75.9	46.0	5.1
Hunan	255	9.5	8.8	16.9	20.2	0.9	75.2	45.0	4.7
Sub-mean	*294*	*10.3*	*9.5*	*17.6*	*18.5*	*0.6*	*63.7*	*48.5*	*6.9*
Western regions									
Sichuan	240	9.9	8.6	17.3	17.8	0.7	66.6	38.1	3.5
Guizhou	168	9.4	6.8	14.1	13.3	0.4	44.0	29.3	3.0
Yunnan	259	10.6	8.8	17.2	18.5	0.3	45.5	28.5	5.3
Shaanxi	265	10.2	9.2	16.8	14.6	1.2	48.8	45.7	5.4
Gansu	226	10.5	6.6	15.7	15.9	0.3	45.9	37.4	3.8
Qinghai	310	8.0	6.5	15.5	12.1	-	27.2	27.2	3.6
Ningxia	284	9.6	7.7	15.1	18.5	0.1	40.8	42.8	4.4
Xinjiang	395	11.1	10.8	19.8	17.0	0.3	24.7	45.9	5.0
Sub-mean	*268*	*9.9*	*8.1*	*16.4*	*16.0*	*0.4*	*42.9*	*36.9*	*4.3*

Notes: Hainan Island and Tibet are excluded due to missing data.; Y is 1991 GDP per capita in US dollars; GDP is the average growth rate of GDP (in per cent) for the period 1982–97; K is the average growth rate of domestic capital stock (in per cent) for the period 1982–97; PRO is the average growth rate of labour productivity (in per cent) for the period 1982–97; INF is the average growth rate of infrastructure (in per cent) for the period 1985–95; FK is the average share of foreign capital stock in total capital stock (in per cent) for the period 1982–97; REF is the output share of the non-state industrial sector in total industry (in per cent) in 1997; HK is the proportion of the population aged six and over with at least six years schooling in 1997; OPEN is the value of exports in GDP (in per cent) in 1993.

Table 14.2 Regression results

Variables	(1)	(2)	(3)	(4)	(5)	(6)	(7)	(8)	(9)
Panel A: 1982–90									
Initial income	-1.567[a] (-3.140)	-1.405[a] (-3.284)	-1.033[b] (-2.282)	-1.790[a] (-3.947)	-0.186 (-0.252)	-0.637 (-0.949)	-1.589[a] (-3.567)	0.451 (0.565)	-0.187 (-0.040)
Domestic capital	0.491[a] (2.763)	0.419[a] (2.736)	0.356[b] (2.284)	0.526[a] (3.303)	0.115 (0.507)	0.354[c] (1.946)	0.518[a] (3.261)	0.022 (0.100)	...
Infrastructure	0.179[a] (3.122)	0.060 (0.410)	...	...	...	...	...	...	...
Productivity	0.289[a] (3.212)	0.225[a] (2.863)	0.209[b] (2.225)	...	...	...	...	...	...
Openness	0.052[b] (2.621)	-0.057 (-0.866)	...	...	...	...	...	...	...
Reform	0.099 (2.376)	0.086[a] (4.126)	0.082[c] (1.833)	...	...	...	...	...	...
Human capital	0.861[c] (1.948)	0.210 (0.463)	...	...	...	...	...	...	...
Foreign capital	0.707[b] (2.619)	0.364 (1.614)	0.873 (1.269)	...	...	...	...	...	...
Constant	13.745[a] (5.778)	11.790[a] (5.563)	7.293[b] (2.569)	14.526[a] (6.776)	6.814[c] (1.874)	6.225 (1.394)	13.569[a] (6.387)	3.404[a] (2.898)	...
Coastal dummy 1	-0.517 (-0.704)	-1.506[b] (-2.148)	-0.772 (-1.235)	-1.282[c] (-1.785)	-2.572[b] (-2.351)	0.044 (0.058)	-1.189[c] (-1.687)	-2.597[a] (-4.085)	-2.582[c] (-2.091)
Central dummy 2	-1.437[b] (-2.147)	-1.623[a] (-2.833)	-1.222[b] (-2.149)	-1.604[b] (-2.670)	-1.818[a] (-2.880)	-1.213[c] (-1.887)	-1.458[b] (-2.439)	-1.495[a] (-3.156)	-1.445[b] (-2.495)
R²	0.353	0.552	0.560	0.507	0.485	0.448	0.507	0.695	0.724
Panel B: 1991–97									
Initial income	-1.517[a] (-4.301)	-1.038[a] (-2.711)	-1.201[a] (-4.022)	-1.657[a] (-4.744)	-0.923[b] (-2.579)	-1.451[a] (-3.671)	-1.470[a] (-4.579)	-0.839[a] (-2.864)	-0.781[b] (-2.098)
Domestic capital	0.702[a] (5.506)	0.569[a] (4.456)	0.375[b] (2.730)	0.712[a] (5.798)	0.534[a] (4.387)	0.679[a] (4.785)	0.694[a] (5.992)	0.333[b] (2.715)	0.330[b] (2.317)

276

The determinants of economic growth

Infrastructure	0.098[b] (2.453)	0.003 (0.071)	:	:	:	:	:	:	:
Productivity	0.389[a] (3.618)	0.294[a] (3.049)	0.286[b] (2.335)	:	:	:	:	:	:
Openness	0.031[c] (1.689)	-0.008 (-0.303)	:	:	:	:	:	:	:
Reform	0.072[a] (3.081)	0.051[b] (2.554)	0.051[b] (2.271)	:	:	:	:	:	:
Human capital	0.078 (0.403)	0.007 (0.046)	:	:	:	:	:	:	:
Foreign capital	0.122[b] (2.427)	0.057 (1.379)	0.076 (0.942)	:	:	:	:	:	:
Constant	11.454[a] (4.370)	6.860[b] (2.268)	5.359[c] (1.978)	12.132[a] (4.751)	6.733[b] (2.481)	11.031[a] (3.845)	11.132[a] (4.669)	3.383 (1.330)	3.106 (1.051)
Coastal dummy 1	4.974[a] (7.145)	4.194[a] (5.937)	3.605[a] (5.310)	4.568[a] (6.420)	2.733[a] (2.908)	4.968[a] (7.002)	4.166[a] (5.831)	1.992[b] (2.554)	1.975[b] (2.315)
Central dummy 2	1.978[a] (3.719)	1.699[a] (3.430)	1.258[b] (2.653)	1.893[a] (3.682)	0.909 (1.590)	1.953[a] (3.583)	1.901[a] (3.927)	0.648 (1.351)	0.662 (1.252)
R²	0.893	0.916	0.933	0.906	0.925	0.894	0.916	0.956	0.957

Notes: [a]Significant at 1 per cent; [b]Significant at 5 per cent; [c]Significant at 10 per cent.

This growth should have contributed positively to the regions' economic performance. The estimation results in Table 14.2 (Model 2) show that the coefficient of the infrastructure variable is positive and significant. Thus, infrastructure development is positively correlated with economic growth in Chinese regions.

Improvement in labour productivity is expected to make a positive contribution to growth. According to Table 14.2 (Model 3), the growth rate of labour productivity is positively related to growth during the two periods considered.

Impact of economic reform and openness

It is argued that economic reform has contributed significantly to China's growth over the past two decades. This claim is supported by empirical studies of the agricultural sector (McMillan *et al.* 1989; Lin 1992). In particular, one of the key reform initiatives was to open China to the world. As a result, China's economic take-off over the past two decades has been accompanied by rapid expansion of international trade. How have domestic reforms and external trade affected growth performance among the regions? To answer this question, reform and openness indicators are developed and incorporated into the growth regressions.

In the growth literature, the ratio of the total value of exports and imports (or the value of net exports) over GDP is employed as an indicator of openness. In the case of the Chinese provinces, it is found that the ratio of the total value of exports and imports over GDP is highly correlated with the ratio of the value of exports.[9] Thus, either ratio can be used as the indicator of openness. In the final estimation, the ratio of the value of exports over GDP is used to represent openness.[10] Not surprisingly, according to Table 14.1, Guangdong and Shanghai have the most open economies in China.

To reflect the progress of economic reform among the regions, the role and development of the non-state sector is examined. As its name suggests, the non-state sector includes all but the state sectors. Three indicators can be used to assess the development of the non-state sector: the shares of the non-state sector in urban employment, industrial output and total retail sales in the Chinese regions. In general, these three shares (which are available for various periods) have been rising over time, implying the deepening of China's economic reform (Figure 14.1). In the empirical models, after preliminary checking, the mean output shares of the non-state sector during 1985–90 and 1990–97 are used to proxy the degree of economic reform during the two periods. Coincidentally, the value of the output share is bound by the value of the employment and sales shares. The estimation results are reported in Table 14.2 (Models 4 and 5). The coefficients of both reform and openness variables

Table 14.3   Selected coefficients of correlation, 1982–90

	Reform	Openness	Productivity
Domestic capital	0.51 (0.68)	0.32 (0.28)	0.14 (0.79)
Infrastructure	0.58 (0.72)	0.91 (0.26)	0.50 (0.76)
Foreign capital	0.35 (0.57)	0.93 (0.86)	0.39 (0.55)

Note: Numbers in parentheses are the coefficients for the period 1991–97.

have the correct signs and are significant, implying that China's reform and openness have contributed positively to economic growth over the past decades.

The role of human capital

The impact of human capital on China's growth has been rarely researched in the literature due to the paucity of data. The exceptions are Wei (1995), Moody and Wang (1997) and Démurger (2000).[11] Wei used the number of scientific and technical personnel as a proxy of human capital. The other two authors employed school enrolment rates. These existing studies focus on one single cross-section only and hence ignore the growth of human capital over time. This study applies information from recent censuses to derive an estimate of human capital stock in the Chinese regions. China conducted population censuses in 1982 and 1990. A sample survey was also carried out in 1997. The census and survey data have now been published in various sources. This study uses two sets of data: the average level of schooling of the population and the level of education of the labour force. Ideally, the latter is an appropriate indicator of human capital but it is available for 1990 and 1997 only. However, statistics on the level of schooling of the population is available for 1982, 1990 and 1997. To justify the use of the 1982 census data, the two sets of data for 1990 and 1997 are compared. It is found that these data sets are highly correlated, with a coefficient of correlation greater than 0.99. Due to this close relationship, the average level of education of the population is used to derive the level and growth rate of human capital stock among the regions.

The average rates of growth of human capital stock during 1982–90 and 1990–97 are employed in the regressions. It turns out that the coefficient of this variable is either negative or insignificant. Other authors have reported the same problem with the human capital stock variable (Benhabib and Spiegel 1994; Pritchett 1997). This may be due to measurement errors and technical constraints in deriving human capital stock data (Temple 1998). To overcome this problem, this study employs an alternative proxy for human capital; that is, the proportion of the population aged six and over with at least six years of schooling (the completion of primary school education). The average growth

Figure 14.1   Selected shares of the non-state sector

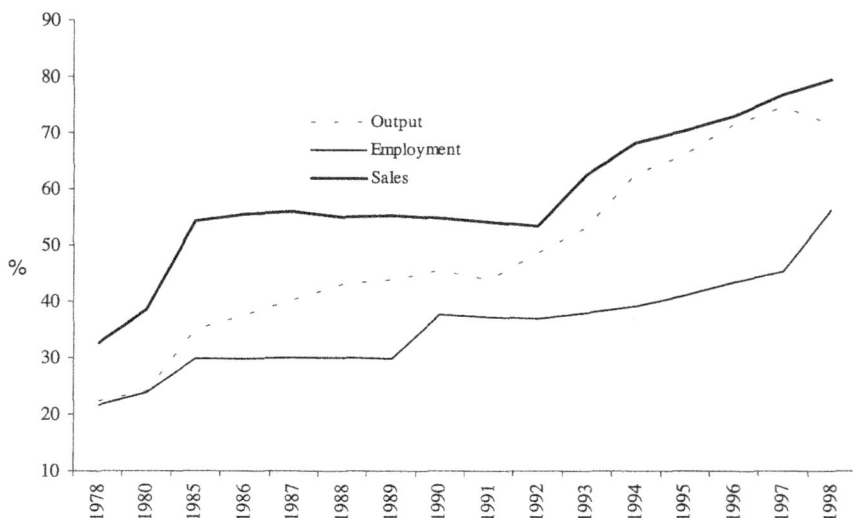

rate of this figure is used in the final estimation. According to Table 14.1 (and as expected) Shanghai and Beijing have the most educated population in China. It is also found that Anhui and Jiangxi—two central regions—have achieved the highest growth in human capital during 1982–97. It is found that the human capital variable has a positive coefficient which is significant during 1982–90 and insignificant during 1991–97 (Model 6 in Table 14.2). Thus, this result may imply that changes in human capital stock growth are positively correlated with economic growth in the Chinese regions. Obviously, this conclusion is subject to further qualification as better data and human capital theories become available in the future.

FDI as an engine of growth

According to new growth theory, FDI has been an important factor propelling economic growth.[12] China's FDI increased significantly in the 1990s but the amount of investment varied considerably across the regions. In particular, some regions experienced hypergrowth in certain years due to the launch of a few large projects. As a result, regional growth rates of FDI vary significantly over time and the outliers in the data sample are problematic. To overcome this problem, the proportion of foreign stock in the total capital stock is employed in the empirical estimations. Foreign capital still plays a minor role in many regions, in particular in central and western China (Table 14.1). The final estimation results are reported in Table 14.2 (Model 7). According to this table, the contribution of FDI to China's growth in the 1980s and 1990s was significant.

Results of pooled estimations

The preceding sections examined the effect of various regional characteristics on economic growth. The objective of this section is to pool the data to investigate the joint impact of the variables on growth. One of the problems with the estimation of the pooled model is the existence of multicollinearity between the growth correlates (Table 14.3). For example, according to Table 14.3, the variables for foreign capital and openness are highly correlated, and thus their appearance in the same growth equation would be problematic. Consequently, several models with different independent variables are estimated. The estimation results from two of those models are presented in the last two columns of Table 14.2. It is clear that those variables considered jointly explain about 70 and over 90 per cent of the growth in the 1980s and 1990s, respectively.

Sensitivity analyses

Estimation results from the growth regressions are vulnerable to the presence of endogeneity and outliers. To check the robustness of the estimates, alternative methods of estimation have been attempted. This section presents the results from the least-trimmed square (LTS) estimation, the first-difference equations and the instrumental variable approach.

The LTS approach treats observations with high residuals as unrepresentative though the cut-off for a high residual is arbitrary.[13] It is apparent that the exclusion of the outliers enhances the explanatory power of the growth regressions, particularly for the period 1982–90 (Table 14.4). In general, the LTS estimation results (for example, directions and magnitudes of the coefficients) are in conformity with the OLS findings in the preceding section (refer to Models 8 and 9 in Table 14.2 and Models 10–13 in Table 14.4). The existence of multicollinearity again prevents the inclusion of all explanatory variables in the same equation.

As capital (domestic, human and foreign) is an accumulated factor, the growth equation has been hampered by the problem of endogeneity. Benhabib and Spiegel (1994) provide evidence of upward biases on the coefficients of capital stock variables. To correct this problem, researchers have resorted to the difference equation and instrumental variable approaches. The estimation results from the difference equation approach are presented in the last two columns

Table 14.4   Estimates of the LTS and difference equation approaches

Variables	1982–90 (10)	(11)	1991–97 (12)	(13)	Difference equation (14)	(15)
Initial income	0.876 (1.264)	-0.760ª (-3.251)	-0.790ᵇ (-2.724)	-4.357ª (-2.674)	-4.697ª (-2.752)	..
Domestic capital	0.168ᶜ (2.013)	-0.038 (-0.196)	0.273ª (2.738)	0.269ᵇ (2.284)	0.215ᶜ (1.738)	0.233ᶜ (1.914)
Infrastructure	0.010 (0.093)	-0.028 (-0.732)	0.086ª (2.577)	0.098ª (3.005)	..	..
Productivity	0.226ª (3.580)	0.225ª (3.217)	0.331ª (4.071)	0.368ª (3.275)	0.231ª (3.840)	0.245ª (4.230)
Foreign capital	0.393ᵇ (2.430)	0.903 (1.423)	0.039ª (1.198)	0.076 (1.223)	0.132ᵇ (2.187)	0.155ᵇ (2.433)
Openness	-0.047 (-0.821)	-0.013 (-0.627)	..	..	..	..
Reform	0.048ᶜ (1.939)	0.079ᵇ (2.210)	0.066ª (3.944)	0.072ª (3.886)	-0.014 (-0.335)	..
Human capital	0.379 (1.259)	0.490 (1.400)	-0.033 (-0.253)	-0.213 (-1.482)	..	..
Constant	1.510 (1.173)	-2.757 (-0.760)	2.267 (1.120)	2.514 (1.101)	-0.256 (-0.188)	-0.406 (-0.248)
Coastal dummy1	-2.060ª (-2.751)	-2.526ᵇ (-2.764)	1.542ᵇ (2.447)	1.394ᶜ (2.058)	4.355ª (7.095)	4.563ª (7.268)
Central dummy2	-1.431ª (-3.588)	-1.518ª (-3.516)	0.196 (0.466)	0.156 (0.348)	2.395ª (5.025)	2.559ª (4.925)
R^2	0.862	0.878	0.977	0.979	0.907	0.915

Notes: [a]Significant at 1 per cent; [b]Significant at 5 per cent; [c]Significant at 10 per cent; Jilin, Heilongjiang, Gansu and Qinghai are excluded from the LTS regressions for the period 1982–90, as are Jilin, Jiangxi and Sichuan for the period 1991–97; The difference equations are estimated by an instrumental variable approach. The instrumental variables include all regressors in the equations and their lagged values.

(Models 14 and 15) of Table 14.4. The results support the claim of biased estimates from the OLS regressions; for example, the coefficients of domestic capital are biased upwards. Finally, the instrumental variable approach is often applied to account for the problem of endogeneity (Barro 1997). The estimation results (presented in Table 14.5) are consistent with the OLS estimation outcomes presented in the last two columns of Table 14.2.

Conclusion

Cross-country studies on economic growth have been criticised for overlooking heterogeneity among world economies. In contrast, studies focusing on a single

Table 14.5   Estimates of instrumental variable models

Variables	1982–90 (16)	(17)	(18)	1991–97 (19)	(20)	(21)
Initial income	..	0.058 (0.113)	0.444 (0.713)	-0.836[a] (-3.376)	-0.817[a] (-3.104)	-0.776[a] (-2.676)
Domestic capital	..	0.107 (0.683)	0.023 (0.135)	0.337[a] (3.252)	0.336[a] (3.059)	0.333[a] (2.997)
Infrastructure	..	0.067 (0.584)	..	0.001 (0.030)	..	..
Productivity	0.224[a] (3.227)	0.211[a] (2.978)	0.207[a] (2.824)	0.292[a] (3.582)	0.289[a] (3.535)	0.285[a] (2.994)
Openness	..	-0.057 (-1.111)	..	-0.008[c] (-0.377)	..	..
Reform	0.086[a] (4.661)	0.068[b] (2.052)	0.081[b] (2.338)	0.051[a] (3.023)	0.050[a] (3.005)	0.051[a] (2.927)
Human capital	..	0.285 (0.841)	0.210 (0.594)	0.024 (0.216)	0.020 (0.161)	..
Foreign capital	0.362[c] (1.812)	0.388[c] (1.940)	0.848 (1.581)	0.057[c] (1.631)	0.055 (1.558)	0.075 (1.192)
Constant	3.406[a] (3.271)	1.714[c] (0.535)	-0.159 (-0.044)	3.366 (1.566)	3.257 (1.453)	3.078 (1.337)
Coastal dummy1	-2.598[a] (-4.610)	-2.295[b] (-2.460)	-2.585[a] (-2.688)	1.989[a] (3.018)	2.003[a] (3.034)	1.976[a] (2.972)
Central dummy2	-1.496[a] (-3.563)	-1.481[a] (-3.310)	-1.454[a] (-3.221)	0.649 (1.602)	0.648 (1.595)	0.658 (1.597)
R^2	0.695	0.711	0.723	0.956	0.956	0.957

Notes: [a]Significant at 1 per cent; [b]Significant at 5 per cent; [c]Significant at 10 per cent; The instrumental variables include all regressors and their initial values.

country may suffer less from this problem. In this chapter, for the first time, several regression techniques are applied to investigate the determinants of recent economic growth in China. This study therefore adds to the existing literature and contributes to the current debate on the sources of economic growth.

Given the available data, the focus of this study is the impact on economic growth of eight region-specific factors (capital formation, initial income, infrastructure, labour productivity, economic reform, openness, human capital and foreign investment). In general, it is found that the growth of physical capital, infrastructure, labour productivity, human capital and foreign investment is positively related to China's economic growth in the 1980s and 1990s. This study also confirms the popular perception that China's economic reform and openness have made positive contributions to recent economic growth. Furthermore, initial income is found to have a negative impact on growth rates, implying conditional convergence among the Chinese regions. This trend of regional convergence was particularly strong in the 1980s. The findings also show that convergence has occurred mainly within the coastal, central and western regions. There is no evidence of the western and central provinces catching up with their affluent counterparts, the coastal provinces. Overall, the empirical estimates show that the eight factors together account for 70–90 per cent of China's growth over the past two decades.

Finally, alternative models are estimated to take account of endogeneity and outliers. The above findings remain unchanged according to the alternative regressions. However, the findings are still subject to further qualifications. One of those is the measurement of human capital which is constrained by both methodology and available statistics (see Sachs and Warner 1997). In addition, there is also scope for improvement in the measurement of economic reform and openness as more information becomes available over time.

Acknowledgments

The author acknowledges the Australian Research Council for financial support under the small grant scheme and Bill Scanlan, Yewliang Lee, Robin Wong and Wana Yang for excellent research assistance. Additional thanks must also go to Cao Yong and an anonymous referee for helpful comments on an early draft.

Notes

1 See for example, Barro (1991), Levine and Renelt (1992) and Sala-i-Martin (1997).
2 See Temple (1999) for a review.
3 According to Sala-i-Martin (1997), the existing literature has employed over sixty variables as the correlates of growth.
4 Capital stock series are also derived by assuming the percentage rates of depreciation of 4, 7 and 10, respectively. Information on the value of depreciation, which is available for the 1980s and 1990s, is then used to test whether the assumed rates are statistically significant. As a result, 4 per cent is accepted and hence used for the final estimation of capital stock series.
5 Guangdong and Fujian are two exceptions. FDI received by these two provinces before 1982 is incorporated into the final estimation.
6 Over the past 50 years, China has only conducted four population censuses; in 1957, 1964, 1982 and 1990.
7 Sala-i-Martin (1997) surveyed around sixty variables and found that the initial income has been included in most empirical studies.
8 Canning (1998) presented a detailed study of estimating indicators for world stocks of infrastructure.

9 The coefficient of correlation is 0.96 according to the statistics in 1993. Regional trade figures are available from 1993 onwards.

10 It should be pointed out that in the early stages of economic reform, export licences were granted to companies in the coastal regions only. Though this policy has been abandoned gradually, it certainly brings about biases in the measurement of regional openness.

11 In addition, Yang (1998) and Cheung and Kwan (1999) investigated the impact of human capital on foreign investment.

12 For a review of the literature, see De Mello (1997) and Wu (1999).

13 See Rousseeuw and Leroy (1987) for details about the LTS estimation.

15

China in international action on climate change

Tingsong Jiang

Since the First World Climate Conference was held in 1979, and especially during the 1990s, climate change has attracted growing attention because of its global and ubiquitous impact on the environment and economy. Some important developments have been achieved since then. For example, the United Nations Framework Convention on Climate Change (UNFCCC), established at the 1992 United Nations Conference on Environment and Development held in Rio de Janeiro, states that advanced industrialised countries (Annex I countries[1]) will reduce their emissions to 1990 levels by 2000, although this is not a binding international agreement. In following Conferences of Parties (COP), countries started to negotiate legally binding targets and timetables and feasible mechanisms to limit emissions in Annex I countries. Most notably, the COP3, held in Kyoto, reached the 1997 Kyoto Protocol of the Framework Convention. The Kyoto Protocol states that the industrialised countries (now called Annex B countries[2]) agree to a legally binding reduction in net greenhouse gas (GHG) emissions that would on average be 5.2 per cent below the 1990 level by 2008–12. The Protocol also includes several flexibility mechanisms to allow nations to meet the targets and timetables in a least-cost manner. These mechanisms, including joint implementation (JI) and the clean development scheme (CDM), fall into the category of emission trading.

Nevertheless, intense debate about the proposed mechanisms and reliable implementation of the Protocol have emerged after Kyoto, and hence, not enough actual effort has been made to implement it. The Protocol will enter into force only after it is ratified by 55 countries, accounting for at least 55 per cent of industrialised country emissions (Article 25). However, only some small island nations have ratified the Protocol so far. In 1997, only three years away from the date when the Annex I countries were meant to stabilise their GHG emissions to the 1990 level as specified in the UNFCCC, most Annex I countries except East Europe and the former Soviet Union countries, had higher emissions than 1990 (Table 15.1).

One issue in the debate is the meaningful participation by developing countries. There are two reasons why the developing countries are being pressed to participate. Industrialised countries are concerned about the effects of a climate agreement on their economies and are reluctant to bear the cost solely. For example, as negotiations proceeded toward the 1997 Kyoto Protocol, the United States Senate passed the Byrd–Hagel resolution by a vote of 95 to zero. The resolution stated that the United States should accept no climate agreement that did not demand comparable sacrifices of all participants (Shogren and Toman 2000).

Another reason is that the extent of required GHG abatement cannot be achieved without the participation of developing countries. Developing countries' GHG emissions have increased proportionally more than the world average, therefore their share in total world emissions has been steadily increasing (Figure 15.1). Often China is taken as an example. China is the second largest GHG emitter in the world, after the United States. In 1996, China emitted 3363.5 million metric tons of carbon dioxide, accounting for 14.8 per cent of the world's emissions (World Bank 2000). Projections show that China will become the largest GHG emitter by 2020 if the current trend of economic development continues (World Bank 1994).

However, global warming is determined by the stock of GHG; that is, the accumulation of past GHG emissions. The industrialised countries have contributed a major part of the stock. In contrast, developing countries have very low per capita GDP and per capita GHG emissions (Table 15.2 and Figure 15.2). Thus, in their view, industrialised nations have the greater responsibility for the solution of global environmental problems—especially because they have been, or still are, the greatest polluters—and should give support to other countries (Vermeer 1998; Zhang 1999). Moreover, like other developing countries, China's priority is to eliminate poverty and enhance economic development. At present, there are about 80 million people in China who do not have enough to eat or to wear (Wu *et al.* 1998). Even in the field of environmental protection, control of GHG emissions is not a priority task. Other more local environmental problems like acid rain, air and water quality, desertification, and so on, are much more urgent issues facing China. Therefore China sets its framework for environmental protection and international cooperation in this field as follows (Wu *et al.* 1998).

- Environmental protection shall be integrated with the needs of economic development.
- Industrialised countries have the main responsibility for environmental deterioration.

Table 15.1   Greenhouse gas emissions, tg of CO₂-equivalent

	CO₂			CH₄			N₂O			Total		
	1990	1997	%	1990	1997	%	1990	1997	%	1990	1997	%
Australia	275.3	..	..	112.2	..	..	23.2	..	..	410.8	..	..
Austria	62.0	66.1	6.48	9.7	9.2	-4.33	2.0	2.3	11.97	73.7	77.6	5.21
Belgium	116.1	..	..	13.3	..	..	9.5	..	..	138.9	..	..
Bulgaria	84.4	59.1	-29.92	29.8	18.7	-37.16	9.2	6.6	-28.62	123.4	84.5	-31.57
Canada	461.3	519.3	12.58	73.5	90.3	22.86	55.8	65.1	16.67	590.6	674.7	14.25
Czech Republic	165.5	137.1	-17.14	16.3	11.8	-27.78	8.0	8.9	11.07	189.8	157.8	-16.87
Denmark	52.3	64.3	23.04	8.8	8.9	0.58	10.5	10.3	-2.38	71.7	83.5	16.53
Estonia	37.8	20.7	-45.19	2.2	2.2	-2.04	0.7	0.2	-69.57	40.7	23.1	-43.28
Finland	59.2	64.6	9.12	7.5	5.7	-23.87	5.8	5.9	1.61	72.5	76.2	5.10
France	395.5	402.2	1.70	63.5	55.0	-13.36	94.6	93.1	-1.57	553.6	550.3	-0.58
Germany	1014.5	894.0	-11.88	117.0	74.8	-36.03	69.6	67.0	-3.83	1201.1	1035.8	-13.76
Greece	85.3	..	..	9.2	..	..	9.3	..	..	103.8	..	..
Hungary	71.7	..	..	11.4	..	..	3.5	..	..	86.6	..	..
Iceland	2.1	..	..	0.3	..	..	0.1	..	..	2.6	..	..
Ireland	30.7	..	..	17.0	..	..	9.1	..	..	56.9	..	..
Italy	432.6	..	..	49.3	..	..	51.0	..	..	532.9	..	..
Japan	1124.5	1230.8	9.45	32.4	29.2	-10.00	18.1	20.4	12.63	1175.0	1280.4	8.97
Latvia	24.8	12.8	-48.16	3.9	1.9	-50.32	7.0	1.2	-83.22	35.7	16.0	-55.26
Liechtenstein	0.2	..	..	-	..	..	0.0	..	..	0.3	..	..
Lithuania	39.5	16.2	-59.02	7.9	6.3	-20.10	4.1	-	..	51.5	22.5	-56.27
Monaco	0.1	0.1	32.41	-	-	..	-	-	200.00	0.1	0.1	32.43
Netherlands	161.4	..	..	27.1	..	..	19.8	..	..	208.3	..	..
New Zealand	25.2	30.3	19.98	35.1	33.5	-4.73	11.5	11.6	1.04	71.9	75.4	4.87
Norway	35.2	41.4	17.69	6.7	7.4	10.41	5.3	5.0	-5.88	47.1	53.7	14.03
Poland	380.7	361.6	-5.01	58.8	47.9	-18.65	19.5	16.7	-14.27	459.0	426.2	-7.15
Portugal	47.1	..	..	17.0	..	..	4.3	..	..	68.4	..	..
Romania	172.5	..	..	41.5	..	..	15.1	..	..	229.1	..	..
Russia	2372.3	..	..	556.5	..	..	70.0	..	..	2998.8	..	..
Slovakia	60.0	..	..	8.6	..	..	3.9	..	..	72.5	..	..
Slovenia	13.9	..	..	3.7	..	..	1.6	..	..	19.2	..	..
Spain	226.4	..	..	45.8	..	..	29.2	..	..	301.4	..	..
Sweden	55.4	56.4	1.78	6.0	5.5	-8.45	8.1	7.4	-7.69	69.5	69.3	-0.20

Switzerland	45.1	43.4	-3.77	5.1	4.7	-8.02	3.6	3.6	1.74	53.7	51.7	-3.81
Ukraine	703.8	322.9	-54.12	197.4	138.7	-29.74	18.0	4.8	-73.10	919.2	466.5	-49.25
United Kingdom	584.2	540.6	-7.45	76.4	57.3	-25.03	66.1	59.5	-9.93	726.6	657.4	-9.52
United States	4928.9	5455.6	10.69	622.9	658.5	5.72	351.2	399.8	13.84	5903.0	6513.9	10.35
Total	14347.7			2294.1			1018.3			17660.1		
Subtotal*	8843.4	9409.2	6.40	1064.5	1039.9	-2.31	702.2	751.0	6.95	10610.1	11200.1	5.56
China	1769.6			25.4			0.19			2361.6		
				-33.9			-0.53			-2624.5		

Note: *Excluding East Europe and former Soviet Union nations and those without data in 1997.
Sources: http://ghg.unfccc.int/; China data from Asian Development Bank, Global Environmental Facility *et al.*, 1998 (Table 1–1).

- The right of developing countries to develop shall be fully recognised.
- A new and fair international economic order shall be established which supports the sustainable development of all countries, especially developing ones.
- International cooperation in the field of environmental protection shall be based on the principle of the sovereign equality of all countries.
- Industrialised countries shall provide enough new and additional funds to developing countries, thus creating the necessary conditions for global environmental protection.

These principles have been termed common but differentiated responsibilities, and are reflected in the Rio Declaration on Environment and Development.

> In view of the different contributions to global environmental degradation, States have common but differentiated responsibilities. The developed countries acknowledge the responsibility that they bear in the international pursuit of sustainable development in view of the pressures their societies place on the global environment and of the technologies and resources they command (United Nations 1992:Principle 7).

The UNFCCC adopted this principle and stated that 'the developed country Parties should take the lead in combating climate change and the adverse effects thereof' (Article 3.1), while the commitment of developing countries is made in Article 4.7 conditional on the performance of developed countries.

The extent to which developing country Parties will effectively implement their

Figure 15.1 Composition of world carbon dioxide emissions

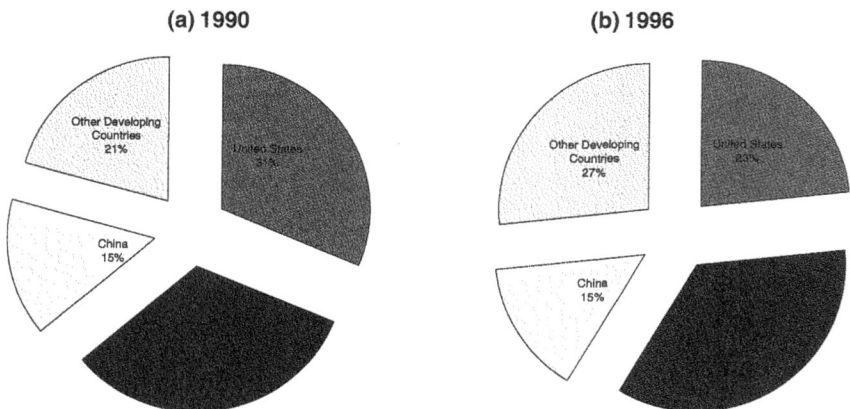

Source: World Bank, 2000. *World Development Indicators 2000*, World Bank, Washington, DC: Table 3.8; International Economic Data Bank, The Australian National University, Canberra.

commitments under the Convention will depend on the effective implementation by developed country Parties of their commitments under the Convention in relation to financial resources and transfer of technology, and will take fully into account that economic and social development and poverty eradication are the first and overriding priorities of the developing country Parties.

In sum, industrialised countries tend to plan their control over GHG emissions conditional on the participation by developing countries, while the latter insists that the former should demonstrate their real effort in the first instance. Many authors try to solve this dilemma by promoting developing countries' participation. For example, McKibbin and Wilcoxen (2000) propose a coordinated but decentralised system of national permit trading, with a fixed internationally-negotiated decentralised price for permits. A permanent endowment of emission rights is allocated to each country; beyond the

Figure 15.2   Per capita carbon dioxide emissions, 1996 (metric tons)

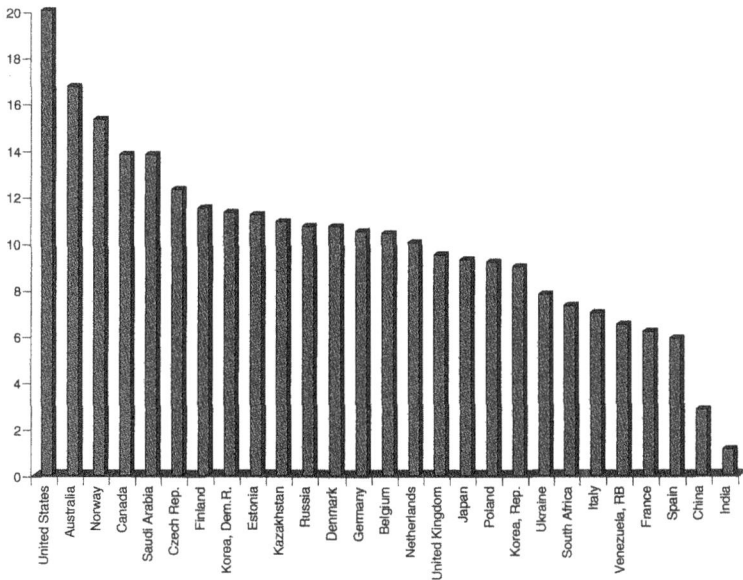

Source: World Bank, 2000. *World Development Indicators 2000*, World Bank, Washington, DC: Table 3.8.

Table 15.2 Carbon dioxide emissions and energy efficiency

| | Carbon dioxide emissions | | | | | | GDP per unit of energy use | |
| | Total Million metric tonnes | | Per capita metric tonnes | | kg per PPP$ of GDP | | PPP$ per kg oil equivalent | |
	1980	1996	1980	1996	1980	1996	1980	1997
China	1476.8	3363.5	1.5	2.8	3.6	1.0	0.7	3.3
United States	4575.4	5301.0	20.1	20.0	1.6	0.7	1.6	3.6
Russia	..	1579.5	..	10.7	..	1.5	..	1.7
Japan	920.4	1167.7	7.9	9.3	0.9	0.4	3.0	6.0
India	347.3	997.4	0.5	1.1	0.8	0.5	1.8	4.2
Germany	..	861.2	..	10.5	..	0.5	..	5.2
United Kingdom	583.8	557.0	10.4	9.5	1.2	0.5	2.4	5.3
Canada	420.9	409.4	17.1	13.8	1.5	0.6	1.4	3.0
Korea, Rep.	125.2	408.1	3.3	9.0	1.2	0.6	2.5	3.9
Italy	371.9	403.2	6.6	7.0	0.7	0.3	3.7	7.3
Ukraine	..	397.3	..	7.8	..	2.3	..	1.1
France	482.1	361.8	9.0	6.2	0.9	0.3	2.7	5.0
Poland	456.2	356.8	12.8	9.2	3.7	1.3	1.0	2.7
Mexico	251.6	348.1	3.7	3.8	0.9	0.5	2.9	5.1
Australia	202.8	306.6	13.8	16.7	1.4	0.8	2.0	4.0
South Africa	211.3	292.7	7.7	7.3	1.3	0.8	2.5	3.3
Brazil	183.4	273.4	1.5	1.7	0.4	0.3	4.4	6.5
Saudi Arabia	130.7	267.8	14.0	13.8	1.3	1.3	2.8	2.1
Iran	116.1	266.7	3.0	4.4	1.1	0.9	2.7	3.0
Korea, Dem. Rep.	124.9	254.3	7.1	11.3	..	..	..	..
Indonesia	94.6	245.1	0.6	1.2	0.8	0.4	2.0	4.5
Spain	200.0	232.5	5.3	5.9	0.8	0.4	3.5	5.9
Thailand	40.0	205.4	0.9	3.4	0.6	0.5	2.9	4.7
Turkey	76.3	178.3	1.7	2.9	0.7	0.5	3.3	5.7
Kazakhstan	..	173.8	..	10.9	..	2.5	..	1.8
Netherlands	152.6	155.2	10.8	10.0	1.1	0.5	2.1	4.6
Venezuela, RB	89.6	144.5	5.9	6.5	1.5	1.1	1.7	2.4
Argentina	107.5	129.9	3.8	3.7	0.6	0.3	4.3	6.9
Czech Republic	..	126.7	..	12.3	..	0.9	..	3.3
Romania	191.8	119.3	8.6	5.3	2.1	0.8	1.4	3.2
Malaysia	28.0	119.1	2.0	5.6	0.8	0.6	3.2	4.0
Belgium	127.2	106.0	12.9	10.4	1.3	0.5	2.2	4.1

Source: World Bank, 2000. *World Development Indicators 2000*, World Bank, Washington, DC: Table 3.8.

endowment, the government of each country could sell an annual emission permit to firms at the negotiated price. The endowment for developing countries could be set far higher than their current emissions. Therefore, developing countries do not need to buy additional permits in the short or medium-run. However, the endowment has a positive price at present, because the holders of the endowment foresee that the endowment will eventually become a binding constraint as long as the countries keep growing. This gives incentives for carbon abatement in developing countries through price signals without imposing short or medium term costs in these economies. Chao and Peck (2000) characterise general conditions under which the Pareto-optimal environmental control will depend on the distribution of the cost burden among nations, and provide a sufficient condition under which a Pareto optimum can be implemented by a market mechanism with tradable emission permits. Ulph (2000) analyses the environmental policy (emission permit) assuming that the costs of environmental damage are only known by state governments. He shows that asymmetric information narrows the difference in environmental policies across states, relative to full information, but does not justify harmonisation (that is, identical environmental policy across states). However, as he assumes that pollution does not cross state boundaries, his findings are not applicable in the GHG emission control.[3] Peck and Teisberg (1999) also analyse the incentives for participation in international carbon dioxide control agreements using tradable emission permits. Their analysis involves two aggregate regions: Annex-I and Non-Annex-I. They define a bargaining range as the range of permit allocations that leaves each region's welfare at least as high as it would be in the no-control solution. From the simulation generated by the CETA-M Model they find that the bargaining range for Non-Annex-I is 70–115 per cent of its optimal emissions.[4] They argue that a bargaining range must be fairly close to each region's optimal emissions so that the interregional income transfers from emission permit trade could not become large enough to cause one of the regions to drop out of the agreement. The asymmetric distribution around optimal emissions for Non-Annex-I contradicts the usual perspective that Annex-I could shift more permits to Non-Annex-I. They argue this is because Non-Annex-I grows faster than Annex-I in both income and population, and its future damage is higher. They also find that the Kyoto Protocol produces a large wealth transfer from Annex-I to Non-Annex-I, but fails to achieve efficiency. Caplan *et al.* (1999) analyse several institutional arrangements in a world with one winner and one loser due to global warming. They show that only in the cases of complete decentralisation and total altruism will the allocation be efficient. Although they doubt the prospect of international policy agreements on the GHG stock level, they suggest that agreements that take the current GHG stock as given are more likely to be successful than agreements that attempt to change the stock. Manne (1996) looks at two cases of GHG abatement. In one, the benefits of abatement enter directly into the utility functions of the individual regions. In the other, the benefits enter into their production functions. He shows that the abatement efforts and the global welfare depend on the region's share of abatement costs in the first case. However, it is possible to separate the issue of equity from those of economic efficiency in the second case.

It seems that emission trade and tax systems are identical with perfect information. However, it is not guaranteed in a multi-country system. It might be true that both instruments will achieve the cost-efficiency to meet certain targets of GHG emission control, but the impact of the two instruments on economic growth and welfare might be different. In spite of implementability, the difference arises from the implicit restrictions on income transfer across boundaries.

This chapter discusses the interaction between China and rest of the world (ROW) in a setting similar to that of Chao and Peck (2000). In addition to analysing the bargaining power and set, the comparison of emission tax and permit trading schemes is highlighted, with particular reference to whether a decentralised and differentiated emission tax scheme improves global welfare.

Developments in China

Since the late 1970s, China has experienced rapid growth, with an annual rate of about ten per cent. Alongside rapid economic growth, total energy consumption—and thus GHG emissions—have increased sharply. Between 1980 and 1998, total energy consumption has more than doubled, with an annual growth rate of 4.63 per cent (Table 15.3), while carbon dioxide emissions grew at an annual rate of 5.28 per cent between 1980 and 1996 (Table 15.2). Zhang (1999) decomposes the change in China's carbon dioxide emissions between 1980 and 1997 into five components. He finds that among a total change in carbon dioxide emissions of 488.65 per cent, economic growth and population expansion have contributed 799.13 per cent and 128.39 per cent, respectively.

However, China's energy efficiency improved during the same period. In 1997, China's energy efficiency, measured in PPP GDP per unit of energy use, was US\$3.3 per kg oil equivalent, which was higher than Canada (3.0) and some Eastern European countries (Table 15.2). In the same study cited above, Zhang (1999) finds that the change in energy intensity actually decreased total emissions by 432.32 per cent. The energy switch played only a moderate role, reducing total emissions by only 6.51 per cent. This can be seen very clearly from the pattern of energy consumption in Table 15.3. From the 1950s to the 1970s, China experienced a major change in the composition of energy consumption. Due to the discovery and exploration of several big oil fields, the share of oil increased steadily from 5 per cent to 20 per cent; consequently, the share of coal decreased from more than 90 per cent to around 70 per cent. The pattern has not changed since.

Although population growth contributes to the increase in carbon dioxide emissions, China's rigorous and controversial population policy plays an important role in the change of emissions. Since the 1970s, due to continuous family planning activities over a long period, China has reduced what otherwise would have been the growth of its population by 300 million people (Wu *et al.* 1998:548). If the population policy had not been implemented, China's total carbon dioxide emissions would had been 4,203.4 million metric tons in 1996, 25 per cent higher than the actual level.

Garbaccio *et al.* (1999) find that technical change within sectors accounted for most of the fall in the energy–output ratio between 1987 and 1992. Another important factor that improved China's energy efficiency was price reform. In order to expand its industry, China had long underpriced energy. The price of coal was set so low that even the best coal mines could not make any profit (Laffont and Senik-Leygonie 1997; Smil 1998). This pricing system hurt the economy through inefficient production and consumption of energy. The Ministry of Finance introduced a two-tier price system in 1984 and by 1994 the government finally freed all coal prices. Subsidies for energy consumption have been reduced significantly. Coal subsidy rates fall from 61 per cent in 1984 to 37 per cent in 1990 and to 29 per cent in 1995, while petroleum subsidy rates fall from 55 per cent in 1990 to 2 per cent in 1995 (Zhang 1999). However, China's energy prices are still lower than those of the resource-rich United States (World Bank 1997:Table 4.4:53).

Although China has significantly improved energy efficiency, it still has a long way to go. First, the current level of energy efficiency is still quite low compared to industrialised countries (Table 15.2). Second, a coal-dominant energy structure is likely to prevail for a long time due to the fact that China is relatively abundant in coal reserves. China possesses the world's third largest coal deposits after Russia and the United States. In any case, its coal resources could last for several centuries at the mid-1990s rate of extraction. In terms of verified coal reserves, China again ranks third in the world with roughly 115 billion tonnes (Gt) or one-ninth of the world's total. In contrast, at the end of 1996, China's proven oil reserves amounted to just over 2 per cent of the world total; and the proven natural gas reserves are much smaller, amounting to a mere 0.8 per cent of the world total (Smil 1998).

The theoretical model

Following Chao and Peck (2000), the model is structured as follows. Suppose there are N nations in the world, the social welfare function of nation i could be written as

$$U^i = P_i U^i(C_i, Q) \tag{15.1}$$

where P_i and C_i are, respectively, the population and per capita consumption of nation i; and Q is the environmental quality, measured by the change in temperature.

The amount of domestic capital goods owned by each nation is denoted by

$\overline{K}_i$. The technology for each nation is represented by a convex and twice-differentiable multi-factor production function. For simplicity, we assume that the production function, F^i (K_i, E_i, Q) has two factor inputs—capital K_i (environmentally benign) and energy, E_i (causing global climate change).[5] Global climate change enters into both utility and production functions because climate change may cause damages that can be valued in a market (crop losses) and damages that do not have established market values (species loss) (Chao and Peck 2000). We further assume that both utility and production functions have the usual properties.

Competitive equilibrium prior to environmental control

Because an individual country cannot control Q, and because the utility function or social welfare function is an increasing function of consumption, the objective of each country is simply to achieve the highest possible output. If the marginal (extraction) cost of energy is c, the net output for nation i, Y_i, can be expressed as

$$Y_i = F^i(K_i, E_i, Q) - cE_i \qquad (15.2)$$

The following conditions are satisfied in a competitive equilibrium prior to

Table 15.3   China's energy consumption

Year	Total energy consumption (million tce)	Coal	Share (%) Petroleum	Natural gas	Hydropower
1957	96.44	92.3	4.6	0.1	3.0
1962	165.40	89.2	6.6	0.9	3.2
1965	189.01	86.5	10.3	0.9	2.7
1970	292.91	80.9	14.7	0.9	3.5
1975	454.25	71.9	21.1	2.5	4.6
1978	571.44	70.7	22.7	3.2	3.4
1980	602.75	72.2	20.7	3.1	4.0
1985	766.82	75.8	17.1	2.2	4.9
1986	808.50	75.8	17.2	2.3	4.7
1987	866.32	76.2	17.0	2.1	4.7
1988	929.97	76.2	17.0	2.1	4.7
1989	969.34	76.0	17.1	2.0	4.9
1990	987.03	76.2	16.6	2.1	5.1
1991	1,037.83	76.1	17.1	2.0	4.8
1992	1,091.70	75.7	17.5	1.9	4.9
1993	1,159.93	74.7	18.2	1.9	5.2
1994	1,227.37	75.0	17.4	1.9	5.7
1995	1,311.76	74.6	17.5	1.8	6.1
1996	1,389.48	74.7	18.0	1.8	5.5
1997	1,381.73	71.5	20.4	1.7	6.2
1998	1,360.00	71.6	19.8	2.1	6.5

Source: State Statistical Bureau, various years. *China Statistical Yearbook*, China Statistical Publishing House, Beijing.

environmental control

$$F_K^i(K_i, E_i, Q) = r \qquad (15.3)$$

$$F_E^i(K_i, E_i, Q) = c \qquad (15.4)$$

$$\sum_{i=1}^{N} K_i = \sum_{i=1}^{N} \overline{K}_i \qquad (15.5)$$

$$P_i C_i = Y_i + r(\overline{K}_i - K_i) \qquad (15.6)$$

$$Q = G\left(\sum_{i=1}^{N} E_i\right) \qquad (15.7)$$

Equations 15.2–15.7 have $4n + 2$ variables in $4n + 2$ equations. Therefore we can solve the system to get the following pre-environmental-control equilibrium values:

$$\hat{E}_i, \ \hat{K}_i, \ \hat{C}_i, \ \hat{Y}_i, \ \hat{Q}, \ \hat{r}$$

Consequently, nation i's social welfare prior to environmental control is

$$\hat{V} = P_i U^i(\hat{C}_i, \hat{Q}) \qquad (15.8)$$

It is clear that this decentralised competitive equilibrium is not socially optimal because the external cost of using energy is not considered by any nations.

Welfare optimum

Let λ_i denote the utility weight for nation i. The global social welfare maximisation problem can be stated as follows

$$\max_{C_i, K_i, E_i, Q} U = \sum_{i=1}^{N} \lambda_i P_i U^i(C_i, Q) \qquad (15.9)$$

subject to

$$\sum_{i=1}^{N} K_i = \sum_{i=1}^{N} \overline{K}_i \qquad (15.5)$$

$$\sum_{i=1}^{N} P_i C_i = \sum_{i=1}^{N} \left[F^i(K_i, E_i, Q) - cE_i\right] \qquad (15.10)$$

$$Q = G\left(\sum_{i=1}^{N} E_i\right) \qquad (15.7)$$

Let π_K, π_C, π_E be the shadow prices associated with the above constraints, respectively. Then the first order condition can be written as

$$\lambda_i U_C^i(C_i, Q) = \pi_C \qquad (15.11)$$

$$\pi_C\left(F_E^i(K_i,E_i,Q)-c\right)=\pi_E G'\left(\sum_{i=1}^{N}E_i\right) \tag{15.12}$$

$$\pi_C F_K^i(K_i,E_i,Q)=\pi_K \tag{15.13}$$

$$\pi_E=-\sum_{i=1}^{N}\lambda_i P_i U_Q^i(C_i,Q)-\pi_C\sum_{i=1}^{N}F_Q^i(K_i,E_i,Q) \tag{15.14}$$

The last condition (Equation 15.14) shows that the shadow price of climate change has two parts: the values derived from the marginal utility and the marginal product of climate change. The condition 15.12 shows that the marginal product of energy reflects both marginal extraction cost and marginal external cost.

Equations 15.5, 15.7 and 15.10–15.14 give $3n + 4$ equations in $3n + 4$ variables. Therefore we can solve them to get the optimal values of the following variables

$$E_i^*,\ K_i^*,\ C_i^*,\ Q^*,\ \pi_C^*,\ \pi_E^*,\ \pi_K^*$$

and the corresponding global welfare is

$$V^*=\sum_{i=1}^{N}\lambda_i P_i U^i(C_i^*,Q^*)$$

Instruments to achieve welfare optimum in a decentralised economy

The above global social welfare maximisation problem is constructed in a centralised pattern. However, the real world is a decentralised one. Moreover, the sovereignty of nations makes the scheme more complicated. For example, an emission tax and/or permit trade may require significant cross-border income transfers. Therefore we have two questions to answer: how to achieve welfare optimum in a decentralised economy? and, is it realistic to achieve the welfare optimum?

Emission tax

It seems straightforward to achieve the welfare optimum in decentralised economy by imposing an emission tax. From Equation 15.12, we know that

$$F_E^i(K_i,E_i,Q)=c+\frac{\pi_E}{\pi_C}G'\left(\sum_{i=1}^{N}E_i\right)$$

Therefore we can set the tax rate as

$$t^*=\frac{\pi_E^*}{\pi_C^*}G'\left(\sum_{i=1}^{N}E_i^*\right)$$

$$=-\left(\frac{\sum_{i=1}^{N}\lambda_i P_i U_Q^i(C_i^*,Q^*)}{\lambda_i U_C^i(C_i^*,Q^*)}+\sum_{i=1}^{N}F_Q^i(K_i^*,E_i^*,Q^*)\right)G'\left(\sum_{i=1}^{N}E_i^*\right) \tag{15.15}$$

Clearly the optimal tax rate is affected by the welfare weight assigned to each nation. This result is in line with the finding of Manne (1996).

This tax rate may induce firms in each country to use energy at the optimal level E_i^*. However, it cannot guarantee that each country has the optimal consumption C_i^*, because the welfare optimum is achieved with the global income constraint 15.10 rather than income constraint 15.6 for each country. This means that in addition to the emission tax, it is necessary to allow income transfers across country borders.

From Equation 15.13 we can derive that the real interest rate for capital as $r^* = \pi_K^* / \pi_C^*$. For nation i, the spending on consumption is $P_i C_i^*$, while total disposable income is $F^i(K_i^*, E_i^*, Q^*) - cE_i^* + r^*(\overline{K}_i - K_i^*)$. It is obvious that only in very rare cases will these two terms be equal, although in aggregate they are equal according to Equation 15.10. Therefore, if they are not equal, some income transfer is necessary to obtain the welfare optimum. Specifically, if $P_i C_i^* > F^i(K_i^*, E_i^*, Q^*) - cE_i^* + r^*(\overline{K}_i - K_i^*)$, then nation i should receive net income support from other countries.

It can be derived that a country is a recipient of such a transfer if it has small capital stock, low productivity and energy efficiency, and thus low product, but has a high propensity of consumption. Applying this in the issue of GHG emission control, we can see that developing countries fall into this category.

However, this income transfer may be beyond our discussion of global warming policy, because if there was no global warming, income transfer would also be necessary to achieve welfare optimality as long as countries were not identical. Therefore it might be better to isolate global warming policy from the general issue of income distribution. This can be done by replacing constraint 15.10 in the global welfare maximisation problem with condition 15.6; that is, each country should satisfy its own budget constraint. But these new constraints make the possibility set smaller, therefore the solution is of the second best property, which we will discuss in more detail later.

Tradable permits

Now consider a global tradable permit scheme. Two issues should be dealt with when such a scheme is designed. First, we should determine the optimal number of permits ($\overline{E}$), which determines the environmental quality through $Q = G(\overline{E})$. Second, we should decide how to allocate these permits. Now the global social welfare maximisation problem can be written as

$$\max_{C_i, K_i, E_i, \overline{E}} U = \sum_{i=1}^{N} \lambda_i P_i U^i \left(C_i, G(\overline{E}) \right) \tag{15.16}$$

subject to

$$\sum_{i=1}^{N} K_i = \sum_{i=1}^{N} \overline{K}_i \tag{15.5}$$

$$\sum_{i=1}^{N} P_i C_i = \sum_{i=1}^{N} \left[F^i \left(K_i, E_i, G \left(\sum_{i=1}^{N} \overline{E}_i \right) \right) - c E_i \right] \tag{15.10}$$

$$\sum_{i=1}^{N} E_i = \overline{E} \tag{15.17}$$

Let π_K, π_C, π_E be the shadow prices associated with the above constraints, respectively. Then the first order condition can be written as[6]

$$\lambda_i U_C^i(C_i, Q) = \pi_C \tag{15.11}$$

$$\pi_C \left(F_E^i(K_i, E_i, Q) - c \right) = \pi_E \tag{15.18}$$

$$\pi_C F_K^i(K_i, E_i, Q) = \pi_K \tag{15.13}$$

$$\pi_E = -G'(\overline{E}) \left(\sum_{i=1}^{N} \lambda_i P_i U_Q^i(C_i, Q) + \pi_C \sum_{i=1}^{N} F_Q^i(K_i, E_i, Q) \right) \tag{15.19}$$

The above conditions are exactly the same as those given by Equations 15.5, 15.7 and 15.10–15.14, except that

$$\pi_E G'(\sum_{i=1}^{N} Ei)$$

in 15.12 and 15.14 is equal to in π_E in 15.18 and 15.19. It can be concluded from these conditions that the initial allocation of permits does not affect the optimal value of capital and energy use and consumption as long as the number of permits is set optimally. It can also be seen that the allocation of permits serves as a tool of income transfer to achieve the first-best outcome, which is problematic with the emission tax scheme. As in the case of an emission tax, we set the permit price and interest rate as

$$P_E^* = \frac{\pi_E^*}{\pi_C^*}, \quad r^* = \frac{\pi_K^*}{\pi_C^*} \tag{15.20}$$

Country i's income other than permit sales is
$F^i(K_i^*, E_i^*, G(\overline{E}^*)) - cE_i^* + r^*(\overline{K}_i - K_i^*)$; while total consumption is $P_i C_i^*$. Therefore, we can carefully choose the initial number of permits ($\overline{E}_i$) such that

$$P_E^* \left(\overline{E}_i - E_i^* \right) = P_i C_i^* - \left(F^i(K_i^*, E_i^*, G(\overline{E}^*)) - cE_i^* + r^*(\overline{K}_i - K_i^*) \right) \tag{15.21}$$

However, it is quite possible that if the value of the right-hand side of Equation 15.21 is too high then we need $\overline{E}_i > E^*$ to equate both sides. Therefore, a tradable emission permit scheme may help to achieve the first-best outcome, but does not guarantee it.

Chao and Peck (2000) claim that the welfare optimum can be achieved in an emission trading system if the initial permits are carefully allocated and provide a proof. However, what they deal with is not what we discuss here. In contrast to condition 15.11 in this chapter, Equation (24) in their paper states that each country should satisfy its own budget constraint, and no income transfer other than emission trading is allowed. What they get is actually a second-best outcome.

In sum, we can make the following statement. Result 1. A pure emission (or energy use) tax cannot achieve the first-best outcome—that is, maximising global welfare, not just meeting emission targets—and an emission (or energy use) permit trading scheme does not guarantee the achievement of the first-best outcome.

Second-best policy

Let us suppose that an individual country should meet its own budget constraint. First let us discuss the emission (or energy) tax scheme. This time we should deal with the problem in a more decentralised way because the interest rate appears in constraint 15.6. It is necessary to distinguish producer and consumer (and social planner). The producer chooses capital and energy use to maximise its profit given the interest rate, energy price and environmental regulation. The resulting first-order conditions are

$$F_K^i\left(K_i, E_i, Q\right) = r \tag{15.22}$$
$$F_E^i\left(K_i, E_i, Q\right) = c + t_i \tag{15.17}$$

At the same time, the global social planner chooses energy supply, consumption and environmental quality to maximise global social welfare (Equation 15.9) subject to constraints 15.6 and 15.7. Let π_C^i, π_E denote the shadow prices associated with constraints 15.6 and 15.7. Then the first-order condition can be written as

$$\lambda_i U_C^i\left(C_i, Q\right) = \pi_C^i \tag{15.23}$$

$$\pi_C^i\left(F_E^i(K_i, E_i, Q) - c\right) = \pi_E G'\left(\sum_{i=1}^{N} E_i\right) \tag{15.24}$$

$$\pi_E = -\sum_{i=1}^{N} \lambda_i P_i U_Q^i(C_i, Q) - \pi_C^i \sum_{i=1}^{N} F_Q^i(K_i, E_i, Q) \tag{15.25}$$

Condition 15.17 is equivalent to condition 15.24, which determines the tax rate of energy use. One important result can be found by comparing condition 15.23 with 15.11. Now the weighted marginal utility of consumption differs across countries. This verifies that the results are not the first-best outcomes. One more important finding is that the tax rates are different across countries. From 15.24, the tax rate should be set as

$$\frac{\pi_E}{\pi_C^i} G'\left(\sum_{i=1}^{N} E_i\right)$$

As π_C^i differs across country, the whole term differs too. If we set a uniform tax rate, then using 15.17, 15.24 can be rewritten as

$$\pi_C^i \cdot t = \pi_E G'\left(\sum_{i=1}^{N} E_i\right) \tag{15.26}$$

This in turn implies that π_C^i should be identical for all i. As the usual optimisation requires different multipliers for different constraints, this restriction further worsens the result. In sum, we have the following result regarding the emission tax scheme if income transfer is not allowed, as in the real world situation.

Result 2. If each country should meet its own budget constraint and an emission tax scheme is considered, then a differentiated tax scheme is the best choice; that is, a uniform tax scheme cannot achieve higher global welfare than a differentiated tax scheme.

Now let us move to the tradable permit system. The problem can be set as follows. The global social planner chooses initial permit allocation, capital, energy and consumption to maximise the global social welfare function.

$$\max_{C_i, K_i, E_i, \bar{E}_i} U = \sum_{i=1}^{N} \lambda_i P_i U^i\left(C_i, G\left(\sum_{i=1}^{N} \bar{E}_i\right)\right) \tag{15.16}$$

subject to

$$\sum_{i=1}^{N} K_i = \sum_{i=1}^{N} \bar{K}_i \tag{15.5}$$

$$\sum_{i=1}^{N} E_i = \sum_{i=1}^{N} \bar{E}_i \tag{15.27}$$

$$P_i C_i = F^i\left(K_i, E_i, G\left(\sum_{i=1}^{N} \bar{E}_i\right)\right) - cE_i + p_E\left(\bar{E}_i - E_i\right) + r\left(\bar{K}_i - K_i\right) \tag{15.28}$$

Let π_K, π_E, π_C^i be the shadow prices associated with the above constraints, respectively. Then the first-order conditions can be written as

$$\lambda_i U_C^i(C_i, Q) = \pi_C^i \tag{15.23}$$

$$\pi_C^i\left(F_E^i(K_i, E_i, Q) - c - p_E\right) = \pi_E \tag{15.29}$$

$$\pi_C^i\left(F_K^i(K_i, E_i, Q) - r\right) = \pi_K \tag{15.30}$$

$$\pi_E + \pi_C^i p_E + G'(\overline{E})\left(\sum_{i=1}^{N} \lambda_i P_i U_Q^i(C_i, Q) + \sum_{i=1}^{N} \pi_C^i F_Q^i(K_i, E_i, Q)\right) = 0 \quad (15.31)$$

$$F_E^i(K_i, E_i, Q) - c - p_E = 0 \qquad (15.32)$$

$$F_K^i(K_i, E_i, Q) - r = 0 \qquad (15.33)$$

The last two are the first conditions of the profit maximisation problem, which imply that $\pi_E = \pi_K = 0$ in 15.29 and 15.30, and 15.31 implies that π_C^i is identical for all i. Thus these conditions are exactly the conditions given in 15.11, 15.13, 15.18 and 15.19. At first glance, it seems that the first-best outcome can be achieved by carefully choosing the initial allocation of permits, as argued by many authors (see, for example Chao and Peck 2000). However, this is not guaranteed. The 'optimal' allocation for some countries could be well above the total optimal number of permits. As we will see, this is exactly the case implied by our numerical model. If non-negative restrictions are imposed on allocations, it turns out that a boundary solution is reached; that is, some countries are not allocated any permits. Therefore we should design the tradable permit scheme in a different way.

An alternative design would involve fixing the total amount of permits, rather than endogenising it. Again, it is possible to get a spurious initial allocation. Another way is to set up certain rules of allocating permits and then to find the optimal number of permits. Without doubt, there are numerous rules to allocate permits, with *pro rata* population and *pro rata* current emissions as two important scenarios.

Before moving on to numerical analysis, we present the following statement to summarise the above theoretical analysis.

Result 3. Emission tax and emission trading schemes are not identical because the latter allows income transfers across borders.

Numerical simulation

In this section, a simple numerical model is presented. There are two regions in the model: China and rest of the world (ROW). In order to illustrate the idea discussed in the previous sections, the values of parameters for ROW are chosen in such a way that they represent a more industrialised world, which is somehow counterfactual.

The climate model

Following Oglesby and Saltzman (1990) and Chao (1995), the relation between the average global climate change (T) and the global energy consumption (E) can be written as

$$T = T_0 \log_2\left(1 + \frac{\gamma E}{X_0}\right) \tag{15.34}$$

where $T_0\,(3°C)$ is the increase from pre-industrial average global temperature as a result of doubling the carbon dioxide concentration in the atmosphere; X_0 is the pre-industrial level of carbon dioxide concentration in the atmosphere, which is about 280 ppm; and γ (0.30 ppm/exajoules/year) is a transfer coefficient which is chosen at the current rate of emission of about 250 exajoules (energy equivalent). The equilibrium carbon concentration will remain at about 335 ppm, therefore γE is the carbon dioxide concentration in the atmosphere (Chao and Peck 2000).

The utility function

Following Chao and Peck (2000), the utility function for each region is assumed to be of Cobb–Douglas form

$$U^i(C_i, T) = \left[C_i^{\theta_i}\left(\overline{T}_i - T\right)^{1-\theta_i}\right]^{1/2} \tag{15.35}$$

The parameter $\overline{T}_i$ is the catastrophic level of average global temperature increase, as perceived by nation i. That is, at that level, the utility becomes zero, which is as bad as when consumption drops to zero. The values of parameters $\overline{T}_i$ and θ_i are highly uncertain and subjective. But one reasonable conjecture is that they are higher for developing countries (China, in this case) than for industrialised countries because developing countries have lower per capita consumption and thus care more about consumption than the environment. Specifically, the values are determined in such a way that the utility reduction from a $3°C$ rise in average global temperature is two per cent for China and four per cent for ROW, and the utility losses increase in a cubic fashion as the average global temperature increases (Chao and Peck 2000; Nordhaus 1994)

$$(1.00)^{\theta_1}\left(\overline{T}_1\right)^{1-\theta_1} = (1.02)^{\theta_1}\left(\overline{T}_1 - 3\right)^{1-\theta_1} = (1.16)^{\theta_1}\left(\overline{T}_1 - 6\right)^{1-\theta_1} \tag{15.36}$$

$$(1.00)^{\theta_2}\left(\overline{T}_2\right)^{1-\theta_2} = (1.04)^{\theta_2}\left(\overline{T}_2 - 3\right)^{1-\theta_2} = (1.32)^{\theta_2}\left(\overline{T}_2 - 6\right)^{1-\theta_2} \tag{15.37}$$

The resulting values are listed in Table 15.4.

The production function

The estimates of the impact of climate change on production are quite diverse and controversial. For example, Nordhaus (1991) estimates that the net economic damage from a $3°C$ warming is likely to be around 0.26 per cent of national income for the United States. Kane et al. (1989) estimate that with a

$2.5°C$ warming, average yields would decline by 20 per cent in the United States and European Community and 18 per cent in Canada, but rise by 15 per cent in Northern Europe and Australia, 10 per cent in Russia, and 4 per cent in Japan. For global warming of $10°C$, it seems likely that crop yields in the mid-latitudes of the United States would collapse toward zero during summer (Cline 1991). Based on these estimates, we conjecture that the impact of climate change on production can be ignored when global warming is not too high, say below $4°C$. Therefore the production function for each region is also assumed to be of Cobb–Douglas form

$$F^i(K_i, E_i, Q) = A_i K_i^{\alpha_i} E_i^{\beta_i} \qquad\qquad (15.38)$$

The technologies employed by the two regions are different in the sense that China has a higher marginal product of capital and higher energy intensity. We follow Chao and Peck's (2000) assumption about the capital value and energy value shares and marginal cost of energy of ROW. However, we make different assumptions about the parameters of China. China has a capital/GDP ratio of about 3.0, which implies that the capital share is about 0.20.[7] The energy/GDP ratio is about 13.33 megajoule/US$, implying an energy share of about 0.06.[8]

China's GDP growth rate was 10.1 per cent per annum between 1980 and 1990, and 11.2 per cent per annum between 1990 and 1998 (World Bank 2000). We assume China will have moderate growth of about five per cent in the next half century, which implies a GDP in 2050 of about US$1,2124.8 billion. The world GDP growth rate was 3.2 per cent per annum between 1980 and 1990, and 2.5 per cent per annum between 1990 and 1998 (World Bank 2000). Assuming that the GDP growth of ROW continues the current trend, the ROW GDP will be about US$100,309.3 billion.[9]

China's annual new capital formation growth was 20.7 per cent between 1985 and 1998 (*China Statistical Yearbook* 1999), while domestic investment growth was 13.4 per cent per annum between 1990 and 1998 (World Bank 2000). If this trend continues, China's capital stock will be as high as US$148 trillion, which is unrealistic. To be in line with the assumptions given above and in Chao and Peck (2000), it is simply assumed that the interest rate and marginal extraction cost of energy are, respectively, 0.05 and US$4.5 per gigajoule. The capital stock and energy consumption are derived from the assumption of their shares in GDP. The capital stock figure implies no cross-border capital flows. Plugging these values into the production functions gives the values of coefficient A_i, which are 4.08 for China and 29.93 for ROW. The difference in the values of this coefficient between China and ROW is mainly because the energy and capital share of total GDP is only 20–26 per cent, and the size of the two economies are quite different. However, the marginal product of capital and energy are of the same order for both regions.

China's population was 1.238 billion at the end of 1998, and the average annual growth rate was 1.3 per cent between 1980 and 1998. The World Bank estimates the annual growth rate will be 0.7 per cent between 1998 and 2015. The world population (excluding China) was 4.658 billion in 1998, and the annual growth rate is estimated at 1.1 per cent between 1998 and 2015 (World Bank 2000). Following these assumptions, in 2050 the population will be 1.78 billion for China and 8.23 billion for ROW.

Numerical results

Without environmental control, the global energy consumption would be 1271.111 exajoules in 2050, and global warming would be $3.72\,°C$. Correspondingly, the per capita utility of China and ROW would be 2.482 and 3.252, respectively, and global welfare would be 31.194 if both have the same power of one (Table 15.5). This is the baseline against which different policy arrangements will be compared.

Introducing environmental control will increase global welfare to 31.655 in a global social optimisation pattern (Table 15.5). However, this global optimisation is not attainable because the underlying assumption is that US$8.812 trillion, amounting to 76.6 per cent of China's GDP, has to be transferred to China from ROW. Correspondingly, China's per capita utility increases to 3.298, while ROW's decreases to 3.133.

Table 15.6 shows the results of imposing energy taxes assuming that both China and ROW have the same bargaining power λ. As previously discussed,

Table 15.4   Numerical assumptions (before environmental control)

Parameter	China	ROW
θ_i	0.9720	0.9489
$\overline{T}_i$	6.03494	6.04728
Production shifter, A_i	4.08	29.93
Capital value share, α_i	0.20	0.15
Energy value share, β_i	0.06	0.05
GDP (US$ trillion)	12.00	100.00
Population (billion)	1.78	8.23
Capital stock, $\overline{K}_i$ (US$ trillion)	48.00	300.00
Energy consumption, E_i (exajoules)	160.00	1,111.11
Marginal cost of energy, c (US$/gigajoules)	4.50	4.50
Interest rate	0.05	0.05

the policy with uniform tax rate creates lower global welfare than that with differentiated tax rates, although both policies can achieve global utility higher than the baseline. Specifically, China's utility is lower while ROW's utility is higher in a uniform tax regime than in a differentiated tax regime.

Figure 15.3 illustrates the bargaining set with a differentiated tax regime. The bargaining set is larger than is usually assumed. The tax rate imposed on ROW could be as high as US\$14.328 per gigajoules for ROW to have the same utility as the baseline if China could impose a tiny US\$0.319 per gigajoules (about 7.09 per cent of the extraction cost of energy) at the same time. However, the bargaining set is not symmetric. The highest tax rate China would accept is only US\$4.84 per gigajoules on the condition that ROW imposes a tax at the rate of US\$4.108 per gigajoules.

Figure 15.4 compares the uniform tax regime with the differentiated tax regime. The optima with varying bargaining power (λ_i)are depicted. The variance of optima with uniform tax is much smaller than that of optima with differentiated tax. All the combinations of (U_1, U_2) under the uniform tax regime, as bargaining power varying from $\lambda_1 = 1$, $\lambda_2 = 0$ to $\lambda_1 = 0$, $\lambda_2 = 1$, are depicted in the diagram, while only a subset of U_1, U_2 under the differentiated tax regime are depicted, with bargaining power varying from $\lambda_1 = 0.375$, $\lambda_2 = 0.625$ to $\lambda_1 = 0.970$, $\lambda_2 = 0.030$. It is clear from Figure 15.4 that the whole utility frontier with uniform tax rate falls into the utility frontier with differentiated tax rates, confirming that a uniform tax regime cannot achieve higher global welfare than a differentiated tax regime. Another observation is that as the bargaining power of ROW increases, these two regimes tend to converge. This can be partly explained by the size differential of China and ROW. When ROW dominates in the negotiation of a global energy tax policy, a uniform tax rate is likely to be adopted.

The results of a tradable permit system with equal bargaining power are listed in Table 15.7. Two scenarios are reported. One is global optimisation by choosing total permit numbers and initial allocations without prior restrictions, in addition to the other control variables like capital and energy use and consumption. As previously discussed, a tradable permit system can achieve the Pareto optimum only if ROW can be allocated a negative amount of permits (-1648.805 exajoules). If a non-negative restriction is imposed on the initial allocation, it turns out that no permits are allocated to ROW. Needless to say, these two scenarios are not realistic and are not worth further exploration. Instead, we try to find the optimal number of permits to use energy with different allocation rules. It can be seen that both allocation rules—that is, allocating permits proportional to the population or pre-control energy use— are in the bargaining set. However, it can also be seen that China benefits less than the ROW from these two allocation rules (Figure 15.5).

It is clear that fixing the total amount of permits at the level of global optimisation with environmental control (652.651 exajoules) is always beneficial to ROW, but not necessarily to China (Figure 15.6).

Both Figures 15.5 and 15.6 show that for China, the allocation of permits proportional to population is not as favourable as people usually assume. This can be explained by the fact that, compared to ROW, China has a higher preference for consumption and higher energy intensity in production. A restriction on the use of energy will hurt China's production more than ROW even if it is offered a seemingly favorable allocation of permits. Because China has to use more energy to produce the same amount of output and has to satisfy its own income constraint, China's benefit from this allocation is limited on the production side. On the other hand, China's benefit from improvement in global warming is also limited due to its preference. Of course, this arrangement is more favorable than the allocation of permits proportional to the pre-control situation. Such arrangements make the ROW much better off while leaving China at the margin if the total permit is endogenous (Figure 15.5). Given this fact, the negotiation of an international agreement on permit allocation is a painful process if developing countries are included.

Table 15.5   Non-cooperative competitive equilibrium versus global optimisation

Indicators	Competitive equilibrium prior to environmental control	Global optimisation with environmental control	
		Absolute value	Change (%)[a]
Capital used in China	48.000	47.632	0.767
Capital used in ROW	300.000	300.368	0.123
Energy used in China	160.000	81.514	-49.054
Energy used in ROW	1,111.111	571.137	-48.598
Output in China	12.000	11.506	-3.255
Output in ROW	100.000	96.745	-4.117
Per capita consumption in China	6.337	11.219	77.040
Per capita consumption in ROW	11.543	10.370	-10.162
Global warming	3.720	2.295	-38.306
Per capita utility in China	2.482	3.298	32.877
Per capita utility in ROW	3.253	3.133	-3.689
Total global utility	31.194	31.655	1.475
China	4.418	5.871	..
ROW	26.776	25.784	..

Note: [a]Percentage change to the baseline outcome, or the competitive equilibrium prior to environmental control.

Table 15.6   Outcome of energy tax with equal bargaining power

Indicators	Global optimisation with differentiated tax rate and individual budget constraint		Global optimisation with uniform tax rate and individual budget constraint	
	Value	Change (%)[a]	Value	Change (%)[a]
Capital used in China	48.125	0.260	47.628	-0.775
Capital used in ROW	299.875	-0.042	300.372	0.124
Energy used in China	93.045	-41.847	80.880	-49.450
Energy used in ROW	552.165	-50.305	566.750	-48.992
Output in China	11.622	-3.150	11.501	-4.158
Output in ROW	96.558	-3.442	96.708	-3.292
Per capita consumption in China	6.291	-0.726	6.267	-1.105
Per capita consumption in ROW	11.431	-0.970	11.439	-0.901
Global warming	2.274	-38.871	2.281	-38.683
Per capita utility in China	2.490	0.322	2.485	0.121
Per capita utility in ROW	3.281	0.861	3.282	0.891
Total global utility	31.436	0.776	31.434	0.769
China	4.432	..	4.424	..
ROW	27.004	..	27.011	..
Marginal cost of global warming	0.210	..	0.136	..
Energy tax in China	2.994	..	4.032	..
Energy tax in ROW	4.244	..	4.032	..

Note: [a]Percentage change to the baseline outcome, or the competitive equilibrium prior to environmental control.

Table 15.7   Tradable permits with equal bargaining power

Indicators	Optimising permit number and initial allocation with individual budget constraint without non-negative restrictions on permit allocation	Optimising permit number and initial allocation with individual budget constraint, with non-negative restrictions on permit allocation
Capital used in China	47.632	47.682
Capital used in ROW	300.368	300.318
Energy used in China	81.514	89.237
Energy used in ROW	571.137	624.502
Permits allocated for China	2,301.457	713.739
Permits allocated for ROW	-1,648.805	0.000
Permit price	3.970	3.280
Output in China	11.506	11.571
Output in ROW	96.745	97.176
Per capita consumption in China	11.219	7.435
Per capita consumption in ROW	10.370	11.215
Global warming	2.295	2.458
Per capita utility in China	3.298	2.699
Per capita utility in ROW	3.133	3.247
Total global utility	31.655	31.529
China	5.871	4.804
ROW	25.784	26.725

Sensitivity analysis

To test the robustness of results we present two sets of analyses. First, we reverse the assumption about the preference; that is, the utility loss from a $3°C$ rise in average global temperature is four per cent for China and two per cent for ROW, and the utility losses increase in a cubic fashion as the average global temperature increases. Second, we assume that China has the same technology as ROW. The results are reported in Tables 15.8 and 15.9.

It is clear from the test that the qualitative result does not change even if the parameters change dramatically: a differentiated tax system is always better than a uniform tax system in terms of global welfare. China suffers from a uniform tax policy even if China cares about global warming more than ROW or has the same technology as ROW.

We also try to test the impact of economic size on the result. We divide the world into three economies: China, rich countries and ROW. We assume China and ROW have the same preferences and production technology, but different levels of population and GDP that are projected based on current and historical data. Rich countries have higher energy efficiency and care more about global warming.

Low and middle-income countries had an annual growth rate of 3.5 per cent between 1990 and 1998, and their GDP (excluding China) in 1998 was US$5,234.8 billion. Following this trend, the GDP in 2050 will be US$31.32

Figure 15.3   Bargaining set with differentiated tax

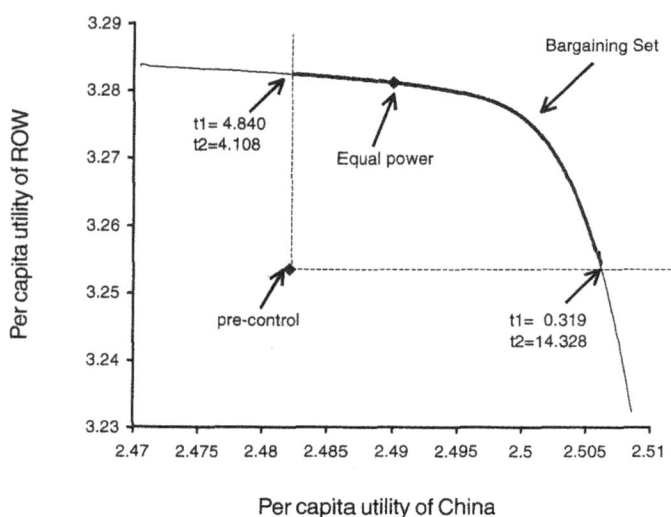

trillion. The population is 3,772 million in 1998. The growth rate is projected as 1.2 per cent between 1998 and 2015. If this trend extends to 2050, then the population will be 7,014 million.

High-income countries had an annual growth rate of 2.3 per cent between 1990 and 1998, and 3.1 per cent during the period 1980–90. Therefore, we assume that rich countries will grow at a rate of 2.5 per cent. The total GDP in 1998 was US$22,543.6 billion, so the level in 2050 would be US$81.41 trillion. The population in 1998 was 886 million. The growth rate is estimated as 0.3 per cent between 1998 and 2015. If this trend extends to 2050, then the population in rich countries will be 1,035.1 million. The assumptions about the parameters are listed in Table 15.10.

Some stylised results are reported in Table 15.11. Again, the qualitative results do not change after the regrouping of the world economy. The differentiated tax system is better than the uniform tax system. China and ROW suffer from the introduction of a uniform tax, while rich countries benefit from it. The welfare optima can not be achieved without income redistribution.

Conclusion

Our theoretical and numerical models show that the emission tax and tradable permit policies are quite different. The main reason behind this difference is that a tradable permit policy allows cross-border income transfers, while a tax

Figure 15.4   Uniform tax versus differentiated tax

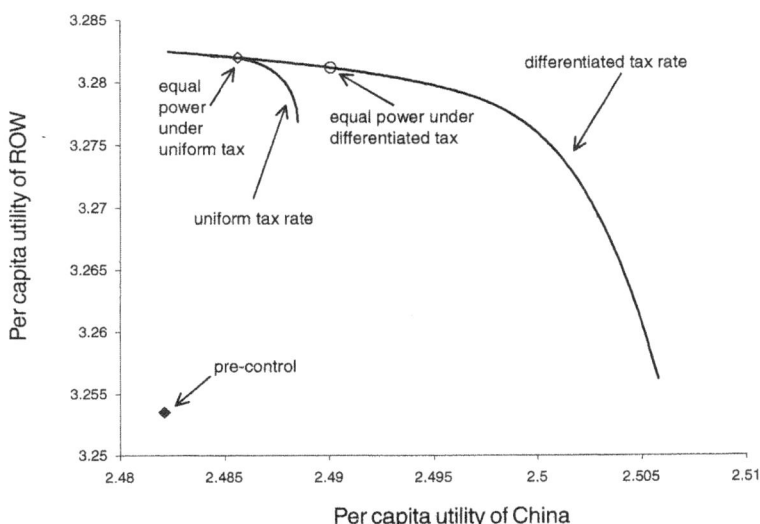

Figure 15.5   Tradable permits with endogenous number of permits and varying initial allocation

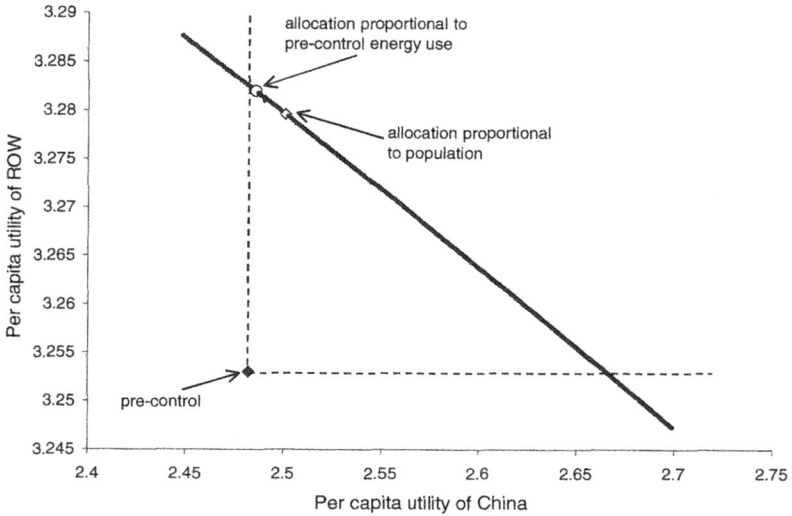

Figure 15.6   Tradable permits with fixed number of permits and varying initial allocation

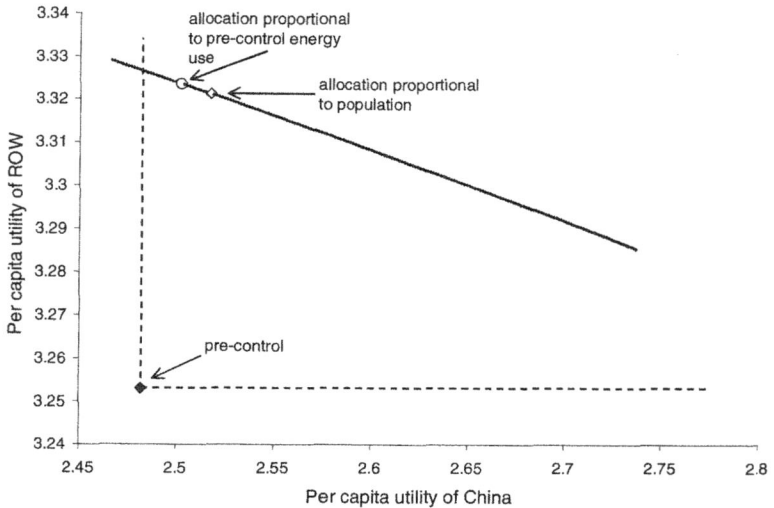

does not. However, both policies cannot achieve the welfare optima. In order to achieve the welfare optima, an emission tax policy should be accompanied by a net transfer of income from rich countries to poor countries, while a tradable emission permit policy requires that rich countries are allocated a negative number of permits. It is clear that neither arrangement is realistic.

In order to achieve the second-best outcome, we find that a differentiated tax system is better than a uniform tax system. The difference in the tax rate is justified by the fact that China and ROW (or, poor countries and rich countries) have different preferences about the environment and consumption, and different production technologies. Because China (or developing countries) prefer consumption more than industrialised countries (and its energy intensity is higher), a lower emission tax (or energy tax) would yield a more favorable environment to produce what it consumes. Because rich countries care more about the environment, their willingness to pay for a clean environment is higher, and therefore they can afford a higher tax rate. Thus, overall welfare could be enhanced by this arrangement.

Another benefit from the differentiated tax system is that it could gradually improve mutual trust and international cooperation because a small unilateral tax could improve individual nations' welfare as well as global welfare. If we could design the tax system carefully in the sense of combining global welfare with each nation's interest, the prisoner's dilemma could be solved.

In theory, a tradable permit system could produce higher global welfare if the initial allocation was chosen carefully. However, this is a centralised system with greater administrative demands. Moreover, the allocation of permits is a very sensitive issue, and it is therefore very difficult to reach international agreement.

The interpretation of these results should be cautious. The model presented here is very simple and it is best for illustrative purpose. For example, the Cobb–Douglas production function may not be the best functional form, as it allows substantial substitution between capital and energy input. After the environmental control is imposed, energy consumption falls by about half. A number of extensions of the model are possible. Because global warming is related to the stock of GHG, one natural extension would be to introduce dynamics. Another might involve dividing energy into several categories to allow energy switch and substitution.

Acknowledgments

I would like to thank Warwick McKibbin, Ben Smith and Yiping Huang for helpful comments.

Table 15.8   Comparison of changing preference assumption

Indicators	Differentiated tax rates		Uniform tax rate	
	Old assumption	New assumption	Old assumption	New assumption
Total energy consumption (exajoules)	645.210	790.630	647.630	792.275
Global warming	2.274	2.656	2.281	2.660
Energy tax in China (US$/gigajoule)	2.994	2.016	4.032	2.547
Energy tax in ROW (US$/gigajoule)	4.244	2.684	4.032	2.547
Per capita utility in China	2.490	2.470	2.485	2.468
Per capita utility in ROW	3.281	3.331	3.282	3.332
Total global utility	31.436	31.815	31.434	31.814

Table 15.9   Comparison of changing technology assumption

Indicators	Differentiated tax rates		Uniform tax rate	
	Old assumption	New assumption	Old assumption	New assumption
Total energy consumption (exajoules)	645.210	630.231	647.630	632.183
Global warming	2.274	2.233	2.281	2.236
Energy tax in China (US$/gigajoule)	2.994	3.011	4.032	4.063
Energy tax in ROW (US$/gigajoule)	4.244	4.240	4.032	4.063
Per capita utility in China	2.490	2.505	2.485	2.501
Per capita utility in ROW	3.281	3.282	3.282	3.283
Total global utility	31.436	31.471	31.434	31.469

Table 15.10   Numerical assumptions

Parameter	China	Rich	ROW
θ_i	0.97	0.95	0.97
$\overline{T}_i$	6.04	6.05	6.04
Production shifter, A_i	4.08	25.04	8.04
Capital value share, α_i	0.20	0.15	0.20
Energy value share, β_i	0.06	0.05	0.06
GDP (US$trillion)	12.00	80.00	30.00
Population (billion)	1.78	1.04	7.01
Capital stock, $\overline{K}_i$ (US$ trillion)	48.00	240.00	120.00
Energy consumption, E_i (exajoules)	160.00	888.89	400.00
Marginal cost of energy, c (US$/gigajoules)	4.50	4.50	4.50
Interest rate	0.05	0.05	0.05

Table 15.11   China, rich countries and ROW

Indicators	Pre-environmental control	Differentiated tax rate	Uniform tax rate
Capital used in China	48.000	48.861	47.652
Capital used in rich countries	240.000	236.369	241.218
Capital used in ROW	120.000	122.770	119.130
Energy used in China	160.000	111.603	61.836
Energy used in rich countries	888.888	334.984	347.798
Energy used in ROW	400.000	298.388	154.590
Output in China	12.000	11.785	11.318
Output in rich countries	80.000	76.016	76.391
Output in ROW	30.000	29.612	28.295
Per capita consumption in China	6.337	6.315	6.211
Per capita consumption in rich	73.077	71.811	71.893
Per capita consumption in ROW	4.023	4.014	3.943
Global warming	4.056	2.540	2.046
Per capita utility in China	2.477	2.492	2.477
Per capita utility in rich	7.755	7.810	7.842
Per capita utility in ROW	1.986	2.000	1.986
Total global utility	26.394	26.575	26.486
China	4.408	4.436	4.409
Rich	8.065	8.122	8.155
ROW	13.921	14.017	13.922

Notes

1   When the Convention was signed, the Annex I countries included the 24 original OECD members (Australia, Austria, Belgium, Canada, Denmark, Finland, France, Germany, Greece, Iceland, Ireland, Italy, Japan, Luxembourg, Netherlands, New Zealand, Norway, Portugal, Spain, Sweden, Switzerland, Turkey, the United Kingdom of Great Britain and Northern Ireland, and the United States), the European Economic Community, and 11 countries with economies in transition (Belarus, Bulgaria, Czechoslovakia, Estonia, Hungary, Latvia, Lithuania, Poland, Portugal, Romania, Russian Federation and Ukraine). The Czech Republic and Slovakia replaced Czechoslovakia later.

2   Croatia, Liechtenstein, Monaco and Slovenia joined at COP3, and Belarus and Turkey were dropped from the list of Annex B countries. There are 39 parties in the Annex B list.

3   However, it is interesting to study the policy implications of information asymmetry about abatement cost of GHG emissions.

4   CETA stands for Carbon Emissions Trajectory Assessment. Introduction to CETA can be found in Peck and Teisberg (1992), while an introduction to CETA-M is in Peck and Teisberg (1999).

5   This assumption implies full employment in the general equilibrium setting.

6   Because the environmental quality is uniquely determined by 19.7, we use Q in these conditions to avoid excessive notation.

7   In 1998, the state-owned and medium and large non-state-owned enterprises had a capital value of 6,483.205 RMB billion, and a value-added of 1,942.193 RMB billion, implying a capital/GDP ratio of about 3.3. The interest rate fell from 10.08 percent on 23 August 1996 to 6.39 percent on 7 December 1998 for capital investment loans of less than one year; and from 12.42 percent to 7.56 percent for loans of more than five years during the same period (*China Statistical Yearbook* 1999). According to Nehru and Dhareshwar (1993), China's capital/GDP ratio was 2.37 in 1990.

8   In 1998, China's total energy consumption was about 3984.8 exajoules, while GDP was US$959 billion (*China Statistical Yearbook* 1999). The resulting energy/GDP ratio was as high as 41.55 megajoule per US dollar. It is still 36.63 megajoules per US dollar even though energy consumption is net of household use. However, the World Bank (2000) estimates that China's energy efficiency is actually 3.3 PPP$ per kg oil equivalent. From this figure, we get a moderate energy/GDP ratio of 13.33 megajoule per US dollar, which implies an energy share of about 0.06.

9   Chao and Peck (2000) assume that OECD countries have an annual growth rate of 2 per cent, while ROW has an annual rate of 3.5 per cent; and GDP in 2050 is US$40 trillion and US$25 trillion, respectively, for OECD and ROW.

References

Abramovitz, M., 1986. 'Catching up, forging ahead, and falling behind', *Journal of Economic History*, 46(2):385–406.

Aigner, D.J., Lovell, C. and Schmidt, P., 1977. 'Formulation and estimation of stochastic frontier production function models', *Journal of Econometrics*, 6(1):21–37.

Ali, A.M.S., 1995. 'Part-time farming in Bangladesh: a village case study of its causes', *Contemporary South Asia*, 4:309–30.

Altinger, L. and Enders, A., 1996. 'The scope and depth of GATS commitments', *The World Economy*, 19(3):307–32.

Amoako, A., Rashid, M. and Steffinds, M., 1992. 'Capital gains tax and equity values: empirical test of stock price reaction to the introduction and reduction of capital gains tax exemption', *Journal of Banking and Finance*, 16(April):275–87.

Anderson, J.R., Dillon, J.L. and Hardaker, B., 1977. *Agricultural Decision Analysis*, Iowa State University Press, Ames.

Ang, B.W., 1987. 'Structural change and energy-demand forecasting in industry with applications to two newly industrialised countries', *Energy—The International Journal*, 12(2):101–11.

Bahl, R. and Wallich, C., 1992. *Intergovernmental Fiscal Relations in China*, World Bank Working Papers WPS 863, World Bank, Washington, DC.

Bai, M., 1997. 'Reducing production costs through energy conservation', *Energy of China*, 1997(9):30–2.

Balassa, B., 1993. 'Outward orientation', in H. Chenery and T.N. Srinivasan (eds), *Handbook of Development Economics*, Elsevier Science Publishers, New York.

——, 1978. 'Exports and economic growth: further evidence', *Journal of Development Economics,* 5:181–9.

——,1965. 'Trade liberalization and revealed comparative advantage', *The Manchester School of Economics and Social Studies*, 33(2).

Balke, N.S. and Slottje, D.J., 1994. 'A macroeconometric model of income inequality in the United States', in H. Bergstrand *et al.* (eds), *The Changing Distribution of Income in an Open US Economy*, North Holland:243–79.

Barkely, D.L., Henry, M.S. and Bao, S., 1996. 'Identifying "spread" versus "backwash" effects in regional economic areas: a density functions approach', *Land Economics*, 72:336–57.

Barro, R.J., 1996. *Determinants of Economic Growth: a cross-country empirical study*, NBER Working Papers No. 5698,Cambridge, MA, August.

——, 1991. 'Economic growth in a cross section of countries', *Quarterly Journal of Economics*, 106:407–43.

Battese, G.E. and Coelli, T.J., 1995. 'A model for technical inefficiency effects in a stochastic frontier production function for panel data', *Empirical Economics*, 20:325–32.

——, 1988. 'Prediction of firm-level technical efficiencies with a generalised frontier production function and panel data', *Journal of Econometrics*, 38:387–99.

Benabou, R., 1996. *Inequality and Growth*, NBER Working Papers No. 5658, Cambridge MA.

Benhabib, J. and Spiegel, M., 1994. 'The role of human capital in economic development: evidence from aggregate cross-country data', *Journal of Monetary Economics*, 34:143–74.

Bierens, H.J., 1987. 'Kernel estimators of regression functions', in T.F. Bewly (ed.), *Advances in Econometrics 1985*, Cambridge University Press, New York:99–144.

Bird, R. and Wallich, C., 1993. *Fiscal Decentralization and Intergovernmental Relations in Transition Economies*, Policy Research Working Papers WPS 1122, The World Bank, Washington, DC.

Blank, R.M. and Blinder, A.S., 1986. 'Macroeconomics, income distribution and poverty', in S.H. Danziger and D.H. Weinberg (eds), *Fighting Poverty*, Harvard Univeristy Press, Cambridge.

Blank, R.M., 1989. 'Disaggregating the effect of the business cycle on the distribution of income', *Economica*, 56:141–63.

Blomstrom, M., 1991. *Host Country Benefits of Foreign Investment*, NBER Working Papers No. 3615.

Bonin, J.P and Huang, Y., 2000. *Dealing with the Bad Loans of the Chinese Banks*, (unpublished).

Boulding, K.E., 1992. 'Appropriate methodologies for the study of the economy', in J.L. Auspitz *et al.* (eds), *Praxiologies and the Philosophy of Economics: the international annual of practical philosophy and methodology*, Volume I., Transaction Publishers, New Brunswick, New Jersey.

Bowen, H.P. and Sveikauskas, L., 1992. 'Judging factor abundance', *The Quarterly Journal of Economics*, 2:599–620.

References

Bowen, H.P., Leamer, E.E. and Sveikauskas, L., 1987. 'Multicountry, multifactor tests of the Factor Abundance Theory', *The American Economic Review*, 5(87):791–809.

BP Amoco, 1999. *BP Amoco Statistical Review of World Energy 1996*, BP Amoco, London.

Bradley, M. and Lumpkin, S., 1992. 'The Treasury yield curve as a cointegrated system', *Journal of Financial and Quantitative Analysis*, 27(September):449–63.

Brailsford, T. and Heaney, R., 1998. *Investments: concepts and applications in Australia*, Harcourt Brace, Sydney.

Brealey, R. and Myers, S., 1996. *Principles of Corporate Finance*, 5th Edition, McGraw-Hill, New York.

Breusch, T.S., 1998. Case Studies in Applied Econometrics: dynamic econometrics 2, lecture manuscript, The Australian National University, Canberra.

Brooke, A., Kendrick, D. and Meeraus, A., 1992. *GAMS: a user's guide*, Release 2.25, Scientific Press, San Francisco.

Brown, L.R., 1995. *Who Will Feed China?*, W.W. Norton, New York.

Brown, L.R. and Halweil, B., 1998. 'China's water shortage could shake world food security', *World Watch*, July/August:10–21.

Buch, C.M., 2000. Is Foreign Control a Panacea? On governance and restructuring of commercial banks in transition economies, mimeo, Kiel Institute of World Economics.

——, 1997, 'Opening up for foreign banks. why Central and Eastern Europe can benefit', *Economics of Transition*, 5(2):339–66.

Byrd, W.A. and Lin, Q., 1990. *China's Rural Industry: structure, development, and reform*, Oxford University Press, England.

Byrne, J., Shen, B. and Li, X., 1996. 'The challenge of sustainability: balancing China's energy, economic and environmental goals', *Energy Policy*, 24(5):455–62.

Cai, F. and Chan, K.W., 2000. The political economy of urban protectionist employment policies in China, paper presented at the international conference China: Growth Sustainability in the 21st Century, The Australian National University, Canberra, 9–10 September.

Campbell, J. and Shiller, R., 1991. 'Yield spreads and interest rate movements: a bird's eye view', *Review of Economic Studies*, 58:295–514.

Canning, D., 1998. 'A database for the world stocks of infrastructure, 1950–95', *World Bank Economic Review*, 12:529–47.

Cao, Y., 1994. 'The impact of partially-introduced market mechanisms on the efficiency of Chinese industry: the case of iron and steel industry', *Economic Systems*, 18:335–62.

Caplan, J.A., Ellis, C.J. and Silva E., 1999. 'Winners and losers in a world with global warming: noncooperation: altruism and social welfare', *Journal of Environmental Economics and Management*, 37(3):256–71.

Carter, C.A. and Zhang, B., 1998. 'The weather factor and variability in China's grain supply', *Journal of Comparative Economics*, 26:529–43.

Cedel Bank, Skadden and Arps, Slate, Meagher and Flom, and NASDAQ, 1996. *Report on Chinese Government Securities Market Regulation and Structure.*

Central Committee of CCP, 1985. 'Ten policies of the CCP Central Committee and the State Council for the further invigoration of the rural economy', in *The Agricultural Yearbook of China*, China Statistical Publishing House, Beijing:1–3.

Chakravarty, S., Sarkar, A. and Wu, L., 1998. *Information Asymmetry, Market Segmentation and the Pricing of Cross-Listed Shares: theory and evidence from Chinese A and B shares*, Federal Reserve Bank of New York Research Paper No. 9820, New York.

Chang, C. and Wang, Y., 1994. 'The nature of the township-village enterprise', *Journal of Comparative Economics*, 19(3):434–52.

Chao, H., 1995. 'Managing the risk of global climate catastrophe', *Risk Analysis*, 15(1):69–78.

Chao, H. and Peck, S., 2000. 'Greenhouse gas abatement: how much? And who pays?', *Resource and Energy Economics*, 22(1):1–20.

Charles, K.W. and Francis, S., 1986. 'The methodological basis of Hirschman's development economics: Pattern Model vs. General Laws', *World Development*, 14:2.

Chen, A., 1998. 'Inertia in reforming China's state-owned enterprises: the case of Chongqing', *World Development*, 26(3):479–95.

Chen, G., 1996. 'Some policy questions on redressing the public finance', *Public Finance*, Ministry of Finance of China, 9:96.

Chen, J. and Fleisher, B.M., 1996. 'Regional income inequality and economic growth in China', *Journal of Comparative Economics*, 22:141–64.

Chen, J.G. and Xu, Y.J., 1993. 'A reflection on the large-scale mobile rural labour force around the country', *Problems of Agricultural Economics*, 6:32–34.

Chen, J.Y. and Han, J., 1994. 'On China's rural reform and Deng Xiaoping's ideas about the development of China's agriculture', *China's Rural Economy*, 10(October) (in Chinese).

Chen, K., Wang, H., Zhang, Y., Jefferson, G. and Rawski, T., 1988. 'Productivity change in Chinese industry: 1953–85', *Journal of Comparative Economics*, 12(4):570–91.

Chen, S. and Ravallion, M., 1996. 'Data in transition: assessing rural living standards in Southern China', *China Economic Review*, 7:23–56.

Chen, T.J. and Tang, D.P., 1990. 'Export performance and productivity growth: the case of Taiwan', *Economic Development and Cultural Change*:577–85.

Chen, X., 1994. 'Substitution of information for energy: conceptual background, realities and limits', *Energy Policy*, January:15–27.

Chen, Z., 1995. *Economic Development and Income Distribution*, Shanghai Sanlian Shudian, Shanghai.

Cheung, L.K. and Kwan, Y.K., 1999. 'Foreign capital stock and its determinants', in Y. Wu (ed.), *Foreign Direct Investment and Economic Growth in China*, Edward Elgar, Cheltenham.

References

China Reform Foundation, 1997. *The Realist Choice: reforms of small-sized state enterprises*, Far East Press, Shanghai.

Chui, A. and Kwok, C., 1997. *Cross-Autocorrelation between A Shares and B Shares in the Chinese Stock market*, Center for International Business Education and Research Working Papers, University of South Carolina.

Chow, G., 1993. 'Capital formation and economic industry growth in China', *The Quarterly Journal of Economics*, 108(3):809–42.

Claessens, S., Demirgüc-Kunt, A. and Huizinga, H., 1998. *How Does Foreign Entry Affect the Domestic Banking Market?*, Policy Research Working Paper No. 1918, The World Bank, Washington, DC.

Clarke, G.R.G., 1995. 'More evidence on income distribution and growth', *Journal of Development Economics*, 47:403–27.

Cline, W.R., 1991. 'Scientific basis for the Greenhouse Effect', *The Economic Journal*, 101(407):904–19.

Coe, D.T. and Helpman E., 1995. 'International R&D spillovers', *European Economic Review*, 39(5):859–87.

Coelli, T., 1996. *A Guide to FRONTIER Version 4.1: a computer program for stochastic frontier production function and cost function estimation*, Department of Econometrics Working Paper, The University of New England, Armidale.

Conroy, R., 1992. *Technological Change in China*, Development Centre Studies, OECD, Paris.

Cowan, A. and Sergeant, A., 1996. 'Trading frequency and event study test specification', *Journal of Banking and Finance*, 20(December):1731–57.

Croome, J., 1999. *Guide to the Uruguay Round Agreements*, published for the World Trade Organisation secretariat by Kluwer, The Hague.

Davidson, R. and MacKinnon, J.G., 1993. *Estimation and Inference in Econometrics*, Oxford University Press, New York.

Dazhong, W., 1993. 'Soil erosion and conservation', in Pimentel (eds), *World Soil Erosion and Conservation*, Cambridge.

De Mello, L.R., Jr., 1997. 'Foreign direct investment in developing countries and growth: a selected survey', *Journal of Development Studies*, 34:1–34.

Démurger, S., 2000. *Economic opening and growth in China*, Development Centre Studies, OECD, Paris.

——, 1998. Infrastructure and economic performances in Chinese provinces, communication at The International Conference on the Chinese Economy, CERDI, France, October.

——, 1997. Openness and Growth: the case of P.R. China, PhD thesis, CERDI, France.

Department of Communication and Energy (DCE), 1997. *Energy Report of China 1997*. DCE, State Planning Commission, China Prices Publishing House, Beijing.

Department of Industrial and Transportation Statistics (DITSa), State Statistical Bureau (various years). *China Industrial Economy Statistical Yearbook,* China Statistical Publishing House, Beijing, (various issues).

Dielman, E.T, 1996. *Applied Regression Analysis,* Wadsworth Publishing Company, United States.

Ding, J., 1995. 'Technical transformation and renovation in PRC industry', in D.F. Simon (ed.), *The Emerging Technological Trajectory of the Pacific Rim,* M.E. Sharpe Inc, New York.

Dollar, D., 1990. 'Economic reform and allocative efficiency in China's state-owned industry', *Economic Development and Cultural Change,* 39(1):89–105.

Dong, X., 1996. 'Two-tier land tenure system and sustained economic growth in post-1978 rural China', *World Development,* 24(5):915–28.

Drysdale, P. and Song, L. (eds), 2000. *China's Entry to the WTO: strategic issues and quantitative assessments,* Routledge, London.

Dutt, S.D. and Ghosh, D., 1996. 'The export growth-economic growth nexus: a causality analysis', *The Journal of Developing Areas,* 30 January:167–82.

Easterley, W. and Fischer, S., 1994. *The Soviet Economic Decline: historical and republican data,* Working Paper No. 4735, National Bureau of Economic Research, May.

Eight Ministries and Bureaus, 1991. Survey Team of the Costs of Industrial and Agricultural Products of the State Statistical Bureau, Finance and Price Bureau and Grain Bureau of the Ministry of Commerce, Ministry of Agriculture, Ministry of Forestry, Ministry of Light Industry, and other Nationwide Data on Costs and Revenues of Agricultural Products, China Price Publishing House, Beijing (in Chinese).

Enders, W., 1995. *Applied Econometric Time Series,* John Wiley & Sons, New York.

Energy Research Institute (ERI), 1997. *Middle and Long term Energy Demand and Supply Analysis in China,* ERI, State Planing Committee, Beijing.

Engelbrecht, H., 1996. 'The composition of the human capital stock and the factor content of trade: evidence from West(ern) Germany', *Economic System Research,* 3:271–91.

Engsted, T. and Tanggaard, C., 1994. 'Cointegration and the US term structure', *Journal of Banking and Finance,* 18:167–81.

Estache, A. and Sarbajit, S., 1995. *Does Decentralization Increase Spending on Public Infrastructure?,* The World Bank, Washington, DC. May.

Fabozzi, F., 1988. *Fixed Income Mathematics,* Probus Publishing, Chicago.

Fabozzi, F. and Fabozzi, D., 1989. *Bond markets, analysis and strategies,* Prentice Hall, Englewood Cliffs.

Fama, E., 1984a. 'Term premiums in bond returns', *Journal of Financial Economics,* 13:529–46.

——, 1984b. 'The information in the term structure', *Journal of Financial Economics,* 13:509–28.

References

Fan, G., 1999a. 'Overcoming deflation and reforming the banking system', *Journal of Economic Research (jingji Yangjiu)*, 1.

——, 1999b. 'On the government comprehensive liability: how to deal with the non-performing loans', *Journal of Economic Research (jingji Yangjiu)*, 5.

——, 1996. *Political Economy of China's Gradual Approach to Transition*, Far East Press, Shanghai (in Chinese).

——, 1995. The locality-initiated monetary expansion: decentralized public-ownership economy and macro-instability in China, communication at The International Conference on the Chinese Economy, CERDI, France.

——, 1994. 'Incremental changes and dual-track transition: understanding the case of China', *Economic Policy*, Great Britain, December.

Fan, G. and Woo, W.T., 1996. 'State enterprise reform as a source of macroeconomic instability: the case of China', *Asian Economic Journal*, 10(3):207–24.

Fan, S.G., 1991. 'Effects of technological change and institutional reform on production growth in Chinese agriculture', *American Journal of Agricultural Economics*, 73:266–75.

Feder, G., 1982. 'On exports and economic growth', *Journal of Development Economics*, 12:59–73.

Feng, G. and Zhu, Z., 1994. *Complete Work of Classification of China's Occupation*, (ZhongGuo ZhiYe FenLei DaQuan), China Labor Publishing House.

Fischer, G., Ermoliev, Y., Keyzer, M.A. and Rosenzweig, C., 1996. *Simulating the Socioeconomic and Biogeophysical Driving Forces of Land-Use and Land-Cover Change: the IIASA Land-use Change Model*, working paper WP–96–010, International Institute for Applied Systems Analysis, Laxenburg, Austria.

Fischer, G. and Velthuizen, H.T. van, 1996. *Climate Change and Global Agricultural Potential Project: a case study of Kenya*, working paper WP–96–71, International Institute for Applied Systems Analysis, Laxenburg, Austria.

Fischer, G., Chen, Y. and Sun, L., 1998. *The Balance of Cultivated Land in China During 1988–1995*, interim report IR–98–047, International Institute for Applied Systems Analysis, Laxenburg, Austria.

Fischer, G., Velthuizen, H.T. van and Nachtergaele, F.O, 2000. *Global Agroecological Zones Assessment: methodology and results*, interim report IR–00–064, International Institute for Applied Systems Analysis, Laxenburg, Austria.

Food and Agriculture Organisation (FAO), various years. *FAO Fertiliser Yearbook*, Rome (various issues).

Fu, J., 1998. 'The enterprise concept in Chinese Law and its application in PRC Company Law', *Australian Journal of Corporate Law*, 8:266–99.

Gaile, G.L., 1980. 'The Spread-Backwash concept', *Regional Studies*, 14:15–25.

Gallant, R.A., 1987. *Nonlinear Statistical Models*, John Wiley & Sons, New York.

Gamble, W., 2000. 'The Middle Kingdom runs dry: tax evasion in China', *Foreign Affairs*, 79(6):16–21.

Gan, L., 1998. 'Energy development and environmental constraints in China', *Energy Policy*, 26(2):119–28.

Gao, X., 1996. 'Developments in securities and investment law in China', *Australian Journal of Corporate Law*, 6:1.

Garbaccio, R.F., Mun, S.H. and Jorgenson, D.W., 1999. 'Why has the energy-output ratio fallen in China?' *The Energy Journal*, 20(3):63–91.

Garnaut, R., Song, L., Yao, Y. and Wang, X., 2001. *Private Enterprise in China*, Asia Pacific Press, Canberra.

General Administration of Customs, 1993. *China's Customs Statistics Yearbook 1992 III*, General Administration of Customs, Beijing.

——, 1992. *China's Customs Statistics Yearbook 1996*, General Administration of Customs, Beijing.

Gibson, M., 1997. *The Bank Lending Channel of Monetary Policy Transmission: evidence from a model of bank behaviour that incorporates long-term customer relationships*, International Finance Discussion Papers No. 584, Board of Governors of the Federal Reserve System.

Goldberg, L., Dages, G. and Kimney, D., 1999. Lending in Emerging Markets: foreign and domestic banks compared, mimeo, Federal Reserve Bank of New York and NBER, New York.

Goldsmith, R., 1969. *Financial Structure and Development*, Yale University Press, New Haven.

Greenaway, D. and Sapsford, D., 1994. 'What does liberalization do for exports and growth', *Weltwirtschaftliches Archiv*, 130:152–74.

Greening, L.A., Davis, W.B., Schipper, L. and Khrushch, M., 1997. 'Comparison of six decomposition methods: application to aggregate energy intensity for manufacturing in 10 OECD countries', *Energy Economics*, 19(3):375–90.

Grossman, G.M. and Helpman, E., 1991. 'Trade, knowledge spillovers and growth', *European Economic Review*, 35(3).

Groves, T., Hong, Y., McMillan, J. and Naughton, B., 1994. 'Autonomy and incentives in Chinese state enterprises', *Quarterly Journal of Economics*, 436:183–209.

Gujarati, D., 1995. *Basic Econometrics*, McGraw-Hill, New York.

Gundlach, E., 1997. 'Regional convergence of output per worker in China: a neoclassical interpretation', *Asian Economic Journal*, 11:423–42.

Gustafsson, B. and Shi, L., 1998. 'Inequality in China at the end of 1980s: locational aspects and household characteristics', *Asian Economic Journal*, 12:35–64.

Halbrendt, C. and Gempesaw, C., 1990. 'A policy analysis of China's wheat economy', *American Journal of Agricultural Economics*, 72(2):268–78.

Hall, A., Anderson, H. and Granger, C.W.J., 1992. 'A cointegration analysis of Treasury bill yields', *The Review of Economics and Statistics*, 74:116–26.

References

Hall, R., 1978. 'Stochastic implications of the life cycle Permanent Income Hypothesis: theory and evidence', *Journal of Political Economy*, 86(5):971–87.

Hasenkamp, G., 1976. *Specification and Estimation of Multiple-Output Production Functions*, Springer–Verlag, Berlin.

Hasenstab, M., 1999. 'Financial system reform and implications', in R. Garnaut and L. Song (eds), *China: twenty years of reform*, Asia Pacific Press, Canberra:117–48.

Hay, D., Morris, D., Liu, G. and Yao, S., 1994. *Economic Reform and State-Owned Enterprises in China 1979–1987*, Oxford University Press, New York.

Hayami, Y. and Ruttan, V.W., 1985. *Agricultural Development: an international perspective*, Johns Hopkins University Press, Baltimore.

Hayek, F.A., 1945. 'The use of knowledge in society', *American Economic Review*, 35.

Heaney, R., Powell, J. and Shi, J., 1998. Share Return Seasonalities and Price Linkages of Chinese A and B Shares, manuscript, The Australian National University, Canberra.

Hicks, J.R., 1969. *A Theory of Economic History*, Claredon Press, Oxford.

Hirschman, A.O., 1958. *The Strategy of Economic Development*, Yale University Press, New Haven.

Hu, A., Wang, C. and Kang, X., 1995. *Regional Disparities in China*, Liaoning People's Press, Shenyang.

Hu, D., 1997. Economic Transition and Regional Disparity, mimeo, CCER, Peking University.

Huang, J.K., Rozelle, S. and Rosegrant, M., 1996. *China and the Future Global Food Situation*, IFPRI 2020 Brief, International Food Policy Research Institute, Washington, DC.

Huang, Y., 1998. 'China's financial fragility and policy responses', *Asian-Pacific Economic Literature*, 12:1–9.

——, 1997. 'Institutional transformation and long-term economic growth', *Journal of Economic Research (jingji Yangjiu)*, 1.

Huang, Y. and Song, L., 2000. 'State-owned enterprise and bank reform: conditions for liberalisation of China's capital account', in P. Drysdale (ed.), *Reform and Recovery in East Asia: the role of the state and economic enterprises*, Routledge, London:214–28.

Huang, Y., Woo, W.T., Kalirajan, K.P. and Duncan, R., 1998. Enterprise Reform, Technological Progress and Technical Efficiency in China's State Industry, paper presented at the international workshop, The Australian National University, Canberra, 17–18 February.

Huang, J. and Zhang, L., 1997. 'The macroeconomic and public expenditure implications of grain policies in China: some selected issues for discussion', *OECD*:180–89.

Hubei Statistical Bureau, 1999. *Hubei Rural Statistical Yearbook 1999*, China Statistical Press, Beijing.

Hughes, D.W. and Holland, D.W., 1994. 'Core-periphery economic linkage: a measure of spread and possible backwash effects for the Washington economy', *Land Economics*, 70:364–77.

Hussain, A., Lanjouw, P. and Stern, N., 1994. 'Income inequalities in China: evidence from household survey data', *World Development*, 22:1947–57.

Information Office of State Council (IOSC), 1996. *Environmental Protection in China*, The State Council, Beijing.

Institute of Agricultural Natural Resources and Regional Planning, Agricultural Academy of China, 1995. *Cultivated Land in China*, China Agricultural Science Press, Beijing.

Institute of Developing Economies, 1969. *One Hundred Years of Agricultural Statistics in Japan*, Institute of Developing Economies, Tokyo.

International Energy Agency (IEA), 1998. *World Energy Outlook 1998*, IEA/OECD, Paris.

Jefferson, G.H. and Xu, W., 1994. 'Assessing Gains in efficient production among China's industrial enterprises', *Economic Development and Cultural Change*, 42(3):597–618.

Jefferson, G.H., Rawski, T.G. and Zheng, Y., 1996. 'Chinese industrial productivity: trends, measurement issues and recent developments', *Journal of Comparative Economics*, 23:146–80.

——, 1992. 'Growth, efficiency, and convergence in China's state and collective industry', *Economic Development and Cultural Change*, 40(2):239–66.

Jian, T., Sachs, J.D. and Warner, A.M., 1996. 'Trends in regional inequality in China', *China Economic Review*, 7:1–21.

Johansen, S., 1988. 'Statistical analysis of cointegrating vectors', *Journal of Economic Dynamics and Control*, 12:231–54.

Johnson, P., 1994. 'On the number of common unit roots in the term structure of interest rates', *Applied Economics*, 26:815–20.

Johnson, D.G., 1999. *Agricultural Adjustment in China: problems and prospects*, Paper No. 99.01, Office of Agricultural Economics Research, The University of Chicago.

Jordan, J.S., 1983. 'On the Efficient Market Hypothesis', *Econometrica*, 51:1325–44.

Judge, G., Griffiths W.E., Hill, R.C., Lutkepohl, H. and Lee, T.C., 1985. *The Theory and Practice of Econometrics*, 2nd Edition, John Wiley and Sons, New York.

Jun An Securities Bond Department, 1997. *Current Market Analysis and Investment Strategies for the Government Treasury Bond Market*, Investor Presentation, 8 December.

Jussaume, R.A., 1991. *Japanese Part-Time Farming: evolution and impacts*, Iowa State University Press, Ames.

Kalirajan, K.P. and Cao, Y., 1993. 'Can Chinese state enterprises perform like market entities: productive efficiency in the Chinese iron and steel industry', *Applied Economics*, 25(8):1071–80.

Kane, S., Reilly, J. *et al.*, 1989. *Implications of the Greenhouse Effect for a World Agricultural Commodity Market*, United States Department of Agriculture.

References

Karfakis, C. and Moschow, D., 1993. *The Information Content of the Yield Curve in Australia*, Working Papers in Economics No. 185, Department of Economics, University of Sydney, Sydney.

Kavoussi, R.M., 1984. 'Export expansion and economic growth: further empirical evidence', *Journal of Development Economics*, 14:241–50.

Keesing, D.B., 1965. 'Labor skills and international trade: evaluating many trade flows with a single measuring device', *Review of Economics and Statistics*, 47:287–294.

Keyzer, M.A., 1998. *Formulation and Spatial Aggregation of Agricultural Production Relationships within the LUC Model*, interim report IR–98–092, International Institute for Applied Systems Analysis, Laxenburg, Austria.

Keyzer, M.A. and Sonneveld, B.G.J.S., 1997. 'Using the Mollifier Method to characterise data sets and models: the case of the Universal Soil Loss Equation', *ITC Journal*, 97(3–4):263–72.

Khan, R.A., Griffin, K., Riskin, C. and Zhao, R., 1993. 'Household income and its distribution in China', in K. Griffin and R. Zhao (eds), *The Distribution of Income in China*, Macmillan Press, Basingstoke.

King, R. and Levine, R., 1993a. 'Finance and growth: Schumpeter might be right', *Quarterly Journal of Economics*,108:717–38.

Kmenta, J., 1971. *Elements of Econometrics*, Macmillan Press, Basingstoke.

Knight, J. and Song, L., 1993. 'The spatial contribution to income inequality in rural China', *Cambridge Journal of Economics*, 17:195–213.

Kohli, I. and Singh, N., 1987. 'Exports, growth and causality in developing countries', *Journal of Development Economics*, 26(June):55–63.

Kong, X., Marks, E.R. and Wan, G., 1999. 'Technical efficiency, technological change and total factor productivity growth in Chinese state-owned enterprises in the early 1990s', *Asian Economic Journal*, 3(3):267–81.

Kornai, J., 1986. 'The soft budget constraint', *Kyklos*, 39(1):3–30.

Kornai, J, 1980. *The Economics of Shortage*, North-Holland Publishing, Amsterdam.

Krasovec, S. (ed.), 1982. Part-Time Farmers and Their Adjustment to Pluriacity, Seminar proceedings, Slovene Academy of Sciences and Arts, Ljubljana, Yugoslavia.

Kritzman, M., 1993. 'What practitioners need to know about the term structure of interest rates', *Financial Analysts Journal*, July–August:14–18.

Kueh, Y., 1984. 'China's new agricultural policy program: major economic consequences, 1979–83', *Journal of Comparative Economics*, 8(2):353–75.

Kung, J.K., 1995. 'Equal entitlement versus tenure security under a regime of collective property rights: peasants' preference for institutions in post-reform Chinese agriculture', *Journal of Comparative Economics*, 21(1):82–111.

Laffont, J. and Senik-Leygonie, C., 1997. *Price Controls and the Economics of Institutions in China*, Organisation for Economic Cooperation and Development, Paris.

Lardy, N., 1998. *China's Unfinished Economic Revolution*, Brookings, Washington, DC.

Leamer, E.E., 1992. *Testing Trade Theories*, Working Paper No. 3957, NBER, Cambridge, MA.

Lee, J., 1994. 'Regional differences in the impact of the open door policy on income growth in China', *Journal of Economic Development*, 9(1):215–34.

Leontief, W., 1954. 'Domestic production and foreign trade: the American capital position re-examined', *Economia Internazionale*, 7:3–32.

Levine, R., 1997. 'Financial developments and economic growth: views and agenda', *Journal of Economic Literature*, 35:688–726.

Levine, R. and Renelt, D., 1992. 'A sensitivity analysis of cross-country growth regressions', *American Economic Review*, 82(4):942–63.

Levine, R. and Zervos, S., 1998. 'Stock markets, banks, and economic growth', *The American Economic Review*, 88:537–58.

Ley, E. and Steel, M.F.J., 1999. *We Just Averaged over Two Trillion Cross-Country Growth Regressions*, IMF Working Paper WP/99/101, IMF, Washington, DC.

Li, S., 1997. 'A model of labor mobility in China's economic transformation', *Journal of Economic Research (jingji Yangjiu)*, 1.

Li, S., Zhao, R. and Zhang, P., 1998. 'China's economic transition and the change in income distribution', *Economic Research Journal*, April:42–52.

Lin, J.Y., 1997. 'The role of agriculture in the transition process in China', in J. Kydd, S. Davidova, M. Mackay and T. Mech (eds), *The Role of Agriculture in the Transition Process Towards a Market Economy*, UN/ECE Economic Studies No. 9, United Nations, New York and Geneva:63–75.

——, 1992. 'Rural reforms and agricultural growth in China', *American Economic Review*, 82(1):34–51.

Lin, J. and Liu, Z. 1998. *Fiscal Decentralization and Economic Growth in China*, Hong Kong University of Science and Technology, Hong Kong.

Lin, J., Liu, Z. and Zhong, F., 1997. *Fiscal Decentralization and Rural Development in China*, China Center for Economic Research, Beijing University, Beijing.

Lin, N., 1995. 'Local market socialism: local corporatism in action in rural China', *Theory and Society*, 24(3):301–54.

Lin, Q. and Du, Y., 1997. *China's Industrial Reform and Improvement of Efficiency: a comparison of state and non-state sectors*, Yunan People's Press, China.

Lin, X.N., 1996. *China's Energy Strategy: economic structure, technological choices, and energy consumption*, Westport, Connecticut, London.

Lin, Y., 1994. 'New forms and organisational structures of foreign investment in China under the Company Law of the PRC', *The Transnational Lawyer*, 7(2):327–436.

Lindert, P.H., 1999. 'The bad earth? China's soils and agricultural development since the 1930s', *Economic Development and Cultural Change*, 47(4):701–36.

References

Liu, G.Y., 1993. The role of coal in China's development, PhD thesis, University of Melbourne, Melbourne.

Liu, L. and Woo, W.T., 1994. 'Saving behavior under imperfect financial markets and the current account consequences', *Economic Journal*, May.

Liu, X.Q., Ang, B.W. and Ong, H.L., 1992. 'The application of the Divisia Index to the decomposition of changes in industrial energy consumption', *The Energy Journal*, 13(4):161–77.

Liu, X., Song, H. and Romilly, P., 1997. 'Are Chinese stock markets efficient? A cointegration and causality analysis', *Applied Economics Letters*, 4:511–15.

Liu, Z. and Liu, G.S., 1996. 'The efficiency impact of the Chinese industrial reforms in the 1980s', *Journal of Comparative Economics*, 23:237–55.

Loyns, R.M.A. and Kraut, M., 1992. 'The family farm in the next decade: the positive role of part-time farming', *Canadian Journal of Agricultural Economics*, 40:591–604.

Lucas, R.E., 1988. 'On the mechanisms of economic growth', *Journal of Monetary Economics*, 22(3).

Lynch, Merrill, 1999. *Asian Strategy Monthly*, Merrill Lynch and Company, various issues.

Lyons, T.P., 1991. 'Interprovincial disparities in China: output and consumption, 1952–87', *Economic Development and Cultural Change*, 39:471–506.

Lyons, T.P., 1997. 'Intraprovincial disparities in post-Mao China: an analysis of Fujian Province', *Journal of Development Areas*, 32:1–27.

McMillan, J., Whalley, J. and Zhu, L., 1989. 'The impact of China's economic reforms on agricultural productivity growth', *Journal of Political Economy*, 97:781–807.

Maddison, A., 1997. *Measuring Chinese Economic Growth and Levels of Performance*, Joint SSB–OECD Workshop on National Accounts, Paper No. 3, OECD, Paris.

Manne, A.S., 1996. 'Greenhouse gas abatement: toward Pareto-optimality in integrated assessments', in K.J. Arrow, R.W. Cottle, B.C. Eaves and I. Olkin (eds), *Education in a Research University*, Stanford University Press, Stanford:391–405.

Markusen, J.R., Melvin, J.R., Kaempfer, W.H. and Maskus, K.E., 1995. *International Trade: theory and evidence*, McGraw–Hill, New York.

Maskus, K.E. and Webster, A., 1995. 'Factor specialisation in US and UK trade: simple departures from the Factor-Content Theory', *Swiss Journal of Economics and Statistics*, 3:419–439.

Maskus, K.E., Sveikanskas, C.D. and Webster, A., 1994. 'The composition of the human capital stock and its relation to international trade: evidence from the US and Britain', *Weltwirtschaftliches Archiv, Review of World Economics*, 130:51–70.

McMillan, J., Whalley, J. and Zhu, L., 1989. 'The impact of China's economic reforms on agricultural productivity growth', *Journal of Political Economy*, 97(4):781–807.

Meeusen, W. and Broeck, J. van den, 1977. 'Efficiency estimation for Cobb-Douglas production functions with composed error', *International Economic Review*, 18(2):435–44.

Meng, X. and Wu, H.X., 1998. 'Household income determination and regional income differential in rural China', *Asian Economic Journal*, 12:65–88.

Merton, R., 1990. 'Financial system and economic performance', *Journal of Financial Services Research*:263–300.

Meulbroek, L., 1992. 'A comparison of forward and futures prices of an interest rate sensitive financial asset', *Journal of Finance*, 47:381–96.

Michaely, M., 1977. 'Exports and growth: an empirical investigation', *Journal Development Economics*, 4:49–53.

Milgrom, P. and Roberts, J., 1992. *Economics, Organisation and Management*, Prenticehall, New Jersey.

Ministry of Agriculture, 1996. *The White Book of China's Agriculture 1995*, Agricultural Publishing House, Beijing.

——, various years. *China's Agricultural Statistics*, China Agricultural Press, Beijing, (various issues).

Ministry of Agriculture–Study Group of Rural Cooperative Economy, 1991. 'A survey of contractual arrangements and cooperative organisation in rural China', *Issues in Agricultural Economy (Nongcun Jingji Wenti)*, 8:30–40.

——, 1988. 'A survey of contractual arrangements and cooperative organisation in rural China', *Issues in Agricultural Economy (Nongcun Jingji Wenti)*, 8:33–40.

Ministry of Water Conservation, 1991–95. *Water Conservation Yearbook of China, 1990–1994*, Hydraulic and Electric Publishing House, Beijing.

Montinola, G., Qian, Y. and Weingast, B. 1996. 'Federalism, Chinese style: the political basis for economic success', *World Politics*, 48(1):50–81.

Mood, A.M., Graybil, F.A. and Boes, D.C., 1974. *Introduction to the Theory of Statistics*, 3rd Edition, McGraw-Hill, New York.

Moody, A. and Wang, F.Y., 1997. 'Explaining industrial growth in coastal China: economic reform and what else?', *World Bank Economic Review*, 11:293–325.

Munasinghe, M. and Meier, P., 1993. *Energy Policy Analysis and Modelling*, Cambridge University Press.

Naughton, B., 1994. 'Chinese institutional innovation and privatization from below', *American Economic Review*, 84(2):266–70.

Nehru, V. and Dhareshwar, A., 1993. 'A new database on physical capital stock: sources, methodology and results', *Rivista de Analisis Economico*, 8(1):37–59.

Nerlove, M., 1958. 'Adaptive expectations and the Cobweb Phenomena', *Quarterly Journal of Economics*, 73(2):227–40.

Nordhaus, W.D., 1994. 'Expert opinion on climate change', *American Scientist*, 82:45–51.

——, 1991. 'To slow or not to slow: the economics of the Greenhouse Effect', *The Economic Journal*, 101(407):920–37.

Oates, W.E., 1972. *Fiscal Federalism*, Harcourt Brace Jovanovitch, New York.

References

Oi, J.C., 1996. 'The Role of the Local State', in A.G. Walder (eds), *China's Transitional Economy*, Clarendon Paperbacks, Oxford.

Organisation for Economic Cooperation and Development (OECD), 1997. *Agricultural Policies in China*, OECD, Paris.

——, 1995a. *Agricultural Policy Reform and Adjustment in Japan*, OECD, Paris.

——, 1995b. *The Chinese Grain and Oilseed Sectors: major changes under way*, OECD, Paris.

Oglesby, R.J. and Saltzman, B., 1990. 'Sensitivity of the equilibrium surface temperature of a GCM to systematic changes in atmospheric carbon dioxide', *Geophysical Research Letters*, July:1089–92.

Ogden, J.P., 1987. 'The end of the month as a preferred habit: a test of operational efficiency in the money market', *Journal of Financial and Quantitative Analysis*, 22:329–43.

Pagan, A., Hall, A. and Martin, V., 1995. Modeling the term structure, manuscript, May.

Park, S.Y. and Reinganum, M.R., 1986. 'The puzzling price behaviour of treasury bills that mature at the turn of calendar months', *Journal of Financial Economics*, 16:267–83.

Park, A., 1996. Household grain management under uncertainty in China's poor areas, PhD thesis, Stanford University.

Patterson, M.G., 1996. 'What is energy efficiency: concepts, indicators and methodological issues', *Energy Policy*, 24(5):377–90.

Peck, S.C. and Teisberg, T.J., 1999. 'CO_2 emissions targets and timetables: an analysis of AOSIS Proposal', *Environmental Modeling and Assessment*, 1(4):219–27.

——, 1992. 'CETA: a model for carbon emissions trajectory assessment', *The Energy Journal*, 13(1):55–77.

Perkins, D., 1988. 'Reforming China's economic system', *Journal of Economic Literature*, 26:601–45.

Perkins, F., 1995. 'Productivity performance and priority for the reform of China's state-owned enterprises', *Journal of Development Studies*, 32:414–44.

Pinstrup-Anderson, P., Pandya-Lorch, R. and Rosegrant, M.W., 1999. *World Food Prospects: critical issues for the early twenty-first century*, IFPRI, Washington, DC.

Poon, J.P., 1995. 'Export expansion, economic growth and economic development revisited', *Journal of Economic Development*, 20(1):75–90.

Pritchett, L., 1997. *Where Has All the Education Gone?*, Policy Research Working Paper No. 1551, The World Bank, Washington, DC.

Prud'homme, R., 1994. 'The dangers of decentralization', *The World Bank Research Observer*, 10(2):201–20.

Qian, Y. and Roland, G., 1998. 'Federalism and soft budget constraint', *American Economic Review*, 88(5):1143–62.

Qian, Y. and Weingast, B., 1997. 'Federalism as a commitment to preserving market incentives', *Journal of Economic Perspectives*, 11(4):83–92.

Qian, Y. and Xu, C., 1993. 'The M-form hierarchy and China's economic reform', *European Economic Review*, 37(2–3):541–48.

Qu, G.P., 1992. 'China's dual-thrust energy strategy: economic development and environmental protection', *Natural Resources Forum*, 16(1):27–31.

Rabin, M., 1998. 'Psychology and economics', *Journal of Economic Literature*, 36(1):11–46.

Raiser, M., 1998. 'Subsidising inequality: economic reforms, fiscal transfers and convergence across Chinese provinces', *Journal of Development Studies*, 34:1–26.

Rao, P. and Miller, P.L., 1971. *Applied Econometrics*, Wadsworth, Belmont, CA.

Rawski, T., 1995. 'Implications of China's reform experience', *The China Quarterly*, 144(December):1150–73.

Reddy, A. and Goldemberg, J., 1991. 'Energy for the developing world', in Scientific American (ed.), *Energy for Planet Earth*, W.H. Freeman, New York.

Renkow, M., 1990. 'Household inventories and marketed surplus in semi-subsistence agriculture', *American Journal of Agricultural Economics*, 72:664–75.

Report of the President's Working Group on Financial Markets, 1999. *Hedge Funds, Leverage, and the Lessons of Long Term Capital Management*, US Department of Treasury, Washington, DC.

Research Group of the Ministry of Agriculture of China, 1995. 'A survey of the status of the mobile rural labour force', *Chinese Rural Economy*, 1:43–50.

Research Team, 1997. 'Analyses and suggestions of urban income disparities', *Economic Research Journal*, August:3–10.

Research Team of Rural Cooperative Economies, 1993. 'A survey of the operation of China's land contract system and cooperative organisations', *Issues in Agricultural Economy (Nongcun Jingji Wenti)*, 11:45–53.

Richardson, H.W., 1976. 'Growth pole spillovers: the dynamics of Backwash and spread', *Regional Studies*:101–9.

Rosenzweig, C., Iglesias, A., Fischer, G., Liu, Y., Baethgen, W. and Jones, J.W., 1998. *Wheat Yield Functions for Analysis of Land-Use Change in China*, working paper, LUC Project, International Institute for Applied Systems Analysis, Laxenburg, Austria.

Rousseeuw, P.J. and Leroy, A.M., 1987. *Robust Regression and Outlier Detection*, Wiley, New York.

Rozelle, S., 1996. 'Stagnation without equity: patterns of growth and inequality in China's rural economy', *China Journal*, 35:63–92.

Rozelle, S., Guo, L., Shen, M.G., Hughart, A. and Giles, J., 1999. 'Leaving China's farms: survey results of new paths and remaining hurdles to rural migration', *China Quarterly*, 158:367–93.

Ruggiero, R., 1995. 'Overview of WTO's first year', *Focus Newsletter*, 7(December):5–17.

References

Rural Sample Survey Office, Ministry of Agriculture and the Policy Study Office of the Central Committee of the CCP, 1994. 'China's peasants in the marketisation process: a survey of peasant households and markets', *China's Rural Economy*, 2:37–43 (in Chinese).

Sachs, J.D. and Warner, A.M., 1997 'Fundamental sources of long-run growth', *American Economic Review* (Papers and Proceedings), 87:184–88.

Sachs, J.D. and Woo, W.T., 2000. 'Understanding China's economic performance', *Journal of Economic Reform* 4(1): 1–50.

——, 1994a. 'Structural factors in the economic reforms of China, Eastern Europe, and the Former Soviet Union' *Economic Policy* 18: 101–45.

——, 1994b. 'Experiences in the transition to a market economy', *Journal of Comparative Economics*, 18:271–75.

Saha, A., 1994. 'A two-season agricultural household model of output and price uncertainty', *Journal of Development Economics*, 45(2):245–69.

Saha, A. and Stroud, J., 1994. 'A household model of on-farm storage under price risk', *American Journal of Agricultural Economics*, 76(3):522–34.

Sala-i-Martin, X., 1997. 'I just ran two million regressions', *American Economic Review* (Papers and Proceedings), 87:178–83.

Schipper, L. and Haas, R., 1997. 'The political relevance of energy and CO_2 indicators: an introduction', *Energy Policy,* 25(7–9):639–49.

Schumpeter, J.A., 1912. *Theorie der wirtschaftlichen entwicklung*, Dunker and Humblot, Leipzig.

Seth, R., Nolle, D.E. and Mohanty, S.K., 1998. 'Do banks follow their customers abroad', *Financial Markets, Institutions and Instruments* 7(4):1–25.

Shah, A., 1998. *Fiscal Federalism and Macroeconomic Governance: for better or for worse?*, World Bank Working Paper No. WPS 2005, World Bank, Washington, DC.

Shan, J. and Sun, F., 1998. 'Export-led growth hypothesis: further econometric evidence from China', *Applied Economics*, 30:1055–65.

Shapiro, S.S. and Wilk, M.B., 1965. 'An analysis of variance test for normality (complete samples)', *Biometrika*, 52:591–611.

Shogren, J. and Toman, M., 2000. *Climate Change Policy*, Resources for the Future Discussion Paper 00–22, Washington, DC.

Simon, D., 1991. 'Segmentation in the treasury bill market: evidence from cash management bills', *Journal of Financial and Quantitative Analysis*, 26:97–108.

Sinton, J. and Fridley, D., 2000. *What Goes Up: recent trends in China's energy consumption*, Lawrence Berkeley National Laboratory, Berkeley, CA.

Sinton, J., Levine, M. and Wang, Q., 1998. 'Energy efficiency in China: accomplishments and challenges', *Energy Policy*, 26(11):813–29.

Smil, V., 1998. 'China's energy and resource uses: continuity and change', in R.L. Edmonds (ed.), *Managing the Chinese Environment*, Oxford University Press, Oxford:211–27.

Song, L., 2002. 'Entry to the WTO and domestic private economy' in R. Garnaut and L. Song (eds), *China 2002: WTO entry and world recession*, Asia Pacific Press, Canberra:97–110.

——, 1999. 'Trade reform and development', in R. Garnaut and L. Song (eds), *China: twenty years of reform*, Asia Pacific Press, Canberra:71–94.

——, 1998. 'China', in R. McLeod and R. Garnaut (eds), *East Asia in Crisis: from being a miracle to needing one?*, Routledge, London:105–19.

State Information Council (SIC) web site. Available at <URL:http://www.chinaeco.com.emon.htm>.

State Statistical Bureau of China (SSB), 1981–99. *China Statistical Yearbook*, China Statistical Publishing House, Beijing (in Chinese).

——, 1996. *Input–output Table of China 1992*, China Statistical Publishing House, Beijing.

——, 1990. *Tabulation on the 1990 Population Census of People's Republic of China*, Volume 2, Population Census Office, State Council and Department of Population Statistics, China.

——, 1982. *1982 Population Census of China*, China Statistical Publishing House, Beijing.

——, various years. *Rural Household Survey Information*, Internal Documents, China Statistical Publishing House, Beijing.

——, various years. *Population Yearbook of China*, China Statistical Publishing House, Beijing.

SSB Survey Team of Urban Socioeconomy, 1992. *Yearbook of Price Statistics of China, 1992*, China Statistical Publishing House, Beijing (in Chinese).

SSB and Centre for Development Studies of the State Council (eds), 1996. *County Economies of China*, China Statistical Publishing House, Beijing (in Chinese).

Sun, H., 2000. 'Economic growth and regional disparity in China', *Regional Development Studies*, 6:43–66.

——, 1998. *Foreign Investment and Economic Development in China 1979–96*, Brookfield, Aldershot and Ashgate, Sydney.

Sun, H. and Chai, J., 1998. 'Direct foreign investment and inter-regional economic disparity in China', *International Journal of Social Economics*, 25(2–4):424–27.

Sun, H. and Dilip, D., 1997. 'China 's economic growth during 1984–93: a case of regional dualism', *Third World Quarterly*, 18(5):843–64.

Tang, K.K., 1998. *Economic Integration of the Chinese Provinces: a business cycle approach*, Working Paper 98/1, National Centre for Development Studies, The Australian National University, Canberra.

References

Tanzi, V., 1992. *Financial Markets and Public Finance in the Transformation Process*, IMF Working Paper, IMF, New York.

Tao, D., 1991. 'China and services negotiations', *Journal of World Trade*, 25(2):23–54.

Temple, J., 1998. 'Robustness tests of the augmented Solow model', *Journal of Applied Econometrics*, 13:361–75.

Temple, J., 1999. 'The new growth evidence', *Journal of Economic Literature*, 37:112–56.

Tian, Y. and Shi, F.Z., 1991. 'On part-time transfer of agricultural labour', *Problems of Agricultural Economy*, 6:54–59.

Tidrick, G., 1986. *Productivity Growth and Technological Change in Chinese Industry*, World Bank Working Paper No. 761, Washington, DC.

Tiebout, C., 1956. 'A pure theory of local expenditures', *Journal of Political Economy*, 64(5):416–24.

Tong, C.S.P., 1997. 'China's spatial disparity within the context of industrial production efficiency: a macro study by the Data-Envelopment Analysis (DEA) System', *Asian Economic Journal*, 11:207–17.

Tse, Y. and Booth, G., 1996. 'The risk premium in foreign currency futures: a re-examination', *Financial Review*, 31(August):521–34.

Tsui, K., 1996. 'Economic reform and interprovincial inequalities in China', *Journal of Development Economics*, 50:353–68.

Tsui, K., 1998. 'Factor decomposition of Chinese rural inequality: new methodology, empirical findings and policy implications', *Journal of Comparative Economics*, 26:502–28.

Tweeten, L., Dishon, C.L., Chern, W.S. and Imamura, N. (eds), 1993. *Japanese and American Agriculture: tradition and progress in conflict*, Westview Press, Boulder, Colorado.

Tyler, W.G., 1981. 'Growth and export expansion in developing countries, some empirical evidence', *Journal of Development Economics*, 9(1):121–30.

Ulph, A., 2000. 'Harmonization and optimal environmental policy in a federal system with asymmetric information, *Journal of Environmental Economics and Management*, 39:224–41.

United Nations, 1997. *China: water resources and their use*, working paper ST/ESCAP/1762, United Nations, New York.

United States Department of Agriculture, 1994. The impact of China's grain reserve system on import demand, mimeo, United States Department of Agriculture.

Vermeer, E.B., 1998. 'Industrial pollution in China and remedial policies', in R.L. Edmonds (ed.), *Managing the Chinese Environment*, Oxford University Press, Oxford:228–61.

Voivodas, C.S., 1973. 'Exports, foreign capital inflow and economic growth', *Journal of International Economics*, November:337–49.

Wan, G.H., 2001. 'Changes in regional inequality in rural China: decomposing the Gini Index by income sources', *Australian Journal of Agricultural and Resource Economics*, 45(3):361–81.

——, 1996a. 'Using panel data to estimate Engel functions: food consumption in China', *Applied Economics Letters*, 3(10):621–24.

——, 1996b. 'Income elasticities of household demand in rural China: estimates from cross-sectional survey data', *Journal of Economic Studies*. 23(3):18–34.

——, 1995. 'Peasant flood in China: internal migration and its policy determinants', *Third World Quarterly*, 16:173–96.

Wan, G.H. and Anderson, J.R., 1990. 'Estimating risk effects in Chinese foodgrain production', *Journal of Agricultural Economics*, 41(1):85–93.

Wan, G.H. and Chen, E.J., 2001. 'Effects of land fragmentation and returns to scale in the Chinese farming sector', *Applied Economics*, 33:183–94.

Wan, G.H., Griffiths, W.E. and Anderson, J.R., 1992. 'Estimation of risk effects with seemingly unrelated regressions and panel data', *Empirical Economics*, 17(1):35–49.

Wang, B., 1995. 'China on the horizon: exploring current legal issues: China's new foreign trade law: analysis and implications for China's GATT bid', *John Marshall Law Review*, 28(Spring):495.

Wang, L, 1998. 'Mountain watershed management in China', in H.P. Blume, H. Eger, E. Fleischhauer, A. Hebel, C. Reij and K.G. Steiner (eds), *Towards Sustainable Land Use: advance in geoecology 31*, Catena Verlag, Reiskirchen, Germany:1017–21.

Wang, P., 1995. 'The implications of cointegration in financial markets', *Applied Economics Letters*, 2:263–65.

Wang, Q., Sinton, J.E. and Levine, M.D., 1995. *China's Energy Conservation Policies and Their Implementation, 1980 to the Present, and Beyond*, Energy Analysis Program, Lawrence Berkeley National Laboratory, Berkeley, CA.

Wang, X.G., 1994. 'Rural economic structural transition and choice of new models: an economic analysis of the phenomenon of large-scale mobile rural labour force', *Problems of Agricultural Economics*, 7:47–52.

Wang, Z., 1996. 'Some reflections on the management of extra-budgetary funds', *Public Finance*, The Ministry of Finance of China.

Wang, Q., Halbrendt, C. and Johnson, S.R., 1996. 'Grain production and environmental management in China's fertiliser economy', *Journal of Environmental Management*, 47(2):283–96.

Wang, X.Y., 1993. 'On the mechanism of land circulation', *China's Rural Economy*, 10(October) (in Chinese).

Wang, Y., Ren, R. and Liu, X., 1998. *Estimation of Physical Capital Stock in China's Manufacturing Sectors*, Institute of Management working paper, Beijing Aviation and Spaceflight University.

Warford, J., Munasinghe, M. and Cruz, W., 1997. *The Greening of Economic Policy Reform, Volume I: principles*, The World Bank, Washington, DC.

References

Webster, A., 1993. 'The skill and higher educational content of the United Kingdom net exports', *Oxford Bulletin of Economics and Statistics*, 2:141–59.

Wei, S., 1995. 'The open door policy and China's rapid growth: evidence from city-level data', in T. Ito and A. Krueger (eds), *Growth Theories in Light of the East Asian Experience*, The University of Chicago Press, Chicago and London.

Wei, W., 1995. *Regional Disparities and Coordination in China*, Anhui People's Press, Hefei. (7)

Wen, G.J., 1993. 'Total factor productivity change in China's farming sector: 1952–1989', *Economic Development and Cultural Change*, 42(1):1–41.

Weiss, C.R., 1997. 'Do they come back again? The symmetry and reversibility of off-farm employment', *European Review of Agricultural Economics*, 24:65–84.

Weimer, C., 1994. 'State policy and rural resource allocation in China as seen through a Hebei province township 1970–85', *World Development*, 22(6):935–47.

Welber, C.K. and Francis, S., 1986. 'The methodological basis of Hirschman's development economics: pattern model versus general laws', *World Development*, 14:81–94.

Williams, J.C. and Wright, B.D., 1991. *Storage and Commodity Markets*, Cambridge University Press, New York.

Williamson, J.G., 1968. 'Personal savings in developing nations: an inter-temporal cross-section from Asia', *Economic Record*, 44(June):194–210.

Woller, G.M. and Phillips, K., 1998. 'Fiscal decentralization and LDC economic growth: an empirical investigation', *The Journal of Development Studies*, 34(4):139–49.

Wong, C.P.W., 1997. *Financing Local Government in the Peoples Republic of China*, Oxford University Press.

Wong, C.P.W., 1991. 'Central-local relations in an era of fiscal decline: the paradox of fiscal decentralization in the post-Mao China', *China Quarterly*, 12(8).

Wong, C.P.W., 1987. 'Between plan and market: the role of local sector in post-Mao China', *Journal of Comparative Economics*, 11.

Wong, K., 1995. *International Trade in Goods and Factor Mobility*, The MIT Press, Cambridge, Mass.

Wong, R.Y., 1993. 'Estimating and interpreting Chinese consumption functions', in T. Hsueh, W. Sun and J. Yu (eds), *Studies on Economic Reforms and Development in the People's Republic of China*, Chinese University Press, Hong Kong.

Woo, W.T., 2001. 'Recent claims of China's economic exceptionalism reflections inspired by WTO accession', *China Economic Review*, 12: 107–36.

Woo, W.T., Wen, H., Jing, Y. and Fan, G., 1994. 'How successful has Chinese enterprises reform been? Pitfalls in opposite biases and focus', *Journal of Comparative Economics*, 18:276–308.

Wood, A., 1991. 'The factor content of North–South trade in manufactures reconsidered', *Weltwirtschaftliches Archiv, Review of World Economics*, 4:719–42.

World Bank, 2000. *World Development Indicators 2000*, The World Bank, Washington, DC.

———, 1997a. *China 2020: food security options: at China's table*, World Bank, Washington, DC.

———, 1997b. *Clear Water, Blue Skies: China's environment in the new century*, The World Bank, Washington, DC.

———, 1997c. *Sharing Rising Incomes: regional disparities in China*, The World Bank, Washington, DC.

———, 1996. *World Development Report 1996*, Oxford University Press.

———, 1995a. *China the Emerging Capital Market*, Volumes 1 and 2, World Bank, Washington, DC.

———, 1995b. *China: agriculture to year 2000*, World Bank, Washington, DC.

———, 1994a. *Report on World Development 1994: an infrastructure for development*, The World Bank, Washington, DC.

———, 1994b. *China: issues and options in Greenhouse Gas emissions control*, The World Bank, Washington, DC.

———, 1994c. *World Tables 1994*, The Johns Hopkins University Press.

———, 1993a. *Energy Efficiency and Conservation in the Developing World: the World Bank's role*, The World Bank, Washington, DC.

———, 1993b. *World Development Report 1993*, Oxford University Press, Oxford.

World Trade Organization, 1998a. 'WTO telecom talks produce landmark agreement', *Focus Newsletter*, 16(February):1–2.

———, 1998b. 'WTO telecoms accord enters into force', *Focus Newsletter*, 27:6.

Wu, B., Kebin, H. *et al.*, 1998. 'The status and trend of China's policies on climate change', in M.B. McElory, C.P. Nielson and P. Lydon (eds), *Energizing China: reconciling environmental protection and economic growth*, Harvard University Committee on Environment.

Wu, X. (ed.), 1997. *Debt Restructuring in China's State Sector: a research report*, China Financial Press, China.

Wu, Y., 2000. 'Income disparity and convergence in China's regional economies', in P. Lloyd and X. Zhang (eds), *China in the World Economy*, Edward Elgar, Cheltenham.

———, 1999a. Income disparity and convergence in China's regional economies, paper from the Annual Meeting of the Association for Chinese Economic Studies (Australasia), 15–26 July, University of Melbourne, Melbourne.

———, 1999b. 'FDI and economic growth', in Y. Wu (ed.), *Foreign Direct Investment and Economic Growth in China*, Edward Elgar, Cheltenham.

———, 1996. *Productive Performance in Chinese Enterprises*, Macmillan Press, London.

———, 1993. 'Productive efficiency in Chinese industry', *Asia Pacific Economic Literature*, 7(2):58–66.

References

Wu, Z., 1996. 'The relationship between Commercial Banking Law of the PRC on management of foreign funded financial institutions', in W. Guiguo and W. Zhenying (eds), *Legal Developments in China: market economy and law*, Sweet & Maxwell, Hong Kong:186–204.

Xie, J. and Jia, K., 1994. *Potential Assessment of Crop Production: China's land resources, use and productivity assessments*, technical report of project CPR/87/029, Volume 3, Beijing.

Yaghmaian, B. and Ghorashi, R., 1995. 'Export performance and economic development: an empirical analysis', *American Economist*, 39(2):37–46.

Yan, C., 1997. *China's Energy Development Report 1997*, Economic Management Press, Beijing.

Yang, Q., 1998. *The Impact of Human Capital on Foreign Investment: the case of China*, OECD Development Centre, Paris, manuscript.

Yang, D.T. and Zhou, H., 1999. 'Rural-urban disparity and sectoral labour allocation in China', *Journal of Development Studies*, 35:105–33.

Yang, T. and Cai, F., 1991. 'Part-time farming households and agricultural labour transfer', *Chinese Rural Economy*, 11:43–50.

Ye, X.Q., 1992. 'Industrialisation, part-time farming and agricultural development', *Rural Economy Forum*, 10:26–33.

Yi, G., 2000. 'Keynote address on financial reforms', international conference on *Globalization and Growth in China*, Pudong, Shanghai, 5–7 July.

Young, A., 1995. 'The tyranny of numbers: confronting the statistical realities of the East Asian growth experience', *Quarterly Journal of Economics*, 110:641–80.

Yu, G., 1997. 'The emerging framework of China's Business Organisations Law', *Transnational Law*, 10:39.

Yunnan Statistical Bureau, 1998. *Yunnan Statistical Yearbook 1998*, China Statistical Press, Beijing.

Zapata, H.O. and Rambaldi, A.N., 1997. 'Monte Carlo evidence on cointegration and causation', *Oxford Bulletin of Economics and Statistics*, 59(1097):285–98.

Zhang, L., 1999. 'Chinese central-provincial fiscal relationships, budgetary declines and the impact of the 1994 fiscal reform: an evaluation', *The China Quarterly*, 157:1158–41.

Zhang, Q. and Felmingham, B., 1999. The relationship between inward FDI and China's provincial export trade, Asian Region International Association of Cooperating Organisations (ARIACO) Conference Paper, November.

Zhang, X.H., Chen, H.S. and Wu, Z.G., 1996. 'Part-time farming and income situations in traditional agricultural regions in China: a comparison', *Agricultural Economics Research Materials*, 4:40–49.

Zhang, Z., 1999. 'Is China taking actions to limit its greenhouse gas emissions', *Weathervane*.

——, 1993. 'Treasury yield curves and cointegration', *Applied Economics*, 25:361–67.

Zhao, R. and Li, S., 1997. 'Increasing income inequality and its causes in China', *Economic Research Journal*, September:19–28.

Zheng, J., Liu, X. and Bigsten, A., 1998. 'Ownership structure and determinants of technical efficiency: an application of Data Envelopment Analysis to Chinese enterprises, 1986–1990', *Journal of Comparative Economics,* 26:465–84.

Zhong, F.N., 1995. *Targets and Scale of Special Grain Reserves in China*, China's Agricultural Press, Beijing.

Zhou, Z.Y., Dillon, J.L. and Wan, G.H., 1992. 'Development of township enterprise and alleviation of the employment problem in rural China', *Agricultural Economics*, 6:201–15.

Zhu, Z., 1993. 'The problem of the large-scale mobile rural labour force around the country: current status, causes, and countermeasures', *Chinese Rural Economy*, 12:33–36.

Zou, H. and Zhang, T., 1995. *Fiscal Decentralization, Public Spending and Economic Growth in China*, Policy Research Working Paper No. WPS 1608, The World Bank, Washington, DC.

Index

Index

* 9 7 8 1 9 2 2 1 4 4 5 8 4 *